Joseph M. McShane. SJ.
Le Moyne College

The Idea of the Victorian Church

DESMOND BOWEN

*A Study of
the Church of
England
1833–1889*

McGill
University Press
Montreal
1968

© McGill University Press 1968
2,500 copies
Printed in Great Britain by
William Clowes and Sons, Limited
London and Beccles
Designed by Robert R. Reid
Library of Congress Catalog Card Number 67-30137

This work has been published with the help of a grant from the Social Science Research Council of Canada using funds provided by the Canada Council.

To Jean

Preface

IN OUR AGE, when the Church of England has been rocked by the disclosures of the Paul Report[1] and so many responsible critics are demanding a new policy of 'worldly holiness' for the Church in modern society, many churchmen look back wistfully at the Church of Victorian England. Asa Briggs has noted in his *Victorian People* that 'the religious climate was more exciting and important than anything else. The amount of pamphlet and periodical literature devoted to religious problems was far greater than that devoted to economic and social problems.'[2]

Most other historians of nineteenth-century England have commented on the same phenomenon. R.C.K. Ensor has gone so far as to say that 'no one will ever understand Victorian England who does not appreciate that among highly civilized, in contradiction to more primitive countries, it was one of the most religious the world has ever known.'[3] Elie Halévy has noted that this religious climate affected even the State which enacted 'that legislation which embodied the dictates of the national conscience.'[4]

There is little doubt that contemporary churchmen were aware of the social power of the Gospel they preached, and the authority of the Church as a corporate body in the nation. Mandell Creighton, in this great period of British imperialism, could exult that 'the Church of England has before it the conquest of the world'.[5] Speaking of the same period Cosmo Gordon Lang has called it a 'Golden Age'.

> I have always considered that the years—say 1890 to 1914—were the Golden Age of parochial work in the towns of England. In spite of all controversies—

1. Leslie Paul, *Deployment and Payment of the Clergy* (1964).
2. Asa Briggs, *Victorian People, 1851–1867* (1954), p. 27.
3. R. C. K. Ensor, *England, 1870–1914* (1960), p. 137.
4. Elie Halévy, *England in 1815* (1961), p. 400.
5. Louise Creighton, *Life and Letters of Mandell Creighton* (1904), II, 302.

the growing pains of the Church—the ideals of the long and steady Church Revival had taken hold. What may be called 'the social consciousness' of the Church had been roused by Maurice and Kingsley and their friends, and more recently by men like Gore and Scott Holland. The work of the Church had grown both in the intensity of faith and worship and in the extent of its range. There were able and devoted men in charge of industrial parishes everywhere; and the public schools and universities and theological colleges were still sending out supplies of keen and healthy young men to help them.[6]

In spite of the fact that the continuing and increasing influence of the Church in national affairs gave a singularly religious atmosphere to Victorian England, few studies have been made of this phenomenon. Kitson Clark of Cambridge University in his *Making of Victorian England* has recently pointed out this oversight, and this book has been written in an attempt to present a view of the Church of Victorian England that will remedy such a scholarly omission. Too often in the past the Church has been dismissed as an Erastian creation of the State which stood in 'resignation to the established order and consideration for the rich'.[7] When note has been made of the role of the Church in Victorian society the tendency of some historians has been to criticize churchmen for not advocating a social policy which could only emerge from a modern welfare state.[8]

Beatrice Webb has suggested in her autobiography that 'it was during the middle decades of the nineteenth century that, in England, the impulse of self-subordinating service was transferred, consciously and overtly from God to man'.[9] The main argument of this work is that churchmen led in the development of this new ethic of service. When a study is made of the writings of churchmen during the period 1833–1889, it will be seen that the 'ideals of the long and steady Church Revival' that Lang speaks of were largely concerned with the role of the church in the nation. Far from immersing themselves totally in theological concerns, or standing in resignation to the established order, the clergy and laity of the Church of England were actively engaged in debating what the mission of the Church to society was throughout this period. The spiritual energy generated by this debate created the 'golden age of parochial work' in pre-1914 England.

Most social historians have noted that the Church of England did

6. J. G. Lockhart, *Cosmo Gordon Lang* (1949), p. 155.
7. J. L. and Barbara Hammond, *Bleak Age* (1947), p. 119.
8. K. S. Inglis, *Churches and the Working Classes in Victorian England* (1963), p. 268 ff. provides an example of this.
9. Beatrice Webb, *My Apprenticeship* (1950), p. 123.

not lose the allegiance of the working classes in Victorian industrial cities, but rather never had any direct significant influence in what was becoming the largest part of the total population.[10] But these same historians tend to overlook another equally noteworthy phenomenon of the time—the acceptance by the English middle class of social values promoted by the Church during this period of revival. Contemporaries certainly recognized the worth of this achievement—as John Morley said, to have changed the promptings of commercial shrewdness into a new enthusiasm for far-reaching principle was no mean accomplishment.[11] This study argues that the Church saw the great danger in class warfare in England and, as part of a deliberate policy of reconciliation, sought to instil in the middle class the spirit of *noblesse oblige* which Victorians assumed the aristocracy still maintained. The success of this venture is reflected in the absence of overt class warfare in the nation, and the growth of the distinctive Christian character which historians attribute to Victorian society.

Much of the evidence to support the thesis that the Victorian Church was prophetically engaged in giving to England a social gospel is to be found in the innumerable tracts and pamphlets which were published throughout the period 1833–1889. In response to each crisis the Church faced there was apt to come forth a clerical broadside from some rusticated but highly literate curate or vicar. Sampling errors are inevitable when one tries to assess the thought not only of major theorists but also of ordinary churchmen during a fifty-year period, but the evidence seems to indicate that abstract theological speculation becomes of less concern to churchmen as the new Idea of the Church and its mission to the nation emerges.

Although I have received help from many sources during the research and writing which preceded the completion of this study, for which I am appreciative, I must acknowledge my particular gratitude for the sorting and cataloguing of the manuscripts and pamphlets at Pusey House first undertaken by Fr. Barry Marshall of the Bush Brotherhood of the Australian Church, and completed by Fr. Hugh Fenwick, s.s.f. I am also grateful for the help given to me as a post-graduate student by Professor W. E. L. Smith and the other members of the History Department of Queen's University, Kingston, Ontario, Canada, and by the Humanities Research Council of Canada, and the Canada Council, both of which assisted me to visit England for

10. E. R. Wickham, *Church and People in an Industrial City* (1952).
11. John Morley, *Life of Richard Cobden* (1881), p. 482.

1*

research purposes. The help given to me during the writing of the work by my colleague, Professor Maureen Hanna, has been greatly appreciated. Finally I must express my deep personal thanks to the Reverend Timothy Sullivan of Bakersfield, California, for his help along the way.

DESMOND BOWEN
Ottawa, Canada
1967

Contents

PART I
CHURCH
AND STATE

*The Defence
of the
Church of
England*

I. The Bishops and the Defence of the Temporalities

*A Season when
the Church is assailed by
so many enemies*
ARCHBISHOP WILLIAM HOWLEY

1. The Church in 1833

IN THE final decades of the eighteenth century no fundamental changes were demanded in England's social order. The ideas of the Enlightenment were not encouraged by the ruling classes, whose members, like the editors of the *Monthly Review*, recognized the more positive value of traditional Christian moral teaching. They believed that 'men are chiefly urged to the practice of moral duties by the dictates of Revelation', and they argued that to 'throw contempt' on the authority of the Christian faith would be 'to sap the foundation of the morals of the people, and this is the same whether that revelation be true or false'.[1] When such latitudinarian religious sentiment was widely expressed, and the 'utility' role of the Church was appreciated by the aristocracy and gentry, the Church was allowed to continue to slumber—as it had since the ecclesiastical storms of the preceding century had abated.

The prelates of the Church relaxed to enjoy the preferment that was theirs in the best of all possible churches. The enthusiasm of the evangelical revival was the only significant religious movement that

EPIGRAPH: *Primary Visitation Charge to the Clergy of Canterbury* (1833).
1. *Monthly Review*, XXXI (1764), 503.

disturbed an otherwise tranquil existence, in which not only bishops and parsons, but the aristocracy and the squirearchy also, took for granted the established order in ecclesiastical affairs.

> The association of the Anglican Church with the governing class has never been more intimate and binding than it was during the eighteenth century. This was true alike of bishops and of clergy. The English bishop was not a gay Voltairean like the French, but was just as zealous a member of the privileged orders, and the system over which he presided and which he defended was a faint copy of the gloriously coloured scandals of the French Church . . . for the English bishops though they were not libertines like the French never learnt so to be Christians as to forget to be aristocratic, and their religious duties were never allowed to interfere with the demands of scholarship or of pleasure.[2]

This social complacency disappeared with the outbreak of the French Revolution. The privileged orders dreaded Jacobinism, and realized that their conventional light attitude towards religion might weaken the moral fibre of the nation during this time when the traditional order throughout Europe appeared to be threatened. Men like Edmund Burke urged the Church 'to exalt her mitred front in courts and parliaments,'[3] and the public-utility role of the Church was emphasized in sermon after sermon. To thoughtful churchmen it seemed as if the argument that a Church is essential to the public tranquillity, and to the safety of the State, alone justified the ecclesiastical establishment in England.[4]

In the post-war period both clergy and laity began to express the fear that the Church had lost its hold on educated opinion during its long period of quiescence and servitude to the State. Arguments about social utility did not have the appeal they once had when it was obvious to all, in the era of Peterloo, that this was a time of rapid social change. Churchmen generally agreed with the sentiments of the *British Magazine* when it said, with reference to the Benthamite *Westminster Review*: 'one shudders in witnessing the horrid display of cold-blooded and unnatural exultation at what it thinks the certain downfall of everything which now is'.[5]

When it became clear that not only was the landowning class under direct attack, but also the Church, whose property, patronage,

2. J. L. and Barbara Hammond, *Village Labourer* (1927), p. 193. Norman Sykes, *English Religious Tradition* (1961), p. 62, speaks of the Church 'at ease in Zion'.
3. *British Critic*, XIV (1833), 151, quotation from 'Thoughts on the French Revolution'.
4. John Bowles, *Dispassionate Enquiry into the Best Means of Public Safety* (1806).
5. *British Magazine*, III (1833), 215.

and privilege came from alliance with the aristocracy and gentry, the unease of churchmen increased. Scurrilous attacks on the Church appeared in print, which sought to expose the 'prevailing immorality among the clergy'.[6] The most abusive of these works was the famous *Black Book* of 1820, which exposed the jobbery and corruption throughout society, and castigated the clergy for acting as 'ministers of the government rather than ministers of the Gospel'. In the eyes of its author the typical establishment cleric was 'rapacious, insolent and luxurious, having no fear of God before his eyes; neglectful of his spiritual concerns; waging increasing war against liberty, knowledge and humanity; exerting all his influence to promote tyranny, and enslave and debase his fellow creatures'.[7]

Such popular criticism was alarming, but what was much more ominous in the eyes of churchmen was the direct interest that Parliament began to take in ecclesiastical affairs. In 1828 the repeal of the Test and Corporation Acts ended the traditional position of privilege of the Church 'without which no clergyman thinks he could sleep with his accustomed soundness'.[8] In the following year came the act for Roman Catholic emancipation; the Reform Bill of 1832 gave added power to the trading class, many of whose members were militant Nonconformists; and then, in 1833, the government announced that it intended to suppress ten of the bishoprics of the Irish Church.

Churchmen knew what lay behind Lord Grey's suggestion that the bishops should begin to put their house in order. The *British Magazine* commented that 'in examining the general question of Church Reform it is too little to say that the immense majority of the people of England demand it in most intelligible language.'[9] Both the Dissenters and secular reformers resented the privileged position of the Church and the scandalous abuse of its wealth. With the dread word 'spoliation' on every lip, the Church realized that a major adjustment in its relationship with the State and Society had once more to be made. The question was—who would begin the new reformation, and what form would it take?

The official leaders of the Church were almost stunned and bewildered by the fierce outbreak of popular hostility. The answers put forth on its behalf to

---

6. William Benbow, *Crimes of the Clergy or the Pillars of Priestcraft Shaken* (1823), p. 4.
7. *Black Book or Corruption Unmasked* (1820), p. 320. The anonymous author of the Black Books was John Wade, a Benthamite Radical.
8. Peter Plymly [Sydney Smith], *Letters on the Subject of Catholics* (1808), p. 67.
9. *British Magazine*, III (1833), 79.

the clamour for extensive and even destructive change were the work of men surprised in a moment of security. They scarcely recognized the difference between what was indefensible and what must be fought for to the death; they mistook subordinate and unimportant points for the key of their position; in their compromises or in their resistance, they wanted the guidance of clear and adequate principles and they were vacillating and ineffective.[10]

In the light of the subsequent political power shown by the cathedral and other ecclesiastical lobbies, which took much of the edge off the temporal reforms initiated by the legislature, it has been questioned whether the Church really had much to fear in 1833. Perhaps it did not; but enlightened men of the time, like Thomas Arnold, believed that no human power could save the Church, and antagonists such as Jeremy Bentham exulted that it was ripe for dissolution. Most churchmen, like the editors of the *British Critic*, believed them, and agreed that the Church was in dire peril.

> We are still in a state of fearful expectation as to the future that awaits us; nor shall we attempt to conceal our apprehension that a blow will be struck at all the institutions and all the property of the country through the side of the Established Church; while the first blow will be struck at the Church itself through the side of the Establishment in Ireland.[11]

When men like James Mill suggested that the Church be turned into a giant mechanics institute, and the Whigs openly expressed their hostility to the black recruiting sergeant who opposed them in every village, it was little wonder that at times the debate over the temporalities of the Irish Church was ugly, and was followed anxiously by churchmen. Time and again the word 'spoliation' arose during the debate. Lord John Russell argued that where Church funds could be more profitably utilized for the moral and religious improvement of the people they should be confiscated. Sir John Graham saw no reason why the State could not redistribute Church property as it saw fit, so long as it was used for Protestant purposes, and Peel said that he could not see why the Church should be treated in a different manner from any other great corporation in the nation. Perhaps Sir John Hobhouse expressed most clearly the mentality of the members of the reformed Parliament when, in a later debate, he expressed his view that the Church was 'the offspring and child of the law and the parent may deal with the child'.[12]

10. R. W. Church, *Oxford Movement* (1891), p. 2.
11. *British Critic*, XVI (1834), 487.
12. *Hansard*, XXVII (1835), 533

The Earl of Eldon saw the Irish Temporalities Bill as a move towards the eventual overthrow of the Church, and said 'I would rather forego my existence than support a Bill which proceeds on a principle that I am satisfied must destroy the Established episcopal form of ecclesiastical discipline in this country.'[13] But even the most loyal of churchmen had to admit that a Church was in need of reform when it still tolerated nepotism, sinecures, pluralities, non-resident clergy, ecclesiastical courts which were complex and inequitable, and Church rates which were a genuine grievance to Nonconformists. Popular resentment of the Church could not be ignored when at a public meeting it was suggested that the Cathedral in Canterbury be used as a cavalry stable, and a dead cat was thrown in the face of Archbishop Howley by a reform mob when he made his primary visitation to Canterbury.[14]

Lord Henley, the brother-in-law of Peel, produced an alarming *Plan of Church Reform* in 1832 which demanded a radical redistribution of ecclesiastical wealth, the reassembling of Convocation, and the withdrawal of bishops from Parliament. The pamphlet went through seven editions in the year. The wide interest shown in such radical ideas led the Archbishop of Canterbury to protest in his primary visitation charge:

> If the House of Commons pass a bill putting an end to the bishops' seats in Parliament, had they better not add a clause abolishing the Church of England at once. If, which is barely possible, the House of Lords shall consent to such a measure, they will avoid a useless struggle, and give some eclat to the movement by sending in their own resignations on the same day.[15]

As public attitudes became more menacing, churchmen began to demand that the Church reform itself before the legislature could act. The urgency of this demand can be seen clearly in the reviews of sermons, and archdeacons' and bishops' charges, which appeared in the *British Critic* in 1833, and in the pamphlets which the clergy wrote. A lowly 'non-beneficed clergyman' addressed an open letter to the primate on the need for reform within the Church because of 'the crisis now at hand'. He said that in the 'last twelve years . . . we have had repeated proofs of the fearful effects of popular feeling', and with much agitation urged 'there is not a moment to be lost; already

---

13. *Mirror of Parliament*, IV (1833), 3413.
14. S. L. Ollard, *Dictionary of English Church History* (1912), p. 289.
15. *British Critic*, XIII (1833), 222.

it is evident that at the meeting of Parliament the first object of public attention will be the Church.'[16]

The Archdeacon of Salop said bluntly that the clergy had to defend their position by making effective use of their social position in the nation, and this theme was taken up by Hastings Robinson, Rector of Great Warley, in an open letter he addressed to the Bishop of London. The question facing the Church, he believed, was not whether temporal reform of the ecclesiastical establishment was to take place, but rather 'to what extent, and by what agency'.[17] A.P. Perceval, the Rector of East Horsley, Essex, said the only chance for the Church was its winning once more the respect and attention of the Christian legislators of the nation.[18] Churchman after churchman sounded similar calls for reformation from within, yet the Church lay, as the *Quarterly Review* said, 'awaiting in helpless nakedness the hostile signal for general plunder.'[19]

The first and most vexatious evil with which the Church had to contend was the tithe system. The Rev. William Jones had noted in his diary that 'the very word "tithe" has ever been as unpleasing and odious, to farmers especially, as "cuckoo" to the married ear',[20] and there is little doubt that the tithe was generally looked upon as a clerical tax, enforced by law. Originally it had been a free-will offering by a churchman; and being attached to a certain field it altered the value of the field, which sold for less because of the tithe rent charge upon it. Parliamentary acts made recoverable at law this part of the proceeds of the land which had been made to the Church. But the tithe was seldom received by the parish priest. Rather, most of it went into the hands of the lay patron, who then gave only a small proportion of what he had received into the pockets of the vicar he had appointed to the living in his gift. As the Hammonds have so vividly said, the tithe-owners 'were stewards of God in much the same sense as George IV was defender of the faith.'[21]

Where the clergyman did directly farm his own tithe he found it a source of great embarrassment, particularly the collection of the tithe in kind. William Jones has recorded that some parsons did not collect any tithe, others only a small portion of what was due to them,

16. Non-Beneficed Clergyman, *Letter to Archbishop of Canterbury on Church Reform* (1833), pp. 3–9.
17. Hastings Robinson, *Church Reform on Christian Principles* (1833), p. 2.
18. A. P. Perceval, *Church of Christ Invulnerable* (1833).
19. *Quarterly Review*, L. (1834), 509.
20. *Diary of the Rev. William Jones of Broxbourne* (1777–1821) (1929), p. 147.
21. J. L. and Barbara Hammond, *Village Labourer*, p. 167.

and though it was expected that the parson would be more lenient than the lay landlord in his tithe visitation, the clergy knew that nothing tended more to alienate them from their flocks than a tithe collection. Parson magistrates were notorious for their harsh treatment of those who refused to pay tithe to the rector of the parish, and men like William Cobbett had harsh words to say about this traditional form of rural taxation.[22]

Few of these disgruntled countrymen realized that about five thousand parsons raised families on less than £150 a year. The second great injustice with which ecclesiastical reformers had to deal was the great inequality in clerical incomes. William Lamb, later Viscount Melbourne, who lived in this hey-day of ecclesiastical jobbery, has recorded that when he chose a vocation he decided on law as a more honourable, if not more lucrative, profession than the Church.[23] Gentlemen of station in society had no difficulty in providing wealth for their sons by the purchase of ecclesiastical preferment, and resentment of the contrast provided by their way of life compared to that of the lesser clergy was great. Why, it was asked, should the Bishop of London receive £12,000 to £14,000 a year, and the Curate of Ashe £125; or the Rector of Stanhope £3,000 and the Vicar of Cranbrook £80 a year? In the 1833 letter of the Rector of Great Warley to the Bishop of London, to which we have already referred, Mr. Robinson said that from his researches it appeared that out of the 7,659 incumbents and 4,254 curates in the Church, 4,361 received less than £150 a year, and nearly two-thirds of these livings were worth less than £100 a year. Half of the curates received less than the legal minimum of £80 a year.[24] Lord Henley in his suggested plan for Church reform reported that some benefices were worth less than £12 a year, and that 4,809 livings did not have habitable houses.[25]

These scandals had to be tolerated because there was no real ecclesiastical authority which could deal with such abuses. In 1813 there had been passed a Clergy Residence Act which stipulated that the minimum stipend paid to curates was not to be under £80 per year; but, as Mr. Robinson of Great Warley pointed out, the provisions of this Act could easily be ignored because of the desperate

22. William Cobbett, *Legacy to Parsons* (1835), pp. 121–22.
23. *Memoirs of William Lamb, Second Viscount Melbourne* (1878), I, 48.
24. Robinson, p. 13. Robinson underestimated the income of the rectory of Stanhope, Northumberland, in the diocese of Durham. The Church Commissioners later revealed its net income to be £4,843, although the two curates who performed spiritual duties there received a total of £270 from W. N. Darnell the absentee rector.
25. Henley, *Plan of Church Reform* (1832), p. 12.

situation of candidates for ordination who came of humble circumstances. He tells in his pamphlet of a friend who was offered a title for orders on the understanding that he pay £10 to the agent who procured him the title, a further sum to the grantor of the title, and sign an agreement to serve for some time without stipend. In the period after the Napoleonic wars, there were many who were willing to accept such conditions for the sake of obtaining the position of social distinction which was granted to any clergyman.[26]

Once a young man was ordained, there was always the chance that some patron might be found who would advance his cause in the Church. Churchmen generally approved of the great inequality in clerical incomes, which Sydney Smith called a system of prizes and blanks, and agreed that the less interference there was with the positions of privilege for which clerics contested the better off the Church would be. William IV had even expressed himself strongly in favour of annexing *commendams* to those bishoprics which were worth less than £6,000 a year.

But the reform temper of the age would not allow the vast inequalities in clerical income to pass unnoticed. The *Extraordinary Black Book* referred to the Church of England as the most unreformed of all churches in temporal matters. It claimed that the revenues of its priesthood exceeded those of either Austria or Prussia, that there was less temporal corruption in 'Popery', and that 'the clergymen of the Church of England and Ireland receive, in the year, more money than all the rest of the Christian world put together.'[27] In the midst of such wealth, humble curates literally starved. Doddington Rectory, with March and Benwick, in the diocese of Ely, whose Rector was Algernon Peyton, and whose patron was Sir H. Peyton, was worth £7,306. Two curates were employed in the living at an aggregate stipend of £385 by the absentee rector.[28]

Enlightened prelates began to put their diocesan houses in order without waiting for the Church as a whole to redress the scandals within the Establishment. No one knew exactly what income the

26. Robinson, p. 20. The Church Commissioners later agreed that for curates to receive no salary at all was not unknown.

27. [John Wade], *Extraordinary Black Book: an Exposition of the United Church of England and Ireland, Civil List and Crown Revenues* (1831), p. 5.

28. *First Report of the Commissioners Appointed to Consider the State of the Established Church* (1835), Table IV, pp. 346–47. Cf. G.R. Gleig, *A Letter to the Lord Bishop of London, on the Subject of Church Reform* (London, 1833). A pamphlet like that of Mr. Gleig had its evidence substantiated when the work of the Commissioners was made public. This report revealed that there were eighteen livings worth over £2,000 a year, and that the average stipend received by the 4,224 curates who did the work for non-resident incumbents was £81 a year.

dignitaries of Durham Cathedral received from local coal fields, but it was obvious that some financial attraction led the Bishop of St. David's to act as Dean of the Chapter, and for him to number among his canons the Bishops of Bristol, Chester, and Exeter. Van Mildert, the Bishop of Durham, knew that lay cupidity was stirred by tales of these 'golden stalls', and he decided in 1832 to begin reform in his diocese before the storm burst upon the Church. His secretary, Prebendary Durrell, wrote at this time:

> It appears to be morally certain that as soon as the Reform Bill is disposed of an attack will be made on Dean and Chapters, and as certain that Durham will be the first object. It has occurred to us that it will be prudent, if possible, to ward off the blow and that no plan is so likely to take as making the public partakers of our income by annexing an establishment of enlarged education to our college . . . no doubt sacrifices would be required of us. We regard them as a premium to be paid to ensure the remainder.[29]

It was this prelatical enlightened self-interest that led to the foundation of the University of Durham in 1832.

Pluralism was another abuse that the reformers could not overlook. Hastings Robinson estimated that in 1832 there were 12,200 preferments in the Church; 11,374 benefices, 668 dignities, and 158 minor canonries. These preferments were not equally divided among the available clergy: 3,853 clerics held only one title, 3,304 held two, 370 held three, 73 held four, and 59 held five or more.[30] Sometimes the holding of more than one benefice could be excused because the clergyman's income was so low that he was threatened by starvation. A bishop of this period told the story of making a visitation of a small benefice only to find the incumbent in bed with his family, where they had retired because of their total lack of either food or fuel.[31] The changing value of land also complicated the whole problem of clerical income, but there was no doubt that scandalous pluralism existed. The son-in-law of Archbishop Manners-Sutton held an archdeaconry, a chancellorship, two prebends, two rectories, and one curacy, worth in all some £10,000 a year.[32] William Cobbett ironically dedicated his *Legacy to Parsons* to the reforming Bishop Blomfield who had conferred a prebendal stall and two rectories upon his son.

29. E. Hughes, 'Bishops and Reform', *English Historical Review*, LVI (1941), 488.
30. Robinson, p. 21. His totals appear to be higher than the number of benefices recorded by the Commissioners of 1835 in their *Report on the State of the Established Church*, p. xi.
31. Convocation of Canterbury, *Chronicle* (1892), p. 225. Reported by the Dean of Chichester.
32. S. C. Carpenter, *Church and People, 1789–1889* (1933), p. 57.

The critics of the Church seldom stopped to inquire whether the prelates of the Church could do anything about unfair distribution of income among the clergy. Robinson, in the plan for Church reform we have referred to, reminded them that of the 4,361 benefices worth less than £150 a year, the Crown held 550, Bishops 650, Dean and Chapters 650, the Universities 270, and lay patrons 2,241. Much of the abuse connected with inequality of clerical income came from this predominant lay control of benefices, and its associated evil, simony, or the sale of spiritual offices, which still haunted the Church of England. The *British Critic* in 1841 said: 'one can scarcely glance one's eyes over any London paper without lighting upon the words, "Next Presentation" or "Perpetual Advowson".' One advertisement which appeared in the *Times*, 5 July, 1838, was so shocking that it was greeted as a malicious or wanton joke.

> To the Clergy: An incumbent would resign directly with patron's consent . . . a beautiful living, a perfect gem, one of the prettiest things in England with excellent new free stone house, in good repair—facing a park in the county of Somerset at the skirts of a small market town, with every necessary of life cheap; productive garden, lawn, pleasure ground . . . stabling for six horses . . . spot healthy, roads and society good; the whole worth £280 a year. Terms: incoming incumbent to pay down £1,900 to indemnify present incumbent's outlay on the spot, and for his fixtures, and his old wine worth £180 . . . piano-forte by Stoddart cost 85 guineas; hand-organ by Flight cost £38 etc.[33]

But reading the *Ecclesiastical Gazette* where 'next presentations' were advertised with the notation 'incumbent is in his 65th year', makes the reader wonder whether the advertisement was a joke.[34] In this paper the ecclesiastical brokers quite baldly advertised their jobbery.

> The Reverend Giles Powell, B.A. offers his services to his brother clergymen on any subject connected with their profession, and other business not inconsistent with it. He makes no charge to incumbents who kindly permit him to recommend Curates to them, but he wishes it to be distinctly understood, that he declines to introduce Gentlemen to employment until he is made acquainted with their age, degree, tenets, and other references they can give when required. Dilapidations, tithes and other ecclesiastical property promptly valued by persons of high character and competency.[35]

33. *British Critic*, XXIX (1841), 395.
34. *Ecclesiastical Gazette or Monthly Register of the Affairs of the Church of England*, II (1839), 116.
35. *Ibid.*, I, 218. The Duke of Norfolk, although he was a Roman Catholic, offered for sale the advowson of Ecclesfield, Yorkshire, for £5,000. *V.* Promotion by Merit, *Cure of Souls by Purchase* (1873), p. 27.

One cannot help suspecting that when a clergyman of the period could offer himself for sale as 'a treasure to any gentleman with whom he might be associated, a very low stipend would be an objection',[36] spirituality would count for very little in these transactions.

The Napoleonic war veteran who had purchased an advowson from a broker at Garraway's Coffee House could be removed from his living only with great difficulty, its emoluments, tithes, and endowments being part of what was, in effect, a freehold tenure. But after ordination he could remove himself from his parish if he was able to persuade his ordinary to dispense him from residence in it. Then from the comfort of some place like Bath or Nice he could direct parish affairs through the office of a resident curate who would be paid as little as possible. In 1809, the curate of All Saints, Sawley, complained that he had served for twenty-four years on a stipend of £40 a year in a living worth £2,400, by caring for three churches separated from each other by a distance of two miles.[37]

The usual excuse given for non-residence was the unhealthy climatical conditions to be found in some parts of England. Essex was notorious for its unhealthy cures, and the *Ecclesiastical Gazette* indicated that high and dry parishes (in a physical sense) were much in demand. A medical certificate would usually be renewed yearly, if it was once obtained, for the bishop was often obliged to grant dispensation for non-residence in this age when there was no other way to provide for ill or incapacitated clergy.

Because curates were expensive, parishes were sometimes abandoned completely, particularly if they were held in plurality. At other times incumbents were ingenious in providing for their cures. In the parish of St. Buryans, Cornwall, the absentee rector found a poor cleric who had had a mental breakdown after ordination. This 'harmless maniac' could provide the necessary Sunday services for the parish, and he was chained to the altar-rail by a chain just long enough to reach the altar and the prayer-desk. On week-days he played the fiddle in the village tavern.[38]

The abuse of non-residence was so widespread, and the law regarding it so complex, that even a reforming bishop could do little about it apart from moral exhortation. The ecclesiastical courts were feeble and unsatisfactory, as well as expensive. Occasionally the diocesan did move to make an example of some offender, but often the culprit was

36. *British Critic*, XXIX (1841), 401.
37. *Hansard*, XIV (1809), 928.
38. Augustus Hare, *Story of My Life* (1896), VI, 177.

someone like the unfortunate curate whom Joseph Hume defended in Parliament in 1829. The father of thirteen children, he held two cures which provided him with a total of £60 a year. The Bishop of Lincoln had proceeded against him for non-residence in one cure, acting through his archdeacon—who lived in Kent.[39]

Inequalities in clerical income, pluralism, simony, and non-residence provided grist for reforming mills; but where the Church was most vulnerable was in its lack of provision of places of worship for the teeming millions in the new industrial areas of the nation. In an age when the Church was still justified by arguments of public utility and the privileged orders were fearful of the destructive power of the masses, such an oversight on the part of the Church was not overlooked by its critics. It was estimated that there were no places of worship for about 6,364,400 of the population, and that most of the neglected lived in the new towns and manufacturing areas. In the metropolis alone 1,425,000 people were left unprovided with spiritual aid.[40] The parishes which attempted to assist the poor of the manufacturing areas were often worth only £150, and did not attract the clergy in the same manner as a rich country living worth £400 with a population of only a hundred souls. Reformers like Lord King suggested that the answer for the Church was to take away the emoluments of Deans and Chapters and to distribute the income of the Church more equally to those 'who did all the work'.[41]

The hierarchy of the Church was well aware of its shortcomings in providing for the spiritual care of those in the cities, a task which was too much for them as long as the Church remained unreformed. In the nation, twenty-six bishops, having on the average 412 parishes in their dioceses, were expected to act as Fathers-in-God to a population of sixteen millions. This they could hardly do when the greatest concentrations of population were in cities like Liverpool, Birmingham, Manchester, Sheffield, or Newcastle, far removed from the oversight of any diocesan.[42]

Though the bishops were generally concerned about the state of the Church, as the charges of the time reveal, few of them provided detailed criticism of the Establishment. This task was generally

39. *Hansard*, XXI (1829), 1826.
40. William Palmer (Worcester College), *Enquiry into the Possibility of Church Extension* (1841), pp. 11–16.
41. *Hansard*, XV (1833), 297.
42. *Report of Commissioners*, XXII (1835), 12, shows that Exeter, with a population of 792,935, and London, with a population of 1,688,899, each had 635 benefices. Norwich, with 568,285 souls, had 809 benefices, while York, with 1,463,503 people, had only 891 benefices.

14

assumed by lesser clergy, like William Palmer of Worcester College, Oxford, and Charles Girdlestone, the Vicar of Sedgley, Staffordshire.[43] These men did not hesitate to call attention to specific corruption and scandal within the Church, which subjected it to popular scorn and threatened to draw down upon it the wrath of the legislature. It was the cumulative effect of the writing of such clerical reformers that reconciled the bishops to the inevitability of a change in the organization of the Church. As we have noted, some like Van Mildert of Durham began on their own initiative to redress obvious grievances.[44]

By 1833 it was clear that the slumber of the eighteenth-century Church had come to an end. Parliament was dominated by reformers, and the new industrial areas that they represented demanded a radical change in the Church so that it could satisfy the needs of a new society. The easy-going latitudinarianism of the eighteenth century had to go. The Church had to find within itself spiritual strength to enable it to bargain with the State. Any weakness that would make it vulnerable to those who would despoil it had to be corrected.

Few contemporaries believed in this dark time that recuperative power would be found in the Church as it then was. Fewer still believed that leadership in reform would be provided by the bishops. This was the age when Sydney Smith could say of the hierarchy of the Church: 'It is vain to talk of the good character of bishops. Bishops are men; not always the wisest of men; not always preferred for eminent virtues and talents, or for any good reason whatever known to the public.'[45] But to the amazement of all, two bishops appeared who showed that a reform of the temporalities of the Church was possible—in terms that would prove acceptable to both clerical and lay critics of the establishment. The work of the two great political bishops, Charles James Blomfield, and Samuel Wilberforce, did much to save the Church of England and its temporal wealth from radical spoliation in the first half of the nineteenth century.

43. Palmer, *Enquiry*, and Charles Girdlestone, *Second Letter on Church Reform* (1833).
44. Parliamentary Papers, *Number of Churches and Livings Augmented in the Diocese of Durham by the Late William Van Mildert*, XL (1836).
45. Sydney Smith, *Works* (1859), I, 122.

2. Bishop Blomfield and Administrative Reform

THE BISHOPS in 1833 knew that in any reorganization of the Church they would need to bear in mind that for centuries Church and State in England had been wedded in practice as well as in theory. The bishops and clergy of the Church would be unable to remedy the evils in the establishment unless the laity supported them; Parliament would have the final say in any redistribution of Church temporalities. This was an age when an existing parish could not be subdivided to create a new benefice unless approval came from the tithe-owner, the patron or incumbent, and finally Parliament.

The bishop who showed the prelates of the Church how to put their house in order was Charles James Blomfield, Bishop of London. He was a man to be reckoned with. Sydney Smith said of him: 'When the Church of England is mentioned it will only mean Charles James of London, who will enjoy a greater power than has ever been possessed by any churchman since the days of Laud, and will become, the Church of England here upon earth'.[1] Blomfield was not another Laud, however. Hugh Trevor-Roper has said that the latter was guilty of a gigantic misconception of the practical, but Blomfield was above all else a political realist. Disraeli believed him to be intellectually limited, but he also recognized him to be a man of great energy and astuteness. He was just the sort of guide the Church had need of in this age of revolutionary social change. He could bring about what was politically possible for the Church by his unique ability of 'recommending himself to the innovator by his approbation of change "in the abstract", and to the conservative by his prudential and practical respect for that which is established'.[2]

Perhaps Disraeli should have qualified his opinion of Blomfield's intelligence, for it was his performance as a Fellow of Trinity College, Cambridge, which first won him the attention of aristocratic patrons who valued him as a tutor for their sons. These friends in high places obtained for him appointment to the see of Chester in 1824. A huge unreformed diocese, one hundred miles long, which contained the cities of Manchester and Liverpool, its income was so low that to support himself Blomfield was allowed to hold the rectory of St. Botolph's, Bishopsgate, *in commendam*. Because of the poverty of the

1. Sydney Smith, *Works*, II, 269.
2. Benjamin Disraeli, *Tancred: or, The New Crusade* (New York, 1877), pp. 72–73. G. F. A. Best, *Temporal Pillars* (1964), p. 330, discusses Blomfield's value to a church 'just waking up to the challenge of the new social order'.

diocese there was always a rapid turnover of bishops in Chester, usually through translation to a richer see. Between 1752 and 1848 there were ten Bishops of Chester, all of whom managed to get themselves translated. A local saying was: 'The Bishop of Chester never dies'.[3]

Blomfield was a reformer but never a radical. He accepted as inevitable certain evils such as pluralism, and, as Cobbett noted, he did not hesitate to provide handsomely for his son.[4] In spite of, or even perhaps because of, his intellectual and moral limitations, he was able to throw himself into the cause of ecclesiastical reform in a way that a more idealistic bishop would have found impossible. Realists like Peel and Disraeli appreciated his capacity for action and, in the words of the latter, recognized him as 'one of those leaders who are not guides'.[5] Such leaders were necessary if the Church was to be saved, and Blomfield revealed himself as one of them by his reforming activities in the diocese of Chester.

When he arrived there he discovered that no questionnaire had been circulated for the information of the bishops since 1788, and that for the last one hundred years no bishop had made more than one perfunctory visitation of each parish. Blomfield with his talent for action threw himself immediately into the work of reforming the diocese, and showed his clergy that he was to be an ordinary to be reckoned with. He began by forbidding hunting and shooting by the clergy, as well as such pastimes as dancing at public balls. He impressed his subordinates with his seriousness when he told each newly ordained man that his licence would be withdrawn if he transgressed any of these new commandments.

For a bishop to take his task as diocesan as seriously as Blomfield did was a revolutionary development. The general standard of clerical behaviour was not high, and causes of scandal such as public drunkenness were not uncommon among them. One cleric disgraced himself by falling into a grave at a funeral he conducted while in his cups. Another defended his conduct before Blomfield by protesting that he had never been drunk while on duty.[6]

In spite of his zeal as a diocesan (he once confirmed 7,991 candidates at six different places in six days) Blomfield was too politically minded to devote himself totally to his see. He was often in London,

3. Alfred Blomfield, *Memoir of Charles James Blomfield* (1864), p. 76.
4. *V. supra*, p. 11.
5. Disraeli, *Tancred*, p. 71.
6. Blomfield, *Memoir*, p. 78.

preaching at St. Botolph's, and making his way in London society and in the House of Lords. Though he was inclined to brusqueness, he could be agreeable, good-humoured, and lively; and Greville has recorded that he could sing a duet with a lady of an evening.[7] His social charm, his influence with Archbishop Howley, and his political ability inevitably made him an object of much suspicion. As a 'priest in the temple of expediency'[8] he was believed to be the bishop who persuaded the episcopate of the inevitability of parliamentary reform in 1832, and the *Edinburgh Review* attacked his 'forwardness of obsequiousness which distinguishes him even on the bench of Bishops'.[9] Many of his detractors who were willing to acknowledge his influence as a reformer refused to lose their suspicion of his real motives. When he missed a dinner party because a dog had bitten him on the leg, necessitating a trip to the hospital, Sydney Smith commented on his absence by saying: 'I'd like to hear the dog's account of the story'.[10]

The combination of great energy, social favour, and political ability brought him his desired translation; and in August, 1828, at the age of forty-two, he became Bishop of London. He was to labour in the metropolis until his death in 1857. During this time he revealed to his fellow prelates not only what was necessary in the way of ecclesiastical reform in industrial areas, but also the way forward to a new relationship between Church, State, and society. Disraeli might sneer that: 'Abstract principles with him ever ended in concrete expediency',[11] but the Church was as much in need of reforming expediency at this time, as it was of the abstract ideas that came out of Oxford.

When the question of suppression of redundant Irish bishoprics arose in 1833, to idealists like Edward Bouverie Pusey, Professor of Hebrew, and Canon of Christ Church, Oxford, they were 'a patrimony which we have received in trust to use ourselves to the service of Almighty God, and to hand down to our successors to be so used'.[12] To the academics of Oxford it was clear that the suppression of the superfluous sees was an act of sacrilege to increase the mammon of the politicians of the day. But to Blomfield, who believed that ideas like apostolic succession had gone out with the Nonjurors, what

7. *Greville Memoirs* (1938), II, 112–13.
8. The jibe is that of the Duke of Newcastle, *Hansard*, XIX (1833), 719.
9. Blomfield, *Memoir*, p. 95, from *Edinburgh Review* (April 1825).
10. *Ibid.*, p. 165.
11. Disraeli, *Tancred*, p. 73.
12. *Pusey House Mss.*, E. B. Pusey to Philip Pusey (1 July 1836).

mattered in this instance was that the Irish clergy were on the point of being reduced to penury because the Roman Catholics were refusing to pay the hated tithes to the Church of Ireland. He viewed the giving up of the ten bishoprics as merely the surrender of an untenable position. As early as 1825, when he was Bishop of Chester, Blomfield had revealed that he was as concerned with the misery of the Irish peasants as he was with defence of ecclesiastical privilege.[13]

He knew that the secular reformers had every intention of devoting their attention to the 'rotten boroughs' of the Church, and the scandalous jobbery connected with the distribution of ecclesiastical wealth. Because of this he was willing to sacrifice what was necessary, including the Irish bishoprics, so that the Church might be strong to withstand its time of trial. Some of his contemporaries, like the Duke of Newcastle, thought his voting for the Irish Bill was merely slippery expediency,[14] but others like Peel had more faith in him. He had been a member of Lord Grey's Royal Commission to 'inquire into the Ecclesiastical Revenues of England and Wales', which had been set up in 1832, continued to serve in Peel's Ecclesiastical Commission of 1834, and Melbourne's of 1835, and finally was appointed in 1836 as a member of the permanent body known as the Ecclesiastical Commissioners for England.[15] He soon emerged as the leading figure on this Commission, which had power to hold real property, to receive episcopal and capitular incomes, and to initiate reforms which, when ratified by Orders in Council, were to have full force of law. Archbishop Vernon Harcourt said of his activities on the Commission, 'till Blomfield comes we all sit and mend our pens and talk about the weather'.[16]

It would be grossly unfair to Blomfield to view him as a mere political careerist in his work on the Ecclesiastical Commission. Regardless of the strictures of Disraeli, his boundless energy reflected more than 'expediency'. He had the abiding ideal of uniting the interests of society with the Church whose 'consolations have been for ages interwoven with almost all the relations and details of civil and of social life'.[17] From the time he became Bishop of London he

13. *Hansard*, XIII, 716–17, *v.* also XIX (1833), 914–18.
14. *Ibid.*, XIX (1833), 915.
15. For the work of these commissions *v.* Olive Brose *Church and Parliament: the Reshaping of the Church of England, 1828–1860* (1959).
16. Blomfield, *Memoir*, p. 167. Best, pp. 296–347, discusses in detail the influence of Blomfield and the other ecclesiastics on the Commission. Even Archbishop Howley had a contribution to make.
17. Brose, p. 83. From C. J. Blomfield, *A Charge Delivered to the Clergy . . . of Chester*. London, 1825.

showed concern for the hard lot of the labouring poor, deplored the employment of children in factories, and agitated for better sanitation to defeat the cholera which was endemic at this time.[18]

He realized that the unreformed Church could do little to alleviate either the spiritual or temporal needs of the poor. In his charge to the clergy of London in July 1834, he told them that many of the troubles besetting the Church came from the attempt 'to do the work of evangelists for a population of more than 14 millions, with a machinery originally constructed for a very small portion of that number'.[19] It was the duty of the Church as the 'great spiritual polity' of the nation to provide for the masses. Ideally each clergyman should have the care of 1,000 souls, but he believed that at this time, even with a redistribution of resource, the Church had the men and resources to serve eleven millions of the population.

The Church had to be reformed so that its resources could be put to better use. Blomfield was enough of a political realist to know that only the power of the legislature could counter the vested ecclesiastical interests that opposed reform, and because of this he devoted himself to working closely with the secular authority.

> I see connected with the Cathedral twenty-nine clergymen whose offices are all but sinecures, with an annual income of about £12,000 at the present moment, and likely to be much larger after the lapse of a few years. I proceed a mile or two to the east and north-east and find myself in the midst of an immense population in the most wretched state of destitution and neglect. . . . I find there, upon an average about one church and one clergyman for every 8,000 or 10,000 souls . . . in one parish . . . one church and one clergyman for 40,000 people. . . . I am told you may not touch St. Paul's. It is an ancient corporation which must be maintained in its integrity. Not a stall can be spared. The duties performed there are too important to admit of any diminution in the number of those who perform them. One sermon is preached every Sunday by a residentiary and another by a clergyman appointed by the Bishop, and paid by the Corporation of London; while the non-residentiaries either preach an occasional sermon on saint's days, or pay a minor canon for preaching it.[20]

Many churchmen regarded the Ecclesiastical Commission as a purely Erastian creation of the State. Its members were few in number, removable at the pleasure of the Crown, and led by the meddlesome ever-busy Blomfield. Ecclesiastical pressure led to a change in the nature of the Commission in 1840, when all bishops

18. Hansard, XI (1832), 109–11.
19. C. J. Blomfield, *A Charge delivered to the Clergy . . . of London* (London, 1834), p. 14.
20. Blomfield, *Memoir*, p. 170.

were made ex-officio members, and the removal threat was abolished. This still did not ease the fears of the High-Church party, in particular, for the industrious Blomfield showed that the Commission was not going to leave the question of reform in the hands of the bishops alone. Church and State were to work closely together to redistribute Church property, and to make more effective the Church's mission to the nation.[21]

Certain matters Blomfield and the other commissioners attempted to avoid; the question of tithe reform,[22] the revival of Convocation, the appointment of suffragan bishops, and the liturgical changes which were beginning to appear. They also steered clear of issues like the sale of next presentation, and other simoniacal practices, which came from the lay control of much of the temporal wealth of the Church. Not until the Benefice Act of 1898 was real progress to be made in these matters.

Blomfield practised the 'art of the possible', and he began the reform activities of the Commission by vesting in the hands of the commissioners, for redistribution, money taken from episcopal and capitular estates. The cathedral lobbies were strong enough to ensure that the Commission's activities never amounted to spoliation, their argument being that the cost of reforming the Church should not be laid on their shoulders alone, but rather on the collective body of the realm. The High-Churchmen supported them and said that the activities of the commissioners would deny to the cathedrals their ideal role in the Church, as schools of discipline, instruction, and prayer. Pusey gloomily prophesied 'we shall live under the supremacy of the Commission, it will be our legislative, executive, the ultimate appeal of our bishops; it will absorb our Episcopate; the Prime Minister will be our Protestant Pope'.[23] The inclusion of the bishops in the Commission led some critics to soften the tone of their opposition, but the resistance to all the commissioners undertook was great.[24]

When they had the revenues of some three hundred and sixty prebends in their hands, the commissioners began to redistribute this income. Blomfield had no difficulty in persuading his colleagues that the wealth they had garnered should be used to provide for the

21. *V. Hansard*, LV (1840), 1115 ff. for clerical opposition to the Commission.
22. The Tithe Commutation Act of 1836 brought the country parson peace for forty years, but with the agricultural depression at the end of the century came a substantial reduction in the Church's real income. *V*. Best, pp. 465–79, for the whole question of tithe.
23. *British Critic*, XXIII (1838), 526.
24. P. J. Welch, 'Contemporary Views on the Proposals for the Alienation of Capitular Property in England, 1832–1840', *Journal of Ecclesiastical History*, V (1954), 192.

spiritual welfare of the poor in the new manufacturing centres. The neglect of the poor by the Church had been scandalous. As early as 1811 the *Quarterly Review*, in a review of the state of the Established Church, had indicated that the parish of Marylebone with a population of 60,000 people had only one church with a seating capacity of 900. It was estimated that in a thousand important parishes the Church was providing accommodation for no more than a seventh of the population.[25] By 1824 it was revealed in Parliament that over four million souls in England had no place in which they could worship. In Manchester, with a population of 187,000, there were church sittings for only 22,468; in Birmingham, with a population of 100,000 people, there were sittings for only 16,000; and Leeds provided church accommodation for only 10,000 of the 84,000 people in that city.[26]

The failure of the Established Church to provide places of worship for the poor in the industrial areas was revealed most clearly by the census of religious worship undertaken by Horace Mann in 1851. Contemporaries believed the result of this census to be substantially accurate. Mann discovered that on census Sunday 7,261,032 people had attended places of Christian worship in England. After making allowance for the people who for various reasons could not attend church, he calculated that 5,288,294 possible worshippers had chosen not to attend church on this day. Most of these absentees were in large industrial towns where, on the average, only one in four inhabitants had worshipped. Churchmen knew that if these non-worshippers had all sought the ministrations of the Church they could not have been provided for.[27]

Between 1840 and 1855 the Ecclesiastical Commission endowed or augmented 5,300 parishes from offices scheduled for abolition by the Cathedrals Act of 1840 (3–4 Vict. c. 113).[28] At the same time the commissioners did not make the mistake of allowing their activities to replace the good works of private benefactors. Wherever possible they sought to make grants where local benefactors would contribute an equal amount. Unfortunately, when this was done, the benefactors tended to provide for churches near their homes. As most of them seemed to live in the south of England, it was in this area that most new churches appeared. In the period 1825–1850, only one church

25. *Quarterly Review*, V. (1811), 365.
26. *Hansard*, XI (1824), 344–45.
27. Parliamentary Papers, *Accounts and Papers: Religious Worship, England and Wales*, LXXXIX (1852–1853), cxix.
28. Parliamentary Papers, *Report of Select Committee of the House of Commons on the Ecclesiastical Commission*, VI (1863), 111.

was erected in Leeds by a private benefactor while five were provided in Brighton.

It must not be thought that all church-building activity was restricted to the efforts of the Ecclesiastical Commissioners. During the early years of the century, before Nonconformity had sufficient political power to oppose such grants, parliamentary aid had been given in 1818 and 1824 to the Church Building Commission, which also sought to provide places of worship for the expanding population of the nation. Blomfield had served on this commission when he was still Bishop of Chester, and one lesson he learned was that not only members of the old landed aristocracy, but also the wealthy among the new manufacturing class could be appealed to when endowments were needed for the creation of new churches.[29]

One of the members of Peel's temporary commission of 1835 was the Honourable and Reverend Baptist Noel. He was appalled at the misery and spiritual destitution of the people of London, and wrote a public letter to Blomfield to urge that the Church remember its duty to the nation. 'I need not remind your lordship that the State has provided the clergy of the Establishment for this very end, that there may be no part of the population without its pastor.'[30] Blomfield, because of his diocesan experience, did not need to be reminded by Noel that the vast majority of the people in the metropolis were 'more untaught in divine truth than the New Zealanders, more unregarded than the Chinese'.[31] His answer to the immediate need of London was to launch an appeal for fifty new churches to be built at once by private subscription.

There was some alarm that an enterprise like this was to be initiated by the ever-busy Blomfield; but, within ten years of the appeal being made, his Metropolis Churches' Fund had provided for the building of forty-four churches, ten more were being built, and nine were about to be built. The Ecclesiastical Commissioners gave some assistance to this work, but most of the money came from private contributions. Pusey made an anonymous gift of £5,000 to the fund, and Blomfield's personal contribution was £2,000, including his building and endowing of St. Stephen's, Hammersmith.

Blomfield's initiative had a beneficial, indirect effect, for it stimulated the work of many other direct-aid societies which were established to relieve the spiritual wants of the poor. In Bethnal

29. M. H. Port, *Six Hundred New Churches* (1961), p. 110.
30. Baptist Wriothesley Noel, *State of the Metropolis Considered: Letter to the Lord Bishop of London* (1835), p. 26.
31. *Ibid.*, p. 12.

Green ten churches were built during the forties.[32] Appeals were also made in the north, particularly in Manchester; and by 1859 Dean Hook had raised money for twenty-one places of worship in Leeds. Blomfield's example also inspired the later appeal of Bishop Tait, who set up the Bishop of London's Fund in 1864 to provide for church building and pastoral work in the metropolis.

During Blomfield's episcopate nearly two hundred new churches were consecrated, and his own philanthropy did much to silence the critics who had feared that he was becoming a mere servant of the State. But Blomfield knew that the Church now could never catch up with the expanding population, and the dream of providing pastoral care for all members of society belonged to the past. When he launched his Metropolis Churches' Fund he said that his wish was to provide church-room for one-third of the population, and one church and minister for every 3,000 persons[33]—a recognition that the ideal of one clergyman for each 1,000 souls, which had once been his, was now abandoned.

An interesting study of the failure of the Church to provide for the spiritual needs of the masses is given in an open letter addressed to Gladstone later in the century. It says that in 1801 when the population was 9,168,000, the Church had 10,600 benefices and 11,000 clergy. By 1841 when the population was 15,914,148, there were 11,438 benefices and 13,960 clergy. By 1871 the population had risen to 22,712,266, but the number of benefices was only 13,725, and the number of clergy 20,694. Furthermore two-thirds of the clergy were in country livings in 1871, providing spiritual care for the 7,500,000 people who remained in rural areas. The endowments of these country livings were worth £2,500,000, but the 5,800 clergy serving the urban masses had only three-quarters of a million pounds endowment.[34]

By the end of the century the Ecclesiastical Commission was using the funds it had built up from episcopal, capitular, and other ecclesiastical estates to distribute over a million pounds a year to sustain work in thickly populated areas of the nation.[35] But the Church was no longer able to dream, as Blomfield once had, of serving its 'obligation to the State', as well as its 'duty towards God', by 'instruction and

32. This was one of the twenty-five parishes in which the population exceeded church-room by 20,000 or more, when the Church Building Commission began its labours.
33. Port, p. 110.
34. George B. Howard, *Future Supply of Clergy for the Service of the Church of England: Letter to Right Honourable W. E. Gladstone* (1875), p. 24.
35. *Year Book of the Church of England* (1900), p. 33.

edification of his people' in the English nation.[36] It did not have the resources to provide for the tremendous increase in population, which was largely concentrated in the urban areas where the Church's temporal strength was weakest. The prophecy of the Rector of Gedling, Nottinghamshire, made in 1833 was fulfilled. 'Our Establishment does not fulfil the purposes of its institution . . . from inherent defects, added to a culpable ministration, it is estranged from the affections of the people, in numbers scarcely national, a sect among the many.'[37]

Why had the Church failed to provide for all Englishmen, to be a national Church in either the way that Hooker or Warburton had believed it could? Why, particularly, had it become in the great cities just one sect among many in its social influence, part of the 'religious kaleidoscope' of the Victorian age?[38]

The answer to both questions lies in the terms of establishment which the Church was forced to accept in the early nineteenth century. The alliance of the Church with the State was such that even when churchmen desired reform, the Church had no means to assert itself as a corporation responsible for its own temporal welfare. Until 1843 it was not possible to create a new parish without an act of Parliament. Whatever the reform of church temporalities that was sought, it could only come through joint endeavour of Church and State to promote legislative action.

When Walter Farquhar Hook became Vicar of Leeds in 1837 he found that the city formed one parish, with 150,000 inhabitants. To assist the vicar there were incumbents of fifteen 'perpetual curacies with cure of souls'. Hook willingly sacrificed a third of his income in order that new parishes might be endowed by a special act of Parliament.[39] Not every rector of a large parish shared the pastoral concern of Hook, who had twenty-one churches built during his incumbency in Leeds; but, even when they did, the law was so complex that change was impossible. George Selwyn, who became Bishop of Lichfield in 1867, desired to sacrifice some of his income to bring the diocese of Southwell into being, but the law demanded that the minimum episcopal stipend be maintained, and this proved a stumbling block to his scheme.

Most churchmen agreed that new dioceses had to be created to deal with the new centres of industrial population in the north. But the

36. From Blomfield's Charge of 1834.
37. Charles Williams, *Considerations on the Present State of the Church* (1833), p. 7.
38. Asa Briggs, *Victorian Cities* (1963), p. 206.
39. C. J. Stranks, *Dean Hook* (1954), p. 64.

creation of new dioceses created constitutional problems which most prime ministers would rather have avoided. Bishops were tolerated in the House of Lords because they had always been there, and it could be argued that they made the State religious. But an increase in their number would make the Church political, and most politicians viewed with considerable suspicion any suggestion that the party in power might increase the size of the episcopate. When the new diocese of Ripon was created in 1836 the dioceses of Gloucester and Bristol were united until 1897 to make room for the new bishop in the House of Lords. When the diocese of Manchester came into being in 1847 the revolutionary step was taken of establishing that the junior bishop for the time being should not sit in the House. Political suspicions were allayed by this manoeuvre, and the bench of bishops became limited to the two archbishops and twenty-four of the diocesan bishops. With this development successive governments allowed the dismemberment of the huge medieval diocese of Lincoln so that the modern dioceses of Oxford, Peterborough, and Ely might come into being. The State also approved the creation of the dioceses of Truro and St. Albans in 1877, Liverpool in 1880, Newcastle in 1882, and Southwell and Wakefield in 1888.

Reform of the Church was slow because of the traditional yoking together of Church and State. It was impossible for one to move without the other in the reformation of ecclesiastical affairs. The Church was an integral part of the English nation, protected by its laws. Any change in its form had to be approved by Parliament, and political considerations influenced every act of the legislature.

Some reforms were easier than others. No one objected very much to adjusting bishops' incomes, to put them on the same level as a Judge of the High Court. Nor was there much opposition to the abolishment of in commendams, and the new policy of frowning upon translations. But any reform that in any way threatened to weaken the prerogatives of the Crown, or to loosen the traditional control of the temporalities of the Church by the laity, was sure to meet great opposition in Parliament. The Crown showed great suspicion of the demand for suffragan bishops in case its power of appointment might be reduced, though by the end of the century most dioceses had suffragans.[40] Lay opposition to the revival of Convocation also revealed a deep distrust of clerical motives.

40. Cf. George D'Oyly (Rector of Lambeth), A Letter to the Ecclesiastical Commissioners of England, on the subject of reviving the institution of Suffragan Bishops (London, 1843). The act for appointing suffragan bishops had been passed originally in 1534 (26 H.VIII, c. 14) and revived in 1559 (I Eliz., c. 1).

The truth was that the abuses in the Church were sustained as much by the laity as they were by the clergy, and the bishops by themselves could not possibly put their house in order. By mid-century the legislature knew that something had to be done for the spiritual welfare of the poor in the cities, but the lobbies that opposed the passing of reform legislation were strong. To promote such legislation, and to sustain the work of the Ecclesiastical Commissioners, bishops like Blomfield were indispensable.

Blomfield was representative of a breed of political bishop that the Church produced in Victorian England. Because their work was plodding, and they had to have the patience of any constitutional reformer, their work has seldom received the appreciation it deserves. But Blomfield and Tait, like Hook of Leeds, who was known as 'the Apostle of the Church to the great middle classes',[41] showed the way forward in the reform of the temporalities of the Church—through legislative action, and through nurturing philanthropy.

Pusey and the other High-Churchmen of Oxford could not appreciate Blomfield's policies. To them it seemed clear that the traditional apostolic government of the Church was being superseded by the Ecclesiastical Commission for the sake of centralization and efficiency. To Blomfield it was clear that in spite of the imperfections which accompanied the crippling alliance of Church and State in England, much could be done to reform the Church without loss of its divine authority. Like Van Mildert of Durham, he was willing to view what the commissioners took from the Church as a premium to be paid, to ensure that the Church might survive and serve the English people. The abstract arguments of the High-Churchmen he was apt to dismiss as the concerns of those ineffectuals who had 'a habit of creating difficulties, and then throwing the onus of them upon the Bishop'.[42]

As a conscientious diocesan, and as a political realist, Blomfield knew that if the Church of England was to be reformed it had to move with the State, in the same direction, at the same rate of speed—as fast as the Common Law would allow both of them to proceed. A modern newspaper has recorded that: 'the State-Church nexus in England is as intimate as that between the hermit crab and the sea-anemone on its back. Examining the relationship, all Commissions, ecclesiastics and academic authorities agree on one point: it is far too late to reorganize the Church of England in accordance with logical

41. Briggs, *Victorian Cities*, p. 159.
42. Blomfield, *Memoir*, p. 105.

principles.'[43] Miss Brose in her excellent study of Church and Parliament during this period says: 'Perhaps even Bishop Blomfield would have said "Amen" to that'.[44]

*3. Bishop Wilberforce
and Pastoral Reform*

WHILE Blomfield was convincing the legislature that it was expedient to work closely with the clergy of the Church in reform of its temporalities, another bishop was showing contemporaries that the new spirit of reform could influence even the pastoral life of the Church. This was Samuel Wilberforce, the friend and ally of Blomfield, and the son of the great Evangelical social reformer. More than any other prelate of this age he put an end to the bad old days of Richard Watson, Bishop of Llandaff from 1782 to 1816, who never settled in his diocese, and by his own admission did next to nothing for the £2,000 a year he received as bishop and professor of divinity at Cambridge.[1]

When Anthony Trollope described the three sons of Archdeacon Grantly in *The Warden* he had in mind Blomfield, Henry Phillpotts of Exeter, and Samuel Wilberforce. There is no doubt that 'Soapy Sam', as he was known, was a political bishop. He became a High-Churchman while he was at Oriel, though he never abandoned completely many of the Evangelical ideas he had inherited. Nor did he hesitate to make use of family connections which could be of help to him. Highly intelligent, with great energy of mind and body, an infinite capacity for work, and native eloquence, he was early marked out for preferment. By 1840 Prince Albert made him one of his chaplains, and he preached often and powerfully before the Queen. His ability as a speaker was such that Wellington confessed that he would 'face a battery sooner' than risk interrupting one of his orations.[2] Peel appointed him Dean of Westminster in 1845. He accepted this dignity but continued to hold the important living of Alverstoke in plurality. Six months later Peel offered him the see of Oxford.

Wilberforce was a different kind of High-Churchman from the

43. Michael Davis, 'A.B.C. of Disestablishment', *Observer*, 20 November 1955.
44. Brose, p. 215.
1. Charles Abbey and John Overton, *The English Church in the Eighteenth Century* (1887), p. 294.
2. A. R. Ashwell and R. G. Wilberforce, *Life of Samuel Wilberforce* (1880–83), I, 108.

academic theorists at Oxford; Newman refused contributions for the *British Critic* which Wilberforce offered, and Pusey and his bishop were in incessant controversy throughout their lives. Wilberforce said of his own theological opinions that he was trying to evolve a living synthesis of the ideas of the Caroline divines and of Hooker. From the former he accepted the idea of apostolic succession, and as early as 1833 preached on 'that unbroken succession whereby those who ordained us are joined unto Christ's own Apostles'.[3] In this he was at one with the Oxford theorists, but he also accepted from Hooker the idea of the national church, and it was at this point that he began to part from them. Just as much as Blomfield, Wilberforce was concerned with the 'art of the possible'. Trollope once remarked that it was the Oxford reformers who 'made episcopal idleness impossible, and clerical idleness rare',[4] but this change reflected the efforts of Wilberforce as well as the theories of the academics of Oriel and Christ Church. There is much truth in S.C. Carpenter's opinion: 'It is not an exaggeration to say that the degree to which the Oxford Movement took hold of the English Church is very largely due to Bishop Wilberforce. The Church accepted it in the same modified sense as that in which he accepted it.'[5] Wilberforce accepted gratefully the exaltation of the episcopal office made by Newman and his followers; but he did this for a definite purpose—to initiate a pastoral revolution in the Church of England.

Wilberforce was concerned that the Church should act as the conscience of the nation, and that the bench of bishops should voice the views of the Church in the legislature. In his maiden speech to the House of Lords he warned that national misdeeds would bring divine retribution—be the victims of these deeds Lancashire mill-hands or Japanese merchants. He continued his father's war against the evils of slavery, and also had much to say about tithe commutation, the repeal of the corn laws, the ten-hours bill, the protection of women acts, penal reform, and national education. His reputation as an orator meant that his services were sought in support of many causes. Sometimes his eloquence carried him into situations where it alone was not enough to sustain him—as in the unfortunate controversy with Huxley over Darwin's hypothesis, to which we will refer later.

Although he was such a powerful figure on the bench of bishops, Wilberforce's greatest contribution to the Church was made in his

3. G. W. E. Russell, 'Samuel Wilberforce' in S. L. Ollard and G. Crosse eds., *A Dictionary of English Church History* (London, 1912), p. 634.
4. Anthony Trollope, *Clergymen of the Church of England* (1866), p. 25.
5. Carpenter, *Church and People*, p. 261.

diocesan administration. A prelate who took as seriously as he did the authority of the bishop was bound to be a diocesan to be reckoned with. In a letter to Lord Shaftesbury he once said: 'The efficiency of diocesan management did not depend merely on the multiplication of clergy and churches . . . it is the Bishop who must be the main instrument in encouraging the zealous, in stirring up the faint-hearted, in animating the despondent; he must be to his clergy the example and the mainspring of holy living and dying for the people committed to their care.'[6]

Episcopal zealousness in diocesan administration was rare in the early nineteenth century. Trollope quipped in *The Warden* that if the archdeacons in a diocese worked there was nothing for a bishop to do; and Richard Bagot, Wilberforce's predecessor, had acted as if he had very active subordinates. He reported that in the Oxford diocese in 1834 there were only 7,000 communicants in a total population of 152,100 souls, and he appeared pleased that since his last visitation one church had been added to the 233 that provided places of worship for the people. Bagot was not unduly upset that these churches were manned by a total of only ninety-two resident clergy and forty-four curates.[7]

Wilberforce put an end to this episcopal lassitude. Ninety days of each year, when the weather permitted travelling, were spent in going about his diocese, personally putting his room of the Church's house in order. Many of these visitations were exhausting. Impassable winter roads meant that confirmations were held in the spring, and Wilberforce was very earnest in his ordering of the Occasional Services of the Church. Until this time confirmations had been considered occasions for revelling, but Wilberforce had such influence among Church people that one publican requested compensation from the bishop for loss of trade since the services had become matters of religion not carousing. The new bishop was very thorough in his ordering of these services, and their length, if nothing else, impressed parishioners. A Sunday morning ordination service was five hours long, with one hundred or more communicants.[8]

On such occasions, and any time that he could gather together a group of his clergy, Wilberforce used his personal powers of persuasion to exhort them to raise the level of parish worship. It was sadly in need of reform. In 1838 Newman was the only cleric in the diocese

6. *Life of Wilberforce*, III, 167.
7. Richard Bagot, *Charge to the Clergy of the Diocese of Oxford* (1834), p. 14.
8. *Life of Wilberforce*, I, 392–94.

who held a weekly celebration of the Eucharist and said the daily office. When T.W. Allies of Launton began a daily celebration as well as daily Matins and Evensong in his parish in the 1840's, his daughter records that this was 'a very unusual practice in those days'. Allies' wife attended the daily Evensong reluctantly after she registered strong protest against such extremism.[9]

Neglect of worship was inevitable when the spiritual zeal of so many of the clergy was low. Francis Pigou, who later became Dean of Bristol, tells in his biography of his curacy at Stoke Talmage at this time, and it makes fascinating reading. The rector of the parish, age 92, took an immediate liking to his new curate when he arrived, and showed his fondness by presenting Pigou with all his old sermons—and those of his father as well. The two clergy drove in a cart pulled by four donkeys, and wherever they went village lads met them with the shout: 'Here come the six!' The aged rector never recognized Pigou when he was clad in his surplice, and when they met after service demanded to know where Pigou had been. Such eccentricities were not unexpected in a man who wore a specially made vest with six pockets for carrying pen, ink, and paper at all times, and allowed the church to fall into such a state of neglect that chickens roosted in the pulpit. No visiting had been done for thirty years when Pigou arrived at Stoke Talmage. He found the village people almost totally ignorant of the Christian faith, or the meaning of the sacraments. When he asked a confirmation class what happened when a child was confirmed, he was solemnly told by one child that that was when she would take upon herself the sins of her godfather and godmother. Because the rector was a pluralist he could afford a good port cellar, and the local gentry showed more interest in this than in the neglect of the parish.[10]

As Pigou noted, this régime began to disappear throughout the diocese during the episcopate of Wilberforce. The work was slow because the bishop did not possess the means to redress many of the evils that were drawn to his attention. The Rector of Baulking with Woolstone wrote to him in 1869 to say: 'I am the incumbent of two churches nearly if not quite three and one half miles asunder, and with an ecclesiastical income of £75 per annum . . . my health and strength are failing me . . . does the Church expect that I am to pay for a curate out of £75 a year?'[11] Before he could help poor clergy

9. M. H. Allies, *Thomas William Allies* (1907), pp. 44–46.
10. Francis Pigou, *Phases of my Life* (1898), p. 122 ff.
11. R. K. Pugh, *Episcopate of Samuel Wilberforce: Diocesan Administration*, Oxford University unpublished D. Phil. thesis (1957), p. 151.

like this, Wilberforce had to have real power, and from the beginning of his Oxford episcopate he set out to build it up. He knew that he had to have power of patronage, as well as spiritual authority, if he was to accomplish what he desired.

When he became Bishop of Oxford, the see was comparatively new and not well-endowed. Only thirteen livings were in the gift of the bishop, and other people were as anxious to gain advowsons as was the bishop. The Evangelical party, in particular, had begun to buy up advowsons, to ensure that only Evangelicals would be appointed to them. One of these was St. Aldate's, Oxford, which had originally been presented to Pembroke College by Charles I. It came up for sale at this time, to be bought for £1,000 by the Simeon Trustees. The story is told that when the purchaser was on his way down the stairway after completing the transaction he met the energetic Samuel Wilberforce on his way up.[12] Such zealousness enabled him to raise the number of livings in his gift to 96 by 1869. This was only a small proportion of the total of 637 in the diocese, but many of those he controlled were in large towns where he could put reforming priests who shared his pastoral concerns.

In spite of all his efforts, Wilberforce's progress was slow. The clergy generally were in a state of apathy. Preaching was avoided whenever possible, Evensong was neglected because of the poor lighting in churches in the winter, and the bishop could do little but exhort delinquent clergy, because of the limitations of his real power. The Church Discipline Act of 1840 was very lenient; and the indolent hunting parson or clerical magistrate was a difficult man to influence, unless his life became the cause of public scandal.

Even an obvious abuse like non-residence was difficult to deal with because at this time there were no clerical pensions. The parson was protected by his freehold, and even an ineffectual like the Rector of Stoke Talmage could not be dislodged. The Rector of Emberton was absent from his parish for fifteen years because a physician had certified that it was necessary for him to live in a more healthy location, which he did until his death in 1860 at the age of eighty-seven. The bishop had no power to force his retirement as an alternative to non-residence. It was not until 1871, when he was Bishop of Winchester, that Wilberforce was able to secure retirement pensions for clergy.[13]

Like his friend Blomfield, Wilberforce knew that to reform the temporalities of the Church he would need to work within the

12. J. S. Reynolds, *Evangelicals at Oxford, 1735–1871* (1953), pp. 134–35.
13. For the problem of non-residence *v.* Diana McClatchey, *Oxfordshire Clergy 1777–1869* (1960), pp. 30–39.

limitations imposed by the Common Law. When he wished to build his theological college at Cuddesdon, he believed that all he needed to do was to separate the village of Wheatley from the parish of Cuddesdon. But he discovered that he was not only Rector of Cuddesdon, but vicar of it also (the vicarage had been granted *in commendam* to the Bishop of Oxford by Charles I). Because of the complexity of the law, he was forced to exchange the lands he held as rector and vicar legally, before he could separate Wheatley and Cuddesdon and build his new college on what had been vicarial land. Fifteen years later the Vicar of Wheatley raised claim to certain lands which he said were vicarial and had been withheld.[14] Such stumbling blocks to reform did not deter Wilberforce, and during his time as Bishop of Oxford he built 106 new places of worship, restored 250, and rebuilt 15. He also built seventy new parsonages, to encourage residence, which now dominate the villages of the diocese 'like so many great white elephants . . . presenting a social and economic problem to the incumbent and his wife'.[15] The teacher's college at Culham and the seminary at Cuddesdon also reflect his reforming zeal.

Wilberforce had no intention of allowing the clergy to share in the direction of his reform programme. His own temperament, as well as his study of the Caroline divines, allowed him to accept the idea that the episcopate was the *esse* of the Church—but he refused to countenance the pretensions of the Tractarians who sought to exalt clerical authority generally. He believed that their form of clericalism sought to take from the layman the direction 'of his own spiritual life', in the manner of the Roman Catholics. He wanted the clergy to support his reform activities, but he was most reluctant to delegate authority, or to encourage clerical associations. The reform of the diocese of Oxford was to be from the top down.

When Pusey showed reluctance to abide by Wilberforce's admonitions regarding the ministry of absolution, he found himself in trouble. Even before Wilberforce reached his diocese he admonished Pusey for 'self-dependence', and his tendency to 'judge the Church which you ought to obey'.[16] By 1850 the bishop was condemning the 'general effect of Pusey's ministry'. The latter assured his diocesan that to ease the tension between them 'All I can do with a safe conscience, I will do.'[17]

14. Pugh, p. 36.
15. McClatchey, pp. 24–25.
16. H. P. Liddon, *Life of Edward Bouverie Pusey* (1898), III, 47–49.
17. *Ibid.*, III, 307.

As far as Wilberforce was concerned, Pusey was the leader of the Oxford theorists; and he knew the trouble their ideas caused among his clergy. They led High-Churchmen to be rigorist in their dealings with Dissenters, refusing to marry or to bury them. This resulted in social bitterness which in no way helped the mission of the Church to the nation. Tract 58 of *Tracts for the Times*, entitled 'Position of the Church of Christ in England Relatively to the State and the Nation', had complained that although the churchwardens of each parish promised the archdeacon on his visitation to give him the names of all in the parish who were leading notoriously immoral lives, no single presentation had been made for a hundred years. Many of the Oxford High-Churchmen believed this situation should be remedied, but Wilberforce knew from his diocesan activities how the laity felt about such ideas. When the churchwarden of Sotwell was asked whether there were any notorious sinners in his parish, he replied: 'Not that I know of, if there were I am certain the Congregation would not care about it. I am not prepared to go back into the dark ages of Popery'.[18] Wilberforce never had any doubt about what was practical, and he knew the popular distrust of Tractarian ideas, which presented the clergy as a caste of intermediaries between God and man and seemed to widen the gulf between clergy and laity. Much of the tension between Wilberforce and Pusey came from the former's suspicion that the ideas of the Oxford reformers were, in fact, impeding the progress of his pastoral revolution.[19]

Wilberforce was as much devoted to the cause of the national Church as Blomfield, and his desire to rescue it from Erastian bondage led him into conflict with the court—a conflict which put an end to much of his personal ambition. As chaplain to Prince Albert he was often at court; and, when he became Bishop of Oxford, the Prince Consort gave him advice regarding his activities in other than purely spiritual concerns.

> A bishop ought to abstain completely from mixing himself up with the politics of the day, and beyond giving a general support to the Queen's government, and occasionally voting for it, should take no part in the discussion of State affairs . . . but he should come forward whenever the interests of humanity are at stake, and give boldly and manfully his advice to the House and Country.[20]

But Wilberforce did not always abide by this caution of Albert's, and many people believed that it was his attempt to promote the interests

18. Pugh, p. 340.
19. *Life of Pusey*, III, 312.
20. *Life of Wilberforce*, I, 276.

of the Church as a corporate body in the nation (as well as his handling of the Hampden affair) [21] which cost him the Primacy of the Church of England. In a sermon which Canon H.P. Liddon preached in 1875 on the work of Wilberforce, he said: 'If he could have brought himself . . . to ignore the spiritual character of the English Church; to treat her practically as a State Department, to appeal to Acts of Parliament for her highest claims . . . the higher ecclesiastical honours could not in the nature of things have been withheld.' [22] Soapy Sam was often pilloried for his charm, and accused of being a political 'trimmer'; but whatever his failings as a person he was not the master of expediency that his enemies believed him to be. As he said of himself: 'You do not suppose that I am so blind as not to see perfectly that I might have headed the Evangelical party and been seated by them at Lambeth'. [23]

Wilberforce first began to lose political favour when he supported the churchmen who desired the revival of Convocation—a project which was of much concern to him. In 1837 an attempt was made in the House of Commons to make Convocation once more 'efficient for the purposes for which it was recognized by the constitution', but the motion was defeated. Lord John Russell remarked at this time that he 'could not see the advantage of reviving the religious disputes of the reign of Queen Anne'. [24] This Erastian viewpoint was shared by the Archbishop of Canterbury, Palmerston, and the press, while many clergy expressed opposition to the idea.

Since 1717, when Bishop Hoadly had been protected from the censure of the Tory clergy of the Lower House of Canterbury, Convocation had been suppressed for all practical purposes by use of the Royal Supremacy. At the opening of each Parliament, Convocation was formally summoned by Royal Writ to meet. But the only business enacted was the drawing up and the sending of a Loyal Address to the Throne. After this formal duty Convocation was prorogued. The effect of this was that the Church was left without any central deliberative or legislative body to redress the grievances which existed in ecclesiastical affairs—at a time when Parliament had less and less time to devote to the Church, as the pressure of secular business increased.

Wilberforce knew from diocesan experience that one of the great weaknesses of the Church was the absence within it of any form of

21. *V. infra* p. 74.
22. H. P. Liddon, *Bishop Wilberforce* (1875), p. 27.
23. *Life of Wilberforce*, II, 360.
24. G. Crosse, 'Convocation', in *Dictionary of English Church History*, p. 145.

centralized government. Even within a diocese there was no synod where ecclesiastical matters might be discussed and regulated; 'every parish seems almost a distinct and complete unit in itself and to be a microcosm, self-sustaining, self-involved, and self-sufficient.'[25] Without the revival of Convocation or the setting up of some similar body, Wilberforce knew that the pastoral reformation, which meant so much to him, could not be extended to the Church as a whole. His enthusiasm was shared by Henry Hoare, a layman and London banker, whom Wilberforce had known since childhood. Hoare was the leading spirit of 'The Society for the Revival of Convocation', a body of churchmen who were concerned for the corporate welfare of the Church in the nation. He did not share Wilberforce's exalted idea of episcopal authority, and preferred to have a synod which included the laity as the central authority for the Church. He knew this was impossible to attain, however, and he agreed to work with the Bishop of Oxford to restore Convocation, in the hope that it would assist the national legislature to become Christian in tone and character.

Wilberforce's cause was helped by the 'papal aggression' of 1850. In that year Pius IX issued a bull which constituted England an ecclesiastical province of the Roman Catholic Church under an Archbishop at Westminster. Hoare argued in a great London meeting of 1851 that this Roman Catholic manoeuvre was due to the 'crippled state of the Church of England'. It was also pointed out that when Parliament was open to non-Anglicans it was in no way now the lay synod of the Church; the revival of Convocation could not be delayed in this time of peril to Protestantism and the Established Church.[26]

Largely because of the perseverance of Wilberforce and Hoare, Lord Derby in 1852 advised the Crown to allow Convocation to resume its functions. In 1854, Lord Aberdeen as Prime Minister (with Archbishop Sumner's only half-hearted approval) allowed a report of a committee on the constitution of Convocation to be considered by Convocation. Archbishop Musgrave of York remained opposed to the revival of Convocation for the northern province, and it did not come into being until 1861, after his death.

When Convocation did meet, it was not an ideal body, particularly in its representation. Only beneficed clergy could elect members, and they were outnumbered by the archdeacons, deans, and representatives of the chapters. Its deliberations should have dealt with matters like

25. *Report of the Proceedings of the Church Congress* (1861), p. iv.
26. *Report of the Public Meeting of Churchmen on the Papal Aggression and For the Revival of Convocation. Henry Hoare Esq. in the Chair* (1851).

the best way of dealing with the crowded poor in the great cities; but, though this and other important problems were discussed, much time was given to issues like temperance, betting, prostitution, better education of the young, and occasionally housing and industrial conciliation. It is doubtful that much has come out of Convocation to significantly influence the history of either the English Church or the English nation in the nineteenth century.

Yet, as Bishop Browne later commented: 'With more life in the Church, the claim for a restoration of the Convocations would have made itself felt long before.'[27] The revival of the ancient governing body of the Church did reflect new life stirring within the Establishment, which was growing restless as reformers like Blomfield and Wilberforce urged that the Church re-discover within itself the resources needed to bring the blessings of the Gospel to the people it had so long neglected. Convocation was but one of the fruits of the pastoral revolution which began in Wilberforce's diocese, and spread far beyond its boundaries.

Henry Hoare's idea of clergy and laity meeting in synods was not completely forgotten. As the pastoral revival took hold, diocesan conferences of clergy and laity began to be held, the first under Bishop Harold Browne in the Diocese of Ely in 1865. Church Congresses, which were unofficial gatherings of churchmen, were held from 1861. At the second congress, which was held at Oxford in 1865, an attempt was made to pass resolutions, but Wilberforce 'saw the peril' and firmly reminded the gathering that it was merely a forum to express opinion.[28] Both the High-Churchmen, like Keble and Pusey, and the bishops were suspicious of the laity having a voice in spiritual matters, in a Church where they in large measure already controlled its temporalities. But as the pastoral revival took hold, they could not be kept out of spiritual deliberations. By 1886 in the Province of Canterbury and 1892 in York, Houses of Laity were meeting, their members elected by Diocesan Conferences, and communication taking place with Convocation by way of the Archbishop of each province. Later the two Convocations and the Houses of Laity met together to form a 'Representative Church Council'. This body of Church opinion was eventually to evolve into the modern Church Assembly.[29]

There were many churchmen who could not appreciate the work of bishops like Blomfield and Wilberforce. As we have seen, Pusey made

27. G. F. Browne (Bishop of Bristol), 'Memorandum on Church and State in English History' in *Report of the Archbishops' Committee on Church and State* (1916), p. 236.
28. *Life of Wilberforce*, III, 51.
29. Guy Mayfield, *The Church of England, Its Members and Its Business* (1958), p. 126.

a contribution of £5,000 to Blomfield's Metropolis Churches' Fund in 1836, and at the time of this 'munificent donation' bishop and scholar respected and appreciated one another.[30] But, when Blomfield rejected two candidates for ordination for asserting the doctrine of the Real Presence and the Real Sacrifice in the Eucharist, they were less in accord. Pusey, the theologian, believed strongly that 'It is every one's duty to maintain Catholic truth, even if unhappily opposed by a Bishop.'[31] By 1845 Pusey's admiration of Blomfield as a pastor was sadly qualified by the theological differences between them. Similarly, Pusey appreciated greatly the pastoral zeal of Wilberforce, but found himself inhibited by him because of theological differences.

This suspicion of 'expediency' governing all that Blomfield and Wilberforce attempted was not limited only to the High-Churchmen of Oxford. No one could deny their zeal, which represented the new spirit in the Church, but even a Broad-Churchman like F. D. Maurice could express a mild cynicism with regard to their efforts to revive Convocation and give direction to a general reform of the Church.

> Even if the Convocation should find out that it existed only to impose taxes on the clergy—which I fancy is the true idea of it—I cannot think that in a day when Blomfield is virtually their ruler, this office should be performed with any safety to that which is abidingly meant for the good of future generations. Everything would be sacrificed to the tastes, fears, or apparent advantages of the moment.[32]

But to put the Church's house in order, to redistribute its wealth, to reform the glaring abuses which gave cause to public scandal, and to persevere in spiritual reform, bishops like Blomfield and Wilberforce were needed. Both of them were political realists. Both of them knew that the Church of England was the Church of the nation, and that to change it sufficiently for it to begin again its mission to the English people, particularly the neglected masses of the industrial areas, the Church had to work with the State. 'What the Church of England wanted', said Wilberforce in 1854, 'was increased liberty to adapt themselves to the present necessities of the people.'[33] This liberty was granted because the labours of prelates like Blomfield and Wilberforce persuaded statesmen like Peel and Russell that the long slumber of the Church was over, that a new sense of mission had arrived.

Blomfield and Wilberforce were the most energetic and dynamic

---

30. *Life of Pusey*, I, 330.
31. *Ibid.*, II, 232–38.
32. Frederick Maurice, *Life of Frederick Denison Maurice* (1885), I, 309.
33. *Hansard*, CXXXIII, 1854, 149 ff.

personalities on the bench of bishops in an age of reform. There were other 'political bishops' at this time—no one could deny that the turbulent Henry Phillpotts of Exeter was anything but a political prelate, and he was also in his own way a reformer. But his love of controversy, his passion for litigation, and his vigorous protection of the rights and privileges of the Church never allowed him to work with the legislature in the way of Blomfield and Wilberforce.

A new spirit was at work in the Church by 1833. Archbishop of Canterbury, William Howley, who was primate from 1828, was representative of the old régime that was passing. He had opposed the Roman Catholic Relief Bill of 1829, the Reform Bill of 1831, the Irish Church Reform Bill of 1833, and Lord John Russell's mild scheme for National Education in 1839. The last Prince-Archbishop of Canterbury, the Ecclesiastical Commission reduced the income of his see to £15,000 a year on his death. Howley had driven to Westminster from Lambeth in a coach flanked by outriders; when he crossed the courtyard of Lambeth Palace, from chapel to Mrs. Howley's lodgings, he was preceded by men bearing flambeaux. Once a week during the season he kept open house. Anyone was welcome at these dinners if he wore court dress. The food and wine was served by thirty flunkeys in livery, and fifteen without livery.[34] The successor to Howley was the pious evangelical, John Bird Sumner, who led at Lambeth the simple life of a country clergyman, lighting his own fires and walking to the House of Lords with an umbrella beneath his arm.

It is difficult to appreciate the herculean labours of Blomfield and Wilberforce, or to appreciate them as churchmen, because of the bad clerical press they received in the late nineteenth century. The situation was unlike that of the mid-twentieth century, when it is considered disloyal to the Church to criticize bishops seriously; the High-Churchmen of Victorian England did not hesitate to castigate the episcopate. No spiritual good was expected of men appointed by the State and intimately connected with its duties. 'The episcopate is not to be expected to initiate any spiritual movement, not to be expected to do anything which will greatly offend the world.'[35]

These High-Churchmen were continuing the critical policies of clergy like Sydney Smith, who, in an article in the *Edinburgh Review* of 1822 entitled 'Persecuting Bishops', had said, 'Prelates are fond

34. For an appreciation of Howley's personal piety v. R. T. Davidson, *Five Archbishops*, (London, 1911), pp. 9–10. For his work on the Ecclesiastical Commission v. Best, *Temporal Pillars*, pp. 345–47.

35. Compton Berdmore, *The Church, the World and the State: Sermon at All Saints, Margaret Street, 13 June 1876*, p. 14.

of talking of my see, my clergy, my diocese, as if these things belonged to them, as their pigs and dogs belonged to them. They forget that the clergy, the diocese and the Bishops themselves, all exist only for the common good.'[36] Whatever the faults of Blomfield and Wilberforce, they never forgot, as many of their High-Church critics did, that the Church was the Church of the nation; that it did exist for the common good. Unfortunately for the peace of the Church, the new order in the Establishment desired by the episcopate and Parliament was not what was desired by many churchmen—particularly the High-Church clergy. Reform was in the air, but it was not limited to the activities of bishops like Blomfield and Wilberforce. The clergy too had rediscovered a sense of vocation.

36. Smith, *Works*, I, 122.

II. The Clergy
and the Defence of
Spiritual Prerogatives

In the year 1831 the whole fabric
of English and indeed
European society was trembling to
the foundations.
Every party, every interest,
political or religious, in this
country, was pushing its claims to
universal acceptance, with the
single exception of the Church of
England, which was folding its
robes to die with what
dignity it could.

THOMAS MOZLEY

1. *The Clergy in 1833*

THE THREAT of spoliation which produced such alarm among the prelates of the Church, who were concerned with the loss of temporal power, had much less effect among the intellectuals of the Church. Unlike the mass of the 'establishment men' or the Evangelicals, who recognized the help given to their party by the State connection, the intellectuals, most of whom were High-Churchmen, toyed in the 1830's with the idea of disestablishment. They believed that advantages, in terms of spiritual licence, might accrue to the clergy if such a move proved necessary.[1] But this blithe moment passed when a series of moves by the State, including the abolition of the redundant Irish bishoprics, seemed to indicate that the secular power of Parliament would consider an invasion of the Church's spiritual life, as well as a reorganization of its temporalities. This fear initiated a clerical counter-reformation to protect the Church, which, in the long run, was at least as important as the labours of prelates like Blomfield and Wilberforce.

EPIGRAPH: *Reminiscences, Chiefly of Oriel College and the Oxford Movement* (1882), I, 273.

1. *Pusey House MSS*, Keble to Newman, July 1833, on 'a little wholesome spoliation' being good for the soul of the Church.

'The bishops wished well to the truth, but they were in fear of the government . . . they were cautious and did not see their way to any action in opposition to the spirit of the times . . . it fell to the inferior clergy to save the Church.'[2]

Cleric after cleric sounded the alarm. At Cambridge the Regius Professor of Greek, James Scholefield, said that without the services of the Established Church: 'The immediate result must be that our villages would at once be abandoned to heathenism.'[3] The *British Critic* agreed 'the permanence even of civilization itself would almost become a problem'[4] if the Church was weakened by a meddlesome legislature. Hugh James Rose, Rector of Hadleigh, Suffolk, who had great influence at Cambridge, as well as among the clergy of London, urged that there not be 'the total abandonment on the part of the State of the paramount duty of providing instruction for all who will have it in that scheme of salvation which is the only source of real and stable comfort here'.[5]

Others urged that the State not abandon Christianity which had contributed so much 'to form the mind and character of Englishmen'.[6]

The most radical study of what was the true position of the Church in the Commonwealth—what were its spiritual prerogatives, and what was to distinguish the authority of the Church from that of the State—was made in Oxford. The traditional date given for the beginning of this reassessment of Anglicanism, which became known as the Oxford Movement, is 14 July 1833. On this day John Keble, Professor of Poetry and Fellow of Oriel College, delivered an assize sermon entitled 'National Apostasy' in the Church of St. Mary the Virgin, Oxford.[7] The church was excessively crowded, but neither the assize judges there assembled nor anyone but a small group of clerical dons who were friends of Keble was much influenced by the sermon. Certainly the newspapers of the day showed little interest in the address. But John Henry Newman was one of the Oxford dons who heard the sermon, and he later said that he always considered it to be 'the start of the religious movement of 1833'.[8]

2. William Palmer, *Supplement to Narrative of Events Connected with the Publication of Tracts for the Times* (1883), pp. 30–31.

3. James Scholefield, *An Argument for a Church Established: Sermon Preached Before the University of Cambridge* (1833), p. 15.

4. *British Critic*, XIV (1833), 298. Review of a tract on Church Reform by the Archdeacon of Colchester.

5. H. J. Rose, *The Churchman's Duty and Comfort in the Present Times* (1833), p. 7.

6. James Mules, *Benefits of the National Church of England* (1833), p. 69.

7. John Keble, *Assize Sermon on National Apostasy*, 1833 (1931).

8. J. H. Newman, *Apologia Pro Vita Sua*, 1864 (1959), p. 122.

The 'movement of 1833' was a clerical revolt against the Erastian position of the Church of England. The latitudinarians of the eighteenth century had seen the ideal Church-State relationship to be 'a politic league and alliance for mutual support and defence; for the State not having the care of souls cannot, itself, enforce the influence of religion, and therefore seeks the concurring aid of the Church; and the Church having no coercive power as naturally flies for assistance to the State.'[9] But by 1833 churchmen wondered whether the State was not about to redefine the terms of the Church-State alliance. They had little faith that the aristocracy would protect the Church when it appeared that they were willing, if necessary, to abandon it as a sop to the new middle class in Parliament. Nor had they much faith that the Erastian bench of bishops would be able to halt the 'frequent craving for such a reform of the Church by authority of the legislature . . . as should extend yet further even to our Liturgy and our articles'.[10] The legislature seemed to be filled with 'vain and foolish men' who 'did not fear to encounter the most important questions in every direction touching on the most essential principles of the Church'.[11] It seemed clear that a situation might arise where 'statesmen not churchmen are to deal with spirituals, a principle which no conscientious churchman can admit.'[12]

> The legislature has ratified to its full extent this principle—that the Apostolical Church in this realm is henceforth only to stand, in the eye of the State, as one sect among many, depending for any pre-eminence she might still appear to retain, merely upon the accident of her having a strong party in the country.[13]

As the 'meddling' in ecclesiastical affairs by the legislature increased, a 'quiet revolution' in the thinking of High-Churchmen, in particular, began to take place. Christopher Wordsworth who had been nurtured on Hooker, Andrewes, Barrow, and Butler said 'when bad men (and bad influences) conspire, then, as it is said, it is high time that good men and good influences should associate.'[14] By 1833 the association of 'good men' was beginning to appear, and to resist

9. Richard King, *Remarks on the Alliance Between Church and State and on the Test Laws* (1807), p. 17.
10. Rose, *Churchman's Duty and Comfort*, p. 10.
11. Palmer, *Supplement to Narrative*, p. 28.
12. Rose, *Churchman's Duty and Comfort*, p. 14.
13. Keble, *National Apostasy*, advertisement from its first edition.
14. Christopher Wordsworth, *Christian Institutes: a Series of Discourses and Tracts* (1842), I, xviii. Wordsworth was Master of Trinity College, Cambridge.

the ideas of men like Brougham who 'loved to frighten the Tories by brandishing Paley's principle and that of the absolute sovereignty of a parliamentary majority before their apprehensive eyes'.[15]

The leadership in this early association was predominantly clerical. 'Our principle was a combination of churchmen . . . and it was of a nature to commend itself to one body and class of men—even the clergy of England'.[16] This is an important point to remember when an attempt is made to understand the significance of the Oxford Movement. Clerics dominated it, and the only layman of any real significance associated with the Oxford reformers was J. W. Bowden, Newman's oldest Oxford friend. James Anthony Froude, the brother of the Oxford reformer, argued that the 'original reformation was a revolt of the laity against the clergy'.[17] Looking at the Oxford Movement of the 1830's, it is difficult not to view it as a clerical counter-reformation, a reaction to the tyranny of an Erastian legislature which said 'so long as we guarantee you your property we will take for ourselves the right of controlling your discipline and of preventing you from exercising any spiritual power over your members'.[18]

Oxford believed that the traditional relationship between Church and State stood in danger of radical alteration. Newman suggested to Bowden that a new study needed to be made along the lines of William Warburton's *Alliance Between Church and State*; a redefinition of 'the relation of the Church as such, to the world and the civil power'.[19] From Oxford came the call for the clergy to associate, to defend the Church against the demonic legislature. The *British Critic* was sure that the Church, led by the clergy, 'the great agents under God of beneficial changes, the chief ministers by his blessing of temporal as of eternal happiness to their fellow creatures', was capable of defending itself.

15. G. F. A. Best, 'Whigs and the Church Establishment in the Age of Grey and Holland', *History*, XLV (1960), 116. William Paley, *Principles of Moral and Political Philosophy* (1811), II, 325, had argued 'there is nothing in the nature of religion as such which exempts it from the authority of the legislator when the safety or welfare of the community requires his interposition.'

16. Palmer, *Narrative*, p. 49.

17. J. A. Froude, *Lectures on the Council of Trent* (1870), p. 102.

18. *Memoirs of Sir Robert Peel, 1828–1846* (1857), I, 84. The words are those of Bishop Charles Lloyd of Oxford. William Paley, *Distinction of Orders in the Church Defended* (1782), p. 12, was willing to maintain the traditional hierarchy of the Church, but only that it might 'supply each class of the people with a clergy of their own level and description, with whom they may live and associate upon terms of equality'.

19. Anne Mozley, *Letters and Correspondence of John Henry Newman During his Life in the English Church* (1891), II, 26.

It has a vast and we believe an increasing proportion of the numerical population of the country; it has a still vaster proportion of its property, its respectability, its talents, its intelligence, improved by the highest advantages of education and association; it has a body of clergy which, from its most elevated grades to its lowest, has never been surpassed; it has great societies of which the energy is such that it requires to be guided than stimulated.[20]

2. The Tractarians

WHEN THE clergy began their association to defend the spiritual prerogatives of the Church, they were a mixed crew of intellectuals, as dismayed and bewildered as the prelates of the Church at the magnitude of the threat that faced them. Generally they were High- or Broad-Churchmen. The Evangelicals showed little interest in the principles which excited the Oxford High-Churchmen; concern with what was 'Catholic, or Church, or sacramental' was dismissed as 'ecclesiastical Christianity'.[1] To be concerned with the Idea of the Church was to turn away from Justification by Faith. They viewed the Establishment as a protection for the Protestant faith, rather than 'an incubus upon the country', as the Oxford dons called it.[2]

Following Keble's Assize Sermon, Oxford was excited by 'the new question of questions for the Oxford intelligentsia—what really was the Church of England'.[3] But each group of intellectuals had a different answer to the problem. There were first of all those who were influenced by the thought of 'High Church dignitaries, Archdeacons, London Rectors and the like, who belonged to what was commonly called the high-and-dry school'.[4] These men who were willing to consider reform possibilities within the Establishment, 'sensible, temperate, sober, well-judging persons', the makers of 'misty compromises', were labelled as 'Z's' by Newman and Froude.[5] Their chief figure at Oxford was Martin Routh of Magdalen, but their real leader was J. H. Rose, whose influence at Cambridge,

20. *British Critic*, XXI (1837), 509–13.
1. E. A. Litton, *The Church of Christ in Its Idea, Attributes and Ministry* (1851), p. ix.
2. William Goode, *Case as It Is: Reply to the Letter of Dr. Pusey to the Archbishop of Canterbury* (1843), p. 35.
3. Geoffrey Faber, *Jowett* (1957), p. 108.
4. Newman, *Apologia*, p. 125.
5. Geoffrey Faber, *Oxford Apostles* (1954), p. 370.

where he was Select Preacher, was reputed to be as great as that of Charles Simeon of Holy Trinity Church. It was because of this school of thought, which contained within the Church the tradition maintained outside it by the Nonjurors, that Keble and Pusey and others had been trained in the faith, practice, and discipline of the Prayer Book, rather than the ideas of the Whig latitudinarians.[6]

In 1832 Rose produced the *British Magazine*, which was dedicated to the defence of Church principles. It contained documents of contemporary interest and bulletins of ecclesiastical and educational affairs from all over England. Rose hoped that this publication could help 'towards reviving the hopes and rekindling the aspirations of English churchmen' in the cause of 'internal union', which he believed to be the best safeguard against the dangers of the Church.[7] Through contributors to his magazine, such as William Palmer, the liturgical scholar of Worcester College, he was introduced to the High-Churchmen of Oxford. He already knew both Pusey and Newman, but a visit to Palmer in the summer of 1832 introduced him to other clerics who shared his concern for the Church: Richard Hurrell Froude of Oriel College, the Honourable and Reverend A. P. Perceval of All Souls, and Isaac Williams of Trinity College. He became a special friend at this time of John Keble; and it appeared that Rose, Palmer, Newman, Froude, Perceval, Williams, and Martin Routh were all on the side of the angels. When Rose was criticized for seeking help exclusively from Oxford, he retorted 'I get no help whatever from Cambridge. . . . I love Cambridge to my heart: but Divinity is not her tower of strength just now'.[8]

As Rose and the Oxford dons continued to meet together, it became clear that the former was a 'Z', an Establishment man, who looked back to Hooker and his judicious interpretation of the marriage of Church and State in the nation. His outlook was that of the clergy of London, who were aware (like Blomfield) of the practical difficulties facing the Church as the society of which it was a part changed rapidly. These men were concerned with questions such as: 'If Convocation were restored and made . . . a Parliament for the clergy, should we be better governed.'[9] They also wondered whether the Church would be capable of governing itself if separated from the State, because of the party strife within it.

6. J. H. Newman, *Lectures on the Prophetical Office of the Church* (1837), in the dedication to Martin Routh spoke of the High-Churchmen as those 'reserved to report to a forgetful generation what was the theology of their fathers'.
7. J. W. Burgon, 'Hugh James Rose', in *Lives of Twelve Good Men* (1891), pp. 83–84.
8. *Ibid.*, p. 86.
9. *Pusey House MSS*, Edward Churton to Perceval, 22 March 1836.

The Oxford clergy tended to gaze at the world from the windows of Oriel, or the lofty heights of the pulpit of St. Mary's. They looked back to the Nonjurors rather than to Hooker, to 'that ancient religion . . . well nigh faded away out of the land, through the political changes of the last 150 years'.[10] They wished to restore the golden age of Laud through a second Reformation. Their passionate call to faith, and Froude's belief that disestablishment would force the Church to find its spiritual resources, 'our only chance',[11] drew from Rose the comment 'I should have very little hope for it . . . very brilliant, very striking, very imaginative, but dreamy, theoretical, not practical.'[12]

The differences between Rose and the Oxford reformers became evident when an organizational meeting was held at Rose's rectory at Hadleigh in midsummer, 1833. Froude, Perceval, Palmer, and Rose were there, but Keble and Newman were not present. As Palmer later said, they had no confidence in meetings or committees, and Newman reveals in his *Apologia* that he was already bent on independent action. The Hadleigh group discussed for three days the dangers to the Church, and the remedies which might be found to protect it. The publication of tracts on Church principles was discussed, but on the whole nothing much came out of the meeting.[13] But back at Oxford, at Oriel College during the long vacation of 1833, there was formed 'The Association of Friends of the Church'. The leading figures in this association were Keble, Newman, and Froude. The members of it were to 'withstand all change involving the denial or suppression of doctrine, a departure from primitive practice in religious offices, or innovation upon the Apostological prerogatives, order and commission of bishops, priests and deacons'.[14]

Newman had come to the conclusion that Rose was a 'practical man' for whom 'existing facts had the precedence of every other idea, and the chief test of the soundness of a line of policy lay in the consideration whether it would work'. Newman knew that Rose had a position in the Church, intimate relations with his own university, and that he had a 'large clerical connection throughout the country'. But he would not agree that such factors of 'expediency' should be able to influence the thought of churchmen who as 'apostolicals' believed themselves responsible to no one but God and His Church.[15]

10. Newman, *Apologia*, p. 128.
11. R. H. Froude. *Remains* (1838), I, Pt. 1, 396.
12. *Keble College MSS*, Rose to Keble, 19 August 1833.
13. Burgon, p. 93.
14. *Life of Pusey*, I, 268.
15. Newman, *Apologia*, p. 124.

In his *Apologia* Newman contrasts the views of Rose with those of Froude, and there is no doubt that the latter influenced him greatly. Froude had all the exuberance of the undergraduate; as Dean Burgon said, he was 'sadly wanting in judgment'.[16] Considering this, his youth, his limited experience, and the extravagance of many of his ideas, filled with the urgency of a dying man, one wonders how seriously his work should be taken. But Newman considered him a man 'of high genius', with an 'intellect as critical and logical as it was speculative and bold'.[17] The production of his *Remains*, after his premature death in 1836, shocked his generation, brought unwanted publicity to Newman and his followers, and aroused widespread indignation. Froude's contemporaries took him seriously, particularly Newman; and in order to understand the schism between the Oxford and London schools of clerical reformers, as well as the beginning of the Tractarian movement, we must try to understand the thought of Froude.

Froude thought the Reformation had been a catastrophe in English history; dismissed Bishop Jewel as an 'irreverent Dissenter'; and among the Protestant reformers saw value only in Calvin, who had had some idea of clerical sovereignty and had been willing to fight for the *jus divinum* even though it was not the true one.[18] Since the seventeenth century, he said, all ecclesiastics had been 'twaddlers',[19] who bowed to the State and accepted a constitutional settlement for the Church in the nation that was theologically unsound.[20] The one bright spot in English ecclesiastical history since the decline of the medieval Church had been the age of Laud, and that of the Nonjurors.

This was an unhistorical idealization of the Caroline era when, Newman and Froude believed, the ecclesiastical power as well as the secular power in the State had rested with the sovereign. All his policies had been formed with advice of prelates and clergy of the Church, who shaped the conscience of the nation. The King with the

---

16. Burgon, p. 93.
17. Newman, *Apologia*, p. 113.
18. *Remains*, I, Pt. II, 386–94.
19. *Ibid.*, I, Pt. I, 355.
20. *Ibid.*, I, Pt. II, 187. Froude might have appreciated High-Churchmen such as Edmund Gibson (Bishop of London, 1720–1748), who had said, *Codex Juris Ecclesiastici Anglicani* (1713), p. xxix, that 'the ancient ecclesiastical power was not . . . extinguished or laid aside, but only subject to greater restraints than it had been before.' Samuel Horsley, Bishop of St. Asaph, had argued in his *Primary Visitation Charge* (1791), p. 36, that 'he who thinks of God's ministers as the mere servants of the State is out of the Church —severed from it by a kind of self-excommunication.'

aid of the Archbishop of Canterbury ruled a truly Christian Commonwealth.

> I never expect the system of Laud to return but I do expect the due continuation and development of his principles . . . the so-called union of the Church and State as it then existed had been a wonderful and most gracious phenomenon in Christian history . . . a realization of the Gospel in its highest perfection when both Caesar and St. Peter know and fulfil their office. . . . Charles is the King, Laud the Prelate, Oxford the sacred city of this principle.[21]

Dean Inge has said that the dictum of Froude, Newman, and their followers was 'Luther is dead, but Hildebrand and Loyola are alive.' Certainly they were guilty of an 'unhistorical idealization of the past', and they did bequeath to the Anglican Church 'the strange legend of an age of pure doctrine and heroic practice to which it should be our aim to return'.[22] Unlike Blomfield, Wilberforce, Hook, or Rose, and the London High-Churchmen, they never reckoned with the reality of the Church's constitutional connection with the State. When Rose attempted to remind them of the need to work together for reform of the Church, within the limitations imposed upon them by the Establishment, they ignored him. 'This our friends will not see, but to all such representations they only answer that this is expediency, humbug, and is the natural and necessary result of living in London, a soil in which they hold that all principle perishes.'[23]

Rose had a passionate interest in Church History. He urged Newman to devote himself to its discipline in 1835, but he knew that their approaches to the subject were going to differ:

> if there was difference as to the character of a particular person (Hildebrand was mentioned) and his views, yet surely two persons differing about them, might be satisfied with the same account, i.e., that account being drawn up not by a partisan of either, but by one, who being aware that men equally capable of judging differed, was anxious to state every act fairly and fully. I at least have often felt and said 'I do not agree with such a view, but the writer is so fair and honest in stating the opinion and views of those from whom he differs that I have no objection to make.'[24]

Newman never approached history in this manner. Like Froude who 'had a keen insight into abstract truth',[25] he viewed the role of men

21. J. H. Newman, 'How to Accomplish It', *Discussions and Arguments on Various Subjects* (1873), p. 22.
22. W. R. Inge, *Outspoken Essays* (1921), p. 184.
23. W. R. Stephens, *Life and Letters of W. F. Hook* (1878), I, 414, a letter from Rose to Hook, December 1837.
24. Burgon, p. 106.
25. Newman, *Apologia*, p. 113.

like Hildebrand or Laud from the standpoint of an 'apostolical'. As Thomas Arnold said in a letter to Hawkins, the Provost of Oriel College, Froude and Newman excluded John Bunyan, Mrs. Fry, and John Howard from Christ's Church, while they exalted the Nonjurors into Confessors and Laud into a martyr.[26] Maisie Ward remarks that they must have been 'rather insensitive not to be haunted by the ears of Prynne and of others severed in the pillory by his orders'.[27] Historically they were insensitive to anything in the history of the Church that did not support their metaphysical ideas. While Newman believed 'no man is certain of a truth who can endure the thought of its contradictory existing or occurring',[28] he had a difficult time to appreciate the thought of Rose.

In one letter to Newman in 1836 Rose said 'I will not talk of the glorious Reformation (you forbid me)—but deliverance is deliverance.' He went on to say that the Church of England should rejoice 'that she was able to escape from pollution, and from the bondage and sin to which a continued stay within the venerable walls would have condemned her'.[29] Such ideas did not endear Rose to Froude, in particular, and the cautions of the London school of High-Churchmen were less and less appreciated in Oxford. Though Rose urged them not to divide the High-Church party, Newman came to the conclusion that 'living movements do not come of committees' and that 'universities are the natural centres of intellectual movements'.[30] Keble said in 1833 'I am getting more and more to feel what you tell me about the impracticability of making "sensible people" enter into our ecclesiastical views.'[31]

Dean Burgon said of Rose: 'Well would it have been for the Church of England had his spirit, his counsels, guided the Tractarian movement of 1833.'[32] But Newman and Froude agreed that Rose was not yet 'apostolical', and the publication of *Tracts for the Times* began without the counsel or help of Rose. He became Divinity Professor at Durham in 1833, but the following year his health began to fail. Before his death in 1838 he had become critical of certain tendencies in the Tracts, and in the writings of Newman and Froude. When the latter wrote a review in the *British Critic* that upset him, Rose said

26. A. P. Stanley, *Life of Thomas Arnold* (1844), II, 43.
27. Maisie Ward, *Young Mr. Newman* (1952), p. 211.
28. J. A. Froude, 'Father Newman on the Grammar of Assent', *Short Studies on Great Subjects* (1900–1), II, 105.
29. Burgon, pp. 113–14.
30, Newman, *Apologia*, pp. 124–25.
31. *Pusey House MSS*, Keble to Newman, July 1833.
32. Burgon, p. 111.

that his 'Oxford friends' were showing 'a disposition to find fault with our Church for not satisfying the wants and demands,—not of the human heart,—but of the imagination of enthusiastic, and ascetic, and morbid-minded men'.[33]

When Rose fell ill, his cautionary role was taken over by William Palmer of Worcester, who believed that Froude, in particular, was 'very deficient in learning and therefore rash'.[34] He tried to persuade Newman that the way to protect the Church was to rally High-Churchmen in support of petitions and declarations addressed to churchmen and statesmen in positions of public authority. But Newman believed that what was needed in the Church was a clerical revival—an association of 'apostolicals' who would lead churchmen to resist the Erastian legislature and free the Church from its bondage.

In 1833, in spite of Palmer's lack of sympathy, Newman wrote what was to be No. 1 of *Tracts for the Times*, 'Thoughts on the Ministerial Commission Respectfully Addressed to the Clergy'. The times are very evil, said the Tract, 'yet no one speaks against them'. Only the bishops, the successors of the apostles, now bear the brunt of the battle. What are the clergy going to do about it?

> Should the Government and Country so far forget their God as to cast off the Church, to deprive it of its temporal honours and substance, on what will you rest the claim of respect and attention which you make upon your flocks? Hitherto you have been upheld by your birth, your education, your wealth, your connexions; should these secular advantages cease, on what must Christ's Ministers depend?[35]

Newman's answer was a call for the clergy to remember 'the real ground' on which their authority was built, their 'apostolical descent'; then to join with the bishops, and support them in their battle to defend the Church. He urged every clergyman to 'make much of' the Spirit of the Apostles which had been granted to them by their bishops 'who have appointed us as their assistants, and in some sense representatives'.

> Keep it before your minds as an honourable badge, far higher than secular respectability, or cultivation, or polish, or learning, or rank, which gives you a hearing with the many. Tell *them* of your gift. The times will soon drive you to do this, if you mean to be still anything. But wait not for the times. . . . Exalt our Holy Fathers, the Bishops, as the Representatives of the Apostles,

33. *Ibid.*, p. 136.
34. Faber, *Oxford Apostles*, p. 330.
35. *Tracts for the Times by Members of the University of Oxford* (1839), No. 1, 1.

and the Angels of the Churches; and magnify your office, as being ordained by them to take part in their ministry.[36]

This tract was published with two others on 9 September 1833. Others followed rapidly. All of them were written by clerics, except for five produced by J. W. Bowden, one of Newman's closest personal friends. The idea of the Tracts was Newman's (Froude was slowly dying in Barbados from November 1833), and he wrote twenty-nine of the whole number, until the series ended after the publication of Tract XC in 1841.

The leaflet form of the Tracts did not assist their sale, and it was not until the first forty-six Tracts were collected into a volume towards the end of 1834 that their influence began to be significant outside of Oxford and its immediate vicinity.

The effect of the Tracts was great. They were intended to be alarming, and alarming they were. The bishops were generally unsure of themselves; like Blomfield they accepted that ideas about apostolic succession had gone out with the Nonjurors, and until Wilberforce showed them how to make use of this Tractarian concern they were unsure about how they should act. Newman never seemed to understand that, apart from the Evangelical bishops in 1833, Ryder of Gloucester, Sumner of Llandaff, and John Bird Sumner of Chester, the episcopate was almost to a man Erastian in its outlook. It was all very well for Newman to speak of Dr. Bagot the Bishop of Oxford as 'my Pope . . . the successor of the Apostles, the Vicar of Christ', but it is doubtful that Bagot ever took his office so seriously. Pusey later said 'if the Bishop of Oxford understood us, and we him, it would be one of the last things which he would desire.'[37]

The Tracts had great influence, however, among the lesser clergy. Few of the parish clergy avowed sympathy for the Oxford Movement; but, as the pamphlets of the period show, the clergy did begin to reckon with their spiritual commission and to follow Newman inasmuch as they told 'the many' of their gift. 'Seeing then my Reverend Brethren that ours is an office of so high a dignity' is the reminder used by the Rector of Haughton, Staffordshire, in a sermon preached before the clergy and Archdeacon of Stafford in 1833.[38] Similar sentiments began to be expressed throughout the nation. To many a humble curate, barely keeping himself and his family alive on a minimum stipend, suffering from the 'contempt of clergy' exhibited

36. *Ibid.*, No. 1, 4.
37. *Life of Pusey*, II, 55.
38. Charles S. Royds, *The Christian Minister a Builder in the House of God* (1833), p. 7.

by the gentry, it meant much to be reminded that he 'as much as his rector had an appointment from the king of kings'. Even the beneficed who prospered in the Establishment discovered that 'it was a new life to feel that this appointment and not the accident of worldly respectability gave him his real power.'[39]

This call to the clergy to realize their divine vocation in the divine society of the Church, visible, catholic, and apostolic, was needed at this time as much as the herculean labours of reforming bishops like Blomfield and Wilberforce. Sydney Smith remarked to Gladstone about 1835 'whenever you meet a clergyman of my age you may be quite sure he is a bad clergyman.'[40] There is little exaggeration in this statement according to the accounts of clerical behaviour which contemporaries have left to us. The mad curate of St. Buryans, and the eccentric Rector of Stoke Talmage were not unique in their approach to spiritual matters. This was the age when the church was dominated by the high three-decker pulpit which was occupied by the clergyman, who leaned his arms on a huge cushion while he addressed himself to the gallery, or to those in the high box pews beneath him. Behind the pulpit was the communion table, covered with a wine-stained, moth-eaten cloth. The clergyman who officiated at the holy table three times a year, and might on occasion preach a sermon of two and one-half hours, was rarely seen in his parish except on Sunday. His coming and going was so casual that often there was no set time for the service—the church bell being rung when the minister came into sight.[41]

An example of the almost total lack of spirituality that existed among many of the clergy at this time is given by C. Kegan Paul, one of the seceders from the Church later in the century. When he was a young curate at Bloxham near Banbury, he had a ninety-year-old vicar, who had been in the parish for fifty years. It was customary in the parish to have the Eucharist celebrated the required minimum of three times a year. In one celebration Kegan Paul remembers, upon the altar, which was covered by a dirty wine-stained cloth, there stood a loaf of bread and a dusty black bottle of wine which were to serve as the elements for the Communion. When the prayer of Consecration was reached, to the horror of this pious curate, the vicar turned to the congregation to ask if anyone present had a corkscrew.[42]

39. F. D. Maurice, *On the Right and Wrong Method of Supporting Protestantism: Letter to Lord Ashley* (1843), p. 11.
40. W. E. Gladstone, *Gleanings of Past Years* (1879), VII, 220.
41. E. B. Ellman, *Recollections of a Sussex Parson* (1912), pp. 155–56.
42. C. Kegan Paul, *Confessio Viatoris* (1891), p. 14.

When scandalous parishes such as this were common, reform had to be legislated by the dignitaries and prelates of the Church, or it had to be a grass-roots movement. As we have seen, the real authority of even a reforming bishop like Wilberforce was so small in disciplinary matters that little could be done to bring new life in the parishes by the ordinary. When William Cockburn, Dean of York, sold Minster lead for personal profit, and disposed of five parishes of which he was the ordinary with the excuse that 'he was a poor man living not at York but at Kalston near Bristol', the Archbishop of York, Harcourt, deprived him of his office. But the Archbishop was overruled by the Court of Queen's Bench, and Cockburn continued to serve as Dean of York until his death in 1858.[43] When even an archbishop could not discipline a nefarious individual like Cockburn, it was obvious that the reform of the Church in spiritual matters had to come from below.

The great contribution of the Tractarians was their spiritual zeal, which inspired a whole generation of clergymen to renew their sense of vocation. At mid-century Bishop Blomfield's biographer could say: 'In character, habits, attainments, social position and general reputation, the ordinary clergyman of 1860 is a very different being from the clergyman of 1810.[44] That they were changed was in large measure due to the Oxford Movement, which had an influence among the clergy of England which has been compared to that of the Evangelical movement.

> If the Oxford Movement had only been a reaction against the wave of political and philosophic Liberalism, a reversion to the ideals of the past, its historical importance would have been inexplicable. . . . It is only as a movement, first and foremost religious and most deeply religious, that the Oxford Movement can be understood. It was a religious revival, insofar akin to the Evangelical Movement, in a manner a continuation and reshaping of it.[45]

A caution is called for here, however. Bishop Brilioth and many other historians of the movement have tended to use as almost interchangeable terms expressions like Tractarian, Anglo-Catholic, Oxford Movement, and Puseyism. But from the very beginning there were differences within the ranks of the Oxford reformers that were as significant as the issues that separated them all from the High-Churchmen of London. Newman, Keble, and Pusey all contributed to

43. R. S. T. Haselhurst, 'Victoriana', *Church Quarterly Review* (1941), p. 69.
44. Blomfield, *Memoir*, p. 41.
45. Yngve Brilioth, *The Anglican Revival* (1925), p. 211.

the religious revival which is associated with the Oxford Movement, but their contributions were different in nature.

3. The Problem of Catholicism

PUSEY said of the beginning of the Tractarian movement 'our first Tracts were the short abrupt addresses of persons who, when the enemy was upon them, seize the first weapon which comes to hand and discharge it.'[1] As we have seen, the Oxford High-Churchmen were sure that 'a sweeping storm' was at hand, and Keble believed that 'anything, humanly speaking, will be better than for the Church to go on in union with such a State.'[2] Both men were sure that the State was about to force on the Church terms of alliance which would amount to 'a renunciation of her fundamental rules'.[3] Their particular fear was that the State, acting through the Ecclesiastical Commissioners, might overwhelm the bishops and clergy and force them all to become mere stipendaries of Parliament. They both believed that the clergy had to organize themselves to defend the Church against an apparently demonic legislature which intended to reform doctrine and discipline. If their association could not resist, at least it would have the strength to exercise the ancient remedy of the martyr: 'leave to suffer when in conscience he dares not obey'.[4]

At first the movement was dominated by Newman and junior men at the university, almost all of whom were Oriel dons. Keble resigned his Oriel fellowship when he married in 1835; and he was absent from Oxford, acting as Vicar of Hursley, near Winchester, from 1836. From this time he acted as the distant 'saint' of the movement, the famous author of the *Christian Year*, the promising intellectual who had given himself up entirely to the charge of his little country parish. He did, however, contribute to the Tracts. But from 1834, when Pusey identified himself with the Tracts, direction of the movement was largely the concern of himself and Newman.

1. *Life of Pusey*, II, 241.
2. *Ibid.*, I, 266.
3. *British Critic*, XXVI (1839), 368.
4. *Ibid.*, p. 390.

Newman admitted in his *Apologia* that 'without him we should have had no chance, especially at the early date of 1834, of making any serious resistance to the Liberal aggression. But Dr. Pusey was a Professor and Canon of Christ Church; he had a vast influence in consequence of his deep religious seriousness, the munificence of his charities, his Professorship, his family connections, and his easy relations with University authorities. He was to the Movement all that Mr. Rose might have been.'[5] Dean Church says that Pusey became the official chief of the Tractarians in the eyes of the world; 'a second head, in close sympathy with its original leader, but in many ways very different from him'.[6]

At first these differences were not apparent. Pusey was never as systematic in his thought as Newman; and, when he preached the Fifth of November sermon at St. Mary's in 1837, he said, 'I feel like a person with a great gun put into his hands, but he does not know exactly with what materials to load it, or how to use it.'[7] This sermon entitled *Patience and Confidence the Strength of the Church* occasioned 'immense excitement' according to J. F. Russell, a young churchman from Cambridge who was in Oxford at this time, and 'even those who did not openly profess themselves "on his side" were imperceptibly adopting his sentiments'.[8] His sentiments then took the form of an anxiety 'to recover forgotten truths and to enable Christianity to encounter its opponents with new courage'.[9]

At this time Newman agreed with Pusey that, while there was need for 'deliverance of the Church from unjust thralldom',[10] the Establishment had to be accepted. 'We find the Church and State united and must, therefore, maintain that union.[11] Meanwhile the Church could concentrate on its essential task of making men into saints, not good citizens,[12] while the State fulfilled its vocation: 'the world in systematically afflicting the Church is but doing its appointed part'.[13]

Pusey wanted the Church of England to be Catholic. This concern for the nature of the Church came from his friendship with staunch

---

5. Newman, *Apologia*, p. 141.
6. Church, *Oxford Movement*, p. 117.
7. *Pusey House MSS.*, Pusey to Newman, 9 October 1837.
8. *Life of Pusey*, I, 406.
9. *Ibid.*, I, 408.
10. E. B. Pusey, *Patience and Confidence the Strength of the Church* (1841), pp. 56–58.
11. Newman, *Discussions and Arguments*, p. 32.
12. J. H. Newman, *Parochial and Plain Sermons*, 1834–42 (1868), IV, 160.
13. J. W. Bowden, 'On the Church Viewed by Faith and by the World', *Tracts for the Times*, No. 58, p. 7.

churchmen such as Dr. Thomas Sikes, Rector of Guilsborough, Northamptonshire, who was known locally as 'the Pope' because of his High Church ideas. Sikes had said to Pusey:

> Wherever I go all about the country I see amongst the clergy a number of very amiable and estimable men, many of them much in earnest and wishing to do good. But I have observed one universal want in their teaching: the uniform suppression of one great truth. There is no account given anywhere, so far as I see, of the one Holy Catholic Church . . . our confusion nowadays is chiefly owing to the want of it.[14]

Sikes also prophesied that much confusion would accompany any revival of interest in the Idea of the Church, and confusion did begin to appear, even among the Tractarians, as Newman and Pusey slowly developed their personal opinions about the nature of the Catholic Church.

The word Catholic was a naughty word in England in the 1830's. To most Englishmen it was an adjective of opprobrium which was attached to the title Roman, and used to refer to the political policies of the Bishop of Rome. Even Newman in his early years spoke disparagingly of the 'grasping ambition' of Roman Catholic policy. In 1837 Sydney Smith preached a sermon, which gossip said was slanted to please the Whigs and earn him a bishopric, on 'the Catholics, the great object of our horror and aversion . . . the Catholic faith (the religion of two-thirds of Europe) as utterly incompatible with the safety, peace and order of the world'.[15]

F. J. A. Hort, the Cambridge New Testament scholar, commented later in the century on 'the total absence of any specific influence of Greek theology upon the Oxford Movement, notwithstanding the extensive reading in the Fathers possessed by its more learned chiefs.'[16] Pusey realized this deficiency and drew Newman's attention to the way Augustine and the Latins equated Regeneration with the death of original sin, and the Greeks equated it with an infusion of new life,[17] but there is much truth in Hort's observation. Newman, in particular, tended to think in Augustinian terms of a basic dualism which existed between the Church and the world. 'All states of the world, all governments, except so far as they are Christian, except so far as they

14. *Life of Pusey*, I, 257–58. Jabez Bunting, the Methodist leader was also referred to as 'the Pope'—because of his Toryism and authoritarianism. *V.* R. F. Wearmouth, *Methodism and the Working Class Movements of England, 1800–1850* (1937), p. 195.
15. Sydney Smith, *Duties of Queen Victoria: Sermon Preached at St. Paul's Cathedral* (1837), p. 19.
16. A. F. Hort, *Life of F. J. A. Hort* (1896), II, 38.
17. *Pusey House MSS.*, Pusey to Newman, 9 October 1837.

act upon Christian principles, are scarcely more than robbers and men of blood.'[18] It may be debated (as in the case of St. Augustine) whether Newman thought in terms of the Church as the Kingdom of God, and of the world outside being evil, but there seems little doubt that he agrees with Augustine that 'true justice is only to be found in that commonwealth of which Christ is the founder and ruler.'[19]

From 1836 Newman and his followers had begun to dominate the editor of the *British Critic*, and from 1838 Newman took it over. As soon as he did so, there was a marked change in emphasis in the magazine. Articles on literature, science, travel, and theology, which had had a wide influence among the learned, began to be replaced by articles which were concerned primarily with the state of the Church. Newman's concern from this time was to be only 'the Church, that peculiar institution which Christ set up as a visible home and memorial of truth'.[20] It was this deliberate narrowing of vision which allowed Newman to say: 'What have we, private Christians, to do with hopes and fears of earth, with schemes of change . . . or dreams of reform.'[21]

As Newman developed this line of thought, he began to separate himself from those High-Churchmen who did not believe that 'the world always lieth in wickedness.'

> The world may be in one age somewhat better or somewhat worse than in another, but it is in substance always the same. I mean that the whole visible course of things, nations, empires, states, politics, professions, trades, society, pursuits of all kinds are, I do not say directly and formally sinful (of course not) but they come of evil, and they are the instruments of evil; they have in them the nature of evil . . . everything in the world is in itself alien from God, and at first sight must be regarded and treated as being so. . . . Satan is the god of this world.[22]

It was becoming clear that what Newman meant by the Catholic Church was not what was intended by Dean Hook when he spoke of the desire 'to imbue the public mind with those Catholic principles by the maintenance of which the English Reformation was gloriously distinguished'.[23]

The first real difference of opinion between Newman and Pusey arose in 1838. Newman was now devoted to maintaining the spiritual

18. J. H. Newman, *Sermons on Subjects of the Day* (1843), p. 263.
19. Terence Kenny, *Political Thought of John Henry Newman* (1957), p. 63.
20. *British Magazine*, IV (1835), 42.
21. Newman, *Parochial and Plain Sermons*, III, 204–5.
22. Newman, *Sermons on Subjects of the Day*, p. 119.
23. W. F. Hook, *Call to Union on the Principles of the English Reformation* (1838), p. 109.

sovereignty of the Church rather than the Establishment. His concern was how to reveal to churchmen the spiritual authority which was vested in the bishops, the successors of the apostles, and in the clergy who shared the power that was delegated to them. He had no idea of the Establishment being recognized as 'catholic' because it acted as the conscience of the nation, and sought to bring the blessings of the Gospel to bear on all parts of the commonwealth. A church was Catholic only because of the spiritual authority within it, which assured salvation to all who sought to enter it. Without this spiritual authority the Church had nothing. It was of no value to the seeker of salvation unless 'it is able to bring our passions into order, to make us pure, to make us meek, to rule our intellect, to give government of speech to inspire firmness, and to destroy self.'[24] If the Church of England did not have this authority it did not 'deserve to be acknowledged as a Church'.

Newman's sermons reveal that Catholicism in terms of spiritual authority meant much to him. No man had faith unless he surrendered himself to the redeemed community governed by the successors of the apostles. 'Obedience is the test of Faith. . . . the whole duty and work of a Christian is made up of these two parts, Faith and Obedience'.[25] Newman's evangel addressed to his contemporaries who were distressed in spirit was simple. 'To all those who are perplexed in any way whatsoever, who wish for light but cannot find it, one precept must be given—obey.'[26]

The source of authority in the Church was the bishop. He provided strength for the hard-pressed clergy who battled Satan in the world. The spiritual power of the bishop should ideally be used in the form of excommunication to cleanse the Church, to strengthen it to withstand the evil outside. Froude had longed for such an exercise of authority by the successors of the apostles whose presence was then 'so slighted both in and out of Parliament'. 'If, indeed, the spiritual rulers of the Church were free to use their apostolical authority their word would be a law to us. . . . we should then be furnished with a guide far safer than our private judgment.'[27] Newman agreed with Froude that this was the time for churchmen to 'humble themselves before the Most High God in the Persons of His Delegates and God on His part will secure them from the terrible consequences of highmindedness'.[28]

24. *British Critic*, XXVII (1840), 'Catholicity of the English Church', 87 ff.
25. Newman, *Parochial and Plain Sermons*, II, 153.
26. *Ibid.*, I, 230–31.
27. *British Magazine*, VI (1836), 52.
28. Froude, *Remains*, II, Pt. I, 272.

There is little doubt that Froude and Newman, because of their fascination with the Middle Ages and the Church of the Caroline divines, dreamed of a theocratic order: 'If we will be Scriptural in our view of the Church we must consider . . . that its officers have great powers and high gifts, that they are charged with the custody of Divine Truth, that they are all united together and that the nations are subject to them.'[29] They wanted the bishops to order their own house—if the house could be identified with the nation, then the idea of a National Church could still be entertained. 'The body of the English nation either are sincere Christians or they are not; if they are, they will submit to Discipline as readily as the primitive Christians did. If not—let us tell the truth and shame the devil; let us give up a National Church, and have a real one.'[30]

The trouble with this line of thought was that it was completely idealistic and abstract; it had no reference at all to the existing order.

In a letter to Pusey, Newman confessed that, when he was in the presence of Bishop Bagot while he was putting on his robes of office, 'I felt it would be such a relief if I could have fallen at his feet and kissed them.'[31] It is interesting to speculate what the reaction of the Bishop of Oxford would have been to such an act of fealty, if Newman had revealed his sentiments. Bagot was a kindly man; but, as Dean Church pointed out, few of the bishops of the time were theologians, or even spiritually minded. Most of them were like Blomfield, frankly puzzled by what was coming out of Oxford.

> Blomfield was not at his best as a divine, and, for a man of his unquestionable power, singularly unsure of his own mind. He knew, in fact, that when the questions raised by the Tracts came before him he was unqualified to deal with them; he was no better furnished by thought or knowledge or habits to judge of them than the average Bishop of the time, appointed, as was so often the case, for political or personal reasons. At the first start of the movement, they not unnaturally waited to see what would come of it. It was indeed an effort in favour of the Church, but it was in irresponsible hands, begun by men whose words were strong and vehement and of unusual sound, and who, while they called on the clergy to rally round their fathers the Bishops, did not shrink from wishing for the Bishops the fortunes of the early days: 'we could not wish them a more blessed termination of their course than the spoiling of their goods and martyrdom'.[32]

Bagot in no way shared this hope for spoliation and martyrdom. Son of the first Lord Bagot, he had married the daughter of the Earl of

---

29. Newman, *Sermons on Subjects of the Day*, p. 355, 'Christian Church an Imperial Power'.
30. Froude, *Remains*, II, Pt. 1, 274.
31. *Life of Pusey*, II, 58.
32. Church, *Oxford Movement*, p. 217; the quotation is from p. 1 of Tract No. 1.

Jersey. His father had presented him to his first living, Leigh in Staffordshire, and his family connections had led to his preferment. He was very upset by the Tractarian controversy, which later precipitated a severe mental breakdown; and theological concerns which he would rather have avoided haunted him all his life—including a dispute with the tendentious Archdeacon Denison of Taunton whom we will meet later.

When Bagot delivered his charge to the diocese in 1838, he had received many anonymous letters complaining of the ideas of the Tractarians. This led him to suggest that these theories might be dangerous when absorbed by young minds, and that the masters at the university who disseminated them should 'mind what they were about'. Newman recognized that this caution was very mild, but it upset him greatly. He came to the conclusion that 'an indefinite censure was cast over the Tracts' and that they should no longer be written.[33] Keble shared Newman's viewpoint at this time. In a Tract he wrote in 1835 he had said: 'By submitting yourself to your Bishop as to Jesus Christ you convince me that you guide your lives by no rule of man's invention, but by the rule of Jesus Christ.'[34] But during the crises of the next few years Keble would begin to change this opinion, and to see that obedience to the will of the bishops was 'necessarily conditional'.[35]

Newman did not immediately inform Pusey about his decision to suspend circulation of the Tracts. Pusey's wife was very ill at this time, but it may be that Newman knew that Pusey would not give his approval to this action as easily as Keble. When Newman did write to him he explained his action by saying 'a Bishop's lightest word *ex cathedra* was heavy. . . . he cannot but act upon me. His word is a deed.'[36] At the same time he admitted that his archdeacon had suggested that Bishop Bagot did not understand the 'jurisdiction' he had over Newman; that Newman was, in effect, taking the matter far too seriously. H. P. Liddon in his *Life of Pusey* gives a succinct description of Pusey's reaction to Newman's letter.

> Pusey was vexed—vexed at what the Bishop had said but still more distressed at Newman's view of what it involved. He did not understand Newman's serious estimate of the disapprobation of his Bishop. This estimate was based on Newman's peculiar theory of the authority of an individual Bishop. 'My own Bishop was my Pope', he says; 'I knew no other; the successor of the

33. *Life of Pusey*, II, 53.
34. *Tracts for the Times*, No. 52, p. 5.
35. Lord Irwin, *John Keble* (1932), p. 232.
36. *Life of Pusey*, II, 53.

Apostles, the Vicar of Christ.' There is no reason to suppose that Pusey ever held this theory; and it may be doubted whether at this time he even understood that Newman did so.[37]

Liddon goes on to say that this issue of Bagot's condemnation revealed a major difference in outlook between Newman and Pusey—which was to influence each of them in their course of action in later years.

> At the close of his life Pusey used to say that Newman had depended on the Bishops while he himself had looked to God's providence acting through the Church. To Newman it was a necessity that his Bishop should approve and support him: Pusey was not indifferent to such a thing if it could be had, but he did not exaggerate its importance, or make it a test of God's approval of his own position and work.[38]

From 1838 Pusey began to suspect that Newman and the young men who were joining the movement were, as much as Laud had been in his generation, guilty of a 'gigantic misconception of the practical'. The bishops they venerated were almost to a man members of the Erastian school that the Tractarians despised. The sovereign in whose royal supremacy they put such faith was a woman of strong personal likes and dislikes, with Lutheran ancestry and with a Lutheran consort.

Pusey and Keble were willing to view the Church as a corporate body in the nation; in times of trial, thoughts of disestablishment came to both of them. They both passionately believed in the cause of defending Church prerogatives in spiritual affairs against meddling by the secular power. They were willing to dispute that the authority of the sovereign, whom they acknowledged to be head of the Church, had been delegated to Parliament, which could now make laws for the Church. But both of them had roots in the English countryside; they understood in a way that Newman never could, the catholic mission to the nation of the Established Church.

When Keble reviewed Gladstone's *State in its Relations with the Church* in the *British Critic* in 1839 he said: 'We should be much obliged to any lawyer who would point out to us the constitutional process by which the Church of England might assert her independence, only giving up her temporal advantages and not incurring the penalties of *praemunire*, except she could obtain the consent of the civil

---

37. *Life of Pusey*, II, 53; The Tracts were continued when Bagot wrote to assure Newman that no censure was intended in his charge.
38. *Ibid.*, II, 57.

government.'[39] Like Pusey he knew that the Church of England existed because of its 'utility' to the nation—'utility' of a spiritual not a political nature. Ten years later in a letter to Gladstone Pusey said:

> I see, with regret, each link of the old system broken, both with regard to the State and to the Church; to the State, because it is dropping the relation on which our prayers for Parliament are founded, and assuming a nondescript character which will in the end be infidel; and to the Church, because having been so long forbidden in any way to act for herself, she is disabled from doing so now, through long disuse.[40]

Both of them knew that the Church could not abandon its Catholic mission to bring Christianity to the nation which 'has no guide but the Church; and if it rejects that, it must flounder endlessly'.[41]

At the same time as Pusey had his first doubts about Newman's concept of the Church and the seat of its authority, unease began to arise over the attitude of Newman, and the young men who now followed him, towards the social needs of the nation. Newman found no difficulty in preaching the doctrine that the individual Christian could safely ignore 'schemes of change' and 'dreams of reform'. As many studies of the Tractarian movement have pointed out, its devotees looked back—to the Fathers, to the Middle Ages, to the Caroline divines. They had little hope for the redemption of the earthly city which did not live by Faith. Pusey, on the other hand, as we shall soon see, was passionately concerned for the lot of the poor. The churchman who gave £5,000 to Blomfield's Metropolis Churches Fund, and was to labour so heroically to improve the lives of slum dwellers could not ignore dreams of change and reform.

When the Tractarians of the Newman school did look at the poor in the 'earthly city', their writings seem to support G. M. Trevelyan, who has said, 'the Tractarians denounced all those who taught the people "to rail against their rulers and superiors".'[42] They feared movements like Chartism, with talk of class war 'which promises success to the poorer party, and threatens property with pillage and law with subversion'.[43] Socially they wanted to retain the status quo, and to see within the traditional social system the increase of Christian influence. They longed for universal 'Christian fellowship which is best cemented as it is best exhibited, by united adoration in

39. *British Critic*, XXVI (1839), 390.
40. *Life of Pusey*, III, 185.
41. *Ibid.*, III, 184.
42. G. M. Trevelyan, *British History in the Nineteenth Century* (1922), p. 281.
43. *British Critic*, XXVIII (1840), 241.

the same temple of the Lord by which the poor are elevated without being made turbulent, and the rich are humbled without being degraded.'[44] Newman said that he believed rebellion to be a sin.[45] Frederick Oakeley said 'the duty of the poor is to submit with cheerfulness . . . and to lend no ear to factious persons who tempt them to break through it.'[46] Froude in his last sermon, 'Riches a Temptation to the High Minded', urged rich and poor alike to submit themselves to their spiritual rulers as the means to a better social order.[47] This was the great panacea the Tractarians sought for the whole of society —the return to a golden age of the past, when 'spiritual rulers' guided secular rulers in an ordering of society where each man 'may do his duty in that state of life wherein God has placed him to the end of his days'.[48]

Until the Church was able to usher in the ideal Christian social order, the rich and poor, now at war with one another, should look back at the example set by ideal squires of other ages, who had done so much to ensure contentment in society. Thomas Mozley, who was married to one of Newman's sisters, in a discussion of the terrible suffering of the ploughboy in the hungry forties, saw this to be but a discipline which would eventually make him a strong and healthy labourer. 'Generally speaking nothing but the deepest and bitterest poverty will subdue the uneducated classes. Were it possible to raise them to comfort and ease and security, what a still worse bondage of sin and punishment would they soon draw on themselves.'[49]

The criticisms of this social outlook have been many. Thomas Arnold saw the ideas of the Tractarians 'a most formidable device of the great Enemy to destroy the real living Church'.[50] F. D. Maurice believed the chief concern of the Tractarians to be the setting up of a Church system, 'Denisonian Chartism about the rights of the clergy',[51] not the caring for the welfare of society as a whole. He believed that those, like the Tractarians, who upheld the right of private property served the cause of the State not the Church: 'the Church, I hold, is

44. *Ibid.*, XXI (1837), 239.
45. *Ibid.*, p. 274.
46. Frederick Oakeley, *Dignity and Claims of the Christian Poor: Two Sermons* (1840), p. 19.
47. Froude, *Remains*, I, Pt. II, 258–73.
48. *British Critic*, XXIII (1843), 261.
49. Thomas Mozley, 'Agricultural Labour and Wages', *British Critic*, XXIII (1843), 261.
50. *Life of Arnold*, II, 53.
51. *Life of Maurice*, II, 61. The reference is to G. A. Denison, the formidable Archdeacon of Taunton.

Communist in principle; Conservative of property and individual rights only by accident; bound to recognize them, but not as its own special work; not as the chief object of human society or existence.'[52]

In a letter to Pusey in 1834, Arnold said he saw 'the system' pursued in Oxford to be a revival of the ideas of the Nonjurors. Success in this venture would 'cause the ruin of the Church of England first,—and so far as human folly and corruption can, . . . obstruct the progress of the Church of Christ'.[53] As Liddon remarks, Pusey was not influenced by Arnold's criticisms at this time. But like Keble, and unlike Newman, Pusey had been a High-Churchman all his life. Both Keble and Pusey 'grasped from the beginning the strength of the Anglican position as opposed to Protestantism and Rationalism, as well as to the yet unappreciated power of Romanism'.[54] They were concerned about the spiritual sovereignty of the Church—but only as a means to an end. Like Dean Church they knew that 'behind the line of immediate struggle still lies the vast thick unshaken mass of human darkness, human barbarism, human selfishness, human degradation.' For this state of affairs, Christianity is 'at once its antagonist and its remedy, here is the true reason why the Christian ministry exists'.[55] Keble and Pusey always understood the need for the Church to engage in a catholic mission to the world.

Another area of possible tension between Newman and Pusey was in university affairs. The tension never became acute because of Newman's departure, but in time it might have, for Pusey was very concerned about university reform. Mark Pattison in his *Memoirs* records A. P. Stanley as once saying: 'How different the fortunes of the Church of England might have been if Newman had been able to read German. . . . all the grand development of human reason from Aristotle down to Hegel was a sealed book to him.'[56] It was not a sealed book to Pusey. He had gone to Göttingen in 1825 to deal with the 'larger questions' which he believed 'could be studied most thoroughly at Universities in which faith and a scarcely disguised unbelief had been in conflict for more than a generation'.[57] He gained much from this apprenticeship, particularly his meetings with Schleiermacher, and the Church historian Augustus Neander. When Hugh James Rose as Select Preacher delivered lectures at Cambridge

52. *Ibid.*, p. 8.
53. *Life of Pusey*, I, 283.
54. *Ibid.*, p. 271.
55. R. W. Church, *Human Life and Its Conditions* (1886), pp. 131–32.
56. Mark Pattison, *Memoirs* (1885), p. 210.
57. *Life of Pusey*, 70.

on 'The State of Protestantism in Germany', and described it as 'an abdication of Christianity', Pusey corrected him. He appreciated Rose's fear of 'intellectual infection', but he had faith in the 'deep moral earnestness' of many of those who 'yet remain strangers to the main Christian doctrines'.[58]

The churchman who could think in this fashion, and who welcomed the introduction of science studies at Oxford,[59] would probably sooner or later have differed with those who would have nothing to do with what was not 'apostolical'. Newman and his followers were obsessed with mustering the clerical forces of the Church to prepare it for a defence against 'liberalism', 'the heresy of Erastus'. Because of this passion and the influence the Tractarians had in Oxford, 'only clerical studies and interests could find a place in the education, and . . . in times of religious controversy the University became an ecclesiastical cock-pit.'[60] Mark Pattison said of the 1830's: 'Probably there was no period of our history during which, I do not say science and learning, but the ordinary study of the classics was so profitless or at so low an ebb as during the period of the Tractarian controversy.'[61] Froude, the historian, agreed with Pattison's criticism and noted that the regeneration of the university intellectually began only with the secessions of 1845. 'Famous as the Tractarians were to become, their names are not connected with a single effort to improve the teaching at Oxford, or to amend its manners.'[62]

Many attempts have been made to apologize for the Tractarian retreat 'to the innermost sanctuary of religion as the only safe and sure refuge',[63] in reaction to the threat of liberalism. Few of them have been successful. As G. C. Binyon has truly said: 'A religion that looks only backward to its base has the key to knowledge but not the knowledge of how to use it.'[64] Yet it must be remembered that the Tractarians, like all their contemporaries, were conditioned by their time. While they were fighting for an ideal ecclesiastical order, radical politicians were devoting themselves to extending the franchise. Just as much as the Tractarians, these men tended to ignore the social distress of the age. No one should assume that 'the political reformers of the early nineteenth century were also the social reformers

58. *Ibid.*, I, 159.
59. *Ibid.*, III, 391.
60. Katherine Lake, *Memorials of William Charles Lake, Dean of Durham* (1901), p. 54. The words of Goldwin Smith.
61. Pattison, p. 237.
62. J. A. Froude, 'Oxford Counter-Reformation', *Short Studies*, IV, 257.
63. W. G. Peck, *Social Implications of the Oxford Movement* (1933), p. 98.
64. G. C. Binyon, *Christian Socialist Movement in England* (1931), p. 70.

who sought to better the lot of the working population.'[65] Those who lived in industrial areas knew only too well that the men who would be elected to Parliament by the Reform Bill regarded the poverty of the working classes as being in the nature of things, just as the Tractarians did. Perhaps any judgment of the Tractarians should include the charity of Dean Church. 'Poor Tractarians . . . it seems that they were expected to exhaust all important subjects in the few years when they were mostly fighting for their lives.'[66]

Slowly Keble and Pusey realized that Newman, and the young men who professed *Credo in Newmannum*[67] were going astray. By the time that Newman was in his 'penultimate stage' in the Church of England, both Keble and Pusey realized that they were no longer able to follow the workings of Newman's mind.[68] It took some time for the followers of each man to realize how deeply they differed in their thought. When their response to the ecclesiastical crises of the age made their differences clear, each group realized that the basis of disagreement was their interpretation of what was 'the Catholic Church' which all professed to desire.

4. The Hampden Crisis and the Jerusalem Bishopric

THE IDEA of the Church and its relationship with the State and society which evolved in the thinking of Newman on the one hand, and Keble and Pusey on the other, did so not through abstract speculation, but through insights gained during the Church's struggle with the legislature. The first enlightenment came during the battle fought over the appointment of Dr. R. D. Hampden to the chair of Regius Professor of Divinity in 1836.

Hampden was a 'gentle, peaceful, diffident' man, 'deeply religious, and carefully loyal to the Church'.[1] He became a fellow of Oriel in 1814, and was a prominent member of the 'Noetic' school of theology,

65. J. C. Gill, *Ten Hours Parson*, p. 1.
66. Mary Church, *Life and Letters of Dean Church* (1895), p. 334.
67. Froude, 'Oxford Counter-Reformation', p. 273.
68. Faber, *Oxford Apostles*, p. 413.
1. W. Tuckwell, *Pre-Tractarian Oxford: Reminiscences of the Oriel 'Noetics'* (1909), p. 128.

together with Richard Whately and Thomas Arnold. The Noetics were devoted adherents of the Reformation settlement, 'these solid Fellowships, Livings, Canonries, Bishoprics, this practical common-sensical reasonable domesticated amalgam of religion, culture and country life.'[2]

An honorary member of the Oriel Common Room was Blanco White, an Anglo-Spaniard who had passed from Romanism to the most extreme liberal Protestantism of his day. He was an influential contributor to the liberal and critical forms of thought which were in the air at Oriel when Newman became a Fellow of the College. He particularly introduced the Noetics to criticism of the scholastic philosophy which had characterized the pre-Reformation period. Unlike Newman, who believed in 'the absoluteness of dogma, as a final revelation of truth by God through the Church',[3] White, Hampden, Whately, and Arnold attempted to restate dogma, implying that it was a human invention. They also disliked clericalism and party spirit within the Church. Politically the Noetics were liberals. Together with Pusey, they opposed Keble, Newman, Hurrell Froude, and Robert Wilberforce by supporting Sir Robert Peel in the Oxford election of 1829 over the issue of Catholic Emancipation, which Peel in large measure brought about.

In 1832 Hampden delivered the Bampton Lectures on 'The Scholastic Philosophy Considered in its Relation to Christian Theology'. The theme of the lectures was the injurious effect of the scholastic way of thought on Protestantism, particularly the excessive veneration of the sacramental system, tradition, and church authority. They attempted to distinguish between the essential content of Scripture and the speculations of the Church at various times which had become dogma.

No one paid much attention to the lectures in 1832. They were not answered or condemned. Pusey later said that he was upset over 'the harsh and often bitter and sarcastic language employed by Dr. Hampden towards the Fathers of the Christian Church'.[4] Hampden did have some interesting things to say when he attempted to account for the ascendency of the Latin clergy over the Greek. He treated St. Ambrose, St. Jerome, and St. Augustine as he would any of his contemporaries. Ambrose had the 'practical dexterity of the man of the world'. Jerome had a 'dark and solitary abstractedness of

2. Faber, *Oxford Apostles*, p. 117.
3. *Ibid.*
4. *Life of Pusey*, I, 415.

mind', and Augustine as a 'shrewd' man was contrasted unfavourably with St. Paul.[5] Pusey said that you might expect such language from Gibbon but not from a Christian theologian.

At the same time, the scholar who had defended the German liberal theologians from Rose's censure saw 'with mingled charity and acuteness' Hampden's intellectual condition. He did not doubt Hampden's personal faith; 'the heart believeth, while the intellect ought consistently to disbelieve'. Hampden was experiencing in his mind a trial which was common to many scholars of the time.

> In a yet extremer case, the Rationalists of Germany have at last seen what had long ago been pointed out to them by the believing writers, that their position was of all the most inconsistent; that they must, if consistent, return to a sounder faith, or plunge deeper into Pantheism. The division is now being made; some sinking into this form of atheism, others returning to Christianity.[6]

In the year that the Oxford Movement began, Hampden was appointed Principal of St. Mary's Hall, Oxford, where he introduced several reforms and spent £4,000 of his own income on college buildings. Then, in March 1834, he was elected to the Chair of Moral Theology—a rebuff to the Tractarians who had counted on the election of Newman. Newman himself had been so sure of his election that he had ordered the new flourish to be put on the title page of a forthcoming volume of sermons.[7] Hampden was assisted in his career by Hawkins, the Provost of Oriel; and though his Bampton lectures were not being widely read, he was regarded as 'a kind of theological authority'.[8]

The tension between Hampden and the Tractarians came into the open when Hampden published a pamphlet, *Observations on Religious Dissent*, which was essentially an extract of his difficult Bampton Lectures. It made clear his central thesis that moral and theological truths are distinct from religion. It also argued that undergraduates should not be obliged to subscribe to the Articles of Religion because of the relative truth of Church formularies.[9] Newman wrote to Hampden to say that his pamphlet advocated Socinianism, and that

5. R. D. Hampden, *Scholastic Philosophy Considered in Its Relation to Christian Theology* (1833), pp. 14–19.

6. *Life of Pusey*, I, 364.

7. A. D. Culler, *Imperial Intellect: a Study of Newman's Educational Ideal* (1955), p. 97.

8. *Life of Pusey*, I, 299.

9. R. D. Hampden, *Observations on Religious Dissent* (1835). A postscript is devoted to the use of religious tests in universities.

'by its appearance, the first step has been taken towards an interruption of that peace and mutual good understanding which has prevailed so long in this place.'[10] As pamphlets were published in answer to Hampden, it became clear that those who opposed the Tractarians, like Provost Hawkins, were primarily concerned for the university and its improvement. The Tractarians' first thought was for the Faith of the Church.

When Hampden published a course of lectures he was giving as Professor of Moral Theology, Newman called them 'a deplorable evil' and agreed with Rose that 'error should be protested against on its first appearing'. Pusey wrote to Newman to say that 'Rose wants you to "bell the cat"'.[11] At the same time he expressed his deep reluctance to enter the controversy which seemed to be beginning.

Controversy became acute conflict early in 1836. The Regius Professor of Divinity, Dr. Burton, died suddenly. The Whigs were back in power, led by Melbourne. The appointment of the new Professor would be by the Crown—that is by Melbourne on the advice of whomever he consulted. Melbourne turned to Archbishop Howley and received from him a list of nine names to be considered. They included Pusey, Newman, and Keble, with Pusey's name coming first on the list. But Melbourne also consulted Whately, now Archbishop of Dublin, and on his advice decided to appoint Hampden.

Immediately Oxford became the ecclesiastical cockpit that Goldwin Smith remembers. A petition of protest, signed by half the resident masters, was drawn up to be sent to the Primate for presentation to the King. When Pusey wrote to Melbourne, the Prime Minister suggested that next time the Oxford people should address their remonstrances to those who could do something about their grievance, rather than the King.

Newman borrowed a copy of Hampden's forgotten Bampton lectures, took extracts from them, and grouped them together, with a preface 'to assist the judgments of those who are in doubt as to his doctrines, and to explain the earnestness of those who condemn them'.[12] Thomas Arnold said of Newman's *Elucidations of Dr. Hampden's Theological Statements*: 'He has in several places omitted sentences in his quotations, which give exactly the soft and Christian effect to what, without, sounds hard and cold'.[13] However 'unjust' Newman's action was it was also 'most effective'. 'Mercy and Truth' were laid

10. *Life of Pusey*, I, 302.
11. *Ibid.*, I, 367.
12. *Ibid.*, I, 371.
13. *Life of Arnold*, II, 23.

aside as the 'agitators'[14] raised a nation-wide clamour against 'a clergyman whose opinions on difficult theological questions are not understood by the mass of his profession'.[15]

Opposition to Hampden's appointment was not confined to the Tractarians, though Newman's pamphlet did much to stir up criticism of Melbourne's choice. After the crisis many churchmen admitted their surprise at discovering how innocuous were Hampden's lectures, compared to the extracts presented to them. But the popular reaction to Tractarian agitation was such that Oxford Convocation, in effect, censured Hampden's opinions. From this time he was held in deep suspicion by most people at Oxford. He attempted to resign but Melbourne would not allow this.

In the long run the Tractarians did not help their cause by this furor. It was quite obvious to Broad-Churchmen like Baden Powell, the Savilian Professor of Geometry, that 'the violent spirit of opposition to Dr. Hampden's appointment . . . originated entirely among the adherents of a peculiar theological school'.[16] F. D. Maurice said that the incessant 'letters of Presbyters' and 'ravings of High Church newspapers' sickened the younger men at Oxford.[17] To many it seemed that they were witnessing deliberate persecution through the actions of Tractarian inquisitors.

Much has been made by various writers of the influence of Newman among undergraduates at this time, but the extent of Newman's spell may be exaggerated. Some of the charm of going to hear Newman's great sermons came from the fact that college dons frowned upon the practice. Even a pious young undergraduate like F. W. Faber found that 'the liberalism of Arnold was almost as captivating as the new Tractarian views.'[18] Canon Richard Gee of Windsor, looking back to this time said 'the Oxford Movement made its way slowly in the undergraduate world. I think we thought more about the Rugby men, late Arnold's famous sixth form, who had then just become university men.'[19] Arnold's influence was great at Oxford, and many waited to see what his reaction to the Hampden controversy would be.

14. Faber, *Oxford Apostles*, p. 350.

15. *Life of Maurice*, I, 446. For a defence of Hampden *cf*. W. W. Hull, *Remarks to Show Dr. Hampden Misunderstood* (1836). Hull, a barrister at Lincoln's Inn, was a close friend of Thomas Arnold.

16. Baden Powell, *Remarks on a Letter from Rev. H. A. Woodgate to Viscount Melbourne* (1836), p. 3.

17. F. D. Maurice, *Letter on the Attempt to Defeat the Nomination of Dr. Hampden* (1847), p. 7.

18. Ronald Chapman, *Father Faber* (1961), p. 20. This is not to deny Newman's power as a preacher. *V. infra* Chapter IV.

19. Richard Gee, *Sixty Years Hence in the Church of England* (1898), p. 10. Gee had come up to Oxford in 1837.

In April, 1836, there appeared in the *Edinburgh Review* Arnold's famous article which was entitled by the editor 'The Oxford Malignants and Dr. Hampden'. To Arnold the inquisitorial tactics of Newman and his followers reminded him of 'the nonjurors reviling Burnet—of the Council of Constance condemning Huss—of the Judaizers banded together against St. Paul'.[20] In his article Arnold used startlingly vehement language in a way that shocked even many of his friends. Newman and his supporters were 'conspirators' and 'obscure fanatics'. He said that the attack on Dr. Hampden bore the character not of error but of moral wickedness. In a letter to A. P. Stanley, which he wrote at this time, Arnold said:

> it is clear to me that Newman and his party are idolaters; they put Christ's Church and Christ's Sacraments, and Christ's ministers, in the place of Christ Himself; and these being only imperfect ideas, the unreserved worship of them unavoidably tends to the neglect of other ideas no less important; and thence some passion or other loses its proper and intended check, and the moral evil follows. Thus it is that narrow-mindedness tends to wickedness, because it does not extend its watchfulness to every part of our moral nature.[21]

The Tractarians were also upset over the advancement in the Church of Connop Thirlwall. A brilliant Fellow of Trinity College, Cambridge, he had been asked to resign his assistant tutorship there because of his advocacy of the admission of dissenters to the university. Lord Melbourne had thought highly of him, however; and, after presenting him to the living of Kirby Underdale, he offered him the bishopric of St. David's in 1840. Archbishop Howley had assured Melbourne of the orthodoxy of Thirlwall, but the Tractarians could not accept a churchman who was willing to concede that having the Judicial Committee of the Privy Council as final court of appeal in ecclesiastical causes might be a good thing for the peace of the Church.

Melbourne's policy, of advancing in the Church only those whom he favoured, confirmed for many High-Churchmen the Erastianism which they believed to be implicit in the Church of England. This in no way perturbed Melbourne. He justified his refusal to allow the Church to have a direct say in ecclesiastical appointments by remarking: 'What have Tory churchmen ever done for me that I should make them a present of such a handle against my government.'[22]

20. *Life of Arnold*, II, 9.
21. *Ibid.*, II, 42.
22. W. M. Torrens, *Memoirs of Rt. Hon. William, Second Viscount Melbourne* (1878), II, 181.

At the same time Melbourne agreed with the Tory High-Churchmen that Arnold was a dangerous man and kept him from a bishopric. Bishoprics, with the attendant right to sit in the House of Lords, were for life; and the government could only be sure of its own creations. Arnold considered himself a strong Whig, but on most issues 'he differed almost as much from them as from their opponents.'[23]

Melbourne felt sure of the allegiance of Hampden, however, as did Lord John Russell, who came to power in 1846. The following year, to spite the Church, or so the Tractarians believed, he appointed Hampden to the see of Hereford. The truth of the matter was that Hampden had written directly to Russell to request promotion, an act that Hampden himself believed to be 'unusual and unwarrantable', though it brought results.[24] The act caused a great storm, and thirteen bishops signed a remonstrance addressed to Russell. A proposal was also made to prosecute Hampden for false doctrine.

Russell was a strong Erastian and a militant Low-Churchman who had no intention of being coerced by bishops or the High-Church party. When the Dean of Hereford, Dr. Mereweather, indicated that he would refuse to vote in chapter for Hampden's election to the see, Russell wrote to him: 'I have had the honour to receive your letter of the 22nd inst. in which you intimate to me your intention of breaking the law.'[25] Though the dean and one canon voted against Hampden, he was duly elected. In his reply to the bishops who had protested against the appointment, Russell referred to the previous furor over Hampden and the bishops' 'ban of exclusion' against a clergyman of eminent learning and irreproachable life. He also said that he had no intention of allowing what the bishops really wanted:

> the supremacy which is now by law vested in the Crown is to be transferred to a majority of the members of one of our Universities. Nor is it to be forgotten that many of the most prominent among that majority have since joined the Communion of the Church of Rome. I deeply regret the feeling that is said to be common among the clergy on this subject. But I cannot sacrifice the rights of Dr. Hampden, the rights of the Crown, and what I believe to be the true interests of the Church, to a feeling which I believe to be founded on misapprehension and fomented by prejudice.[26]

Henry Phillpotts, the High-Church Bishop of Exeter, expressed

23. *Life of Arnold*, I, 194.
24. *Later Correspondence of Lord John Russell, 1840–1878*, ed. G. P. Gooch (1925), I, 178.
25. G. Crosse, 'Renn Dickson Hampden', *Dictionary of English Church History*, p. 258.
26. Henry Phillpotts, *Reply to Lord John Russell on the Bishops' Remonstrance Against the Hampden Appointment* (1847), p. vi.

the sentiments of his party when he said the Erastianism of the Church of England could not be denied if the King, the recognized head of the Church, opposed this appointment; the bishops believed the man to be made bishop was a heretic, and still the legislature was about to proceed with his advancement. 'Never before was any person recommended by the Crown to a bishopric against whom there stood a formal legal judgment affirming the unsoundness of his doctrine.'[27]

Another of the bishops who signed the remonstrance was Samuel Wilberforce. As a professor of the university, Hampden was exempt from episcopal control, but he was also Rector of Ewelme, and this made him subject to the jurisdiction of the Bishop of Oxford. When approached by Charles Marriott, who represented Keble and others who were interested in instituting a suit against Hampden in the ecclesiastical courts, Wilberforce granted Letters of Request to enable the case to be taken to the Court of Arches. It was only after this action that Wilberforce undertook to read Hampden's much maligned Bampton Lectures which were reputed to be heretical. When he did so he found nothing in them that he could consider heretical. Eight days after granting Letters of Request he withdrew them, bringing the suit to an abrupt close. All those who would have liked to see Hampden tried, High- and Low-Churchmen alike, were furious, and Phillpotts wrote Wilberforce an astonishing rebuke. The Court and the Government were also annoyed because he had allowed the suit to get under way. Canon Liddon believed this loss of court favour saved Wilberforce's soul by cutting off his ambitions, sending him back to his conscience and his diocese.

Keble showed much more interest in Hampden's elevation than Pusey did, and was the real instigator of the agitation against him. Pusey's relation to this last phase of a controversy was 'inconsiderable and indirect'—though he did assist Keble to pay for the £2,000 expense incurred by a last-ditch attempt to object to Hampden's appointment in the Court of Queen's Bench.[28] Pusey was more distressed over Wilberforce's failure to censure Hampden's writings than he was over the question of Lord John Russell's choice of bishop. 'The mischief of the Bishop's letter is that it pronounces almost *ex cathedra*, that the language of the Bampton Lectures is hardly an object of slight blame in the English Church. . . . it is far more injurious to the Church than Dr. Hampden's appointment. An act of tyranny hurts

27. *Ibid.*, p. 13.
28. *Life of Pusey*, III, 161.

not the Church; the betrayal by her own guardians does.'[29] At the same time he indicated that his own faith in the Church of England was not shaken by this latest revelation of episcopal folly. 'I am not disturbed because I never attached any weight to the Bishops. It was perhaps the difference between Newman and me: he threw himself upon the Bishops and they failed him; I threw myself on the English Church and the Fathers as, under God, her support.'[30]

Perhaps some of Pusey's concern over Wilberforce's failure to move against Hampden reflected the fact that this same bishop had admonished Pusey, five days after his consecration, and before he had even reached his diocese, for his 'self-dependence': 'your being ready to give up any one of our Formularies . . . if you, as an individual, think that you can find in early Christian writers contradictions of them'.[31] The violent reaction to poor Hampden was unfortunate. Pusey and Keble spent time and money which neither could well afford, to block the appointment of a man who, after an undistinguished, quiet, studious career, died as Bishop of Hereford in 1868. The main result of the whole sorry affair was that the Oxford High-Churchmen had as their implacable foes all those who had supported Hampden.

By the time of Hampden's elevation, Newman had already left the Anglican Church. From 1839 he had had doubts about the *Via Media*, and was influenced by W. G. Ward and other extreme young men who joined the movement. In 1841 he had written Tract XC, the last of the series, which endeavoured to show that the Thirty-Nine Articles might be interpreted in a Catholic sense. This had resulted in a great storm, criticism by bishop after bishop, and Newman's retirement to a semi-monastic existence at Littlemore. He might have weathered this time of trial, but the issue of the Jerusalem Bishopric brought him to what was the 'beginning of the end'. As he later confessed in his *Apologia*: 'From the end of 1841, I was on my death-bed, as regards my membership with the Anglican Church'.[32]

Frederick William IV, King of Prussia, in the summer of 1841 sent to London as his special envoy the Chevalier Bunsen with a scheme to set up an Anglo-Prussian bishopric in Jerusalem. The bishop of this see was to provide for any members of the Church of England, or German Protestants, who chose to put themselves under his jurisdiction.

29. *Ibid.*, III, 162.
30. *Ibid.*, III, 163.
31. *Ibid.*, III, 48.
32. *Apologia*, p. 209.

He was also to develop friendly relations with the Orthodox and to promote conversions among the Jews. For political as well as religious reasons the English government favoured the design. Blomfield and the Archbishop of Canterbury, Howley, both gave it their blessing, and Bunsen also gained the support of Lord Palmerston and Lord Ashley, leader of the Evangelicals. It was agreed that the British and Prussian Crown should nominate alternately to the bishopric; that both countries should contribute to the endowment of the see; and that the bishop might ordain German ministers who subscribed to the Confession of Augsburg, or Anglicans who subscribed to the Thirty-Nine Articles and the Prayer Book.

Archbishop Howley introduced the Bill creating the bishopric into the House of Lords. The new bishop was to exercise jurisdiction over congregations in Syria, Chaldea, Egypt, and Abyssinia who chose to accept his authority. The first bishop consecrated was Michael Solomon Alexander, a Jewish convert who had been born in Posen, and ordained in Ireland. Although he was limited as a scholar—he knew no Greek and but little Latin—he had been appointed as Professor of Hebrew at King's College, London.

Opinion was divided about the merits of the proposal—even among the High-Churchmen. Dr. Hook of Leeds supported it.[33] Pusey hoped that it might lead to the absorption of the Protestants who met with Anglicanism in this see. 'I trusted to the Catholicity of our Church to win those who were brought within the sphere of her influence'.[34] But his faith in the power of a Catholicism of mission was not shared by Newman:

> at the very time that the Anglican Bishops were directing their censure upon me for avowing an approach to the Catholic Church . . . they were on the other hand fraternising, by their act or by their sufferance, with Protestant bodies, and allowing them to put themselves under an Anglican Bishop without any renunciation of their errors or regard to the due reception of baptism and confirmation: while there was great reason to suppose that the said Bishop was intended to make converts from the orthodox Greeks, and the schismatical Oriental bodies.[35]

Ever since Nicholas Wiseman, the future cardinal, had published his 1836 lectures on the *Principal Doctrines and Practices of the Catholic Church*, which had stressed authority as the essence of the Catholic Church, Newman had been haunted by the question of what

33. W. F. Hook, *Reason for Contributing to the Jerusalem Bishopric* (1842).
34. *Life of Pusey*, II, 250.
35. *Apologia*, p. 206.

authority justified the Church of England.[36] He was convinced that no authority justified Protestantism, yet now the Church of England 'was not only forbidding any sympathy or concurrence with the Church of Rome, but it actually was courting an intercommunion with Protestant Prussia and the heresy of the Orientals'.[37] Such an alliance was anathema to the cleric who believed 'Lutheranism and Calvinism are heresies, repugnant to Scripture, springing up three centuries since, and anathematised by East as well as West.'[38] He could no longer remain within a Church which was 'the corroboration of a present, living, and energetic heterodoxy'.[39]

On 7 November 1841 Dr. Alexander was consecrated as the Bishop of Jerusalem. Not only Newman, but the enemies of the Oxford reformers knew what was implied by the creation of the bishopric. The anti-clerical Earl of Radnor took great delight in mocking the spiritual successors of the apostles who were not free to consecrate without licence from the Crown. As he said it was 'somewhat of an anomaly that archbishops and bishops who claimed the right of ordination by virtue of their spiritual succession from the apostles . . . should still consider themselves not entitled to exercise that power without licence from the Crown'.[40] Newman believed that not only the licence to consecrate, but the very desire to create the bishopric came from the State not the Church—that it was a 'catholicity of extent' against the pretensions of Rome, and another manoeuvre by Ashley and the Evangelicals at the expense of the Tractarians.[41] 'As to the Jerusalem matter the simple case is this—our government wants a resident religious influence there such as the Greek Church is to Russia and the Latin to France.'[42] Newman viewed the whole enterprise as an attempt to join with Protestant Prussia to found a sect for political purposes. The appointment of the bishop was merely an attempt to give ecclesiastical sanction to what had been done.

From this time Newman and men like Ward and Oakeley lost their faith in the Anglican Church. Oakeley confessed to Pusey that 'the idea of a national Church in itself I cannot but regard as essentially uncatholic.'[43] Ward believed the Church of England to be 'decayed

36. *British Critic*, XX (1836), 373–403, Newman's review of Wiseman's lectures.
37. *Apologia*, p. 206.
38. *Ibid.*, p. 208.
39. *Ibid.*, p. 209.
40. *Hansard*, LIX, 496, speech of 7 September 1841.
41. Robert Ornsby, *Memoirs of J. R. Hope Scott* (1884), I, 305.
42. *Correspondence of John Henry Newman with John Keble and Others 1839–1845* (1917), p. 148.
43. *Life of Pusey*, II, 254.

and degraded'.[44] Newman quietly began his withdrawal from the Church of England, dismayed by the episcopal censures of Tract XC, and bewildered by the separation which was taking place between himself and men like Pusey, Keble, and William Palmer. He no longer showed interest in contributing to the *British Critic*, now under the editorship of Thomas Mozley—though it was largely taken over by Ward and Oakeley.

Pusey was alarmed by the alliance with Prussian Protestants, but he did show satisfaction at the 'consecration of a Bishop to represent our ancient British Church in the city of the Holy Sepulchre . . . and united around it representatives of the three branches of the Church Catholic'.[45] Pusey never lost his faith in God's guidance of the English Church, and the good which could come out of a creation like the Jerusalem Bishopric—inspired though it originally was by secular motives. Newman could only pray, ' May that measure utterly fail and come to nought, and be as though it had never been.'[46] Keble sympathized with Newman but suggested 'a little expression of reverence to those whom you are censuring'.[47] This was an interesting caution when one considers that it came from a priest who believed that obedience due to bishops was 'necessarily conditional', while Newman had proclaimed that 'a Bishop's lightest word *ex cathedra* is heavy'.[48] Palmer was disturbed over the creation of a bishopric within the diocese of the Oriental Churches,[49] but he was much more disturbed, as he showed in his writings, by the extreme statements of Ward and Oakeley in the *British Critic*.

Keble and Pusey showed their loyalty to Newman during the crisis over Tract XC, but although both of them were desperately concerned over 'the practical failure of the English Church',[50] neither of them could consider seceding to Rome. As Keble said, the High-Church party had not been happy over Archbishop Howley's elevation of his friend Samuel Hinds to the see of Norwich, but they had patiently borne this affliction (Hinds resigned after marrying his cook in 1857). 'If persons have thought it their duty to bear with the Puritans and Latitudinarians of times past, so far as not to give up the Church of England to join them, nor to acquiesce in their interpreta-

44. Faber, *Oxford Apostles*, p. 400.
45. *Life of Pusey*, II, 259.
46. *Ibid.*
47. *Ibid.*, II, 256.
48. Cf. *supra*, p. 61.
49. William Palmer, *Aids to Reflection on the Foundation of a Protestant Bishopric at Jerusalem* (1841).
50. J. T. Coleridge, *Memoir of John Keble* (1869), p. 299.

tion of its formularies, what is there in this case to make them take a different view.'[51] In saying this, Keble was echoing the thought expressed by Pusey in his 1837 sermon *Patience and Confidence the Strength of the Church.* 'We may not be over-anxious even about holy things, such as the deliverance of the Church. . . . God allowed his chosen people to live in bondage 400 years, and not till the set time was come did He judge that power which enthralled them.'[52]

Both Keble and Pusey knew of Newman's development of thought, and both were alarmed over the excesses of Newman's followers. They were anxious about the fear in the public mind of 'a secret spreading disloyalty to Anglicanism'.[53] Both of them urged Newman, for the sake of the Church, to do nothing further to foment discord. When Newman suggested that he might reprint Tract XC, Keble said that he should re-read his Hooker and Hammond before he did so.[54] Newman's public 'retraction' of his earlier indictment of the Church of Rome as a 'lost Church' which served the 'cause of Antichrist', and the extreme statements of men like Ward also perplexed Pusey.[55] Pusey's loyalty to Newman was such that 'he constantly threw himself into Newman's language and position, out of love and trust and deference, and in cases where his own unbiased inclinations would have counselled hesitation'.[56] But it was clear to both of them by 1842 that they were following different paths.

By the time of his secession Newman was convinced that the Church of England 'was in the position towards Rome of the heretical and schismatical bodies towards the primitive Church'. He had to become a Roman Catholic or 'sink into a dead scepticism, a heartless *acedia*'.[57] Concern with the 'schismatical' state of the Church of England allowed him no peace of mind to appreciate its spiritual mission to the English nation. Neither Keble nor Pusey shared his concern. Neither of them had misgivings about the claims of the Church of England. Rather they began to see that Newman and men like Ward and Oakeley had wandered far from their original starting point. In effect they had become a mere schismatic group who failed to look beyond concerns like 'authority' in the Church, or the need for secular submission to clerical power. Keble, Pusey, and Maurice seldom saw

51. Irwin, *John Keble*, pp. 127–28.
52. Pusey, *Patience and Confidence*, p. 50.
53. *Pusey House MSS*, Newman to Pusey, 9 June 1843.
54. *Ibid.*, Keble to Newman, 19 February 1841.
55. *Life of Pusey*, II, 299.
56. *Ibid.*, II, 371.
57. *Ibid.*, II, 450.

eye to eye, but by 1845 they realized what Maurice had meant when nine years earlier he had cried 'Oh that our High Churchmen would but be Catholics.'[58]

Newman had argued that the Church had to be a political power, 'formidable and influential'. 'It is the plain duty of its members not only to associate internally, but also to devote that internal unity in an external warfare with the spirit of evil whether in king's courts or among the mixed multitude.'[59] Keble and Pusey had agreed that churchmen had to associate to resist the designs of an Erastian legislature, but they began to realize as time went on that the Tractarian party was so concerned with evil in 'king's courts' which threatened the temporal and spiritual privileges of the Church, that it had no time to wage war with the evil 'among the mixed multitudes'. They began to see that an ecclesiastical party which was concerned only for the welfare of the Church was in truth not 'catholic'.

Newman believed that the external warfare around which Augustine had built so much of his theology was waged eternally by Rome against Liberalism, and every secular movement which threatened the Church. He left the Church of England to commit himself to support of this 'catholic' and imperial power. With his departure, Keble and Pusey gave up their earlier ecclesiastical concerns to devote themselves to serving the spiritual needs of the English people. Keble said to Isaac Williams, 'now that I have thrown off Newman's yoke . . . things appear quite different'.[60] He realized that the apostasy of the nation had to be combated in the countryside as well as at Westminster. When the High-Churchmen who followed Newman wavered in their loyalty, he proclaimed 'If the Church of England were to fail altogether yet it would be found in my parish.'[61] Deliberately he turned his back on the ecclesiastical concerns of Oxford to devote himself to the parish of Hursley. There he gave to the Church a new standard of parochial work, and a type of piety that was almost forgotten; serious, cultured, and dutiful, dedicated to the revelation of the divine Love which Keble knew abided in the Church of England.

Pusey's answer to Newman's secession was to turn his full attention to the cause which was nearest to his heart; the destitution of the 'mixed multitude'. As early as 1828 he had written to his fiancée on the social horrors of the industrial metropolis. 'London often appears to me like a great lazar-house which I would willingly visit as a

58. *Life of Maurice*, I, 188.
59. J. H. Newman, *Arians of the Fourth Century* (1833), p. 276.
60. Georgina Battiscombe, *John Keble* (1963), p. 275.
61. *Ibid.*, p. 303.

physician; but not as a spectator, less as a patient.'[62] He knew that a Church was 'catholic' not by virtue of purity of doctrine alone, or assurance that it was divinely vindicated by the mystique of Apostolic Succession, but only when its spiritual authority, which was revealed in mission activity, was relevant for every soul in every stratum of society throughout the nation.

> The Church must meet in her synods, to remedy the evils which hinder or check the fulfilment of her Divine mission. . . . she herself ought to debate upon remedies and should not leave to individual effort the work of the whole. We need missions among the poor of our towns; organized bodies of clergy living among them . . . to grapple with our manufacturing system as the Apostles did with the slave system of the ancient world . . . if by God's help we would wrest from the principalities and powers of evil those portions of His Kingdom, of which, while unregarded by the Church, they have been taking full possession.[63]

For the Church of England to be 'catholic' it had to have the power to raise up men within it and 'call forth self-sacrificing efforts, proportionate to the greatness of the needs in the whole length and breadth of our land'.[64]

A few months after Newman's departure, Pusey wrote to Keble: 'If we could once gain the idea (and I suppose it is fixing itself) that we do need for our towns, mines, manufactories, real missionaries, one might hope that a new day would dawn upon our Church.'[65] But Pusey had not waited for other churchmen to begin to share his vision. He had already contributed substantially to the Bishop of London's scheme for building churches in East London. Then in 1839, when the anti-Tractarian party were discussing the erection of the Martyrs' Memorial in Oxford, Pusey received a letter from Hook, the Vicar of Leeds, asking for help to build churches in his city. Pusey's reply to Hook's plea was characteristic. In the same month in which Newman joined the Church of Rome, the Church of St. Saviour's, Leeds, built entirely by Pusey's liberality, was consecrated. Few churchmen knew the identity of the donor. Within the Church was the inscription 'Ye who enter this holy place pray for the sinner who built it.'

Another answer to the need of the age, which revealed the 'catholicism' sought by those members of the Tractarian party who remained loyal to the Church of England, was the founding of *The*

---

62. *Life of Pusey*, I, 130.
63. E. B. Pusey, *Councils of the Church A.D. 51–A.D. 381* (1857), pp. 4–5.
64. *Ibid.*
65. *Pusey House MSS.*, Pusey to Keble, 21 April 1846.

Guardian. This weekly Anglican religious newspaper was the creation of R. W. Church, the future Dean of St. Paul's, and Frederick Rogers, later Lord Blatchford. It upheld Church principles, but at the same time it was dedicated to showing their relevance to the best secular thought of the age. A paper of discernment, it was widely respected, as it sought to bring the light of the Gospel to bear on all aspects of Victorian intellectual life—even the revolutionary theories of Charles Darwin.

At the end of his life, Pusey said that where he and Keble differed from Newman was over the question of authority in the Church. In the midst of his trials Newman had said 'My sole comfort has been that my Bishop has not spoken against me, in a certain sense I can depend and lean, as it were, on him. . . . I cannot stand if he joins against me. . . . I am a clergyman under the Bishop of Oxford and anything more is accidental.'[66] Pusey never shared Newman's faith in bishops. In a long letter to W. J. Copeland, which he wrote shortly before his death, he said that he believed Lord Liverpool to have been the first Prime Minister (1812–1827) in a long while who had nominated bishops out of principle.[67]

> In the last century persons were taken out of the priesthood for the higher office of Bishop; whence there grew up that habitual mistrust of Bishops which is not easily shaken off. The laity bartered their 'birthright for a mess of potage'. Church patronage was at the best employed for purposes of this world. The laity had the Bishops whom they desired, and when they had them despised them.[68]

Pusey was bred in the High-Church tradition, and though he had absolute faith in the Church of England he knew that by the very nature of the Church its bishops could not be 'leaned on'.

Canon Liddon has said in his biography of Pusey that 'in Newman's mind a single and present authority took the place which Pusey assigned to a more remote and complex, but at the same time more really authoritative guide. . . . had he been a Roman Catholic he would have leant on Councils rather than on Popes; in the Church of England he leant on her collective voice in her formularies rather than on particular and contradictory interpretations of them by some of her rulers.'[69]

Looking back at the years when the Tractarians were most under

66. *Ibid.*, Newman to Pusey, 26 August 1838.
67. *Ibid.*, Pusey to Copeland, 17 July 1882.
68. Pusey, *Councils of the Church*, p. 14.
69. *Life of Pusey*, II, 238.

assault, Pusey said: 'What might not the movement have been if the Bishops would have understood us! I remember Newman saying to me at Littlemore, "Oh, Pusey! we have leant on the Bishops, and they have broken down under us!" It was too late then to say anything: he was already leaving us. But I thought to myself, "At least I never leant on the Bishops: I leant on the Church of England." '[70]

With the departure of Newman and the two dozen or so clergy who followed him to Rome at this time,[71] the interests of those clergy who had been influenced by the Tractarians, yet remained loyal to the Church of England, moved outside Oxford. As the 'Puseyites' began to make their presence felt in the nation as a whole, in a very real and practical sense, they became aware of the true nature of the Established Church. We must now look at their relationship with the Judicial Committee of the Privy Council in the Gorham Case and other crises —and their revelation, in the midst of conflict, of what was the Church of England.

70. *Ibid.*, p. 237.
71. H. Daniel-Rops, *The Church in an Age of Revolution, 1789–1870* (New York, 1965), p. 436; estimates over three hundred conversions within a year of Newman's departure, 'all of them intellectuals'. Authorities differ about how many actually seceded.

III. The Church
and the
Establishment

*Whether it were right or wrong
to allow Justinian, Charlemagne,
or Charles I to appoint Judges of
Doctrine, it was not the same
thing as allowing a modern Prime
Minister to do so.*

JOHN KEBLE

1. The Anglican Episcopate

IT SEEMED clear by the time of Newman's secession that the Tractarian ideology was not going to have substantial influence in the Church of England. The bishops had proved themselves to be Newman's 'broken reed'; Keble and Pusey revealed that they had never shared their fellow reformer's veneration for the episcopal office; and no one else in the Church seemed to be concerned about the extravagant claims made for episcopacy by the Tractarians. But the Tractarians sometimes had influence of which they were unaware. They had their times of trial in their relationship with Samuel Wilberforce; but, as we have noted, 'Soapy Sam' took his episcopal office as seriously as any of them. He was not the only prelate who began to consider thoughtfully the role of the Anglican bishop in the period after Newman's departure. The original Idea of the Tractarians proved to be most attractive to the bench of bishops.

Since the Elizabethan settlement, the Church of England had done little to exalt the episcopal office. Many scholars have noted that the judicious Mr. Hooker nowhere insisted upon the episcopate as the

EPIGRAPH: 'A Call to Speak Out', *Church Matters in 1850* (1850), p. 30.

esse of the Church—much to the disappointment of Keble when he edited *Of the Laws of Ecclesiastical Polity*.[1] Hooker thought the form of Church government to be of secondary importance compared with the spiritual well-being of *Ecclesia Anglicana*. There is little doubt that ideas of apostolic succession, the bishops' 'pedigree', were not taken seriously until after the Restoration of 1662. In fact, Elizabeth had carefully admonished her bishops not to take on spiritual airs.

> The Bishops of this realm do not . . . nor must not claim to themselves any greater authority than is given them by the Statute of King Henry VIII revived in the first year of Her Majesty's reign . . . for if it had pleased Her Majesty, with the wisdom of the realm, to have used no bishops at all, we could not have complained justly of any defect in our Church . . . but sith it pleased Her Majesty to use the ministry of Bishops, and to assign them this authority, it must be to me, that am a subject, as God's ordinance.[2]

There was no widespread objection to bishops in the sense of their being 'senior presbyters' necessary for regional administration, even in the minds of many Puritans. But there was little encouragement given by anyone in the Church to the idea that the bishops were monarchical prelates providing the only channel of Divine Grace for the ministry. 'A Bishop that is the same with a Presbyter is of fifteen hundred years standing; but a Bishop "phrasi Pontificia" that is, a distinct Order superior to a Presbyter invested with sole power of Ordination and Jurisdiction is but a novel institution.'[3] Most churchmen accepted the confusion of interests of Church and State which Hooker had identified. They believed that the final authority in ecclesiastical causes was 'that which by common consent of the whole State, King, Nobles, Bishops, Judges, Commons in Parliament is taught and commanded; whatsoever cometh hence, cometh from the complete body of the Church of England'.[4]

The Tractarians never appreciated how comprehensive the post-Reformation Anglican Church had been. William Whittingham, Dean of Durham from 1563 to 1579, who had served as a minister in Geneva had never received episcopal ordination, nor had Hooker's scholarly friend, Hadrian Saravia, a prebendary of Gloucester, nor Isaac Casaubon, the French classical scholar, who was appointed to a prebendal stall at Canterbury by James I. Even after the Restoration, Archbishop Thomas Tenison made zealous efforts to reunite the more

1. Richard Hooker, *Works* (1888), I, lxvii of Keble's Preface.
2. John Strype, *Life and Acts of John Whitgift* (1822), III, 222.
3. F. J. Shirley, *Richard Hooker and Contemporary Political Ideas* (1949), p. 126. The words are those of 'Smectymnuus', a body of Presbyterians.
4. John Sprint, *Cassander Anglicanus* (1618), p. 265.

moderate Nonconformists with the Church of England. He vigorously opposed the Occasional Conformity Act of 1711 which restrained Dissenters from receiving the Sacrament in the Church of England in order to qualify for government posts. He noted that communicating with the Church of England was no new practice among the Dissenters, but had been used by 'some of the most eminent of our ministers ever since 1662'.[5] Edward Stillingfleet, Bishop of Worcester, advocated a union between Episcopalians and Presbyterians, and reminded his contemporaries that 'They who please but to consult the third book of learned and judicious Master Hooker's *Ecclesiastical Polity* may see the mutability of the form of Church Government largely asserted and fully proved'.[6]

Though the Tractarians tended to dismiss such Latitudinarian extravagance, it did represent a continuing tradition in the Church of England which influenced all churchmen who thought in terms of a national Church. Many accepted this comprehensiveness because they wished to avoid religious dissension which would hinder the Church's mission to serve the nation. But others, because of honest scepticism, rejected ideas which exalted the episcopal office. Benjamin Hoadly, the great opponent of the Nonjurors, said that he believed the myth of apostolic succession was something to be avoided because harm could come to a Church which made 'the eternal salvation of Christians to depend that uninterrupted succession, of which the most learned must have the least assurance, and the unlearned can have no notion, but through ignorance and credulity'.[7]

As we have seen, from 1833 churchmen realized that the Church was very much on its own in its relationship with the State. The aristocracy were on the defensive in this era of reform, and they could not be counted upon to defend the Church. Nor could the Church count on the royal supremacy when it was clear that the real legislative power now lay with Parliament. The Church had to discover justification for its existence other than the tolerance extended to it by a Parliament which now contained both Nonconformists and Papists.

Hugh James Rose believed that much of the weakness in the Church came from its failure to govern itself through the episcopate—the form of Church government of the Apostolic Church. He quoted with approval from the letters of Cyprian: 'the contempt of the authority

5. Thomas Tenison, *Occasional Conformity a Wooden Leg* (1705).
6. Edward Stillingfleet, *Irenicum, a Weapon-Salve for the Churches Wounds or the Divine Right of Forms of Church Government Examined* (1662), p. 394.
7. Benjamin Hoadly, *Answer to the Representation Drawn up by the Committee of the Lower House of Convocation* (1717), pp. 89–91.

of the Bishops presiding over every Church is the root of schism and of heresy.'[8] Rose's argument was essentially utilitarian when he pleaded for the bishops to protect the Church they represented from schism and heresy within and aggression from without. He quoted from Hooker when he presented the Church as a visible society in need of the freedom to make its own laws of policy, and to protect itself from those political reformers who would have it 'poor as the Apostles of Christ were poor'.[9]

We have noted how Newman and those who dwelt upon the episcopate as the *esse* of the Church had little sympathy for the 'expediency' of men like Rose. But when the bishops they leaned upon proved to be Newman's 'broken reed' in the midst of ecclesiastical controversy, those who continued to share the Tractarian view of the episcopate, and remained in the Church of England, were a minority. Most High-Churchmen, like Pusey, returned to the traditional position with regard to the episcopate which had been held by men like Rose. 'Single bishops or an association do not commit the Church. . . . Dear J.K. and I never did lean on the Bishops, but on the Church. We, or rather the whole Church, have had plenty of scandals as to Bishops and shall always have them.'[10]

So, at mid-century, it seemed as if the emphasis given to the episcopal office by the remnants of the Tractarian party was going to be ignored by the Church at large. But this was not to be. The *Edinburgh Review* had noted in 1844 that it was remarkable to find bishops opposing the Tractarians 'considering the soothing flatteries and obsequious professions of obedience of which the Tracts were full'.[11] The bishops continued to oppose the Tractarians, particularly after publication of Tract XC, but Samuel Wilberforce led the way in accepting gracefully what was provided by the Tracts 'to gratify Episcopal vanity, and to strengthen Episcopal pretensions'.[12] Most bishops during the century followed Wilberforce's example. They did not like to admit this, and were hesitant about publicly supporting the doctrine of apostolic succession; but, at a time when the power of the establishment was waning, the compensation provided by it was irresistible.

Frederick Temple was tutored by W. G. Ward and was much

---

8. H. J. Rose, *Internal Union the Best Safeguard Against the Dangers of the Church* (1822), p. 26.
9. *Ibid.*, p. 7.
10. *Pusey House MSS.*, Pussy to Liddon, 2 July 1870.
11. *Edinburgh Review*, LXXX (1844), 310–11.
12. *Ibid.*, LXXVII (1843), 508.

interested in the Tractarian movement, though he never joined it. When a young man, he wrote tentatively to his mother: 'With regard to preaching on apostolical succession, I think it is certainly a part of God's truth, and I do not think it ought to be dropped out of sight.'[13] He was ordained priest by Samuel Wilberforce in 1847. He then went to Rugby as Headmaster, contributed to *Essays and Reviews*, the controversial publication of 1860 which we will presently refer to, and was generally believed to be a Broad-Churchman. But, after Gladstone appointed him to the see of Exeter in 1869, people began to recognize him as a stiff and rigorist High-Churchman.

Apparently his attitude towards the doctrine of apostolic succession was slowly changing. He saw dangers in it: 'if it be taught as a means of separating the clergy from the laity and giving them a position of their own, it will become a hard unspiritual thing which will repel many noble minds—as it repelled Dr. Arnold's.'[14] At the same time he appreciated why the Church had ensured that its bishops would remain in the succession as a branch of the Holy Catholic Church, and approved that 'all her ministers shall have that succession as a matter of fact.'[15] He was Bishop of London when the bishops of the Anglican Communion at the Lambeth Conference of 1888 approved the 'Lambeth Quadrilateral' as the basis for any movement towards reunion in the Christian Church—including the demand for the 'historic episcopate'. There is little doubt that the one-time Broad-Churchman who became Primate of the Church in 1896 believed fully in the doctrine of apostolic succession.[16]

Temple's development was common among the Anglican bishops, and among the members of the old high-and-dry school of churchmanship. By the end of the century what Hensley Henson labelled the 'Tractarian revival of the medieval doctrine of the hierarchy' had at last proved irresistible to the episcopate, as the *Edinburgh Review* had believed it would.

> The decay of the Establishment, the development of Tractarianism, and the rapid expansion of Anglican Christianity had largely altered the character and functions of the English bishop, weakening his local importance, limiting his personal independence, emphasizing mistakenly his extra-national obligations, and facilitating, if not even compelling, his acquiescence in the exorbitant episcopalian theory of his office.[17]

13. E. G. Sandford, ed., *Memoirs of Archbishop Temple* (1906), I, 55.
14. *Ibid.*, II, 10–11.
15. Frederick Temple, *Letter of 16 July 1873*.
16. G. W. E. Russell, 'Frederick Temple', *Dictionary of English Church History*, p. 585. Russell's account is based on personal recollections.
17. H. H. Henson, *Retrospect of an Unimportant Life* (1942), I, 265.

The bishops became Tractarian in their outlook because during the nineteenth century they found themselves, through unforeseen circumstances, forced to exercise authority which the State could not in the direction of ecclesiastical affairs. By the time of the Lincoln Judgment of 1890, churchmen realized that the putting of their house in order was a task that the State really wanted the bishops to assume —they were to look to Lambeth not to Westminster in matters of Church order. With this task thrust upon it, the episcopate began to take itself much more seriously. Few late nineteenth-century bishops would have agreed with Blomfield that ideas of apostolic succession had gone out with the Nonjurors. The growth of the Anglican communion added to the sense of episcopal importance, and the influence of Tractarianism spread far beyond England. The result of this has been, in the words of Norman Sykes, a radical departure in the development of modern Anglicanism: 'by its doctrine of the Church and of Episcopacy it has altered profoundly the balance of the Anglican tradition; and in all modern discussions of ecclesiastical re-union it has forced episcopacy into the foreground.'[18] This new concern about episcopacy would not have been understood by many churchmen of the pre-Tractarian period, who would have agreed with Dean Sherlock that 'a Church may be a truly Catholic Church, and such as we may and ought to communicate with, without bishops. . . . I do not make episcopacy so absolutely necessary to Catholic communion as to unchurch all Churches which have it not.'[19]

'The unforeseen circumstances', which led the Anglican bishops to reconsider thoughtfully the prerogatives that the Tractarians had claimed for them, were a series of crises which revealed the reluctance of the State to continue dealing with matters such as ecclesiastical discipline. A new spirit was at work in the Church of England after 1850; zealous young churchmen who adopted Pusey as their 'Father-in-God' dedicated themselves to a new Catholic mission to the nation. Wherever they went, their zeal upset the established order, and forced a reconsideration of what was the role of the Church of England. This debate, and the issue of what was Catholicism, was of less and less concern to the legislature as time passed. The obvious failure of the Judicial Committee of the Privy Council in its handling of ecclesiastical affairs resulted in a general feeling of relief—especially when the bishops began to show interest in establishing peace in the

18. Norman Sykes, *English Religious Tradition* (1961), p. 81.
19. Anonymous, *Ought Clergymen with Foreign Orders to be Reordained in the Irish Church* (1877), p. 19.

Church—bolstered by the Tractarian ideology which most of them began to take seriously.

2. The Victory of the Common Law

NEWMAN and most of the churchmen who left the Church of England with him did so because they were convinced of its Erastianism. They were dismayed by the Church's failure to resist when the legislature chose to ignore religious controversy, and to order ecclesiastical affairs by itself—as it had done in the Hampden affair and the Jerusalem Bishopric. But the clearest revelation of the state of bondage in which the Church found itself was made through a series of legal judgments, which began with the Gorham crisis of 1850, and reached an embarrassing climax in the Lincoln Judgment of 1890. In order to understand the extent to which the State could regulate the Church at this time, we must first look at the development of ecclesiastical courts and ecclesiastical law since the Reformation.

By the Statute of Appeals, 1533, final appellate jurisdiction in the Church of England was taken from the pope. A year later, the Act 25, Henry VIII, c. 19, established the Court of Delegates to hear and pronounce final sentence upon appeals from the archbishops' courts, which hitherto had gone to Rome. This was not a permanent court. Delegates were to be appointed by the King in Chancery to hear appeals in matters such as matrimonial and testamentary cases. In 1545 ecclesiastical courts were opened to married laymen who were doctors in civil law, and it was these civilians who heard the cases in the Court of Delegates.

These ecclesiastical lawyers formed an association known as Doctors' Commons, a restricted body which excluded clerics from its ranks. The members of this college of advocates practised not only in the ecclesiastical courts, but also in the Admiralty Court. In 1568 they acquired Mountjoy Place, near St. Paul's Cathedral, for the use of the Advocates and Doctors of the Arches. The dean of the Court of Arches, the consistory court of the Province of Canterbury, acted as president of the college. There were also in Doctors' Commons proctors, who corresponded to solicitors in other courts. They prepared the cases for the advocates. The membership of this college was never very large—in 1843 the number of advocates totalled only twenty-three—but Doctors' Commons virtually controlled the administration of the ecclesiastical law in England from the Reformation to the nineteenth century.

No one was pleased with the state of the ecclesiastical courts by the time the reform era burst upon the Church. The Court of Delegates was accepted as a convenient means by which the Royal Supremacy could be exercised in quasi-ecclesiastical matters, to which its jurisdiction was in practice confined. Only seven cases involving doctrine or discipline came before the Delegates during their whole history, and in none of these was the decision taken to reverse the decision of the provincial court. Churchmen were bothered that the common law and civilian judges who served as Delegates were appointed without regard to their fitness for such a position, but the work of the court was unobtrusive and aroused little dissatisfaction. The Court of Arches, the consistory court of the Province of Canterbury, and the Chancery Court for the Province of York, were also tolerated because they were staffed by the Advocates in Doctors' Commons. But below these courts were diocesan courts whose judges often lacked proper legal training, and smaller courts of Peculiar Jurisdiction which numbered in all 386 in 1832.[1] In these lesser courts an anachronistic system of written depositions taken from witnesses without the presence of counsel was used, instead of evidence being given *viva voce*.

It was impossible for the reformers to overlook the cumbrous and antiquated ecclesiastical courts. In 1823 and 1824 reports were submitted on the courts of the Archbishop of Canterbury and those of the Bishop of London. Then recommendations were made by the Ecclesiastical Courts Commission, including the suggestion that appeals should be made to the King in Council rather than to the King in Chancery, the jurisdiction which the Court of Delegates represented. The reasons given were the manner in which the Delegates were appointed, their costly and dilatory procedure, and the fact that they gave no reasons for their decisions, which were not always uniform.

These reports led to the abolishment of the Court of Delegates in 1832 (2 & 3 Wm. IV, c. 92), and the transfer of its jurisdiction to the Privy Council as a whole. The following year the appellate jurisdiction

1. Robert J. Phillimore, *Study of the Civil and Canon Law in Its Relation to the State, the Church and the Universities* (1843), p. 51.

4*

of the Privy Council was transferred to the Judicial Committee of the Privy Council as the supreme ecclesiastical court of appeals. It was to consist of the Lord Chancellor and a number of judges and ex-judges. Only the judge of the Prerogative Court of Canterbury and the Lord Chancellor had to be churchmen, or even Christians. Other reform measures abolished the peculiar courts and customs such as written depositions submitted as evidence. By the Church Discipline Act of 1840 all archbishops and bishops who were Privy Councillors were made members of the Judicial Committee for hearing appeals under that Act. This provision was repealed by the Appellate Juris-diction Act of 1876, and bishops then attended the court as assessors, not as members. This deprived the Court of any semblance of spiritual authority in the eyes of High-Churchmen.

In 1857 Parliament deprived the remaining ecclesiastical courts of the right and duty of supervising and administering the probate of wills, by setting up a Court of Probate to be presided over by a judge who was to be the same person as the Judge of the Court of Admiralty. In the same year Parliament withdrew from the ecclesiastical courts matrimonial jurisdiction, investing it in a new court whose judges were to be the Lord Chancellor, the chief justices, the judge of the Probate Court, and certain common-law judges. At this time Parliament also granted Doctors' Commons power to surrender its charter, to sell all its property, and to divide the proceeds among the Fellows. In 1861 the Advocates sold by auction their magnificent library. Dickens' 'lazy old nook near St. Paul's churchyard' was gone within another five years, and the legal profession was deprived of the college which for so long had provided ecclesiastical lawyers trained in the Roman civil law.[2]

Much of the unfortunate ecclesiastical legislation in the late nine-teenth century reflected this suppression of Doctors' Commons, and the gradual disappearance of ecclesiastical lawyers who were trained in the civil law. Very soon the common-law lawyers who staffed the Judicial Committee of the Privy Council, when it was the final court of appeal in ecclesiastical causes, found themselves in a very unhappy predicament. The proceedings in ecclesiastical causes could not be governed by the rules of the common law, nor by any analogies it could furnish. One of these lawyers, Sir James Parke, later Lord Wensleydale, said 'With respect to the Common Law Judges, not-withstanding their great learning and experience in the Law of their own courts . . . they must occasionally, perhaps not infrequently,

2. *London Topographical Record* XV (1931), 86.

rely for the law of the Ecclesiastical Court on the Civilian Con-delegates.'[3]

This situation arose because of the long and tortuous development of English ecclesiastical law. At the time of the Reformation the statute for the Submission of the Clergy and Restraint of Appeals (25 Henry VIII, c. 19) had enacted that a commission of thirty-two persons, half clergy and half members of the two houses of parliament, should review and report on the existing canons of the Church. Those that the commission approved were to be revalidated by the king's assent under the Great Seal, and such as they disallowed were to be abolished. In the meantime it was ordered that all existing canons which were not contrary to the king's prerogative were to be used and executed. But this commission never met nor acted, and attempts to bring it into operation fell through under both Edward VI and Elizabeth, and were never renewed. The legal result was that the statute of Henry VIII remained the ruling one upon the subject, and thus approximately all the ancient canon law of the Church of the Middle Ages which did not conflict with former or later canons or civil statutes was still binding in ecclesiastical law.

> No one, I think, can read the published reports of the cases in the ecclesiastical courts down to the middle of the last century without being struck by the familiarity of the advocates not only with the medieval canon law and its commentators, but also with the continental canonists of the sixteenth and seventeenth centuries such as Sanchez, the great authority on the law of marriage, Pierre de Marca, the Gallican archbishop of Paris, and Van Espen, the celebrated doctor of Louvain. The Ecclesiastical Law in England was not regarded as an isolated system, but as a part, albeit with its own special rules, of a much greater system.[4]

The common-law lawyers and judges of the J.C.P.C. were greatly embarrassed by their lack of knowledge of both procedure and precedent in the field of ecclesiastical law. In 1848 Mr. Mavor, perpetual curate of Forest Hill, accepted a living in Essex without resigning his original benefice. Criminal articles were preferred against him for accepting a benefice with cure of souls while in possession of another. The articles alleged that by Canon XXIX of the Fourth Lateran Council of 1215 he was *ipso jure* deprived of the first living. The judge, Sir Herbert Jenner Fust, finally agreed that the Council of the Lateran set forth the law in this case, and Mavor lost the perpetual curacy of Forest Hill. Poor Mr. Mavor accumulated

3. G. C. Brodrick and W. H. Fremantle, *Collection of the Judgments of the J.C.P.C. in Ecclesiastical Cases Relating to Doctrine and Discipline* (1865), p. lxii.
4. E. W. Kemp, *Introduction to Canon Law in the Church of England* (1957), p. 62.

such costs during this trial that he died in Debtor's Prison, Oxford, in 1853.[5]

The new ecclesiastical lawyers were also called upon to have some knowledge of the canon law which was peculiar to the Church of England. William Lyndwood, an English canonist who was Dean of the Arches from 1426 to 1433, published in the latter year a digest in five books of the synodical constitutions of the Province of Canterbury from the time of Archbishop Stephen Langton to the time of Archbishop Henry Chichele. Lyndwood's *Provinciale* provided a 'body of domestic ecclesiastical law' which Robert Phillimore believed 'the common law was always disposed to recognize' although it was averse to countenancing much of the general canon law.[6] Added to this domestic law were 151 canons passed by the Convocation of Canterbury in 1604 and of York in 1606. In the nineteenth century they were still technically binding on the clergy.

> The Law of the Church of England, and its history, are to be deduced from the ancient general Canon Law—from the particular constitutions made in this country to regulate the English Church—from our own Canons—from the Rubric, and from any acts of Parliament that may have passed upon the subject; and the whole may be illustrated also, by the writings of eminent persons.[7]

The result of this was that when the Court of Delegates was replaced by the J.C.P.C. all the complexities produced in a system of ecclesiastical law that was hundreds of years old were placed upon the shoulders of a group of amateurs. The members of the new court had not usually, and were not obliged to have, any legal training in the law they were expected to administer. They were acquainted with some matters that were of concern in ecclesiastical law, property, revenues, and personal freedom; and perhaps statutory legislation was the best way to regulate them. But other matters such as the administration of the sacraments, the conduct of public worship, and the outward pattern of devotional life required a different approach. Admonition was of more use here than the imposing of ecclesiastical discipline upon tender consciences. The long history of the Church had taught the lawyers of the old Court of Delegates that any attempt to enforce the strict letter of the law by coercive measures had usually proved disastrous.

5. Robert Phillimore, *Principal Ecclesiastical Judgments Delivered in the Courts of Arches, 1867–1875* (1876), pp. 36–37.

6. *Ibid.*, p. 36.

7. Kemp, p. 58, the words of Sir John Nicholl, Dean of Arches at the beginning of the nineteenth century.

Unfortunately those who staffed the J.C.P.C. in ecclesiastical cases had little knowledge of the *Corpus Juris Canonici*, Lyndwood's constitutions, or the history of canon law regulation in England. The result was 'hasty and crude legislation'[8] which reflected a lack of knowledge of both the law and the history of the Church. When the learned Robert Phillimore was called upon to judge the presence of heretical doctrine in the Eucharistic teaching of W. J. E. Bennett of Frome Selwood, Somerset, in 1867, he was able to refer to and discuss the teachings of Paschasius Radbertus, the ninth-century Benedictine theologian of Corbie, and those of his opponent, the monk Ratramnus. He also made mention of Aelfric of Malmesbury, the Fourth Lateran Council, and the teachings of Luther, Ridley, Matthew Parker, Hooker, Laud, Andrewes, and Bellarmine before the final summing up and the verdict that 'Mr. Bennett, by his language respecting the visible Presence of our Lord, and the adoration of the Consecrated Elements, has contravened the law of the Church.'[9] Phillimore could make such a long and reasoned judgment. Son of the Regius Professor of Civil Law at Oxford, he was a trained civilian, Advocate of Doctors' Commons, Judge of the High Court of Admiralty, and Dean of the Arches. But few of those who served the J.C.P.C. in ecclesiastical causes had had this lengthy and rigorous training.

> It can scarcely be denied that the substitution of the Judicial Committee of the Privy Council for the Court of Delegates operated not only unfavourably but unjustly upon our profession. In the latter Court five civilians sat with three Common Law Judges in all cases of appeal; in the new tribunal it may and does sometimes happen that no civilian at all sits, but that four judges from the Common Law or Chancery determine even upon points of practice in the Ecclesiastical courts. It would be a curious sight to behold four civilians sitting in judgment as Court of Appeal upon cases—especially cases of practice—from Westminster Hall and Lincoln's Inn; though it would be difficult to say why the injury done would be greater or the injustice more flagrant in the latter than the former case.[10]

In the acute conflict between churchmen and the J.C.P.C. which occurred in the late nineteenth century, much of the tragedy of what happened came from the inability of the lawyers who staffed this ecclesiastical court to deal with problems that were peculiarly religious —matters of ritual and discipline that only someone with the training of Robert Phillimore and others like him could appreciate. By the

8. Phillimore, *Study of the Civil and Canon Law*, p. 52.
9. Phillimore, *Principal Judgments*, pp. 332–33.
10. Phillimore, *Study of the Civil and Canon Law*, p. 43.

time of the Public Worship Regulation Act, and the imprisonment of pious and popular clergy for ritualistic offences, public embarrassment was beginning to demand that the bishops be encouraged to tidy up their house in spiritual as well as temporal matters. It was now impossible for the Anglican episcopate to follow the easy-going life of the eighteenth century. In 1777 the case of Havard vs Evanson was directly concerned with the charge of heresy, yet it was judged by common-law judges and civilians with no bishops in commission— without any outcry on the part of anyone.[11] By the time of the Lincoln Judgment of 1890, it was impossible for the bishops to be kept out of such cases. A new spirit was at work among churchmen, which demanded a different adjustment in the relationship of Church and State.

3. The Gorham Controversy

THE QUESTION of where lay the ultimate source of authority for the Church in matters of doctrine became a national issue in 1847. The Bishop of Exeter since 1830 had been Henry Phillpotts, a vigorous Tory High-Churchman of the old school, who had a love of litigation which had been fostered during the years he served as a clerical magistrate. An unpopular man in his diocese, he had a reputation for nepotism, time-serving, and pluralism. He was continually quarrelling with someone, and during his episcopate he engaged in more than fifty law-suits which cost him in all between £20,000 and £30,000.

In 1846 Bishop Phillpotts instituted as Vicar of St. Just-in-Penwith, Cornwall, G. C. Gorham, a Low-Church cleric who had attained some distinction as an antiquary and botanist, and had at one time been a Fellow of Queen's College, Cambridge. His theological opinions were so pronounced that Bishop Dampier of Ely had threatened to refuse him ordination in 1811 because of his interpretation of baptismal regeneration. Phillpotts had great sympathy for the Tractarians, and shortly after he instituted Gorham he rebuked him for advertising for a curate 'free from Tractarian error'. On 2 November 1847, Gorham was presented by the Crown to the vicarage of Brampford Speke, also

11. Brodrick and Fremantle, p. lvii.

in the Diocese of Exeter. When he applied to the bishop for institution to his new benefice, he was told that before the bishop would comply with his request Mr. Gorham would be obliged to undergo examination to ensure that he was sound in Christian doctrine.

When Gorham submitted himself for examination, he discovered that he had to answer one hundred and forty-nine questions which took him fifty-two hours, spread over eight days in December 1847, and March of the following year. He protested against the intricate nature of the questions, complaining that the whole procedure was virtually a 'penal inquisition'—as in fact it was. Gorham had distinct Calvinistic ideas with regard to the sacrament of baptism, and because of them Phillpotts eventually refused to institute him.

Gorham immediately sought a monition from the Court of Arches, which directed the Bishop of Exeter either to institute Mr. Gorham or to show cause why he should not do so. The case was argued at length in January and in June 1849. On August 2 of that year, the Dean of Arches, Sir Herbert Jenner Fust, gave judgment that as the Church of England held the doctrine of spiritual regeneration of infants in baptism, Mr. Gorham did in fact oppose the teaching of the Church when he insisted that baptismal regeneration was conditional upon worthy reception of the sacrament, and that infants never benefited in baptism except by some other gift of Grace. When the judgment was received, Gorham appealed from the Arches Court of Canterbury to the Judicial Committee of the Privy Council.

When the new secular court had been set up to take the place of the old Court of Delegates in 1833, no bishop or other representative of the Church, apart from Robert Phillimore, had paid much attention to the change. But when Gorham made his appeal churchmen were filled with great anxiety. An essential doctrine of the Church was in question and many wondered what kind of adequate spiritual judgment could be given by such a civil court. Bishop Blomfield suggested that because the Committee might find difficulty in deciding doctrinal matters it might follow the opinion of 'the collective episcopate of England'.[1] Lord John Russell rejected this suggestion as an attempt to impose the 'dogmatic decrees of a dominant hierarchy', which would alter the Protestant nature of the Church and eventually substitute the supremacy of the Pope for that of the Queen.

The elevation of Hampden had convinced many churchmen that the Crown was quite capable of advancing to the episcopate a clergyman

1. *Speech of the Bishop of London in the House of Lords, 3 June, 1850, on the Bill Relating to Appeals from the Ecclesiastical Courts* (1850), p. 50.

whose doctrine might be seriously questioned. Now it seemed as if in its handling of the Gorham case the Crown might reveal a tendency to mould the doctrines of the Church as well as to appoint its rulers. It was all very well for the court of appeal to claim that it had no intention of affecting the doctrine of the Church, but only intended to make clear what that doctrine was. As Keble pointed out, *cujus interpretatio, ejus lex*: 'a judicial sentence contrary to a prevailing construction though its force be short of legislation, cannot be denied to be a practical change in the Law.'[2]

Pusey, Keble, and Gladstone all wished that the Bishop of Exeter had instituted Gorham and tried, through kindness, to win his allegiance to the cause of true religion rather than through litigation. Looking back at the Gorham case, Gladstone later said of Phillpotts, 'all who knew that remarkable Prelate are aware that he was a man of sole action, rather than of counsel and concert; and it was an individual, not a body, that was responsible for striking the blow, of which the recoil so seriously strained the Church of England.'[3] Pusey expected the worst to happen and once more called for passive resistance to temporary tyranny. 'A judicial decision on a doctrinal question reversing an ecclesiastical judgment and deciding against the Creeds, would be a miserable thing, though one must, if God avert it not, make the best of it, and sit down by the waters of Babylon, toiling on under bondage.'[4]

The case came before the court on 11 December 1849. Acting on it were J. B. Sumner, the Evangelical Archbishop of Canterbury, Thomas Musgrave, the Evangelical Archbishop of York, Bishop Blomfield of London, and seven lay judges. When it was reported that both the Archbishop of Canterbury and Blomfield were ready to treat 'the grace and efficacy of Baptism as an open question',[5] Keble and Pusey were shocked but not altogether surprised, and expressed a new depth of sympathy for the Nonjurors of the seventeenth century. On 9 March 1850 the Judicial Committee announced their award. The opinions of Mr. Gorham were not 'contrary or repugnant to the declared doctrine of the Church of England as by law established',[6] and Mr. Gorham ought not, by reason of the doctrines held by him, to have been refused admission to the vicarage of Bramford Speke. Of the lay judges, only Vice-Chancellor Knight Bruce dissented from the

2. John Keble, 'Call to Speak Out', *Church Matters in 1850*, p. 27.
3. W. E. Gladstone, *Is the Church of England Worth Preserving?* (1875), p. 70.
4. *Life of Pusey*, III, 204.
5. *Ibid.*, p. 225.
6. *Ibid.*, p. 229.

judgment. Blomfield also opposed it, but the archbishops concurred with the other lay judges.

The Gorham Judgment of 1850 marked a time of great crisis in the Church. When a court that was secular in origin, with two dissentients among its members, would choose to reverse a decision made by a Church court, in a matter of doctrine, and the two archbishops could agree with such a judgment, it appeared to many churchmen that the Erastianism of the Church of England could no longer be denied. Royal Supremacy now meant Parliamentary Supremacy. In no way could Parliament be viewed as a lay synod of the Church, when it included both Nonconformists and Roman Catholics, yet it could not be withstood when it chose to interpret Church doctrine, and force into a living a cleric whom a bishop believed to be heretical.

Another wave of secession to Rome followed the judgment. Those who departed were led by Henry Manning, Archdeacon of Chichester, who could not accept the supremacy of a court unless both the tribunal and its judge were purely spiritual and within the Church. Robert Wilberforce, Archdeacon of the East Riding, son of the great William Wilberforce and brother of the Bishop of Oxford, followed Manning in 1854. A theologian of note, his loss was grievous. As a result of this unfortunate judgment the Church also lost James Hope-Scott, one of Gladstone's most intimate friends; William Maskell, the liturgical scholar, who had conducted the examination of Gorham in his capacity as chaplain to the Bishop of Exeter; and T. W. Allies, one time friend of Pusey, who became a prominent apologist for Roman Catholicism.

As was to be expected, Phillpotts did not accept the reversal of his own decision quietly. He protested to the Archbishop of Canterbury against the judgment, and went so far as to say that anyone who supported Gorham in any way until he retracted his views was 'a favourer and supporter of those heresies'. Furthermore, Phillpotts would himself refuse to have communion with anyone who would abuse 'the high commission which he bears' by refusing to condemn Gorham.[7] The bishop's protest was of little avail. On 6 August 1850, Gorham was instituted to the living of Bramford Speke by the Dean of Arches under the fiat of the Archbishop of Canterbury.

As had happened in 1845, churchmen waited to see what would be the response of Keble and Pusey. Keble reacted by writing two pamphlets which proved to be the most searching criticisms to come from

7. Henry Phillpotts, *Letter to the Archbishop of Canterbury* (1850), p. 90.

the High-Church party—'Trial of Doctrine' and 'A Call to Speak Out', which were published later as *Church Matters in 1850*. In the first pamphlet he began by pointing out that the ecclesiastical court of the Judicial Committee of the Privy Council was set up by Parliament. The Church had never assented to the authority claimed by this court, which sought now to perform a task granted by Christ to His Church, His Apostles, and their successors. He argued that at the time of the Reformation the clergy had submitted to Henry VIII only because they understood that in temporal matters they would be governed by the law of the land, and in spiritual matters by the law of the Church. In Canon XXXVI of 1604 the clergy had reaffirmed the Royal Supremacy in both temporal and spiritual causes, but in Article XX of the Thirty-nine Articles the Sovereign had agreed that the Church had authority in articles of faith, and in Article XXXVII she had agreed to sanction the Church's doctrine by the civil sword. This being so, no doctrinal decision of the Judicial Committee of the Privy Council could make the Church of England formally heretical.

Keble's answer to what he believed to be usurpation by the State of spiritual prerogative that belonged to the Church was a call for the revival of Convocation. He said that when appeals to Rome had been taken away by Henry VIII, the Upper House of Convocation had been authorized to act as a court of appeal in spiritual causes. He was quite willing to agree to the House of Lords acting as court of appeal in temporal matters, if Convocation were allowed to fulfil the same function in matters of doctrine.

The second pamphlet was written and published after the decision of the Judicial Committee had been revealed. Keble confessed that he was filled with horror that 'the Primate has signified his willingness to institute the clerk condemned by his own Court for denial of sacramental Grace'.[8] He questioned whether a break should be made with the archbishop who had condoned such heretical procedure. What is the priest to do, asked Keble, when he has sworn in his ordination vows 'to banish and drive away all erroneous and strange doctrines contrary to God's word'? Should the example of the people and clergy of Constantinople be followed, who withdrew from Nestorius because of his heresy? No, said Keble, the Church will be reformed and neither it nor the State should be abandoned in their need. Rather let the clergy look to the history of their Church and nation, and from the experiences of reformers of other ages, find their way forward.

8. Keble, 'Call to Speak Out', p. 1.

What has been the course of constitutional reformers in this country, when their (seemingly) just demands have been doggedly refused by their Governments of the time? This set them on examining the whole theory and system of those institutions, and if they had, or seemed to have, a good moral case, a fair appeal to the equity and good sense of their countrymen . . . they have in general, sooner or later, carried the mind of their country with them, not only for redress of the special wrong, but (if need were) for the general remodelling of the institution which seemed committed to the wrong.[9]

Like Manning and the other seceders, Keble was forced by the Gorham judgment to consider where the ultimate authority of the Church of England lay. A High-Churchman with roots deep in the English countryside, he had advised Newman to re-read Hooker and Hammond when he was perplexed, and in this time of crisis for himself he returned once more to a study of the historical development of the Church of England. Ideally Keble would have liked to agree with Henry Phillpotts, who told his diocesan synod that the bishops should have the authority to act as judges of divinity within the Church. But his Tractarian days were behind him, and he realized the futility of seeking a readjustment in the relationship between Church and State that would allow 'the practical exercise of the judicial as well as the legislative functions which are inherent in the bishop's office.[10] He was convinced that the ultimate authority which sustained the Church, and upon which churchmen had to rely, was not the bishops, as Newman had thought, but the whole people of the Church.

He said that churchmen should not be satisfied with any court which had not the sanction of Convocation, 'nor with Convocation itself, unless we had a better way of appointing Bishops'.[11] He considered that the bishops might depute seven or nine of their number to advise the Queen in matters of doctrine, ritual, or discipline, but only if they were assisted in their decision-making by historians, lawyers, and theologians. Like Hooker, whose writings he knew so well, Keble found ultimate authority in the Church in the people—not in the bishops who had proved to be Newman's 'broken reed'. Referring to the promises made to the Church in Magna Carta and the Coronation Oath, Keble said: 'When the whole case of the Church, not in regard of this doctrine, nor of this tribunal only, but in all its relations to the State and Law of England, is fairly and fully set before the people of England, we shall carry them with us in our

9. *Ibid.*, p. 10.
10. H. P. Liddon, *Difficulties in the Relations Between Church and State by the Late John Keble* (1877), p. x of Liddon's Preface.
11. *Life of Pusey*, III, 223.

demand for redress.'[12] By 'the people' Keble meant ideally the communicants of the Church of England only. But in this time of crisis he was not going to question too closely the doctrinal exactitude of even a nominal churchman's position. He was disappointed that Sir Robert Phillimore was made Dean of Arches because he considered him to be in many ways only a nominal churchman, but he preferred his judgments to the harsh Erastianism which Keble believed the Privy Council court represented.[13] In the Church's time of trial he refused to consider either secession, leading to a nonjuring movement, or acceptance of the authority of the Judicial Committee. He had faith in the apostolic foundation of the Church of England, in the continuing power of the Holy Spirit within it, and in the godly people of England, who would one day demand that the Church be set free from its bondage. He urged the people of his own parish to unite together to save their Church, which seemed about to 'consent to heresy and throw away faith'. It was at the suggestion of Keble that Phillpotts held a diocesan synod at Exeter to resist the Judicial Committee.[14]

Pusey wrote in 1850 his fragment entitled *The Royal Supremacy Not an Arbitrary Authority But Limited by the Laws of the Church of Which Kings are Members*, which was supplemented later by his work on the Councils of the Church. Like Keble he believed the ultimate authority in ecclesiastical affairs to lie within the whole Church. The bishops derived their spiritual jurisdiction from their sees, and the Crown was only the power within the Church 'which put into motion a jurisdiction existing independently of itself'.[15] Because of this he would refuse to follow those who would force Keble and himself into a nonjuring schism, 'bind us to withdraw' from the Church.[16] Nor would he at this time attempt to divide churchmen when the whole Church was in peril; he resisted those who expected from him some 'statement which should summarily force Low-Churchmen either to accept the Catholic doctrine unhesitatingly and in its fullness, or to leave the communion of the Church of England'.[17]

Pusey's importance at this time was not as a controversialist. In the minds of churchmen, even more than Keble who remained at Hursley, he represented the *via media* party of Oxford, the High-Churchmen who were attempting to reclaim something out of the disintegration

---

12. Liddon, *Difficulties*, p. xx.
13. *Ibid.*, pp. xvi–xviii.
14. *Life of Pusey*, III, 226.
15. *Ibid.*, p. 259.
16. Keble, 'Trial of Doctrine', *Church Matters in 1850*, p. 23.
17. *Life of Pusey*, III, 262.

of the old Tractarian party after the secessions of 1845. Because of this position, Pusey found himself a very unpopular figure in the Church. He belonged to the Bristol Church Union, one of the associations to defend Church principles which had come into being in the wake of the Gorham judgment. The Vice-President of the Union was William Palmer of Worcester College, an old-fashioned and rigid High-Churchman who supported the 'Branch Theory' in defence of the Catholicism of the Church of England.[18] When asked to prepare 'resolutions and statements of principles' for the Bristol organization, he included an anti-Roman declaration. Keble did not object to 'a very moderate but quite real disavowal of Rome',[19] but Pusey opposed it on the grounds that churchmen like Archdeacon Manning, who had not yet seceded, might be given fresh impulse to leave the Church of England. He knew that such a declaration could be misunderstood and that, among the members of the old Tractarian party, 'some will be made desperate and the rest remain hopelessly disunited'.[20]

Many of Pusey's enemies interpreted this reluctance of Pusey to ally himself with those opposed to Rome as a *de facto* avowal of Roman sympathies. Other churchmen, like Palmer, Hook, and Samuel Wilberforce, could not understand at the time what seemed to them to be evasiveness. Palmer later wrote of his misapprehensions at this time.

> I should gladly have seen Pusey attempt to reform mistakes introduced by Newman, and endeavouring to correct, instead of seeming to go along with, the ultra-Tractarian mistakes. . . . but in the end I became satisfied that the position he occupied was for the good of the Church. . . . He had to control a very uncertain party, open to Newman's influence for some time—a party which was unsettled in principle and might easily be driven into secession. . . . I should myself have often been in favour of a sterner and more direct policy towards all who shared in semi-Romanizing and Ritualistic opinions, and whom Pusey conciliated; but my own opinions were proved to be faulty by the result; for by mild methods the Church has been saved from further disruption and retains all the energies which a different mode of proceedings might have lost.[21]

Pusey was also attacked by those who left the Church for Rome, particularly by T. W. Allies and W. Dodsworth, who accused him of

18. *V.* William Palmer, *Treatise on the Church of Christ* (1838), II vols. Palmer viewed the Anglican Church as one 'branch' of Catholicism, whose roots were in the Church of the Fathers.

19. *Life of Pusey*, III, 276.

20. *Ibid.*

21. William Palmer, *Supplement to a Narrative of Events Connected With Tracts for the Times* (1883), pp. 240–41.

double dealing. The latter charged Pusey with leading the members of the Tractarian party on the road to Rome, then of shrinking from the front rank when the moment of crisis came.

> By your constant and common practice of administering the sacrament of penance; by encouraging everywhere, if not enjoining auricular confession, and giving special priestly absolution; by teaching the propitiatory sacrifice of the Holy Eucharist, as applicatory of the one sacrifice on the Cross, and by adoration of Christ Really Present on the altar under the form of bread and wine; by your introduction of Roman Catholic books 'adapted to the use of our Church'; by encouraging the use of rosaries and crucifixes, and special devotions to our Lord . . . you have done much to revive among us the system which may be pre-eminently called 'Sacramental'. And yet now, when, by God's mercy to us, a great opportunity has occurred, of asserting and enforcing the very keystone of this system . . . you seem to shrink from the front rank.[22]

Pusey failed to satisfy Dodsworth and Allies because he could not share their exaggerated estimate of the damage done to the Church by the Judicial Committee's judgment. Nor did he really believe that the Low-Church views, which the court had sustained, were as widely removed from what he considered to be the Catholic position as did those who left the Church. He continued to believe that within the Catholic comprehensiveness of the Church of England there was room for different expressions of doctrine.[23] But inevitably, in the eyes of those who left, he appeared both timid and compromising, when he refused to accompany them on their quest for an ecclesiastical system which Pusey believed to be based on abstract and *a priori* considerations 'unwarranted by primitive precedent'.[24]

Pusey was very upset by Dodsworth's charges, which seemed to try him more than the suspicions of Palmer and the High-Churchmen who remained in the Anglican fold. He confessed that Dodsworth put him in a 'sort of moral pillory',[25] but he was content to attempt to weather the storm while he kept as many within the Church as possible, through a policy of comprehensiveness and conciliation. He never expected that Dodsworth's charges would be taken seriously by the bishops—least of all by his own diocesan.

This might not have happened except for Roman Catholic provocation. Nicholas Wiseman, Vicar Apostolic of the London District, hailed the Gorham judgment as a 'providential event, overruled by

22. W. Dodsworth, *A Letter to the Rev. E. B. Pusey* (London, 1850), pp. 16–17.
23. *Life of Pusey*, III, 264.
24. *Ibid.*, p. 268.
25. E. B. Pusey, *Renewed Explanation in Consequence of Rev. W. Dodsworth's Comments* (1851), p. 2.

God for the advancement of His holy religion, and the triumph of His Universal Church',[26] in a lecture delivered at St. George's Cathedral, Lambeth. He believed that the secessions of 1850 might be but the beginning of a 'return to the bosom of the Catholic Church'. This misconception was shared by many Low-Church bishops. When Pius IX, in September 1850, established a new Roman Catholic episcopate in England, this 'papal aggression', which referred to the Church of England as 'the Anglican schism', aroused an almost fanatical storm of indignation throughout the nation. Meetings were held all over the country, bishops wrote letters, and Lord John Russell introduced into Parliament the Ecclesiastical Titles Bill which was carried amidst great excitement.[27] It forbade the Romans to assume territorial titles within the United Kingdom, but remained a dead letter from the time it was passed until it was repealed twenty years later.

Russell did much to inflame popular passion by a public letter which he wrote to Edward Maltby, Pusey's old tutor who was now Bishop of Durham. In it he denounced the 'mummeries of High Church superstition'. Pusey was well-known as the leader of what was left of the Tractarian party because of the writings of Dodsworth and the others who had attacked him, and Pusey accepted as inevitable the public scorn which came his way. But he never expected the bishops to 'throw the weight of their authority on the side of popular and short-sighted passion'[28]—which they did with the exception of the intransigent Phillpotts.

As Canon Liddon remarks in his biography of Pusey, timidity has always been thought to be an episcopal distinction in the Church of England; *Episcopi in Anglia semper pavidissimi*.[29] It certainly was characteristic of the bishops of 1850. In sheer terror of Rome and the Erastianism of Russell, bishop after bishop joined in the general denunciation of Pusey and all who sympathized with him. Lord John Russell had made use of Dodsworth's criticism of Pusey in his letter to Bishop Maltby, and this expedient was used by others who joined in the attack. When Blomfield delivered his sixth charge to the clergy of his diocese in 1850, he poured scorn on those who had paved the way for secession to Rome by teaching and practice which revealed a belief that the Church of England was 'separated from that of Rome

---

26. N. P. S. Wiseman, *Final Appeal in Matters of Faith* (1850), p. 20.
27. 14 & 15 Vict., cap. 60.
28. *Life of Pusey*, III, 292.
29. *Ibid.*, p. 293.

by a faint and almost imperceptible line'.[30] In a letter to Pusey, Blomfield made quite clear that he had him in mind, 'amongst others', when he delivered his charge.

The pamphlet war of 1850 was fierce. Pusey was bewildered by the distress of the time, and found that everyone who called on him had a tract to press into his hand: 'Pamphlets come like hailstones by every post, and from the hands of friends.'[31] When he protested to Blomfield about the talk of 'putting down Tractarianism', and urged the bishop to realize that 'the remedy for secessions from the Church is her own health and well-being',[32] Dodsworth, now a Roman Catholic, jumped back into the fray with 'A Few Comments on Dr. Pusey's Letter'. But most serious of all the correspondence that Pusey received at this time was a series of letters, which came as private correspondence, from Samuel Wilberforce.

This correspondence indicates that Pusey's diocesan did not like the tendency of Pusey to initiate devotional and sacramental practices without first seeking the approval of his ordinary. Pusey believed that the true authority for all he did came from the tradition and teaching of the Church, which Pusey knew as well as any man of his time. Wilberforce had accepted from Tractarianism exalted ideas about the jurisdiction of his office, and he had no intention of allowing Pusey to exercise in these matters what was a private judgment of the Church's position on controversial matters. The bishop's viewpoint was to govern the thinking of the clergy of his diocese, and he did not appreciate the originality of Pusey's independent line of thought.

On the day that Blomfield delivered his charge, Wilberforce wrote to Pusey saying that not only did he condemn Pusey's adaptation of Roman Catholic books of devotion as an attempt to spread 'Romanism' in the Church, but he also opposed the general 'effect of Pusey's ministry'. He admitted that his convictions regarding Pusey's activities reflected his reading of Dodsworth's published letter, and he called on Pusey to give an answer to the charges laid against him, as well as a promise 'as shall satisfy me that they (his practices) will no longer lead any of the flock committed to me as chief pastor of this diocese, to the corruptions or the communion of the See of Rome'.[33]

Pusey indicated in his reply that the main reason for the recent secessions was the failure of the bishops to reaffirm the faith of the

---

30. *Ibid.*, p. 294.   31. *Ibid.*, p. 297.

32. E. B. Pusey, *Letter to the Bishop of London in Explanation of Some Statements Contained in a Letter by the Rev. W. Dodsworth* (1851), p. 259. Pusey's explanation took some 276 pages.

33. *Life of Wilberforce*, II, 79–81.

Church after the Gorham judgment. Wilberforce then repeated his previous blanket condemnation of Pusey's ministry and inhibited him from preaching anywhere in the diocese except at Pusey, where his influence could not harm anyone. When Keble heard of this he was upset that Wilberforce distinguished between himself and Pusey, and he and Charles Marriott both wrote to the bishop on Pusey's behalf. But Wilberforce was adamant. His private inhibition of Pusey was to continue until an answer to Mr. Dodsworth was published to the satisfaction of the Bishop of Oxford.

Keble encouraged Pusey to withstand this tyranny. 'Whether we are suspended or no, we must go on in a disowned and crippled state, as far as these State Bishops are concerned.'[34] Wilberforce refused to see Pusey, or to make specific charges against him. He told Keble that he was a man of action without time and leisure for the theological exercise of answering Dr. Pusey's writings. But he knew that Pusey was a danger to the Church 'if young men, some very slightly instructed, some struggling out of gross sin, some loving novelty and excitement, were brought under his spiritual guidance'.[35] Keble countered by saying 'My own conviction is that [Pusey] has been the greatest drag upon those who were rushing towards Rome. . . . whenever the attention of thoughtful persons should be generally drawn towards the doctrine of the one Catholic and Apostolic Church, Pusey was raised, as it were, for this very purpose, to hinder their defection, as by other ways, so especially by showing them that all their reasonable yearnings are sufficiently provided for in the English system rightly understood'.[36]

Pusey believed that the inhibition from officiating was unjust. He begged the bishop to make specific charges against him, so that he might be tried by the whole Church in a court of law. He even offered to pay the costs of such a prosecution. 'If I have taught anything contrary to the Church of England, I have no wish to avoid being convicted; but I do deprecate any extra-judicial condemnation'.[37] Pusey also suggested that if the bishop was not prepared to say that Pusey's doctrine and practice were opposed to that of the Church of England in a court of law the inhibition ought to be removed. Pusey accepted the inhibition at the moment only because Keble urged him to do so to avoid scandal.

Wilberforce kept avoiding Pusey's suggestion that the bishop grant

34. *Life of Pusey*, III, 310.
35. *Ibid.*, p. 312.
36. *Ibid.*
37. *Life of Wilberforce*, II, 107–8.

him an interview. He also said that he would avoid prosecution because it would not be good for the state of the Church. Wilberforce believed that a bishop had the right to express a private wish that a presbyter not officiate in his diocese without taking formal proceedings. These evasions did not satisfy Pusey.

> I see no satisfactory way open except that I should be admitted formally to clear myself, or not be condemned and punished without form of law. I am willing to be punished if I have offended against the rule of the Church. If not, I cannot but think that the punishment is arbitrary and unexampled. If your Lordship adopt this course of punishing me without a hearing, and refusing the opportunity of explanation, the only course which I see before me (in behalf of those who, equally with myself, may suffer by these unofficial suspensions, or who may be distressed by them) would be publicly to call upon your Lordship to sustain in a court of law, if your Lordship can, any grounds for this virtual suspension.[38]

The bishop began to relent when both Gladstone and Mr. Justice J. T. Coleridge of the King's Bench interceded for Pusey. The latter, in very strong language, pointed out the danger of proclaiming by this inhibition that Pusey's teaching was incompatible with that of the Church of England. But he still maintained that he did not think 'that the highly responsible power now possessed by a Bishop of preventing in his diocese ministrations which he deems injurious to the Church by one without cure of souls in it, ought to be limited to cases of heresy and false doctrine, which would warrant the infliction of punishment by the Courts. To this view I adhere, and upon it I shall act.'[39]

This was not Pusey's view of the matter, however. He was willing to submit to inhibition only if it was proved that he opposed the teaching of the Church. But if the only charge against him was that he offended the theological sensibilities of the Bishop of Oxford, Pusey wished the inhibition to be lifted. Wilberforce took his office so seriously that he could not consider any limitation to his authority within his own diocese. Pusey considered that the law of the Church limited every action of the bishop, who was bound to abide by it as well as Pusey. Unless he showed where Pusey offended the Church's teaching, he was acting unlawfully by maintaining this prohibition.

Gladstone urged Keble to restrain Pusey. He believed that Wilberforce, for all his gifts, was not yet mature in much of his thinking, and a crisis 'would precipitate in fixed forms his cruder ideas and check the free growth of those which, but for that crisis, may be destined to correct and overrule them'.[40] Just as Pusey had urged that a con-

38. *Life of Pusey*, III, 321.
39. *Ibid.*, p. 323.   40. *Ibid.*, p. 324.

ciliatory attitude might keep many in the Church of England until they had outgrown their 'Roman fever', so Gladstone urged moderation upon Wilberforce's victim.

Finally Pusey met face to face with Wilberforce on the occasion of a confirmation at St. Peter's-in-the-East, Oxford, in August 1851. The bishop knew from the cautioning of Justice Coleridge how serious the situation was, and he asked Pusey to allow matters to remain as they were until he delivered his episcopal charge in the autumn. When the charge was delivered in November 1851 the bishop deliberately did not mention Pusey's name, and no inhibition was published. But comment was made on passages in certain theological works to which the bishop took exception. He still did not tell Pusey that his private inhibition had been lifted. This did not come until the following May when, in reply to a specific request from Pusey to have it removed, he said that because of Pusey's private assurances of anti-Roman convictions and the large liberty allowed to Anglican clergy in these matters, Pusey was once more free to preach. Pusey sent to Keble the good news of this 'certain progress in the episcopal mind',[41] together with Wilberforce's admission that Pusey's teaching was not directly condemned by the teaching of the English Church.

Pusey's sturdy refusal to bow to Wilberforce's will, when this attempt was made to bring him to heel, forced the bishop, in effect, into the position where he had to admit that Pusey's teaching was not 'directly condemned by the judgment of the English Church'[42]— regardless of his own personal distrust of Pusey's thought and practice. Pusey never failed to recognize the important position of the bishops in the Church, but he knew that the ultimate ecclesiastical authority belonged to the whole Church and was not to be found in the episcopate alone. 'A Bishop's office was not arbitrary; he had only to bear witness to that which he had received.'[43] Pusey knew as a scholar that what he taught and acted upon was an integral part of the teaching and tradition of the Church of England.

At mid-century Pusey and Keble had both come to the conclusion that the bishops were not of the *esse* of the Church in the sense that churchmen could lean upon them. When the question of lay representation in synods arose, Pusey admitted that he was filled with 'terror' at the prospect, for he did not see how the laity could be kept from encroaching on the clerical prerogative of declaring what was the

41. *Ibid.*, p. 327.
42. *Ibid.*
43. *Ibid.*, p. 354.

doctrine of the Church—the traditional prerogative of Convocation. 'The Church meets, not to settle what the faith shall be, but to declare what it always has been. The Bishops primarily, and presbyters as delegated by them, declare this. . . . If the Bishops are not heretical, the laity ought to receive their statement of faith. If they are, the appeal ought to lie to some large body.'[44] In his pluralistic view of the Church, both laity and bishops had their peculiar function to perform; and neither was to encroach on the prerogatives of the other, nor upon those of the clergy. But his thought was confused about the role of the bishops in the Church. When he argued against lay representation in Church synods, he said 'It was forgotten that Bishops already represent the laity; they are virtually chosen by the laity.'[45] The proper concern of the laity was for the temporalities of the Church which, presumably, their representatives, the bishops, maintained. But the bishops were also the traditional guardians of the doctrine of the Church, with which he did not want the laity to interfere.

Pusey's thought about the role of the bishops in the Church, and the nature of the Establishment, was further formed in the midst of acute ecclesiastical conflict, just as it had been earlier by the Hampden and Gorham crises. He found himself the leader of the rump Tractarian party which remained in the Church after the great secessions between 1845 and 1850—a party which was increasingly concerned about matters which had never been of importance to the early leaders of the movement. In the 1840's the work of the Tractarians in the parishes was like that of the Rev. W. J. Palmer of Finmere parish in Oxfordshire.

> He had to invite his parishioners to daily service, when every one of them was all day at work, generally far away from the Church. He had to inculcate fasting when most of them fasted already in the poverty and scantiness of their daily fare. He had to invite them to confession, those whose daily practice and antecedents were already well before the eyes of their neighbours. . . . He had to urge the new doctrine in season and out of season, especially among the few educated neighbours who could understand him, and who soon settled the question by reducing their intercourse to occasional and unavoidable civilities. As often as not he found his own household incapable of going along with him. His wife had children to look after, his servants were no more than the work absolutely required.[46]

By mid-century the dogged adherents of the Tractarian party were

44. *Ibid.*, p. 347.
45. *Ibid.*, p. 354.
46. McClatchey, *Oxfordshire Clergy*, p. 90.

moving into a new phase of development. Their uphill labours in the parishes of the nation, especially those of the cities, led them to discard much of their early rigorism, and to lessen their concern for ecclesiastical doctrines like that of the apostolic succession. Oxford was no longer the real centre of the Church revival, and pastoralia became of greater importance to the new High-Churchmen than abstract theological ideas. Experience was teaching them that clericalism and purely clerical concerns were of little interest to their flocks.

They were still devoted to preaching the Catholic faith which they found in the Prayer Book—but it was not a faith in theological principles which were of concern only to university dons. Their Catholic faith was that which could influence all men, in all stations of life, in all parts of the nation. Because of the universalistic nature of their Gospel, they were willing to use means to present it which had appeal to men and women of all classes. This was the age of the Romantic revival, and a hard-headed individual like Samuel Wilberforce was willing to admit that there was 'in the English mind a great move towards a higher ritual',[47] which he believed was influencing even Dissenters and the Established Church in Scotland.

The new evangelists of the High-Church party were called either Ritualists or Puseyites. Like the Tractarians they emphasized sacramental worship, were concerned with refitting churches which had been allowed to fall into neglect during the latitudinarian era, and did not hesitate to adore and beautify both the altar and the celebrant at the Eucharist which was of so much importance to them. Their opponents criticized them for pressing aesthetic concerns of the clergy upon their parishioners; but, as the congregation of St. Alban's, Holborn, told the Bishop of London in 1874, 'The ritual that has been gradually developed has been requested at each successive stage by the laity, so that there is no pretence for saying that it has been forced upon an unwilling congregation.'[48] Ritual to them was a pastoral aid, which brought, through medieval pageantry, colour and meaning to the worship of people whose secular lives were drab and without significance. This was particularly true in the slum parishes of the great industrial cities where Ritualism flourished, and devoted priests gave themselves unreservedly to the service of the Gospel without the benefit of either blessing or direction from the bishops.

47. *Life of Wilberforce*, III, 189.
48. E. F. Russell, *A. H. Mackonochie: a Memoir* (1897), p. 161.

4. The Episcopate and the Ritualists

WHEN the question of using ceremonial to express doctrine began to arise, Pusey found himself in the centre of the controversy. Instinctively he distrusted Ritualism as a movement. He saw that it led to individualism in religious practice whereas 'the very spirit of Catholicity is to make the individual sink in the body whereof he has been made a member.'[1] When he wrote in 1839 to J. F. Russell, who was Vicar of St. Peter's, Walworth, Pusey said he feared that concern with ritual could lead to vanity and 'unsubduedness'.

> On this ground among others, I should deprecate seeking to restore the richer style of vestments used in Edward the Sixth's reign. . . . It seems beginning at the wrong end for the ministers to deck their own persons: our own plain dresses are more in keeping with the state of our Church, which is one of humiliation: it does not seem in character to revive gorgeous or even in any degree handsome dresses in a day of reproach and rebuke and blasphemy: these are not holyday times.[2]

He confessed to Russell his fear that, just as frequent mention of the Cross by the Low-Church party now signified very little, so the new High-Church peculiarities might turn out to have no real spiritual meaning.

Pusey was drawn into the midst of the ritualistic controversy soon after the consecration of St. Saviour's, Leeds, 'the offering of a penitent' (Pusey) to the poor in the slums of this industrial city. The first vicar of the parish, Richard Ward, requested Pusey to spend some of his long vacations at Leeds. This was not possible for Pusey, who sent instead the Rev. R. G. Macmullen, an able and energetic priest who was very interested in the liturgical experiments some of the High-Church party were excited about. At St. Saviour's the vicar and his curates used a translation of the Roman Breviary in the prayer-room at the vicarage. Macmullen increased their interest in such 'popish' activity, and called the censure of the Bishop of Ripon upon the St. Saviour's clergy when he preached a sermon on the Intercession of the Saints on All Saints' Day, 1846. W. F. Hook, the Vicar of Leeds, then wrote a rather bitter letter to Pusey accusing him of planting 'a colony of Papists' in the heart of Leeds. Without intending to do so, Pusey had established what was to become a prototype 'Ritualist' parish.

1. *Life of Pusey*, II, 142.
2. *Ibid.*

112

Pusey tried to placate Hook by assuring him that he stood 'on no other ground than yourself, that of Ken, Andrewes, and Bramhall—the primitive, undivided Church'.[3] But Hook said he believed Pusey guilty of 'building a church and getting a foot in my parish to propagate principles which I detest'.[4] Pusey found this charge of 'Jesuitism' very distressing, as he did the labelling of the clergy of Leeds 'perverts' in a 'nursery of Romanism', who were cunning enough to keep just within the letter of the Church law in order to teach popish principles. He was also upset by Hook's demand that Pusey persuade Richard Ward to resign, and then give the patronage of St. Saviour's to the Bishop of Ripon.

Hook had a difficult time in Leeds. The population had risen from 53,162 in 1801 to 123,393 in 1831. In 1825 there were four churches in the town, besides the parish church, and nine in the suburbs. The total number of clergy was eighteen. Though four more town churches were built in the next ten years, they were mere chapels of ease for the parish church, without endowment, and poorly attended.[5] The gift of St. Saviour's had been much appreciated.

Leeds was full of Dissenters and Socialists, and both groups 'entertained the most implacable animosity'[6] against the Church. Only Hook's strength of character allowed him to make any progress at all during his first few years in the city. When he attended his first vestry meeting, he found the holy table in the church covered with hats and coats, when the churchwardens were not sitting upon it. Hook's cleansing of the temple identified him as an impossible High-Churchman; and he fought a running battle with his vestry. The churchwardens, in particular, grumbled over the expenditure of sacramental wine which accompanied the institution of a weekly celebration of Holy Communion. They also disliked Hook's suspicion of their motives when they insisted on remaining in the vestry during the administration to guard the wine. Hook resented the Ritualists at St. Saviour's not only for what they were, but because they gave his enemies a stick to beat him with.

St. Saviour's had just become a distinct parish under the Leeds Vicarage Act when Macmullen preached his disturbing sermon, and

3. *Ibid.*, III, 115.

4. *Ibid.*, p. 120. James F. White in his *Cambridge Movement* (1962), p. 153, discusses how romanticism linked the Oxford Movement and the Gothic Revival in church building. Only Mozley showed sustained interest in matters of ecclesiology. The architecture of St. Saviour's is discussed on p. 72.

5. Stephens, *Life and Letters of W. F. Hook*, I, 371.

6. *Ibid.*, I, 373.

this lessened Hook's influence with Ward and Macmullen. On New Year's day 1847, after being told that Macmullen and four other people from St. Saviour's had just gone over to Rome, he wrote to a friend:

> I suppose that my usefulness here is over, and indeed, in the Church of England. . . . My desire was to exhibit a parish well worked on the Church of England system; to show that the *via media* could be carried out. I had gained the confidence of my people; my opponents were softened and coming around, I was beginning to feel that Leeds had become to me a perfect Paradise, and now it is a howling wilderness.[7]

Hook viewed St. Saviour's as a 'hornet's nest planted at my garden gate'. A pen-and-ink etching made by one of his curates at this time shows him fleeing from a church on a hill (St. Saviour's) pursued by hornets and attempting to escape stones hurled at him by the Protestant press and a mob.[8]

At the request of the Bishop of Ripon, Mr. Ward resigned the living of St. Saviour's in January, 1847, and one of his curates went with him. Subsequently they both seceded to Rome. The 'Romish extravagances' continued at St. Saviour's under his successors. Poor Hook entered his period of greatest trial in 1848 when one of the curates at the parish church resigned and then seceded to Rome. The anti-popery uproar which accompanied this latest defection came at a time when Hook was nearly exhausted from his parochial labours. A malignant kind of fever raged among the Irish in the city, trade was depressed, workmen were thrown out of work in great numbers, and their destitution was appalling. At one time during the year, 15,000 people were receiving public relief from the soup kitchen of the city, and average weekly earnings did not reach 10d. a head. The following summer Leeds was struck by a major cholera epidemic. The heroic labours of the clergy of both St. Saviour's and the parish church drew Hook and the Ritualists closer together for a time, but Hook still distrusted their tactics.

Hook said that what he objected to most was the tendency of the clergy at St. Saviour's to 'tell people that their views and mine are the same. . . . when they set up a confessional they said they only carried out my principle.' Hook's primary concern was to 'obtain unity of action' between the Ritualists and 'the rump of the Evangelical party, which . . . having degenerated into Arnoldism is seeking to support itself by Rationalistic principles'.[9]

7. *Ibid.*, II, 197.
8. *Ibid.*, p. 203.
9. *Ibid.*, p. 255.

The crisis over St. Saviour's came with the 'papal aggression' of 1850 when Pius IX announced his intention of organizing the hierarchy in England. Lord John Russell sent to the Bishop of Durham his famous public letter which revealed his belief that the teaching and practice of the High-Church clergy were far more formidable sources of danger to the Church of England than any aggression on the part of Rome. 'All over the country a wild cry of "No Popery" was raised; moderate High-Churchmen were denounced as Papists, a decent and orderly ceremonial was stigmatised as Popish mummery.'[10] This resulted in the Bishop of Ripon holding an inquiry in the Parish Church of Leeds with Hook present. The clergy of St. Saviour's and several witnesses were examined. They admitted teaching the duty of confessing to a priest before receiving Holy Communion: 'deadly sin after baptism must end in spiritual death unless penance was resorted to, and unless the sinner confessed his offences to a priest'.[11] The result of the bishop's inhibition of one of the clergy was a wholesale secession of clergy and many laity to Rome. Out of the fifteen clergy associated with St. Saviour's since 1845, nine had seceded to Rome, and only one remained at his post by 1851.

At the end of 1851 a new vicar was found for St. Saviour's, the secessions to Rome ceased, and the parish relapsed into quiescence and insignificance.

What was the significance of this melancholy history? Both Pusey and Hook had had high hopes for St. Saviour's. Set in the very midst of poverty and vice, staffed by clergy willing to accept apostolic poverty for the sake of the work to which they were called, it was supported zealously by both clergy and laity. Under the energetic, zealous, and warm-hearted Ward, 'the whole band of workers, clerical and lay, harmoniously strove together to enlighten the ignorant and reclaim the vicious who lay so thickly round about.'[12]

St. Saviour's represents a completely new movement in the Church of England. This was the age when, in the wake of the Gorham decision, men like Archdeacon Manning seceded to Rome, and the time when Pusey had his most unhappy relations with Samuel Wilberforce. Pusey was obliged to give new direction to the old Tractarian party; and, in the words of Thomas Minster, the Vicar of St. Saviour's in 1848, the hope of all the supporters of the new parish was 'that it

10. *Ibid.*, p. 290.
11. *Ibid.*, p. 291.
12. *Ibid.*, p. 293.

must eventually rise and be a model for the working of other manufacturing towns'.[13]

Both Hook and the Evangelicals in Leeds viewed the concern for the confessional at St. Saviour's as an exhibition of 'priestcraft', an exaltation of the clerical office. From the standpoint of Minster and his associates, the first problem that had to be dealt with in the slums about their church was the appalling viciousness in the lives of the people who lived there. Rather naïvely Minster wrote to Bishop Longley, the future Archbishop of Canterbury, 'giving him a full and very particular account of the work going on at St. Saviour's, and the awful depths of sin we had to contend with in very many of the people who came to us'. In his reply Longley indicated that he was more concerned with the 'sins of former incumbents' of St. Saviour's than he was with the pastoral work that was being carried on among the poor.[14]

Longley had made up his mind to suppress the 'Romanizing' at St. Saviour's. He did not hesitate to reveal in public that he had lost confidence in the work of the clergy there, and this attitude contributed much to the despondency of those who seceded to Rome. The Bishop, like Hook, was influenced by the general alarm over the 'papal aggression', and the secessions. His sentiments were not far removed from those of the intemperate Hook who wrote to Gladstone in 1851:

> I am boiling over with indignation at the attack which has been made upon the institutions of my country, my Church, and my religion, by an avowed, wicked and unscrupulous enemy. I believe that assailant to be the enemy of God and man, for although the Pope be the antichrist employed against the cause of my Saviour and my God in this country, the real author of the movement is he who is the author of all evil.[15]

Both Hook and Longley knew of 'the savage ignorance, the embittered barbarism'[16] in the manufacturing centres of the nation; they recognized the pastoral zeal of the St. Saviour's clergy, especially during the outbreaks of Irish fever and cholera in 1848 and 1849; but the religious hysteria of the age never allowed them to put in perspective the means the Ritualists used to reach the poor. Together with most High-Churchmen and Evangelicals they put theological

13. *Life of Pusey*, III, 356.
14. *Ibid.*, p. 357.
15. *Life of Hook*, II, 295.
16. *Ibid.*, p. 308.

concerns and good order in the Establishment ahead of the pastoral mission of the Church.

This may seem unfair to Hook, who loved greatly the people of Leeds. But he was a sober defender of the *via media*, a student of history who loved the Church as it was, a 'Reformed Branch of the Church Catholic'.[17] 'To the Church of England, to the Primitive Church, to the Greek Church, and to the written and infallible Word of the Living God, the Church of Rome stands opposed.'[18] Hook loved his people in Leeds, but the man who said 'we can only be good Church of England men by loving the Church of England',[19] loved the Established Church more.

The uproar over St. Saviour's, Leeds, marked the real beginning of the Ritualist controversy. There were theological reasons why clergy encouraged auricular confession, faced the altar while celebrating, or wore certain vestments; but it was the latter aberration which drew the most public attention and caught the attention of bishops. Most of them followed the example of Longley. Through courts of inquiry they sought to determine whether ritualistic practices were authorized in the Church of England, and whether such erring clergy should continue to be licensed. Very rarely did a bishop override Protestant protest to support a Ritualist on the grounds that he was a good pastor.

Writing in 1875, Gladstone said that the Ritualist movement began about thirty-five years earlier. At that time some High-Churchmen began to wear waistcoats buttoned all the way up to the cravat. 'This was deemed so distinctly Popish that it acquired the name "the Mark of the Beast"'; and it is a fact that among the tailors of the west-end of London this shape of waistcoat was familiarly known as 'the M.B. waistcoat.'[20] Interest in such matters had increased substantially by the time that trouble arose at St. Saviour's.

As the patron of St. Saviour's, Pusey had been drawn into the controversy. Bishop Longley accused him of attempting to 'force a system of his own imagining, copied to a certain extent from medieval practice, upon the Church at Leeds'.[21] After affairs had quietened down, Hook began to appreciate better the position of Pusey in the midst of this controversy, and ended up by calling him 'that saint whom England persecuted'. But to most churchmen, Pusey was

17. *Ibid.*, p. 198.
18. *Ibid.*, p. 220.
19. *Ibid.*, p. 222.
20. W. E. Gladstone, *The Church of England and Ritualism* (1875), p. 25.
21. *Life of Pusey*, III, 366.

looked upon as the father-in-God of every Ritualist. During the disgraceful riots at St. George's-in-the-East in the years 1859 and 1860, the cry of the mob was 'Down with the Puseyites'.

Pusey confessed in a letter of 1851 that 'I was not ritualist enough to know, until the other day, that the act of turning had any special meaning in the Consecration.'[22] But ten years later he wrote to Bishop Tait of London to say 'my name is made a byword for that with which I never had any sympathy, that which the writers of the Tracts, with whom in early days I was associated, always deprecated —any innovations in the way of conducting the Service, anything of Ritualism, or especially any revival of disused Vestments.'[23]

Perhaps the secret of Pusey's support of the Ritualists is revealed by his biographer Liddon when he says: 'Whatever mistakes were made by the clergy at St. Saviour's (and they were many) there can be no reasonable doubt that both Dr. Hook and the Bishop were endeavouring, under the terror of the Roman phantom, unduly to limit the frontier of the Church of England.' Pusey felt that 'a generation which had but lately become aware of the real strength of their own Church was entitled to special patience and sympathy.'[24] He understood then about the Ritualists what the episcopate discovered many years later—that those 'who hate all real Church progress are the people who object to them'.[25]

We will look in detail at the heroic labours of the Ritualists, in the slums of England, in Chapter VI. At the moment our concern is the failure of the Establishment to comprehend the spiritual significance of the Ritualist movement, and the tension between Church and State which resulted from this lack of comprehension.

In an established Church it was inevitable that the State, represented by Parliament and ecclesiastical courts, should concern itself with public worship in the parishes of the nation, when such worship was apparently becoming a cause of public scandal. Both the bishops and the legislature should have paid more attention to churchmen like those of St. Alban's, Holborn, who told the Bishop of London in 1874 that their ritual represented the religious enthusiasm of the laity as well as that of the clergy.[26] Samuel Wilberforce was one of the few bishops who understood the spiritual zeal which lay behind Ritualism. He said he was very doubtful 'how far we can go in repression without

22. *Ibid.*, IV, 210.
23. *Ibid.*, p. 211.
24. *Ibid.*, III, 368.
25. *Life of Wilberforce*, III, 183.
26. *V. supra*, p. 111. E. F. Russell, *A. H. Mackonochie: A Memoir*, p. 161.

repressing that development of real Church life in which is our hope'.[27] The bishops, the legislature, and the judges appointed to try the Ritualists all failed to understand the genius of the Church of England. 'The Judges in their decisions have wholly ignored a leading feature in the history of the Church, "The Church of England is legally a compromise".'[28]

The Establishment attempted to deal with the Ritualist movement through prosecution of offending clerics under the Church Discipline Act of 1840, which empowered the bishop in the case of an alleged non-criminal offence to issue a Commission of Inquiry, or to transmit the case by Letters of Request to the Provincial Court of Appeal. Final appeal could be made to the Judicial Committee of the Privy Council. By 1856 the militant Church Association, composed of leading Evangelical churchmen, was sending spies to churches like St. George's-in-the-East to note deviations in traditional ritual. Numerous prosecutions began, some cases being brought before the Privy Council as the court of final appeal. Not all the judgments pleased the Church Association and the Evangelicals. When W. J. E. Bennett, Vicar of Frome Selwood, Somerset, wrote of the Real Presence in the Eucharist in a public letter to Pusey, his teaching was allowed by the Privy Council. But the trial of John Purchas of St. James, Brighton, led the final court of appeal to rule that Eucharistic vestments, the eastward position, the mixed chalice, and wafer bread were illegal during the celebration of Holy Communion. This judgment, which was delivered in 1871, marked a turning point in the Ritualist controversy. From now on those who persisted in such practices were regarded as law-breakers. The judgment was widely disobeyed, however, as being without spiritual authority; and the eastward position was maintained even in St. Paul's Cathedral. In the trial of C. J. Ridsdale, Vicar of St. Peter's, Folkestone, in 1877, the judges reversed their earlier decision and allowed the eastward position, provided it did not conceal manual acts from the congregation.

Lord Shaftesbury led the Evangelical and Low-Church opposition to the Ritualists and introduced into the House of Lords bill after bill to do away with Ritualism, between 1865 and 1872. The opposition to the Ritualists was great throughout the Church, but many churchmen realized that the activities of these law-breakers represented a new spirit within the Church. There was a desperate need for more interest to be shown in matters of ritual and ceremonial.

27. *Life of Wilberforce*, III, 183.
28. Grueber, C. S., *Decisions on Ritual: an Appeal to the People* (1874), p. 12.

Robert Gregory, who was influenced by the Tractarian Movement while at Corpus Christi College, Oxford, in the 1840's, became a Canon of St. Paul's in 1868, and Dean of the cathedral in 1890. He collaborated with R. W. Church and H. P. Liddon in making the cathedral a centre of religious life in London, and he early realized that if this task was to be accomplished more attention had to be paid to the externals of religion. He found that on Sunday mornings it was not unusual to find no one in the cathedral; the number of communicants was always very small. Few people attended the daily services. It was little wonder that the populace found the services unattractive.

> The most ordinary improvements with respect to the dress of the clergy officiating, and the ordering of the services that were found elsewhere, had not been introduced at St. Paul's. No clergyman wore a cassock; there was little or no order in entering the Cathedral at service time. . . . the choir was wretched; it consisted of six or eight boys and two, three, or four men, just as they happened to turn up. . . . At the Celebration of Holy Communion there was no credence table for the Elements, but all were placed on the Altar just as they would have been in a Dissenting Chapel. . . . the choir men read letters and talked during the service, and it was never known for more than one member of the Chapter to be present at a service except on very special occasions.[29]

Unfortunately the revival of interest in ceremonial in services was a grass-roots movement. The bishops realized that it represented an attempt to change the whole tenor of churchmanship, and because it was not under their direction they were frightened by it. As Father Rowley (Dolling of St. Agatha's, Landport) exclaimed in Compton Mackenzie's novel *The Altar Steps*: 'Bishops are haunted by the creation of precedents. A precedent in the life of a bishop is like an illegitimate child in the life of a respectable churchwarden.'[30] Ritualism in public worship was a precedent the bishops found specially upsetting.

One of the most 'advanced' Ritualists was A. H. Mackonochie, who from 1867 was under almost constant prosecution by the Church Association in his parish of St. Alban's, Holborn. The prosecutions finally forced him to resign his living in 1882. Before he was forced to leave, many churchmen began to identify themselves with his cause, and to view A. C. Tait, Bishop of London, 1856–1868, and Archbishop of Canterbury, 1868–1882, as another Laud whose 'true memorial is his perhaps unparalleled chastenings, accompanied by the highest

29. W. H. Hutton, *Robert Gregory, 1819–1911* (1912), p.164.
30. Compton Mackenzie, *Altar Steps* (1922), p. 183.

worldly success'.[31] T. T. Carter, Rector of Clewer and founder of the Community of St. John the Baptist, one of the earliest sisterhoods, believed that the persecution of the Ritualists led many churchmen to resist the authorities in the Church for the same reason that the Archbishop of Canterbury and the six bishops had resisted James II.[32]

In 1867 the government created a Royal Commission to inquire into the variations in ceremonial practice in the Church of England. Among the Commissioners was the Archbishop of Canterbury, Longley, who had dealt with the refractory clergy of St. Saviour's, Leeds; Tait, who was then Bishop of London; and Samuel Wilberforce, the Bishop of Oxford. They issued four reports between 1867 and 1870. The Commissioners were almost unanimous in their wish to forbid the use of vestments, but they had great divergences of opinion among themselves over other matters. Their final proposals were much criticized. It was this disagreement among churchmen that led to the passing of the Public Worship Regulation Act in 1874.

Drafted by Archbishops Tait and Thomson, the bill was presented to a turbulent House by Disraeli as a bill 'to put down Ritualism'.[33] Many churchmen supported the bill; the previous year a deputation representing 60,000 persons had called at Lambeth to request action against changes in ceremonial. But Tait did not consult with the Convocations before drafting the bill, and the Church as a whole had no say in the measure of 1874. Lord Shaftesbury seized the opportunity to amend the bill drastically in Parliament in a more Protestant and Erastian direction.

Instead of the establishment of a diocesan advisory board to assist the bishop in cases concerned with public worship, Shaftesbury's amendment called for the appointment, by the two archbishops, of a single lay judge to act as judge of the provincial courts of Canterbury and York in ritual cases. Final appeal was still to be made to the Judicial Committee of the Privy Council. In a House so frenzied that, as one eyewitness said, 'if it had been proposed to cut off the hands of all offending clergymen, they would have carried it',[34] the bill with the amendment was passed and became the Public Worship Regulation Act of 1874. Against Shaftesbury's wishes, Tait secured provision for the bishop's veto of proceedings under the act. The first judge appointed was Baron Penzance, an ex-judge of divorce.

Tait believed that only a minority of churchmen wanted freedom

31. Churchman of the Diocese of Canterbury, *Laud and Tait* (1883), p. 37.
32. T. T. Carter, *Things of Caesar and the Things of God* (1877), p. 11.
33. R. T. Davidson and W. Benham, *Life of Archibald Campbell Tait* (1891), II, 213.
34. *Life of Dean Church*, p. 245.

from such 'lay control' of the Church,[35] but the truth of the matter was that only a minority of churchmen chose to support the action taken against the Ritualists under the terms of the new act. Most of them belonged to the militant Church Association, which sent around informers to various parishes to gather evidence by which offending priests might be prosecuted.

Four priests were imprisoned for contumacy between 1877 and 1882 when they refused to acknowledge the validity of the new court and carried on ritualism in their services. The imprisonment of three of them, Arthur Tooth of St. James, Hatcham, in the Diocese of Rochester, Pelham Dale of St. Vedast's, in the City of London, and R. W. Enraght of Holy Trinity, Bordesley, were for short periods of time. But the fourth offender Sidney Faithorn Green, Rector of St. John's, Miles Platting, was imprisoned for a year and seven months. He was a priest of exemplary life and devotion, much beloved by his congregation. Archbishop Tait thought that his diocesan, James Fraser, might have refused to allow the Church Association to press their suit against him, but Fraser's attitude to the Ritualists was much like that of Hook of Leeds. He was devoted to his task of bringing spiritual life into the new diocese of Manchester, and he refused to countenance any clerical insubordination. He apologized for allowing the Church Association to initiate their suit by saying 'I do not see how I could have acted otherwise. My one aim has been to put on record a protest against that spirit of lawlessness which in its principle strikes at the life of all organized society. . . . I am not activated by any partisan still less by any intolerant motives.'[36]

The reaction of the Ritualists to this 'Erastian tyranny' was intense. After his first interview with Arthur Tooth, Tait recorded 'I fear I shall not find him . . . amenable to authority.'[37] Tooth and the other Ritualists believed their use of ceremonial was authorized by the Church, and they refused to accept the judgments made by the Privy Council or the lay authority represented by the Public Worship Regulation Act. Tooth wrote to Tait: 'The Church of England by the synodical acts of her Convocation in 1661, adopted a particular order of ritual, which I, at my ordination, pledged myself to obey, and your Grace does not show me, and I cannot discover, any ordinance

---

35. A. C. Tait, *Church and Law: a Letter in Answer to Rev. Canon Carter of Clewer* (1877), p. 15.

36. Thomas Hughes, *James Fraser, Second Bishop of Manchester, 1818–1885: a Memoir* (1888), p. 278.

37. *Life of Tait*, II, 245.

provincial or synodical act repealing that order of ritual, or dispensing with obedience to it.[38]

When Enraght of Holy Trinity, Bordesley, was condemned by Lord Penzance, as Dean of Arches, for ritual irregularities, which included the use of wafer bread in Holy Communion, one piece of evidence produced was a consecrated wafer which had been kept by a communicant. After the trial the wafer was placed in the Registry of the Court of Arches along with documents and other materials of evidence. Churchmen of all parties appealed to the Archbishop of Canterbury to remove the consecrated wafer from the custody of the court, but he found that it took him from August until December to overcome the legal obstacles which prevented him from obtaining the wafer and reverently consuming it. During this time the wrath of the Ritualist party knew no bounds. The object of much of their scorn was the unfortunate Tait, who was remembered as the author of the Public Worship Regulation Act, and was deluged by abusive mail. Bewildered by the extravagance of the Ritualist outcry, he said:

> Will any Christian man, unless he is blinded either by superstition or by partisanship, dare to deny that these letters, with the outcry and strife they have fomented, are out of all proportion to the real importance of this misguided wrong act? Can these clergy, in face of the glaring sins and vices of our day, be right in giving such a picture of what they deem to be the great and the little things of faith and life as these stand in the sight of Almighty God?[39]

Pusey's attitude to the Ritualists was paradoxical. Not only did he avoid using excess ceremonial in his own ministrations, but he disliked the sectarian temper of the Ritualist party as it developed. He decried the agitators among them, who were 'outdoing one another, their organ the *Church Times* ridiculing and abusing the Bishops pouring contempt on all who did not agree with them, exasperating by extremes the English people'.[40] He particularly disliked their 'infallibilist air', and doubted the acceptability to the English people of their 'un-understood' rites.[41]

A vigorous and well-written ecclesiastical newspaper, the *Church Times,* had been founded in 1863. Costing one penny, it was intended to be a popular publication which could bring the cause of the Ritualists before the Church as a whole. One of its early leading

38. *Ibid.*, p. 252.
39. *Ibid.*, p. 266.
40. *Pusey House MSS.*, Pusey to Hon. C. L. Wood, 7 January 1864.
41. *Ibid.*, Pusey to Wood, 2 January 1875.

articles said that the campaign the *Church Times* directed against the bishops reflected resistance to 'not our fathers-in-God but our would be fathers-in-law'.[42] The *Church Times* had little sympathy for Archbishop Tait, or the other occupants of the episcopal bench—almost all of whom were regarded as avowed enemies of the progressive party in the Church—that of the Ritualists.

> As matters stand, the mass of correspondence and purely routine business which a bishop has to get through somehow keeps him fully occupied, and he has but little leisure for doing mischief. But there can be no doubt how he would employ himself if his tasks were lightened by one-half: not in more active visitation, not in theological composition, not in sedulous promotion of practical reforms, but in bullying those of his clergy who belonged to the unpopular school.[43]

This same article expressed the opinion that no more than six of the bishops in 1867 had 'any tolerable acquaintance' with theology, and that the learning of twenty diocesans was 'utterly inadequate'.

Scorn was also heaped upon Lord Penzance, who was proclaimed to be incompetent after the Ridsdale judgment of 1877. He was a judge

> grossly ignorant of the law which he professes to administer, as guilty of wholly illegal acts, and as entirely destitute of a shadow of that jurisdiction as Dean of Arches to which he pertinaciously lays claim. This authoritative exposure of his true judicial character has practically ended his nominal authority, for even though his statutory jurisdiction is not affected . . . yet his name as a trustworthy lawyer is gone, as well as his factitious title as Dean of Arches, so that no weight, personal or official, will henceforth attach to any ecclesiastical judgment he may pronounce.[44]

Pusey objected to the ridicule and sarcasm which was found in articles of this nature because such criticism promoted disobedience to authority. He could not see how the evils in the Church could be overcome by individual priests disobeying their bishops. He always hoped, as he had in his Tractarian days, that the bishops would see the light and take over direction of this new movement of the Spirit in the Church, instead of inhibiting it. But his own treatment by Bishop Wilberforce, and his observation of the episcopal mind at work, slowly convinced him that real spiritual progress in the Church would come in spite of, rather than with, the blessing of the episcopal bench. Reluctantly Pusey emerged as the champion of the persecuted Ritualists in their war with episcopal authority.

42. *Church Times*, 8 February 1963, p. 12.
43. *Ibid.*, 9 March 1867.
44. *Ibid.*, 28 December 1877.

At the same time Pusey never became a supporter of the more radical Ritualists who advocated Disestablishment of the Church. Like Keble he had come to the conclusion that ultimate sovereignty in the Church rested not with the bench of bishops, either as representatives of the State or of the mystique of apostolic succession, but with the whole people of the Church. He agreed with the *Union Review*, which appeared in 1863 to further the Ritualist cause, when it said to the bishops: 'Be Cyprians. As you have one and all his authority, use it one and all as he did. Lay down for yourselves the rule he laid down for himself . . . "I determined to do nothing of my private opinion without the consent of the people".'[45]

5. The Ritualists and Disestablishment

THE WAR that the Ritualists carried on with the bishops soon led them to look critically at the Establishment as a whole.

> The attitude of resistance towards the episcopate into which the whole active section of the High Church school has moved of late years, naturally provokes much comment and some sarcasm from critics of other parties. . . . [the]he conclusion drawn from this fact is that the theoretical champion of Apostolical Succession is in practice a rank Presbyterian or Independent.[1]

By the time of the Public Worship Regulation Act, the Ritualist or Puseyite criticism of the episcopate was that all its energies were devoted to maintaining the temporal blessings of the Establishment. The bishops were not interested in spiritual reform, as were the Puseyites, if it offended the vested interests in the Church. To cover up the grave spiritual abuses that the Ritualists were exposing, the bishops were willing to collaborate with the secular power in a policy of persecution. They understood that the man at the helm seldom appreciates the man who rocks the boat.

Exposure of the lack of spirituality within the Establishment became a passion with the Puseyites. When the 1864–1873 average of 598 ordinations a year rose to 644 in 1874, then dropped sharply to 590 in 1875, the *Church Times* attributed the decline to public disgust

45. *Union Review* (1871), IX, 248, 'On Synods and the Laity'.
1. *Church Times*, 9 February 1877, p. 81.

with the Established Church after the passing of the Public Worship Regulation Act. The people of England no longer wanted the 'quiet old-fashioned churchmanship of fifty years ago . . . where there was no new territory to reclaim and no serious onslaught to repulse'.[2]

The *Church Times* saw itself engaged in a great battle to liberate the Church from the tyranny of the bishops and the judiciary of the State. Every week from March 25, 1881 to November 3, 1882 a notice appeared above the newspaper's leading article which read:

> ARRESTED MARCH 19th, 1881.
> The Prayers of the Church are desired for
> SIDNEY FAITHORN GREEN,
> Priest,
> IN PRISON
> For Obedience to the Church's Law.

In this cause both clergy and laity were united. 'We have constantly pointed out that as the so-called ritualist's phase of the Catholic revival is due to the laity far more than to the clergy, and as it concerns them most, it is their part to bear the brunt of the struggle.'[3]

The Puseyites had little tolerance for the remnant of the old Tractarian school which still sought the authority of the apostolic succession in the bishops.

> In their view a mitre confers if not absolute infallibility at any rate immunity from criticism and a claim to unquestioning obedience, . . . but why should a clergyman who yesterday was an unconsidered nobody . . . be treated as inspired because he has the 'luck' to be selected for a mitre? . . . this is no attitude for a *freeborn Englishman*, it is simply a fetishism, as degraded as that of a negro of the Gaboon and the sooner it gives way to a dispassionate recognition of the true limits of Episcopal qualities and powers, the better for the Church of England.[4]

The oppressed Ritualists compared themselves to John Wesley that 'simple, earnest man'. Like themselves he had suffered at the hands of the bishops of the Establishment, who 'opposed him in every possible way and drove him from the pulpit and altars of the Church he loved'.[5] They longed for the appearance of another Wesley to lead the Puseyites in freeing the Church from the tyranny which kept it

2. *Ibid.*, 7 January 1876, p. 8.
3. *Ibid.*, 26 May 1876, p. 263.
4. *Ibid.*, 16 November 1877, 'Anglican Superstition', pp. 645–46.
5. A. H. Mackonochie, 'Disestablishment and Disendowment', *Nineteenth Century* (1877), I, 698.

from fulfilling its catholic mission to the nation—the tyranny of vested interests represented by the prelates of the Establishment.

> If Wesley had flourished in our days how different might the result have been. We need now a man of his marvellous energy, courage and perseverance to form, organize and carry into work, a religious society of priests and lay brothers who shall be of the Church of England, but not under the rules of the Establishment, who might act as freely as did Wesley or the Friars of old, wherever work is calling for workers, wherever souls are perishing for lack of pastors.[6]

The Puseyites did, in fact, consciously combine old Evangelical piety with their new emphasis on sacramentalism, as we will see when we look at their pastoral importance in Chapter VI. They loved the poor of the slums with a fervour that was rare in the Church, and their complaint was that the bishops were trying to drive them not only from their pulpits and altars, but also from the people whom they loved. Unfortunately, their 'sectarian temper' and 'infallibilist air', which Pusey so disliked, blinded them to the presence of bishops who were equally devoted pastors, though not sympathetic to Ritualism. One of these was S. F. Green's diocesan, James Fraser, Bishop of Manchester. A hard-working bishop, dedicated to improving the social and educational facilities offered to the slum-dwellers of Manchester by both Church and State, he was popular with every class of people in his diocese—except the Ritualists. He wanted his clergy to work as a team under diocesan direction, and foolishly, as we have noted, allowed Green to be tried and imprisoned. When he urged Green to submit to the courts and be released, the recalcitrant cleric told the bishop that he was no longer legally his ordinary.

> It can hardly have escaped your notice that I can at any time obtain my release from prison by what your lordship calls submission to the Bishop, without troubling the Bishop at all. Surely then it would be inexcusable in me to waste your valuable time calling upon you to do for me what I am quite able to do for myself. . . . The law *De haeretico comburendo* was only repealed in the latter part of the XVII century. Had that law been unrepealed people are asking with some interest at what point of such proceedings your lordship would be prepared to say 'Hold! Enough!'.[7]

This attitude to episcopal admonition was more representative of some extreme Dissenters than of the old Tractarians.

The *Church Times*, which did not then have its present-day policy

6. *Union Review*, 'The Church of England and the Establishment' (1869), VII, 405.
7. Hughes, *James Fraser*, pp. 298–99.

of cautious non-partisan reporting, never glossed over the failings of the Establishment—which the bishops tried to overlook. The Puseyite party had no intention of leaving the task of 'putting the house in order' to the bench of bishops—few of whom were as energetic as Blomfield, Wilberforce, or Fraser. Its editors asked embarrassing questions about scandals like 'absenteeism'. 'How many clergymen live in or conveniently near their parishes? How many have no parsonages and do not want to have them? How many having parsonages let them?' They pointed out that the incumbent of All Hallows, Barking, a nominee of Archbishop Sumner, had an income of £2,000 *per annum* in 1872, yet lived in Gordon Square; Blomfield's son, an infamous pluralist, received £2,000 a year as Rector of St. Andrew, Undershaft, and lived at Lancaster Gate.

> Pull these gentlemen down first is our counsel. Waste no time in prating over vested interests, but dock the incomes of the living incumbents who can show no congregations, and apply them to the augmentation of poor suburban livings. . . . Then every clergyman holding a City living who could not or would not work his Church, and get a congregation should be forced to resign on a modicum of the income and a better man put in his place, besides handing over a handsome surplus to other and needy districts. There is a good deal of wholesome sweating to be done by some of these two thousand pounders who are such exceedingly bad bargains for the Church. . . . the men who do nothing but draw funds which they have not earned in any fashion deserve severe treatment.[8]

They believed that the wrath of the episcopal bench should have been directed against clerical delinquents like Blomfield's son, rather than devoted pastors like Mackonochie or Green, who at least lived and worked in the parishes the Church entrusted to them. Alfred Blomfield admitted that his father 'never, to the end of his days recovered his former spirits' after he drove W. J. E. Bennett from his living of St. Paul's, Knightsbridge. Blomfield's unease came from the accusation that 'he did have recourse to a measure apparently coercive, he sacrificed a clergyman who, whatever his opinions, had been more than ordinarily zealous and conscientious in the discharge of his duties, to the clamours of the public press and the tyranny of the mob.'[9] On the other hand Blomfield had no qualms about holding a parish *in commendam* when he was a bishop, nor did he hesitate to promise ecclesiastical preferment to one of his sons while he was still at Oxford, though he did say 'the better you acquit yourself at College, the less scruple I shall feel in providing for you.'[10]

8. *Church Times*, 4 February 1876, p. 55.
9. *Memoir of Blomfield*, II, 151.
10. *Ibid.*, p. 224.

The Church Times also attacked the scandalous sale of livings which the prelates of 'the right reverend bench regarded everywhere with suspicion and dislike', yet did so little to halt. Rev. S. Hornibrook, Chaplain of the Kent County Lunatic Asylum at Maidstone said that in 1873, out of 13,000 parishes almost half were in the hands of private patrons, and some 1,200 livings were constantly for sale. Clerkenwell was cited as an example of a town where, in the midst of a teeming population, the church was supported only by pew-rents and offertories, while a layman enjoyed some £10,000 a year income from the rectory. He also mentioned the living of Falmouth, worth £1,700 a year, where an aged vicar of seventy-seven was appointed (livings could not be sold while vacant) so the advowson could be purchased in a public auction in London by a north-of-England gentleman, with the power of next appointment.[11] The Ritualists believed the bishops could expend their disciplinary zeal on many clergy who, unlike themselves, had little or no interest in being good pastors.

Because the Ritualists were generally good pastors, and as concerned for the temporal well-being of their people as they were for the state of their souls, they also indicted the bishops for their lack of social conscience—particularly towards the end of the century. An interesting record of the episcopal attitude to social reform was drawn up by Joseph Clayton, a prominent layman in Puseyite circles, and Rev. Stewart Headlam, whose Guild of St. Matthew was one of the first socialist societies in England, in a work entitled *Bishops as Legislators*.

Headlam provided the introduction to the work by remarking that English bishops were all men of good character, and usually of blameless private life. They were neither worldly nor ambitious above their fellows. Rather they were clerical 'insiders'; men 'who have proved themselves good organizers or great scholars, or successful schoolmasters. . . . men of conspicuous courage or devotion are rarely selected as bishops for those qualities imply enemies.'[12] Seldom were they indolent. Headlam confessed that in the last fifty years of the nineteenth century the 'bishops worked as hard as cabinet ministers', and yet 'as legislators they were the despair not only of politicians but of the plain average citizen. . . . they were in the House of Lords to maintain the rights and privileges of the Established Church. . . . Erastian and unashamed . . . when reforms were proposed the bishops

---

11. S. Hornibrook, *Sale of Livings* (1873), p. 5.
12. Joseph Clayton, *Bishops as Legislators* (1906), p. 14.

first asked: " Will this proposal improve the position of the Established Church ?" '[13]

In the body of the work, Clayton admitted that bishops had improved during the century. In 1820 they had striven to retain hanging as a punishment for cutting down trees, or killing cattle, the bad old days when 'the poor and needy were strung up in batches by the hangman . . . without prayer for mercy from the prelates in the Lords.'[14] They had also improved from 1839 when the Bishop of Exeter had observed: 'Looking to the poor as a class, they could not expect that those who were assigned by Providence to the laborious occupations of life should be able largely to cultivate their intellects.'[15] And he admitted that with regard to social reform, particularly factory legislation, the bishops were more favourable towards it than the trading classes in the Commons.[16] But their great failing was to put the well-being of the Establishment before the pastoral care of souls. In no way had they encouraged the spiritual revival in the Church led by the Ritualists, nor the efforts of those concerned to bring the blessings of Christ into the slums.

The call of Clayton and Headlam was for the people of the Church to shrug off the bondage of the Establishment and its Erastian bishops. 'It is illogical on account of the crimes and follies of the Bishops to condemn the Church which is essentially democratic and liberal in its doctrines and institutions, and which, if the people were wise, they would in spite of this damning episcopal record, claim and use as their own Church.'[17]

When Joseph Chamberlain brought out his radical programme in 1885, which included 'religious equality', disestablishment became a living issue in English politics. Pamphlet after pamphlet poured out of the vicarages of the country to warn churchmen of the danger posed by Chamberlain and his followers.[18] But other voices, particularly those of the Puseyites, argued that only disestablishment would free the Church from its bondage to the State. The *Church Times* cried ' we are fighting for the very life of the Church. Disestablished in some form she must clearly be.'[19] Stewart Headlam viewed the move

13. *Ibid.*, p. 12.
14. *Ibid.*, p. 47.
15. *Ibid.*, p. 60.
16. The bishops were cooler towards rural social reform, or reform of conditions in mines where they had a direct interest.
17. Clayton, *Bishops as Legislators*, p. 7.
18. Constantine Frere, *The Coming Election and the Coming Danger: a Letter to the Electors of Finningham, Suffolk* (1885).
19. *Church Times*, 2 March 1877.

towards disestablishment as a transcendent summons: 'to turn from the Bishop of London to the Bishop of all the earth, and from the judgment of society to the judgment of Jesus'.[20] Their confidence that disestablishment would mean spiritual advance for the Church came from their interpretation of the Puseyite movement: 'had the Ritualists obeyed the bishops and the lawyers this revival of the Church of England with all the Church restoration and the work of social reform in our towns that it has meant would have been impossible.'[21] Writing to the *Times*, Mackonochie said in 1869:

> Once free from State control we shall begin, I trust, to feel as a body and not merely as individuals, that we belong to a 'kingdom which is not of this world'. Our bishops will know that their power is that of servants of Christ not Lords of Parliament. We of the clergy shall be free from the temptations to worldly gain and ambition with which an Establishment surrounds men; and our people will receive or reject us for Christ's sake, not as ministers appointed by the State.[22]

This same sentiment was given a more radical interpretation by Stewart Headlam in 1882: 'When we are really free, free from State fathers and wealthy patronage, forced to throw ourselves—as we are bound being followers of Jesus to do—on the sympathies of the people; free to develop ourselves as the great Socialistic Secular Society; then I foresee a glorious future for the despised Church of England.'[23]

Pusey often considered disestablishment as a possibility for the Church because he believed that the State connection impeded the mission work of churchmen. 'I have for many years made up my mind that some sort of denominationalism or Disestablishment must come. I have thought so in reference to the populations of our great towns, of whose spiritual destitution we have been so accustomed to speak that we have been almost inured to it as a remediless evil.'[24] But at other times he confessed that he shrank from actively participating in desecration of what had once been given to God by churchmen of another age. He also realized that as long as the Evangelical party was dominated by the fanatical Church Association there would be real danger of the Church of England breaking up into warring parties, if the Church was disestablished.

20. S. D. Headlam, *Sure Foundation: an Address to the Guild of St. Matthew* (1883), p. 9.
21. Clayton, *Bishops as Legislators*, p. 109.
22. A. H. Mackonochie, *Times*, 16 January 1869, p. 5.
23. S. D. Headlam, *Service of Humanity* (1882), p. 134.
24. *Voices from Within: or Disestablishment as Viewed by Churchmen* (1871), p. 17. A speech to the English Church Union in June 1868.

The bishops were the object of Pusey's suspicion, and of Ritualist resentment, because it was believed they served the State and the Establishment, rather than the will of the whole Church. Inasmuch as the Ritualists reflected the influence of the Holy Spirit in the Church, Pusey believed they were justified in their resistance to the episcopate. As early as 1842 he had stated that when episcopal declarations were injurious to the true interests of the Church, the conscientious Churchman had to speak out against his bishop. 'If unhappily . . . he contravene his commission . . . it becomes a duty in any one (while ready patiently to take any consequences) to speak in behalf of the common faith.'[25] But resisting Erastian bishops in their folly, and seeking disestablishment, with the hope that spiritual bishops might be elected in diocesan synods, were two different matters.

The *Church Times* argued that episcopal authority was to be recognized only if it was (1) in accordance with Holy Scripture; (2) used to promote love, quietness, and peace; (3) directed to the restraint and punishment of the disorderly and ill-conducted; and (4) not used in any respect contrary to the traditional doctrine, ritual, and discipline of the Church of England.[26] The *Union Review* believed that the proper sort of diocesan would only appear when synods of both clergy and laity met, where the bishop would come 'face to face with his flock, to take common counsel with them as a father with his children'.[27]

Disestablishment did not come because the majority of churchmen realized, as did Pusey, that at least the State connection kept the Church from suffering schism, which was so common among the Free Churches. The churchmen who were most vocal in their support of disestablishment, like Dean Hook, Archdeacon Denison, H. P. Liddon, and Leslie Stephen, were the sort of individuals who loved ecclesiastical controversy, and contributed much to the sectarian strife in the Church. A prelate such as the Evangelical John Charles Ryle, Bishop of Liverpool, had an attentive and thoughtful audience of all schools of churchmanship when he warned the Church in 1885:

> I know there are some enthusiastic Churchmen here and there who fancy that freedom from State control would be a real benefit to the Church of England. They have pleasing visions of a free, rich, and powerful Church, no longer fettered by connection with the State, guided by perfect Bishops, no longer

25. E. B. Pusey, *Letter to the Archbishop of Canterbury on Some Circumstances Connected with the Present Crisis in the English Church* (1842), p. 48.
26. 'Obedience to the Bishop', *Church Times*, 8 June 1877, p. 329.
27. 'On Synods and the Laity', *Union Review* IX (1871), 249.

interfered with by naughty Parliaments and wicked Courts of Law, possessing perfect unity, and able to do a hundred things which it cannot do now. These amiable enthusiasts would soon find, if they had their own way, that a Free Church is a fine thing to talk about, but not so free as it appears. There are other chains and screw-presses besides those of Parliament, secular Law Courts and the Royal Supremacy. . . . When I hear an English Churchman expressing a wish for Disestablishment, I always think of the famous epitaph which said: 'I was well; I would be better: I took physic, and here I am.'[28]

Ryle was a superior bishop who commanded a hearing not only because of his power as a speaker, or his reputation as one of the greatest of evangelical tract writers, but also because of his able and conscientious administration of the diocese of Liverpool which the State had created by order in council in 1880. Ryle refused to countenance a proposal to erect a costly cathedral, preferring to devote his energies and the offerings of the faithful to the endowment of parish churches and other pastoral enterprises. Respect for him grew also because of his refusal to use his authority as ordinary of Liverpool in partisan activity. His personal theology became less hard and formal from the time he became bishop, and he tried to persuade the Church Association that their attitude to the Ritualists should be 'educate not litigate'.[29]

Peace began to settle in the Church over the issue of Ritualism after the Church Association attempted its greatest coup—the prosecution of Edward King, Bishop of Lincoln. A disciple of Charles Marriott of Oriel College, Oxford, the editor of the Tractarian *Library of the Fathers*, King was almost universally loved by the clergy of the Church. He was the saint of the episcopate, simple, sensible, and strong, his life totally committed to God and the care of the souls in his diocese. If ever a bishop was a 'father-in-God' to his clergy and his people, it was Edward King. H. P. Liddon, who preached King's consecration sermon entitled 'A Father in Christ', had feared that the see of Lincoln might have been offered to himself. When he heard of King's appointment he said 'I am altogether wanting in the sympathy and lofty spirituality of character which are so full of the highest promise for the Episcopate which is about to begin in the throne of St. Hugh.'[30]

To the shock of many churchmen, the Church Association, with the concurrence of a layman of the diocese, petitioned King's metropolitan to cite him for illegal ritualistic acts such as using the eastward

28. J. C. Ryle, *Our Position and Our Dangers* (1885), p. 22.
29. Carpenter, *Church and People*, p. 348.
30. J. O. Johnston, *Life and Letters of Henry Parry Liddon* (1904), p. 315.

position, altar lights, the mixed chalice, the *Agnus Dei*, the sign of the cross, and the ablution of the sacred vessels at the altar. There was much ancient authority for archbishops sitting as sole judge in their own courts, but the court of the Archbishop of Canterbury had been in abeyance for two hundred years. Edward White Benson, the primate, was an antiquarian and liturgical scholar, however; and, after assurance by the Privy Council that he might exercise his jurisdiction in person, he declared his own competence to try the case of Bishop King, with five bishops as his assessors. The constitution and the procedure of the court were held to be defective by some authorities—William Stubbs, the ecclesiastical historian and new Bishop of Oxford described it as 'an archbishop sitting in his library',[31] but King accepted the tribunal. The hearing took twelve months, and the detailed judgment, which was based on much historical research, required almost another year for preparation.

Benson did not consider his court to be bound by existing judgments of the Privy Council. He allowed all the points at issue to be argued afresh, and came to conclusions which ignored earlier decisions. The continuity of the Church before, through, and after the Reformation was assumed, and constant reference was made to the rubrics of the Prayer Book, and the traditional practice of the Church. Narrow rules of interpretation were avoided. Benson argued that important points of Church law could not properly be decided unless full consideration was given to history and liturgiology. When judgment was given, it was ruled that the sign of the cross in absolution and benediction was illegal, otherwise the court ruled in favour of Bishop King, and the judgment was received by the majority of churchmen with satisfaction. When the prosecutors appealed to the Judicial Committee of the Privy Council in 1892, the appeal was dismissed, the archbishop's decision being upheld. The appeal court did have some doubts about the matter of altar lights, but avoided contention by saying that the bishop himself was not directly responsible for lighting them. King had been represented in Archbishop Benson's court by counsel, but not before the secular court whose jurisdiction he had refused to recognize.

This case destroyed completely the authority of the Privy Council in matters of ritual. It showed clearly that its previous decisions, which had led to the imprisonment of dedicated clerics, were not

---

31. G. W. E. Russell, 'Edward White Benson', *Dictionary of English Church History*, p. 52. King preferred to be tried by all the bishops of the province, but accepted Benson's overruling of his objection.

infallible or irrevocable, but could be reconsidered in the light of greater historical knowledge and liturgiology. No one could accuse the Archbishop of being a sympathizer of the Puseyites, and his devotion to the principle of Establishment was almost monomania. He was also respected for his fervent piety. Without violation of conscience or principle, the clergy felt they could yield to the Archbishop's court an obedience which they denied to the tribunals of Lord Penzance and the Privy Council.

The acceptance of the Lincoln Judgment by churchmen showed the way ahead—the solution to the long-protracted struggle between the bishops and the Ritualists. The epoch of ritual prosecutions was at an end. Later suits dealing with ceremonial matters were few and unimportant, and the bishops were left to deal with them through exercise of their spiritual authority, in accordance with the laws of the Church, unhampered by secular interference. Through the good fortune of having the statesmanlike Tait succeeded by the imaginative, learned, and catholic-minded E. W. Benson, a way of satisfying all parties had been found.

The Lincoln Judgment also put an end to the serious discussion of disestablishment. The persecution of the Ritualists by the bishops had made many churchmen wonder if Pusey and his followers would not have been driven out of the Church, if the common law had not restrained the disciplinary powers of the episcopate. It was the Establishment which refused to allow outright proscription of the Ritualists as a party. S. L. Ollard, in his study of the early Tractarians and the Puseyites who succeeded them, believed that the great opposition to the revival associated with their movement came from the bishops rather than from the State.

> 'The evil that men do lives after them'. Just as the heads of Houses in Oxford had striven by means which were cruel and unintelligent to arrest the Movement in its earlier years, so did the English bishops in their turn, from 1840 to 1890, strive to crush those who were reviving the lawful ceremonial of the English Church. The Heads, in the event, lost their authority when the time of change came, the bishops impaired for a generation at least the influence of their order among clergymen and laymen of the persecuted school.[32]

Archbishop Benson represented a new consciousness among the bishops of the value of the Establishment in terms of catholic mission to the nation. He was one of the prelates who listened to churchmen like the Earl of Carnarvon when he urged both the bishops and the Ritualists to 'push on the work of the Church'.

32. S. L. Ollard, *Short History of the Oxford Movement* (1932), p. 142.

135

The more freely and boldly the Bishops exercise the power which they now possess in preventing litigation and strife the more effectually will they maintain the peace of the Church. We may, I believe, have a substantial unity on the greatest questions; but we must forego the attempt at an impracticable and unwholesome uniformity in matters of detail. We look to the large-mindedness and courage of the Bishops to use their powers, and to save us from a great danger.[33]

Benson was devoted to resisting 'the attack which is based upon the assurance that we are a very divided house'.[34] In the year that he delivered his celebrated judgment, Brooke Foss Westcott was consecrated Bishop of Durham, and it became clear to most churchmen that the Church was entering into a new 'golden age of pastoral endeavour'. Even the Ritualists were less likely to say 'when the clergy turned to their leaders, the bishops, for direction they met commonly with repression and rebuke.'[35] Bishops, clergy, and laity were uniting to make use of the tactical advantages provided by the Establishment for the Church to persevere in its vocation to overcome the world. 'We have nothing whatever to fear for the connection of Church and State, if Churchmen will only awake, arise and do their duty.'[36]

Finding a better relationship with the State was only part of the accomplishment of the Church, however—a means to an all important end. The second part of this study will examine the Church's mission to society in Victorian England—sometimes in spite of, but usually in alliance with, the secular power of the State.

33. Earl of Carnarvon, *Advantages of an Established Church* (1885), p. 9.

34. *Speech of the Archbishop of Canterbury at Church Defence Institution Annual Meeting, 9 July 1883*, p. 8.

35. Ollard, p. 143.

36. J. C. Ryle, *Disestablishment: Thoughts for Thoughtless People, and Churchmen Who Wish for Disestablishment* (1885), p. 6.

PART II
CHURCH
AND SOCIETY

*The Mission
of the
Church of England*

IV. The Church
and the
Intellectual Revolution

Unless all existence is a medium of revelation, no particular revelation is possible.

ARCHBISHOP WILLIAM TEMPLE

*1. Revelation and Reason
   in Victorian England*

IT WOULD be unwise for any historian to underestimate the power and influence of the Victorian pulpit. Christian preachers succeeded in feeding both the hearts and minds of generations of earnest believers, however lacking in refined rhetoric, philosophy, or theology their discourses may have been. Like many poets, novelists, and essayists, they presumed to give to society the moral exhortation and theological assurance which they believed was needed in a time of religious and intellectual uncertainty. They were listened to by a vast and earnest audience of privileged and socially powerful people. In the long run they probably had a greater influence than the writers, for, however sentimental it was, Victorian worship was popular worship. Through the medium of the Bible, the Prayer Book, hymns, music, and other devotional aids, the clergy succeeded in persuading most members of the upper classes to become a noticeably religious people.[1] As Lady Tweedsmuir has reminded us,

---

EPIGRAPH: Loren Eiseley, *Immense Journey* (1958), p. 1.

1. Horton Davies, *Worship and Theology in England from Watts and Wesley to Maurice 1690–1850* (1961), p. 239, notes how Christian worship inspired the 'efflorescence of Christian philanthropy' which was characteristic of the age.

the question that Victorians of the privileged classes asked each other on Sunday was not 'Will you, or won't you go to Church?' but 'Where will you go to Church?'[2]

Sermon-tasting for the Victorian was not only a duty but a delight. During the middle years of the century, sermons were the most popular forms of reading.[3] When Disraeli told Dean Stanley of Westminster Abbey, 'Mr. Dean, no dogmas, no deans',[4] he was well-acquainted with the liberal theology which characterized Stanley's sermons. When R. W. Dale of Birmingham, one of the most impressive of Free Church preachers, exhorted his congregations to the practice of civic virtue in the commercial and industrial society of late Victorian England, his pleas were heeded by many of the shrewd merchants of the north. Respectful attention was paid to the dramatic Joseph Parker of City Temple when he preached on Armenian atrocities, and concluded his sermon with the ringing words, 'God damn the Sultan!'[5]

Just as Keble's *Christian Year* appealed to the Romanticism of the age,[6] so the 'sweet persuasiveness' of John Henry Newman fascinated generations of Oxford undergraduates. They thronged dimly lit St. Mary's on Sunday afternoons to hear the sermons of the man whom James Anthony Froude, Matthew Arnold, and many others acknowledged to be 'a peerless preacher'.[7] Through his 'refinement and delicacy of feeling, the reserve and carefulness of statement, the humility',[8] as well as the sentiment and pathos which the age desired, Newman captivated those who listened to his Oxford sermons. He was a devout and mystic soul, who was able to use his great gifts of imagination and scholarship 'to invest abstract and complex philosophical theology with movement and life'.[9] After Newman's secession, the great preacher in the Tractarian tradition was Canon H. P. Liddon. From the pulpit of St. James', Piccadilly, and after his

2. S. C. Buchan, *The Lilac and the Rose* (London, 1952), p. 85.

3. Horton Davies, *Worship and Theology in England from Newman to Martineau 1850–1900* (1962), p. 282.

4. L. E. Elliot-Binns, *English Thought 1860–1900: The Theological Aspect* (1956), p. 223.

5. Davies, *Newman to Martineau*, p. 284.

6. For the influence of Romanticism on the Tractarians v. W. Ward, *Life of Newman* (1912), II, 354–55 and B. H. Smith, *Dean Church* (1958), p. 27. The *Christian Year* went through 43 editions. H. A. L. Jefferson, *Hymns in Christian Worship* (1950), p. 119, says that Newman could never understand the appeal of 'Lead Kindly Light'. He attributed its popularity to the romantic tune of J. B. Dykes.

7. Froude, *Short Stories*, IV, 278 ff.

8. Davies, *Newman to Martineau*, p. 304.

9. *Ibid.*, p. 308.

preferment in 1870, from the pulpit of St. Paul's, Liddon's sermons became an important part of London life. He gave to an uneasy generation the religious certitude that so many longed for. Hearing Liddon preach was an event long remembered by those who visited London.

F. W. Robertson of Holy Trinity Chapel, Brighton, emerged as a great master of psychological preaching during the years 1848–1853. He appealed to the emotions as well as to the minds of his congregation, as he stressed the humanity of Christ, and the need for social justice—a subject that many preachers of the period chose to ignore. He belonged to no ecclesiastical party, but his thought was influenced by F. D. Maurice, who was then preaching his sermons of quiet devotion at Lincoln's Inn, for the spiritual enrichment of many.

Whatever his taste in sermons, the Victorian churchman could usually find someone to satisfy him. Stopford Brooke (the biographer of F. W. Robertson), who was a literary critic, and a chaplain to the Queen, had his own special following. Thomas Binney delighted Nonconformity by his thundering denunciation of the Establishment from the pulpit of the Congregationalist King's Weigh-House Chapel. At the Unitarian Chapel in Little Portland Street, James Martineau appealed to the minds as well as the hearts of the intellectuals who came to hear him. The incomparable C. H. Spurgeon opposed the intellectual tide of the age with his Calvinistic theology, but he was listened to by 10,000 people a Sunday in his Metropolitan Tabernacle between 1868 and 1892. His sermons were carried in full by daily newspapers as far away as America and Australia.[10]

During the later years of the century, following the American-inspired 'revival' movement of 1858–1859,[11] the Victorians were swayed by the devout, unsophisticated preaching of Dwight L. Moody, and the rhythmical hymn tunes of his fellow-evangelist, Ira D. Sankey. These years also saw the appearance of the Salvation Army, and the growth in appeal of popular-worship services. They were usually held outside regular church buildings, and were supported by both the Establishment and the Free Churches. On the surface, the English people seemed to be at least tolerant, if not enthusiastic supporters of every new wave of religious emotionalism that appeared.

Yet many churchmen were dismayed by the growing emotionalism and the lack of intellectual appeal in much of late Victorian worship.

10. *Ibid.*, p. 286.
11. J. E. Orr, *Second Evangelical Awakening* (1955), p. 125 ff.

They feared that it might conceal an undercurrent of religious un-certainty, perhaps even scepticism, which they knew was appearing among even the most loyal of churchmen. They noted that interest in ecclesiastical controversy was beginning to decline, and they wondered what intellectual resources the Church could find when it attempted to bring the Gospel into the new world of science which was beginning to fascinate the Victorians. The anxiety of these sensitive churchmen was noted by several observers of the religious scene.

John Stuart Mill noted in his diary for 13 January 1854, 'Scarcely anyone in the more educated classes seems to have any opinions . . . or to place any real faith in those which he professes to believe. . . . the multitude of thoughts only breeds increase of uncertainty. Those who should be the guides of the rest, see too many sides to every question.'[12] There is little doubt that Mill was right in his observation; in almost every field of intellectual inquiry traditional viewpoints were being discarded, and among thinking men there was a general 'increase of uncertainty'. The reaction of most churchmen to this confusion of belief was a rejection of intellectual speculation and a reassertion of the power of Christian Revelation. John Henry Newman wrote for a sympathetic public when he said:

> In a state of society such as ours, in which authority, prescription, tradition, habit, moral instinct, and the divine influences go for nothing, in which free discussion and fallible judgment are prized as the birthright of each individual, I must be excused if I exercise towards this age, as regards its belief in this doctrine, some portion of that scepticism which it exercises itself towards every received but unscrutinized assertion whatever.[13]

We noted in Chapter II that the early Tractarians showed little or no interest in secular affairs and that, because of this, education generally was at a low ebb in Oxford during their ascendancy. They were not unique in this regard. In the same diary entry to which we have referred above, Mill asks: 'What is it that occupies the minds of three-fourths of those in England who care about any public interest or any controversial question? The quarrel between Protestant and Catholic; or that between Puseyite and Evangelical.'[14] The truth was that combatants of both extreme parties in the Church of England were so caught up in theological dispute that they had little time, energy, or even interest to give to secular intellectual concerns until the latter years of the century.

12. J. S. Mill, *Letters* (1910), II, 359.
13. J. H. Newman, *Idea of a University* (1912), p. 37.
14. Mill, *Letters*, II, 359.

James Anthony Froude, the historian brother of Richard Hurrell Froude, was a typical disenchanted churchman. He knew Newman and the Tractarians at Oxford when they were at the apogee of their influence—the time when 'for hundreds of young men *Credo in Newmannum* was the genuine symbol of faith'.[15] But during the time that Newman was at Littlemore, Froude was thrown on his own resources. He began to read Carlyle, Goethe, Lessing, Neander, and Schleiermacher. As he studied, he began to suspect the obscurantism of the Tractarians. When they persuaded him to assist in a production of the lives of the saints he found that his faith was not equal to the task. 'St. Patrick I found once lighted a fire with icicles, changed a Welsh marauder into a wolf, and floated to Ireland upon an altar stone. I thought it nonsense. . . . I had to retreat out of my occupation, and let the series go on without me.'[16]

Froude never lost his respect for men like Newman and Pusey, but he did begin to see that a kind of anti-intellectualism accompanied the Tractarian revival.

> This became clear to me, that the Catholic revival in Oxford, spontaneous as it seemed, was part of a general movement which was going on all over Europe. In France, in Holland, in Germany, intellect and learning had come to conclusions from which religion and conscience were recoiling. Pious Protestants had trusted themselves upon the Bible as their sole foundation. They found their philosophers and professors assuming that the Bible was a human composition—parts of it of doubtful authenticity, other parts bearing marks on them of the mistaken opinions of the age when these books were written; and they were flying terrified back into the Church from which they had escaped at the Reformation, like ostriches hiding their heads in a bush. Yet how could the Church, as they called it save them? If what the philosophers were saying was untrue, it could be met by argument. If the danger was real, they were like men caught in a thunder-storm, flying for refuge to a tree which only the more certainly would attract the lightning.[17]

No one could deny the intellectual capabilities of the Tractarian leaders—certainly the Evangelical school never produced their equals —but even Pusey, who was acquainted with German rationalism, held in deep suspicion the scepticism inherent in secular thought.[18]

The Tractarian movement was a religious revival. When a study is made of the view of history taken by Newman, in whose thinking 'a strong logical faculty went with an extraordinary credulity about

15. Froude, 'Oxford Counter-Reformation', *Short Studies*, IV, 283.
16. *Ibid.*, p. 323.
17. *Ibid.*, p. 312.
18. *Life of Pusey*, I, 83. 'Pusey always distrusted philosophical methods of handling theology; he took refuge in authority, whether that of Scripture or of the Primitive Church.'

matters of fact', [19] and consideration is given to his view of fallen humanity—in contrast to the *Zeitgeist* which had interpreted and rationalized away so many dogmas of the Christian religion—the significance of Tractarian thought becomes clear. It was, as J. A. Froude discovered, 'an intense revolt against every kind of latitude'. [20] Reasoning about Christian 'evidences' may be plausible, but it will never convince.

> It is indeed a great question whether Atheism is not as philosophically consistent with the phenomena of the physical world, taken by themselves, as the doctrine of a creative and governing Power. But, however this be, the practical safeguard against Atheism in the case of scientific enquirers is the inward need and desire, the inward experience of that Power, existing in the mind before and independently of their examination of His material world. [21]

On the title page of his *Grammar of Assent*, Newman quoted St. Ambrose, 'It pleased not God to save his people by force of logic.' Newman believed that religious truth is never proved by interpretation of evidence, by scientific demonstration, or even by logical argument. The Christian will 'look for certainty by modes of proof which, when reduced to the shape of formal propositions, fail to satisfy the severe requisitions of science'. [22] The primary assumptions of religion are supplied by the conscience rather than by reasoning; and this is to be expected, for religion has to do with the whole of man, not just his intellect.

> If religion is to be devotion, and not a mere matter of sentiment, if it is to be made the ruling principle of our lives, if our actions, one by one, and our daily conduct, are to be consistently directed towards an Invisible Being, we need something higher than a balance of arguments to fix and control our minds. Sacrifice of wealth, name, or position, faith and hope, self-conquest, communion with the spiritual world, presuppose a real hold and habitual intuition of the objects of Revelation, which is certitude under another name. [23]

Because of this lack of interest in almost everything that was not purely religious, the Tractarians failed to contribute significantly to the development of the arts in England—unless you consider the Gothic revival, and the follies of the 'restorers' like Sir Gilbert Scott,

---

19. A. W. Benn, *History of English Rationalism in the Nineteenth Century* (1962), I, 366.
20. A. P. Stanley, 'The Oxford School', *Edinburgh Review*, cliii, 309.
21. J. H. Newman, *Oxford University Sermons* (1872), p. 59. These sermons form an introduction to his *Grammar of Assent*.
22. J. H. Newman, *Grammar of Assent* (1870), p. 407.
23. *Ibid.*, p. 230.

to be artistic endeavour. Although he became a High-Churchman, Scott originally came from an earnest Evangelical household and considered himself a servant of the Lord 'raised up by Providence for his work, and guided by Providence in it'.[24] Much of his work, and that of his fellow 'restorers', reflects the anti-intellectualism, particularly the lack of historical knowledge, of the Tractarians and their successors. Although many of the churches they restored were Norman or even Saxon in style, they had to be altered because they were 'primitive, undeveloped and unsymbolic'. The desecrations of the 'restorers' came from the ideal they had of what a church should look like; 'the ecclesiological theory of pure style and correct arrangement'.[25] It was their duty to impose on their generation the style of thirteenth-century Geometrical and fourteenth-century Decorated churches of which the Tractarians approved, because of their fascination with the Middle Ages.[26]

There is much truth in Ronald Chapman's comment about the artistic contribution made by churchmen of the Tractarian school.

> The truth, as we know it now, is that the Oxford Movement produced no poetry, no painting, no architecture. It did indeed produce the greatest prose writer of the 19th century. . . . But there is no poetry even to compare with Wesley's hymns, the architecture is second-hand, the painting non-existent. . . . In itself the Movement was artistically dead. Looking back we find it strange, and it was considered strange at the time, for the Tractarians were no Philistines. They were intensely interested in the arts. . . . But there was a fatal malady somewhere. Tractarian art was second-hand, derived. It could produce nothing. Whether Evangelicalism which played so much greater a part in the Movement than is generally allowed blighted such art as there was; or whether, more charitably, it may be supposed that strong religious feeling may best be expressed in other ways than art; or whether the Movement was too short, too broken, too torn by controversy to be creative; or whether the fact of its deliberate reaction against the Liberal and Utilitarian stream of the time rendered it sterile . . . the Movement contained innumerable amateurs of art but no creators.[27]

The early Tractarians and the old Evangelicals had much in common. A. W. Benn is one scholar who does not hesitate to identify the Oxford Movement as part of an over-all religious revival which existed 'during the century which began with Wesley's call and ended with the last "Tract for the Times".'[28] Yngve Brilioth, in his studies

24. Basil Clarke, *Church Builders of the Nineteenth Century* (1938), p. 161.
25. *Ibid.*, p. 230. *Cf.* Peter Anson, *Fashions in Church Furnishings, 1840–1940* (1960), p. 44 ff.
26. White, *Cambridge Movement*, p. 155 ff.
27. Ronald Chapman, *Father Faber* (1961), p. 64.
28. Benn, I, 362.

of the Oxford Movement, which he called the *Anglican Revival*, agreed with that 'highly competent judge', W. E. Gladstone, that there was a close connection between Evangelicalism and the Tractarians. The former movement provided the 'spirit which was so to fertilise the organism of old High Churchmanship that it once more could bear offspring'.[29] Gladstone had argued that this was an unquestionable fact that 'since the date of the Tracts—*since* and not before it—the juice and sap of the Evangelical teaching has in a very remarkable manner coursed through "the natural gates and alleys of the body" of the English Church.'[30] In our own generation Dieter Voll in his study of *Catholic Evangelicalism* has said 'It is of course unquestionable that without the Evangelical impulse the Oxford Movement would have hardly been possible.'[31]

Whether or not the charge of obscurantism can be directed at the early Tractarian party may be a matter of question. But few people would dispute Gladstone's opinion that the Evangelical movement 'did not ally itself with literature, art and general cultivation.'[32] It may be argued that the Tractarians had no time to consider other than ecclesiastical matters until after Newman's secession, but it seems to be clear that the Evangelicals deliberately turned their backs on both spiritual and secular speculation. Mark Pattison believed the Evangelical party grew in the Church as 'a reaction against High Church "evidences"; the insurrection of the heart and conscience of man against an arid orthodoxy. It insisted on a "vital Christianity" as against the Christianity of books. Its instinct was from the first against intelligence. No text found more favour with it than, "Not many wise, not many learned".'[33]

Some of the eighteenth-century Evangelicals such as Isaac Milner, Thomas Scott, and John Newton, had been concerned with theology, but a major difference between the Tractarians and the Evangelicals of the mid-nineteenth century was that the anti-intellectualism of the latter party led them to ignore even theology. Newman said of the Evangelicals of 1839 that their party 'had no intellectual basis; no internal idea, no principle of unity, no theology . . . no straightforward

29. Brilioth, *The Anglican Revival*, p. 30.
30. Gladstone, *Gleanings of Past Years*, VII, 221.
31. Dieter Voll, *Catholic Evangelicalism* (1963), p. 133.
32. Gladstone, *Gleanings of Past Years*, VII, 219.
33. Mark Pattison, 'Learning in the Church of England', *Essays* (1889), II, p. 268. Davies, *Worship and Theology in England from Watts and Wesley to Maurice, 1690–1850*, p. 239 describes the Evangelicals' defect as 'their overwhelming emphasis on the Atonement as effecting a salvation out of this world'. H. D. McDonald, *Ideas of Revelation, 1700–1860* (1959), pp. 218–24, discusses Evangelical suspicion of 'natural religion'.

view on any one point, on which it professes to teach, and to hide its poverty, it has dressed itself out in a maze of words'.[34] It was this failure to provide a theology which led many Evangelicals, such as Samuel Wilberforce, Gladstone, Mackonochie, and Liddon to give their allegiance to other Church parties, and for Newman, Manning, Faber, and R. I. Wilberforce to go over to Rome. The pages of a publication such as *The Record* show the decline of the Evangelical party from a position of extreme piety and charity until it became 'a virulent and uncharitable accuser of the brethren'[35]—the Low-Church party of the nation.

The failure to provide a theological basis for the Evangelical position is clearly revealed in the writings of two of the intellectuals of the party—William Goode, who became Dean of Ripon, and Edward Arthur Litton, who was successively Dean of Oriel, Vice-Principal of St. Edmund's Hall, Rector of St. Clement's, Oxford, and Rector of Naunton, near Cheltenham.

Goode was one of the intransigents of the Low-Church party, acting as the Evangelical counterpart to Archdeacon Denison, who represented the extremists among the High-Churchmen. His writings are interesting because they reveal that the Evangelicals were willing to support the Establishment against the Tractarians or Papists, but that their enthusiasm for the Reformation settlement was always qualified. They were never happy about a Hookerian identification of the cause of Church and State. Goode's obituary in the *Clerical Journal* referred to him as a 'zealous supporter of Scriptural and Protestant principles',[36] but it is quite clear that the former was more important in his thinking. The Church to Goode was really an invisible body devoted to serving only spiritual causes.[37]

It was all very well for Goode to view the rise of Tractarianism as part of the continuing contest between 'Reformation and Romish principles',[38] and to say that Newman and his party opposed the Establishment as 'an incubus upon the country',[39] but he never

---

34. Newman, *Apologia*, p. 173.

35. G. W. E. Russell, *Short History of the Evangelical Movement* (1915), p. 109. Samuel Wilberforce was 'a Papist in reality' to the editors of *The Record*—leading men away from the way of salvation. *V. Life*, II, 223.

36. *Obituary of Very Rev. William Goode, Dean of Ripon* (1883), p. 6.

37. William Goode, *Reply to the Letter and Declaration Respecting the Royal Supremacy Received from Archdeacons Manning and Wilberforce and Professor Mill* (1850), p. 10.

38. William Goode, *Some Difficulties in the Late Charge of the Bishop of Oxford* (1842), p. 9.

39. Goode, *Case as it is: Reply to the Letter of Dr. Pusey to the Archbishop of Canterbury* (1843), p. 35.

6+I.V.C.

committed himself to a theological defence of the Reformation settlement—not even when the 'papal aggression' of 1850 was viewed as an 'outrage upon the dignity and sovereignty of the Crown'.[40] He merely reminded his readers that the bishops could conceivably be won over to the cause of Ritualism, as they were in the days of Laud,[41] but as always the 'preservation of our Church has been due to a power altogether extraneous to the Episcopate.'[42] The authority of the Church came from God's Word, and was not found in Catholic theology or practice, which led to Rome, or in rationalistic thought of any sort, which could lead to unbelief.[43] Man was to bow to the sovereignty of God revealed in the Word, not to exalt himself through theological or philosophical speculation.

The innovations of bishops like Samuel Wilberforce not only received hostile criticism from the editors of *The Record*, but protest from zealous Evangelicals who served in the diocese of Oxford. Litton was one of these objectors. He was upset by the processions, the chanting, and the wearing of the surplice at Cuddesdon; and outrage over these developments blinded him to the value of Wilberforce's pastoral revolution. There is much evidence that he was one of those who, so Wilberforce said, carried on a pamphlet war which disturbed 'God's work'. These Evangelical pamphlets reflected a 'querulous, suspicious temper'[44] which led churchmen to whisper insinuations and to stir up strife, and which militated against Christian charity.

Litton was more thoughtful than Goode and recognized that the Evangelicals needed 'something more than the protest of a healthy Christian instinct, such as the laity of this country have given expression to'.[45] But when an attempt is made to read his extremely bulky work entitled *The Church of Christ in Its Idea, Attributes and Ministry*, Newman's opinion that Evangelical theology was a 'maze of words' comes to the reader's mind. Litton believed there was need for the 'adherents of the Reformation to justify their faith',[46] but Litton's works are no more successful than those of Goode in fulfilling this

40. William Goode, *Address to the Inhabitants of All Hallows the Great and Less on the Recent Act of Papal Aggression* (1850), p. 4.

41. William Goode, *Remarks on the Episcopal Resolution Passed in the Upper House of the Southern Convocation on the Subject of Ritualism* (1867), p. 13.

42. *Ibid.*, p. 11.

43. William Goode, *The Doctrine of the Church of England on the Two Sacraments of Baptism and the Lord's Supper* (1864), p. 7.

44. *Address to the Bishop of Oxford of Rev. E. A. Litton and other Clergymen of the Diocese Together with His Lordship's Reply* (1859), p.14.

45. E. A. Litton, *The Church of Christ in Its Idea* (1851), p. vi.

46. *Ibid.*

task. Like the Dean of Ripon, he continually falls back on the 'evidences of the heart' not those of the mind, and speaks of the invisible Church of the spiritually elect. He has little faith in Hooker's view of the Church in the nation because 'there is nothing in the State, as such, directly leading to Christ';[47] there is no moral law incorporated in the civil code.

Not only was Litton suspicious of what man might accomplish by the use of his reason in the State or in society, but he was also cautious about undue use of rational processes in discussing religion. He believed that 'Romanism and Rationalism coincide in more points than might be supposed.' In both systems there is 'a defect of personal sensitiveness, an absence of awareness of the heinous nature and tremendous consequences of sin, and of personal implication therein'. Litton opposed any attempt to 'transform the Gospel into a philosophical system'. He also opposed those who would 'by means of improved social institutions, and the force of education, irrespectively of spiritual influences . . . recover man from the moral ruin occasioned by the Fall'.[48]

After mid-century the degeneration of the Evangelicals into the Low-Church party was more marked. Though the Evangelicals offered no alternative policy for the Church, any who supported the Tractarian, Puseyite, or High-Church cause were bitterly resisted in their reform activities. Wilberforce found that they opposed even the physical restoration of 'churches with their green walls, damp stones, and mouldy furniture'.[49] Lord Shaftesbury said to his biographer that all his life his only enemies had been the Evangelicals. When, in 1869, they were mounting their bitter attack on the nomination of Frederick Temple to the see of Exeter, Shaftesbury rejected the 'coldness and insincerity of the bulk of the Evangelicals. . . . they have much political and personal and little spiritual Protestantism.'[50] By the 1880's, when the Church was entering its golden age of pastoral influence, a writer in the *Contemporary Review* compared the circulation of *The Record* with that of the liberal *Guardian* and concluded 'that the Evangelical party has declined in influence and in numbers will hardly be denied.'[51]

47. E. A. Litton, *Connection of the Church and the State: the Question of the Irish Church* (1868), p. 5. In his *Introduction to Dogmatic Theology* (1860), p. 420, he says 'Church and State can never formally be one.'
48. E. A. Litton, *Intellectual Religionism Portrayed* (1853), p. 10.
49. *Address to the Bishop of Oxford of E. A. Litton*, p. 13.
50. Russell, *History of the Evangelical Movement*, p. 123.
51. R. E. Bartlett, 'Church of England the Evangelical Party', *Contemporary Review* (1885), XLVII, 66.

When *Lux Mundi* appeared in 1889 to show that the Church was willing and able to comprehend and assimilate the new intellectual developments of the age, Hensley Henson believed that the new liberal Catholic school, which its writers represented, was able to have the influence it had because the old Evangelical and Low-Church party was dying. No longer could it attempt to dominate the hierarchy as in the days of Palmerston, who had been Shaftesbury's stepfather-in-law.

> The Evangelicals were exhibiting all the marks of a moribund party. They were out of touch with the prevailing tendencies, social and intellectual, of the time. In a rapidly changing world they were still immersed in the interests, and bound by the prejudices of a past generation. Thus, in spite of their accord with the Protestant sentiment of the nation, which their rivals alienated, they could neither command public regard nor secure any measure of official preferment at all commensurate with their number. Not the choice of Governments, but their own inferiority in personal quality, was the key to their weakness in the hierarchy.[52]

Many contemporaries noted the limitations of Evangelical religion. The sermon was used to present its theology; and, because of Victorian delight in sermon-tasting, many Evangelical clergymen sought to limit themselves to the role of professional preacher. The great Charles Simeon, Vicar of Holy Trinity, Cambridge, gave up his pastoral work to his curate from 1827. This curate, who later became an Archdeacon, then passed on the pastoral work to the second curate, who did the whole pastoral work of the parish in return for a small gratuity. Thomas Mozley said of the Evangelical preacher of Victorian England:

> The great mass of people committed to his care he assumed to be utterly bad or hopelessly good. . . . he delivered his message and that was enough, for him at least. He could thus reserve his attention for a few. Relieved thus from the dull reiteration of house to house work, and from close parochial work generally, he became mobilized. . . . the Evangelical preacher very soon discovered that his vocation was not in cottages and hovels, or in farm houses, or in garrets and cellars . . . in dirty lanes and courts.[53]

There were notable exceptions to this pattern of Evangelical clerical behaviour, such as the heroic pastoral work of W. W. Champneys in Whitechapel, but there is much truth in Mozley's observation.

William Hale White in *The Autobiography of Mark Rutherford* tells

52. Henson, *Retrospect of an Unimportant Life*, I, 157.
53. Mozley, *Reminiscences of Oriel*, I, 185.

of his conversion at the age of fourteen, in 1846, and how formalized this event had become for so many.

> I was told that it was time I became converted. . . . I knew that I had to be 'a child of God', and after a time professed myself to be one, but I cannot call to mind that I was anything else than I always had been, save that I was perhaps a little more hypocritical; not in the sense that I professed to others what I knew I did not believe, but in the sense that I professed it to myself. I was obliged to declare myself convinced of sin; convinced of the efficacy of the atonement; convinced that I was forgiven; convinced that the Holy Ghost was shed abroad in my heart; and convinced of a great many other things which were the merest phrases.[54]

The tragedy of Evangelicalism was that many who believed its tenets to be 'merest phrases' were in a position where they should have been developing a theology that was intellectually acceptable to the age. But because of the influence of Evangelicalism, which up to mid-century 'set the tone of almost the entire Church',[55] many intellectuals in the universities chose to continue to accept and teach ideas in which they no longer believed. Leslie Stephen remembered the Cambridge don of the 1850's as a man who accepted matters like 'verbal inspiration', or the traditional concept of Hell, in some sense or other. But he 'did not ask too closely in what sense. . . . He shut his eyes to the great difficulties or took the answer for granted.'[56]

The spiritual needs of the nation were so great that the Evangelicals believed that they had no time to devote to abstract theology, such as that which occupied the Tractarians. Nor did they have time for the intellectual speculation and sober piety of the middle-of-the-road churchmen, 'moderate men who love God moderately and their neighbours moderately and hate sin moderately and desire Heaven and fear Hell moderately.'[57] God had called them to the task of making England 'a righteous nation'.[58] Their authority was the Bible, whose commandments could be disobeyed only at the cost of moral peril.

It is easy from the standpoint of the twentieth century to be critical of the obscurantism of the Evangelicals and the Tractarians. How could any Victorian churchman in the years after 1850 not be influenced

54. Mark Rutherford [W. H. White], *The Autobiography of Mark Rutherford* (1881), p. 9.
55. Elie Halévy, *Victorian Years, 1841–1895* (1961), p. 346.
56. F. W. Maitland, *Life of Leslie Stephen* (1906), p. 152.
57. Chapman, *Father Faber*, p. 19. The words are those of Charles Simeon, the Cambridge Evangelical.
58. J. B. Sumner, *Charge to the Diocese of Chester* (1838), p. 19.

by the 'blizzard of intellectual doubt which blew across from Germany during the rest of the century'?[59] Did the new ways of thought not liberate the human psyche? As T. H. Huxley later said, the people who talked about the comforts of belief appeared to forget its discomforts: 'the fear of theological error, and the overpowering terror of possible damnation, which have accompanied the Churches like their shadow'. He acknowledged that blessings could accompany loss of faith: 'If agnostics lose heavily on the one side, they gain a good deal on the other.'[60]

After years of anxiety over the 'superstition which fails to make happy, fails to make good, fails to make wise',[61] Harriet Martineau, who collaborated with Henry Atkinson to give Victorians a full creed of scientific materialism, described her conversion to atheism in terms which reflect the Evangelical influence of the age.

> My labouring brain and beating heart grew quiet and something more like peace than I had ever yet known settled down upon my anxious mind. . . . a new vigour pervaded my whole life, a new light spread through my mind, and I began to experience a steady growth in self-command, courage, and consequent integrity and disinterestedness. I was like a new creature in the strength of a sound conviction. Life also was like something fresh and wonderfully interesting now that I held in my hand this key whereby to interpret some of the most conspicuous of its mysteries.[62]

Yet few Victorians were willing to make the leap of faith of Harriet Martineau or Leslie Stephen. Most were like Thomas Arnold, who could point out the 'equal or greater difficulties of Atheism or scepticism'.

> If I were talking with an Atheist, I should lay a great deal of stress on faith as a necessary condition of our nature. . . . for faith does no violence to our understanding; but the intellectual difficulties being balanced, and it being necessary to act on the one side or the other, faith determines a man to embrace that side which leads to moral and practical perfection; and unbelief leads him to embrace the opposite, or, what I may call the Devil's religion, which is, after all, quite as much beset with intellectual difficulties as God's religion is, and morally is nothing but one mass of difficulties and monstrosities.[63]

Rather than commit themselves to the unknown, Victorian churchmen in their moments of doubt, 'the great and terrible battle of faith and

59. Smith, *Dean Church*, p. 137.
60. T. H. Huxley, 'Agnosticism', *Science and Christian Tradition: Essays* (1894), p. 242.
61. Harriet Martineau, *Autobiography* (1877), II, 356.
62. *Ibid.*, I, 109–10.
63. *Life of Arnold*, I, p. 179, letter of 15 February 1832.

doubt', [64] usually chose to listen to the voices of the spiritual masters of their age—men like Robertson of Brighton.

> In such moments you doubt all—whether Christianity be true: whether Christ was man, or God, or a beautiful fable. You ask bitterly, like Pontius Pilate, 'What is Truth'? In such an hour what remains? I reply, Obedience. Leave those thoughts for the present. Act—be merciful and gentle—honest: force yourself to abound in little services: try to do good to others: be true to the Duty that you know. . . . Do that much of the will of God, which is plain to you, 'You shall know of the doctrine, whether it be of God.' [65]

Much of the anti-intellectualism of both the Tractarians and the Evangelicals came from the practical nature of their religion. Even John Stuart Mill admitted that 'the special characteristic of Christianity as opposed to most other religions' was its insistence that 'religion does affect this world'; [66] and, as historians like G. M. Young [67] and Kathleen Heasman have pointed out, it is impossible to ignore the value of Christian philanthropy in Victorian England. 'The Evangelicals are remembered for what they did rather than for their theology.' [68] Both the Tractarians, who ignored secular thought deliberately to get on with their task of reviving a theology of the Church, and the Evangelicals, who feared and despised the vain thought of the world which might impede their mission work, bowed to the authority of Revelation rather than Reason. But they did so for no negative reason. Both parties were devoted to building the Kingdom here upon earth in their own fashion—except when they forgot their purpose in Church-party warfare—and both feared intellectual confusion because it might interfere with what they were about.

Their reaction to the intellectual challenges of the age was like that of Charles Kingsley when he read *Essays and Reviews*. In a letter to Charles Sumner, Bishop of Winchester, Kingsley says that the work aroused in him the old 'doubts and puzzles' which 'have passed through the mind of every thinking man in the last twenty-five years'.

> I confess to having thrust the book away in disgust, as saying once again, very weakly, what I had long put out of sight and mind, in the practical realities of parish work. When my new curate came back to me after ordination, having heard your lordship's allusion to these 'Essays and Reviews'

64. Charles Kingsley, *Letters and Memories of His Life* (1883), II, 183.
65. F. W. Robertson, *Sermons on Religion and Life* (1906), p. 136, a sermon of March 1851.
66. Mill, *Letters*, II, 144.
67. G. M. Young, *Early Victorian England* (1934), II, 346.
68. Kathleen Heasman, *Evangelicals in Action* (1962), p. 15.

and asked me whether he should read them, I told him, 'By no means. They will disturb your mind with questions which you are too young to solve. Stick to the old truths and the old paths, and learn their divineness by sick beds and in every-day work and do not darken your mind with intellectual puzzles, which may breed disbelief, but can never breed vital religion, or practical usefulness.'[69]

Kingsley might protect his curate from disquietude in this fashion in 1861, but he knew himself that the power of secular science had to be reckoned with. Two years later he said to F. D. Maurice 'Darwinism is conquering everywhere, and rushing in like a flood, by the mere force of truth and fact.' Churchmen were being forced to choose between 'the absolute empire of accident, and a living immanent ever-working God'.

> Grover's truly great mind has seized the latter alternative already, on the side of chemistry. Ansted is feeling for it in geology; and so is Lyell; and I, in my small way of zoology, am urging it on Huxley, Rolleston, and Bates, who has just discovered facts about certain butterflies in the valley of the Amazon, which have filled me, and, I trust, others with utter astonishment and awe. Verily, God is great, or else there is no God at all.[70]

Kingsley was not the only clergyman who began to admit that the 'greatness, wisdom and perpetual care' of God had never really been understood until he 'became a convert to Darwin's views'. Those like him, who believed that Darwin's work 'helps mine at every turn',[71] were a minority in the Church—but they were an important and creative minority, representative of the intellectual power which churchmen could put to work, when they decided to 'baptize' the intellectual ferment of the age.

69. Kingsley, *Letters*, II, 123.
70. *Ibid.*, p. 155.
71. *Ibid.*

2. The Church and Darwinism

THE IMPORTANCE of Darwinism was that it brought traditional meta-physics down to earth, and introduced the idea that chance, rather than divine providence is responsible for the natural order. If man could discover how this system of chance developed, he might be able to influence it, and even produce a way of life where he could attain perfection and happiness by complete adaptation to the conditions of existence. The introduction of a new scientific metaphysics was more upsetting to traditional religion than the suggestion that the accepted story of mankind's origin was erroneous.

Darwin himself wrote as a naturalist, wisely limiting himself to the field of natural history in the production of his *Origin of Species*, which came out in 1859. He admitted that he was not the only thinker who had considered 'modification of species' rather than 'separate acts of creation', and that others had believed that the modification was affected by natural selection. In fact, in the later editions of his *Origin of Species*, he lists thirty-four authors who had come to these opinions independently of his teaching. He also left room for the action of a Creator in his hypothesis. 'There is grandeur in this view of life, with its several powers, having been originally breathed by the Creator into a few forms or into one; and that, whilst this planet has gone cycling on according to the fixed law of gravity, from so simple a beginning endless forms most beautiful and most wonderful have been, and are being evolved.'[1]

Prior to Darwin, scholars generally made a rigid distinction between the world of matter and the world of life. The material world was one order of existence, but man, mind, and morals were viewed as part of a spiritual order. But Darwin demonstrated that individual species of plants and animals evolved by natural means from previously existing plants and animals. Once Darwin had provided the hypothesis of evolution with a solid basis of scientific fact, metaphysical specula-tion began about the origin of life, and the ultimate origin of species. Man was swept into the evolutionary pattern of life, and the logic of the new science was applied to all forms of human activity—to mind, to morals, and to society. A revolution began to take place, not only in science, but in philosophy, in man's concept of himself and his works.

After 1859 there began to appear a new ethics, a new psychology, a

1. Charles Darwin, on the *Origin of Species* (London, 1906), p. 670. In his *Life and Letters* (1887), I, 282 he says it is 'impossible to conceive this immense and wonderful universe . . . as the result of blind chance or necessity'.

new history, a new philosophy, all influenced by the new logic of science; as it was generally accepted that knowledge of the universe yielded knowledge of society. Ideas of struggle of the 'fittest' and survival of the 'best' were used to justify many forms of social conflict, like those of class, of nation, and of race.[2] Herbert Spencer became famous as the popularizer of the new theory of evolution. He was dismissed by some as the philosopher whom those who have no other philosopher can appreciate, but nevertheless he had great influence. The idea was now in the air that, with sufficiency of scientific knowledge, society would become utopian. Spencer believed the evolutionary process was slow, but there was beginning to 'arise in human nature and institutions, changes having that permanence which makes them an acquired inheritance for the human race'.[3]

Beatrice Webb believed that this 'belief in science and the scientific method' was 'certainly the most salient, as it was the most original element of the mid-Victorian Time-Spirit'.[4] She recognized the limitations of people like Spencer, who wrote his *Biology* without having read *Origin of Species*, and she was as much distressed as Leslie Stephen over the 'scientism' of the period—like that of the critics of the popular reviews, 'young gentlemen . . . who have a jaunty mode of pronouncing upon all conceivable topics without even affecting to have studied the subject'.[5] But people like Beatrice Webb and Leslie Stephen knew that slowly a new concept of the meaning of human existence was beginning to appear, and it was based on popular 'scientism'. The young Lord Balfour reported in the 1860's that his barber talked of 'the doctrine of evolution, Darwin and Huxley and the lot of them—hashed up somehow with the good time coming and the universal brotherhood, and I don't know what else'.[6]

The acceptance of 'scientism' as a faith can be seen clearly in the thought of the physicist, John Tyndall. Darwin had expressed himself willing to admit a Divine Creator as the first cause of evolutionary life, but Tyndall thought this unnecessary and unreasonable. Through

---

2. Andrew Carnegie, *The Gospel of Wealth and other timely essays* (New York, 1900), p. 13, used Darwinian philosophy to justify the evolution of an ideal State in which 'the surplus wealth of the few will become . . . the property of the many, because administered for the common good.' He believed economic individualism led to 'the elevation of our race'.

3. Herbert Spencer, *Study of Sociology* (1873), p. 349.

4. Webb, *My Apprenticeship*, p. 123.

5. Leslie Stephen, 'The First Edinburgh Reviewers', *Hours in a Library* (1899), II, 248–49.

6. C. F. Harrold and W. D. Templeman, *English Prose of the Victoria Era* (1938), p. lvii.

what he called 'intellectual necessity' and a 'vision of the mind', he made a leap of faith into agnosticism.

> Believing as I do in the continuity of Nature, I cannot stop where our microscopes cease to be of use. Here the vision of the mind authoritatively supplements the vision of the eye. By an intellectual necessity I cross the boundary of the experimental evidence, and discern in that Matter which we, in our ignorance of its latent powers, and not withstanding our professed reverence for its Creator, have hitherto covered with opprobrium, the promise and potency of all terrestrial life.[7]

Others joined him in this act of 'intellectual necessity'. When Harriet Martineau and Henry Atkinson produced their 'exposition of avowed atheism and materialism', Charlotte Brontë recorded her horror over what it implied: 'If this be Truth, man or woman who beholds her can but curse the day he or she was born.'[8] Like Carlyle she realized that, if man was no more than a developed animal, then 'moral sentiments were only a disguised form of selfishness, and life was without any moral purpose'.[9]

Their anxiety was justified; there were men in the Victorian age who were eager to use Darwinian 'scientism' to justify selfish social attitudes, in the same way that Benthamite arguments had been used in an earlier time. Herbert Spencer taught that the 'purifying process' by which the animal kingdom rid itself of its sickly, crippled, and aged could also be discerned at work in human society: 'The poverty of the incapable, the distresses that come upon the imprudent, the starvation of the idle, and those shoulderings aside of the weak by the strong, which leave so many "in shallows and in miseries" are the decrees of a large, far-seeing benevolence'.[10] Like Andrew Carnegie and John D. Rockefeller in America, he justified the rapacity of the aggressive man of business as 'a survival of the fittest . . . the working out of a law of nature and a law of God.'[11] He also used Darwinism to justify the 'jingoistic' war and militarism of the last half of the century, while contemporaries saw in the new gospel support for their theories of white racial superiority.[12]

All the intellectuals influenced by Darwin were not conservative in their social policies, however, and their liberalism was also stimulated by the new concepts. If there was mutability in nature, and in the

7. D. C. Somervell, *English Thought in the Nineteenth Century* (1929), p. 134.
8. E. C. Gaskell, *The Life of Charlotte Brontë* (London, New York, 1908), p. 329.
9. J. A. Froude, *Thomas Carlyle: A History of his Life in London, 1834–1881* (London, 1884), II, 259.
10. Herbert Spencer, *Social Statics* (1851), p. 323.
11. W. J. Ghent, *Our Benevolent Feudalism* (1902), p. 29.
12. W. E. Houghton, *Victorian Frame of Mind* (1959), pp. 209–13.

human organism, why not in human society? Perhaps man altered himself by attempting to change environmental forces? If all thought of cosmic determinism was left out of the picture, could man, with his intelligence, not be viewed as a being living in a new stage of evolutionary development—a stage when man transformed his life by creating culture? Darwinists of this school were not willing to adopt the idea of people like Spencer which identified the 'prosperity of the wicked' with the 'success of the Adapted'.[13] The progress they were interested in was social; and it would come about, they believed, not through the survival of the fittest, but through education and through social reform. Thomas Huxley, in the address entitled *Evolution and Ethics*, which he delivered shortly before his death, reminded his contemporaries that those who survived in the human as well as in other species tended to be the strongest and most self-assertive, rather than the ethically best. Man still had the problem of curbing his passions in society.[14]

Society and its problems became of great importance to the Victorians in the latter half of the century, and this new interest reflected the appearance of the new Darwinian metaphysics. Beatrice Webb suggested that 'it was during the middle decades of the nineteenth century that, in England, the impulse of self-subordinating service was transferred consciously and overtly from God to man.'[15] Most Victorian intellectuals who were influenced by the new 'scientism' were aware of how *they* ought to behave in society, for their conscience formed by generations of Christianity, told them that clearly enough. But with their doubts about traditional religion, they wondered why they should continue to do so, and what ethics should be developed for society with the aid of the new scientific outlook. The attempt of men like Auguste Comte to develop a 'religion of humanity', which was propagated in England by Frederick Harrison and others, was dismissed by Miss Webb as an attempt by 'poor humanity' to turn 'its head round and worship its tail'.[16] She believed that the authority of most of the secular idealists of the time came from public opinion, for which she had little respect. With most of her thoughtful contemporaries she was unwilling to jettison completely the Christian concepts upon which society had hitherto been built.[17] The Social

13. E. A. Ross, *Social Control* (1904), p. 392.
14. T. H. Huxley, *Evolution and Ethics* (1894), pp. 80–85.
15. Webb, *My Apprenticeship*, p. 123. *Cf. supra*, p. viii.
16. *Ibid.*, p. 129.
17. N. G. Annan, *Leslie Stephen* (1951), p. 198. 'I now believe in nothing, to put it shortly, but I do not the less believe in morality etc.'

order had to be reshaped, because the new service of man demanded reform, but few were willing to abandon completely the idea of transcendental authority. 'Practically we are all positivists; we all make the service of man the leading doctrine of our lives. But in order to serve humanity we need inspiration from a superhuman force towards which we are perpetually striving.'[18]

The truth was that even in the universities there were few men who could come to terms intellectually with the new ideas of the Darwinists. The reviewers and the polemicists of the 'Halls of Science' of the age, like Charles Bradlaugh, had their day because most educated people had no tradition of serious reading apart from divinity and the classics. The good news that 'religion was exploded' could be preached by men unqualified to discuss physical science, let alone pronounce upon metaphysical truths, because of the narrowness of English education.

The reading public of Victorian England was much larger than it had been in the eighteenth century, but formal education had broadened very little. T. H. Huxley said that in 1868 the public schools taught mathematics and classics, but ignored geography, history, literature and 'the whole circle of the sciences, physical, moral and social'. A young man of privilege could attend one of the great public schools yet never be taught 'that the earth goes around the sun; that England underwent a great revolution in 1688, and France another in 1789; that there once lived certain notable men, called Chaucer, Shakespeare, Milton, Voltaire, Goethe, Schiller'.[19] Although reform began at Oxford in the 1850's, the university had for so long been 'a citadel of ecclesiasticism and the arena of ecclesiastical dispute' that science was virtually exiled from the university and mathematics had but a slight influence.[20] Walter Besant claimed that the young men who came up to Cambridge in the fifties had seldom travelled beyond their villages or country towns. They were 'wholly ignorant of the world, of society, of literature, of everything. . . . It is difficult in these days to understand the depth, and the extent, and the intensity of the ignorance of those lads.'[21] The new prophets of secular dogma had little to fear in the way of rebuttal from the literate

18. Webb, *My Apprenticeship*, p. 129. H. G. Wood, *Belief and Unbelief Since 1850* (1955), p. 102, says that for many Victorians 'the foundations of morality seemed more secure than the foundations of their religious faith, or rather the firmness of the foundations of morality underpinned and helped to secure the structure of their religious faith.'
19. T. H. Huxley, 'A Liberal Education and Where to Find It', *Science and Education, Essays* (1893), p. 94.
20. Goldwin Smith, *Reminiscences* (1910), p. 99.
21. Walter Besant, *Autobiography* (1902), p. 83.

public who were so influenced by the writers of the popular reviews, to the distress of Beatrice Webb and Leslie Stephen.[22] What secular opposition was encountered by the Darwinists came from those who censured the new ideas from the point of view of the property-holder. They were not pleased that Darwin published his *Descent of Man* in 1871, 'revealing his zoological conclusions to the general public at a moment when the sky of Paris was red with the incendiary flames of the Commune'.[23]

3. Essays and Reviews

WHEN AN attempt is made to judge the reaction of the Church to Darwinism and its new mythology, the encounter of the two systems of belief must not be taken out of historical context. Victorian England was subject to the pressures of the increase in population, the Industrial Revolution, and the turbulent political forces which were at work in the 1860's. It was also in the midst of a great religious revival. As Professor Kitson Clark has reminded many secular historians who tend to abstract from history only what they wish to emphasize, 'it is necessary to think of the years which followed 1859 not as years of an acute crisis of the mind but rather as the years of the great religious revivals among people who were probably little troubled by Darwinism and had certainly never read *Essays and Reviews*.'[1] The Church, as a whole, can hardly be blamed if it was primarily concerned with what it considered to be a time of Christian 'break-through' in England, rather than with the uncertainties raised by Darwinism in the minds of an intellectual minority. The Church took seriously its role as the conscience, or soul, of the whole nation, and because the privileged and socially important classes were directly influenced by Christianity, it was concerned first of all with their attempt to make all England Christian.

22. *V.* Alvar Ellegard, *Darwin and the General Reader* (1958).
23. John Morley, *Recollections* (1921), I, 92.
1. Kitson Clark, *Making of Victorian England* (1962), p. 148.

All religious denominations engaged with ever-increasing zeal in the attempt to re-convert England, churches and chapels were built, missions despatched, revivals staged; what was spent on that work in the way of human effort and sacrifice, and for that matter of financial expenditure, is one of the really important facts of English history of the nineteenth century. Indeed, if it were possible to add up the numbers of hours spent by human beings hoping, planning and working for selected objectives in the reign of Queen Victoria, it seems possible that the re-conversion of England and the achievement of democracy and abolition of privilege would come highest on the list.[2]

When intelligent agnostics, or militant atheists of the artisan or small shopkeeper class 'were the exception'[3] in society, the Church must surely be excused for paying more attention to the important middle class which was then so enthusiastically Christian.

On the other hand, no excuse could be made for the Church if it deliberately avoided the issues raised by Darwinism, and refused to see in them a challenge which the Christian faith had to meet and encompass, if it was to be truly catholic. *Essays and Reviews* of 1860, and *Lux Mundi* of 1889 both reveal that within the Church there was a creative minority which was able and willing to challenge both the science and the metaphysics of the Darwinists.

Since the publication of *Origin of Species*, much has been made of the conflict of religion and science, and in the popular imagination the typical Victorian cleric has been cast as a blind obscurantist—someone like Samuel Wilberforce, who had his unfortunate dispute with T. H. Huxley at the Oxford meeting of the British Association in 1860. Wilberforce was pressed into service by conservative scientists at the meeting because of his speaking ability. Then, 'crammed to the throat' with scientific information which he did not really understand he ridiculed Darwin badly, and Huxley savagely. Finally, with smiling insolence, he begged to know from Huxley whether it was through his grandfather or his grandmother that he claimed to be descended from a monkey. The 'agnostic' gleefully murmured to his neighbour, Sir Benjamin Brodie, 'the Lord hath delivered him into mine hands', and proceeded to make a speech which ended with the words: 'If I am asked whether I should choose to be descended from the poor animal of low intelligence and stooping gait, who grins and chatters as we pass, or from a man endowed with great ability and splendid position who should use these gifts to discredit humble seekers after truth, I hesitate what answer to make.'[4] The press largely ignored the Wilberforce-Huxley clash,[5] but Huxley's encounter with clerical

2. *Ibid.*, p. 284.   3. *Ibid.*, p. 148.
4. L. Huxley, *Life and Letters of T. H. Huxley* (1903), I, 268–69.
5. Ellegård, *Darwin and the General Reader*, p. 68.

obscurantism has become an important story in Darwinian hagio-graphy.

What is often overlooked is the conservatism of the British Association at this time, with regard to Darwin's theory. The Presidential Address by Lord Wrottesley contained several references to the Deity, but none to Darwin. Wilberforce was not versed in science, but he was speaking on the soundness or unsoundness of the Darwinian theory as a philosophy, after reading *The Origin of Species*. His speech made 'a great impression'[6] among most scientists at the meeting who objected to Darwin's theories, rather than to the scientific evidence upon which they were based.

The fact of the matter was that churchmen responded just as other Victorians did to the popular presentation of what amounted to a new teleology. In a letter to Lyell, which he wrote in December, 1859, Darwin remarked on a zoologist friend who had promised to read Darwin's book only after he had solemnly assured the author he would never believe it.[7] Some churchmen responded to the new challenge in this fashion. But others wondered why it was more irreligious to explain the origin of man as a distinct species from some lower form than to explain the birth of the individual through the laws of ordinary reproduction.

Charles Kingsley had doubts about the wisdom of his curate engaging in abstract speculation about the issues raised by *Essays and Reviews*, but he himself managed to explore the new ways of thought intelligently. In a letter to Darwin dated November, 1859, he said: 'I have gradually learnt to see that it is just as noble a conception of Deity, to believe that He created primal form capable of self development into all forms needful *pro tempore & pro loco*, as to believe that He required a fresh act of intervention to supply the *lacunas* which He himself had made. I question whether the former be not the loftier thought.'[8] Three years later he became vice-president of a club, with T. H. Huxley as president, which had the purpose of bringing together in London 'scientific and philosophic men ... who care to know and speak the truth'. This society 'for the propagation of common honesty in all parts of the world' accomplished little, but it is significant that it contained churchmen like Kingsley.[9]

The scholarly F. J. A. Hort of Trinity College, Cambridge, after

6. *Life of Wilberforce*, II, 451.
7. Francis Darwin, *Life and Letters of Charles Darwin* (1921), II, 237.
8. *Ibid.*, p. 287.
9. *Life of Huxley*, I, 214 ff.

reading Darwin's works and those of the popularizers, said: 'the scientific question is a very complicated one—far more complicated than Darwin seems to have any idea.'[10] He considered *The Origin of Species* 'a book one is proud to be contemporary with',[11] but as a scholar he knew how much more evidence had to be found before the extreme claim of the Darwinists could be seriously considered. He refused to say anything about it himself in scholarly journals because he would need to spend 'months and months of thinking' about Darwin's theories, or be guilty of uttering 'brief and cloudy oracles'.[12]

The obscurantists among the clergy, particularly those of the Evangelical school, and many of the Tractarians, made a great deal of noise over the acceptance of some of the Darwinian insights by liberal churchmen; but, as we shall see in our discussion of *Essays and Reviews*, much of their reaction reflected anxiety about Church-and-State tension, and revealed party struggle within the Church rather than an outright and blind rejection of science as such. By 1870 a conservative churchman like H. P. Liddon could write: 'Evolution from a Theistic point of view is merely one way of describing what we can observe of God's continuous action upon the physical world.'[13] In the north, the Archbishop of York, William Thomson, sought to find a meeting ground for religion and science throughout the 1860's.[14] On the whole, it seems that the clergy bided their time to see what could be made of the new scientific insights from the philosophical and theological standpoints. John Tyndall, the agnostic physicist and one-time colleague of Michael Faraday, admitted the open-mindedness of most of the clergy whom he met. In one meeting in 'an ancient London College with three or four hundred of them, who were, I should say, to be ranked among the finest samples of their class' he observed that because of the new ideas that were in the air they 'had entirely given up the ancient landmarks, and transported the conception of life's origin to an indefinitely distant past'.[15]

One of the reasons why the clergy did not panic over the theories of the Darwinists was the influence of *The Guardian*, the weekly Anglican newspaper founded in 1846 by R. W. Church, Frederick Rogers, and others to show the relevance of the Church and its doctrines to the best secular thought of the age. The writers in *The*

10. Hort, *Life and Letters of F. J. A. Hort*, I, 433.
11. *Ibid.*, p. 416.
12. *Ibid.*, p. 415.
13. H. P. Liddon, *Some Elements of Religion* (1881), p. 56.
14. H. Kirk-Smith, *William Thomson* (1958), p. 139.
15. J. Tyndall, *Fragments of Science* (1889), II, 130.

Guardian believed that 'only a religion which is a way of living in every sphere either deserves to or can hope to survive.'[16] They believed that Anglican assumptions had to be 'closed with and tested face to face in the light of fact and history',[17] and they tried to welcome what they saw to be of benefit to society. When the French had their revolution in 1848, Church said of the Socialism of the time:

> Socialism adopts the great commandment of charity as the scientific and practicable basis of civilized legislation. . . . It does not reject religion like the old infidels; it but professes to complete Christianity. It takes up, not with less faith, but with more philosophy, what Christianity failed in. Christianity it says started from the right point, the poor; it took them, and not the rich, as the true essence of society, not with modern economists, as an inconvenient accident.[18]

Church was just as willing to welcome the insights of Darwinism as he was to justify what he saw to be beneficial in Socialism.

Because of his sound Incarnational theology, Church could say: 'Surely a Christian need not be afraid to honour all that is excellent in civilization as being in whatever way from His own Master, Whose awful mind and will is reflected in the Universe.'[19] The review of *Origin of Species* which appeared in *The Guardian*, 8 February 1860, was almost certainly written by him. Not only was the review sympathetic to Darwin's startling hypothesis—'time alone and the discussion of the learned will set the seal of value upon his speculations'[20]—but it also revealed an ability to cope with scientific detail, and recognition of the value of the vast research which underlay Darwin's theory.

Church was an amateur scientist with a small laboratory in his rectory in which he dabbled in chemistry. He was also a close friend of Dr. Asa Gray of Harvard University, who was a devout Christian as well as the man who made Cambridge the American centre for botanical study. Both Church and Gray knew Darwin personally, and because of this association, and Church's critical reading, he had given Darwin's ideas much thought before the *Origin of Species* appeared.

---

16. *Church Quarterly Review* (1955), CLVI, 9. Words of A. C. MacIntyre.

17. Smith, *Dean Church*, p. 51. When John Seeley's *Ecce Homo* appeared in 1865, Church thoughtfully reviewed it in *The Guardian*, although Shaftesbury called it 'the most pestilential book ever vomited from the jaws of hell'. *V.* S. L. Ollard and G. Crosse, *Anglo-Catholic Revival in Outline* (1933), p. 53.

18. R. W. Church, *Essays and Reviews* (1854), p. 294. First published in *Christian Remembrancer*, July, 1848.

19. R. W. Church, *Gifts of Civilization* (1898), p. 11.

20. Smith, *Dean Church*, p. 136.

He failed to see how the theory of evolution necessarily postulated the atheistic inferences which so many people found in it. 'Mr. Darwin's book . . . is the book of science which has produced most impression here of any book which has appeared for many years. . . . One wishes such a book to be more explicit. But it is wonderful 'shortness of thought' to treat the theory itself as incompatible with ideas of a higher and spiritual order.'[21]

One churchman who was a self-confessed evolutionist was Baden Powell, Savilian Professor of Geometry at Oxford. A mathematician, he arrived at his conclusions through deductive reasoning; he accepted the new geological evidence which seemed to indicate that new species originated from pre-existing organic forms. He also accepted evolution as an evidence of divine design in the universe. To Baden Powell the real issue between the evolutionists and their opponents was 'whether we suppose the Creator to construct a machine which, once adjusted, shall go on fulfilling its work, or one which at successive periods shall require manual interposition'.[22]

Baden Powell welcomed controversy and was a respected opponent of both Tractarianism and Evangelicalism. He particularly detested the Sabbatarianism of the latter party, which taught that after twelve o'clock on a Saturday night it was sinful to read off a scientific scale. Because of this, 'extensive tables' were printed in his day with every seventh entry filled up with the word 'Sunday' instead of degrees, minutes, and seconds.[23] The biblical fundamentalism of the Evangelicals, especially in Old Testament study, also filled him with fury. He scornfully proclaimed that anyone who believed in the Mosaic cosmogony ought, 'by party of reason', to also believe in the Ptolemaic system and in transubstantiation.[24]

He was very upsetting to his contemporaries. In one work entitled *The Order of Nature* he brought the new insights in astronomy, geology, and natural history to bear on theology, and argued that miracles, such as those recorded in Scripture, could not be accepted by an enlightened man of the age.[25] To the great annoyance of the Evangelicals, he argued that there was as much evidence for the ecclesiastical miracles that the Tractarians had loved as there was for the Gospel miracles. As far as Baden Powell was concerned, if the

21. J. J. Gray, *Letters of Asa Gray* (1893), II, p. 264.
22. Benn, *Rationalism in the Nineteenth Century*, II, 94.
23. *Ibid.*, p. 95.
24. Baden Powell, *Revelation and Science* (1833), p. 6, a discourse at St. Mary the Virgin, Oxford, 8 March, 1829.
25. Baden Powell, *The Order of Nature* (1859), p. 202.

Evangelicals labelled the Fathers of the Church and their miracles untrustworthy, the Evangelists also had to be accepted as untrustworthy, and their miracles equally incredible.

The academic liberalism of a clerical scientist like Baden Powell brought angry protests from many conservative churchmen; but outside clerical and anti-clerical party circles his ideas excited little attention. This changed, however, when he joined together with a group of Broad-Churchmen like Benjamin Jowett, the Regius Professor of Greek at Oxford, and Mark Pattison, the Rector of Lincoln College, Oxford, in the writing of *Essays and Reviews* which was published in 1860.

The volume contained seven essays, each written by a different churchman. A notice to the reader explained that each writer was responsible for his own work, but that all of them hoped that the volume would 'be received as an attempt to illustrate the advantage derivable to the cause of religious and moral truth, from a free handling, in a becoming spirit, of subjects peculiarly liable to suffer by the repetition of conventional language and from traditional treatment'. Jowett said they produced the volume in reaction to the 'terrorism' of the ecclesiastical conservatives at Oxford who had crushed the Tractarians and were now turning on the liberals.[26]

Jowett never referred directly to the idea of evolution which was 'in the air' by the time of *Essays and Reviews*, but it appears everywhere in his thought. He argued that there were 'two witnesses of the Being of God; the order of nature in the world, and the progress of the mind of man'.[27] His acquaintanceship with evolutionary thought was strengthened by what he considered to be the greatest progress yet made by man in theological thought—the liberalism of German theologians like Ferdinand Baur of the Tubingen school. He devoted himself to using 'those principles, whether of criticism or of morality, which in our age we cannot but feel and know'.[28] As a student of Hegel and Comte, as well as the German theologians like Baur, Jowett was far ahead of the educated public opinion of his day, and many suspected his orthodoxy. They were also suspicious of Mark Pattison, who had a wide range of out-of-the-way knowledge and a dislike of all systems which conceived religion as supernatural and historical—as did Tractarianism.

Within a year of its publication, the little book of essays by six

26. 'Essays and Reviews', *Dictionary English Church History*, p. 208.
27. Benjamin Jowett, *Epistles of St. Paul* (1859), II, 414.
28. Benn, II, 88.

priests and a pious layman produced the same sort of hysteria which had earlier been associated with *Tracts for the Times*, the Hampden case, and the Gorham controversy. The authors of the book were denounced as 'Septem Contra Christum', and both the press and the pulpit throughout the nation spread indignation and panic.

Jowett and other churchmen of the liberal school, like A. P. Stanley and F. J. A. Hort, had foreseen the uproar; and Hort had expressed his fear that 'a premature crisis would frighten many back into the merest traditionalism.'[29] But the public reaction was even greater than that anticipated. This was a 'fallen languid' age, as Carlyle said, not one of 'peaceful triumphant motion'. When so many Victorians of the educated classes were 'destitute of faith, but terrified at scepticism', the attempt of the essayists to bring the Gospel to society in terms of the most advanced idiom of the age was sure to provoke intense reaction.[30] They forced upon an unwilling public open discussion of religious questions which it preferred to ignore. This was the great service rendered by the seven revolutionaries.

The theological liberalism of men like Thomas Arnold, eclipsed as it had been for so long by the Tractarian controversy, was bound to reassert itself. Able churchmen like Jowett could not in conscience keep quiet while they beheld 'the steady, inch-by-inch retreat of "religion" before geology, and the vain attempts to preserve it by making it fill up the remaining interstices of science'.[31] They knew that the 'God of the gaps' would never satisfy the minds of the young intellectuals at the universities. Convinced as they were that the Incarnation influenced all aspects of the created world, they believed they could present the Gospel to a sceptical generation in terms other than those used by 'conventional Christianity into which no one is to enquire, which is always being patched and plastered with evidences and apologies'.[32]

The first essay, 'The Education of the World', was by Frederick Temple, then Headmaster of Rugby, later Archbishop of Canterbury. It had provoked little opposition, when first presented as a sermon, or when it was expanded into essay form for *Essays and Reviews*. It was a mild and temperate account of the progressive understanding of revelation in the light of the conscience. The essay written by the

---

29. Hort, I, 400.
30. Thomas Carlyle, 'Sir Walter Scott', *Critical and Miscellaneous Essays* (London, 1857), IV, 159.
31. Basil Willey, *More Nineteenth Century Studies* (1956), p. 140.
32. Evelyn Abbott and L. Campbell, *Life and Letters of Benjamin Jowett* (1897), II, 348.

Cambridge layman, C. W. Goodwin of Christ's College, was more upsetting because it protested against the 'theological geologists' who attempted to reconcile the Mosaic story of Creation with what was being discovered in astronomy and geology. The 'Mosaic Cosmogony' could not be explained away as having poetic, mystical, or symbolical meaning. It represented the speculation of the Hebrew Descartes or Newton of that day—the most probable account that could be given of God's universe by another age.

The essays of Rowland Williams, Vice-Principal of Lampeter, and H. B. Wilson, Vicar of Great Staughton, were considered to be especially offensive because they dealt in an irreverent manner with Scripture. Williams discussed 'Bunsen's Biblical Researches' in what even A. P. Stanley called a flippant and contemptuous tone, and Wilson called for a relaxation of subscription to formularies—greater freedom in teaching for the clergy, and latitude in belief for the laity, including some 'demythologizing' of the Bible. The popular indignation was so great against these two writers that legal proceedings were instigated, and both of them were condemned by the Dean of Arches, Dr. Lushington, in December, 1862. When they were suspended from service in their benefices, they appealed to the Judicial Committee of the Privy Council. It found that the appellants had not, in the passages their accusers criticized, directly contradicted the formularies of the Church; and their sentence was reversed in February 1864. The two archbishops dissented from part of the Privy Council judgment, and public interest in the proceedings was such that a petition of thanks for their abstention was received by the two prelates, signed by 137,000 laymen. Previously they had received a declaration on the Inspiration of Scripture signed by 11,000 clergy.

Mark Pattison's 'Tendencies of Religious Thought in England, 1688–1750' was a piece of original research. It was disturbing because it introduced the concept that religious ideas had a history whose origins and growth had to be explained. If religious ideas had a history, and changed with the times, perhaps contemporary beliefs reflected the needs of the Victorian age, just as the rational and utilitarian teachings of the eighteenth century satisfied the Christians of that time?

Professor Baden Powell entitled his essay 'On the Study of the Evidences of Christianity'; and, as might be expected from such a thorough-going evolutionist, it appeared to be the Tract XC of the new Oxford movement. In substance it was a summary of the arguments already put forward by the Savilian Professor in his work,

168

Order of Nature; and in many ways it was his philosophical testament, for he died immediately after the volume was published. He directly referred to Darwin, and rebuked those who opposed the spirit of the age by attacking honest doubters on moral grounds. Miracles he dismissed as something at variance with both nature and law, together with other historical 'facts' accepted as evidences for Christianity, but without usual historical tests being applied to them. Baden Powell's convenient demise probably spared him the embarrassment of also being hailed before the Dean of Arches.

The last essay, by Benjamin Jowett, was the longest and weightiest of all. It demanded that the Bible be read 'like any other book', and was the well-thought-out work of one who was 'determined not to submit to this abominable system of terrorism, which prevents the statement of the plainest fact, and makes true theology or theological education impossible'.[33] The time had come when advanced criticism of the Bible could no longer be ignored in England. No longer could a rearguard action be fought with the geologists, biologists, and philologists—rather, the results of new scientific criticism of the natural order and of the Bible had to be welcomed. No Christian should be forced to feel obliged to apply to the Bible methods of interpretation which they would think dishonest to use in studying a classical author.

The condemnation of the volume did not really begin until Frederick Harrison reviewed it in an article entitled 'Neo-Christianity' in the *Westminster Review* for October 1860. A one-time High-Churchman, by 1860 he had become a devoted disciple of Comte with the belief that Christianity, as the ultimate form of theology, was now approaching extinction. In the article he says that the 'crumbling edifice' of the Church is too ruinous to be repaired, and he welcomes the work of the essayists who are helping in the work of demolition. At the same time he displays a certain jealousy over the work of the essayists who are trying to put forth a Neo-Christianity, a living organism with powers of growth and adaptation to a changing environment. Harrison did not appreciate a new form of Christianity succeeding the old, rather than his new faith in Humanity. He wanted the essayists to reveal their true colours as Positivists, or else react to the new environmental challenges in the way that Harrison expected all 'English Protestantism' would react. As far as Harrison was concerned, churchmen who, like Jowett, were not biblical fundamentalists were not Christian. The new disciple of Comte had a premonition that if Neo-Christianity was accepted by the educated classes in England it

33. *Life of Jowett*, I, 275.

would likely absorb the religion of Humanity, rather than be absorbed by it.

The reaction of the episcopate to the essayists was conditioned by the conduct of Samuel Wilberforce, who rushed to the defence of orthodoxy to save the Church from contagion. Like Carlyle, he considered the liberals sentries who ought to be shot for deserting their posts at a time of crisis when the Church needed to be defended, but privately Wilberforce may have shared many of the doubts of Carlyle about matters like miracles and the personality of God.[34] What he chiefly objected to was the 'infidelity' of the work, which weakened the Church in its mission.

The anxiety of Wilberforce was shared by most members of the Church because, at the time of the crisis over *Essays and Reviews*, J. W. Colenso, the Bishop of Natal, brought out his critical works on Romans and the Pentateuch. He had been asked by an intelligent native, who was helping him translate the Pentateuch into Zulu, whether he really believed stories like that of the Deluge were all true. Colenso found that he was unable to say that they were. This led him to approach the Old Testament critically and, because of his training, from the standpoint of a mathematician. He said, for example, that he could not see how it was possible for the seventy souls who accompanied Jacob down into Egypt to grow into the two and a half to three million souls who left Egypt in the Exodus. When Colenso also began to question matters like the traditional authorship of the books of the Pentateuch, conservative churchmen reacted almost as strongly to his ideas as they had to those of the essayists.[35]

Not only did Wilberforce persuade the whole episcopal bench, including Connop Thirlwall of St. David's, and R. D. Hampden of Hereford, to join in a collective denunciation of *Essays and Reviews*,[36] but he preached against it at Oxford, and wrote an article in the *Quarterly Review* of January 1861 which agreed with Harrison's earlier article about the tendencies of the writers. Especially he deplored the biblical criticism of the essayists which tended to destroy all notion of inspiration. Gone, he said, are the old inspired Scriptures, and what is left is a collection of legends, traditions, and poetic writings, which can be identified and interpreted by the intellectuals of each age in the way that is most appealing to them. Holy Scripture

34. This was Carlyle's opinion. *V*. Froude's *Life of Carlyle*, IV, 419.
35. Peter Hinchcliff, *John William Colenso* (1964), p. 81, indicates how Colenso upset contemporaries by suggesting toleration of polygamy.
36. *Life of Wilberforce*, III, 5.

is either a system of supernaturalism or a falsehood; and those who are tainted by German theology, like the English Deists and French Atheists of an earlier age, need to recognize this. To advance the views found in *Essays and Reviews*, and to continue to serve as Church of England clergymen was moral dishonesty.

The essayists had few open defenders. Dean Stanley attempted to defend them in a partial and apologetic spirit in the *Edinburgh Review* of April 1861, but the public panic did not subside when he assured his readers that half the rising generation of churchmen, including a quarter of the bishops and the leading spirits among the clergy, accepted much that was taught by the new theology coming out of Germany.[37] Because of this panic, the liberals among the clergy bided their time and tried to avoid adding to already existing controversy. But their influence was considerable; and, as Dean Stanley said, the ideas of Neo-Christianity were widespread. Pusey drew up the declaration on the Inspiration of Scripture which 11,000 clergy signed —but many may have signed it through fear of man rather than love of truth. Many prominent churchmen did not sign it. Out of thirty deans only eight adhered to Pusey's declaration; out of forty Oxford professors only nine signed it; and only one professor at Cambridge agreed with Pusey's document which called upon the clergy to sign it 'for the love of God'.[38]

Many churchmen were thankful for the established position of the Church during this time of ecclesiastical hysteria. Without the possibility of appeal to the Privy Council as a caution to clerical extravagance, a full-scale witch-hunt might have occurred. Wilberforce engineered a synodical condemnation of the essayists in Convocation but the lawfulness of this action was questioned in the House of Lords, and Lord Chancellor Westbury described the so-called synodical judgment as 'a well-lubricated set of words, a sentence so oily and saponaceous that no one can grasp it—like an eel it slips through your fingers, and is simply nothing'.[39] 'Soapy Sam' delivered a weighty rebuke to such secular ribaldry, but from this time, apart from the flurry of excitement over the appointment of Temple to the see of Exeter in 1869,[40] the issue of *Essays and Reviews* was allowed

37. *V.* the reaction of the *British and Foreign Evangelical Review* (1861), pp. 407–30, in its article on 'The Oxford Essayists—Their Relation to Christianity and to Strauss and Baur'.

38. Benn, p. 134.

39. A. O. J. Cockshut, *Anglican Attitudes* (1959), pp. 79–80.

40. *V.* William Keane, *Protest Against Dr. Temple's Consecration to the Bishopric of Exeter* (n.d.), p. 3, where the Rector of Whitby refers to the possibility of 'sin against the Holy Ghost' in the appointment.

to die, and slowly its ideas were accepted and became commonplace. Because of the intellectual adaptation of churchmen over the next thirty years, the climate of opinion which radically opposed *Essays and Reviews* could give way to the welcome which was extended to *Lux Mundi*. By 1889 most churchmen were willing to agree with Dean Church when he said: 'It seems to me that our apologetic and counter-criticism has let itself be too much governed by the lines of attack and that we have not adequately attempted to face things for ourselves, and in our own way, in order not merely to refute but to construct something positive on our own side'.[41]

4. Lux Mundi

ONE OF those who believed it was imperative that the position taken by the essayists should be seriously questioned, in a reasonable manner, was Brooke Foss Westcott, the future Bishop of Durham, who was then an assistant master at Harrow. He was most indignant at bishops like Prince Lee, the first bishop of Manchester, who merely shrieked abuse at the writers of the controversial essays. His solution to the problems raised by the crisis was the publication of a work, which would be 'a mean between *Essays and Reviews* and Traditionalism'.[1]

> I look on the assailants of the Essayists, from Bishops downwards, as likely to do far more harm to the Church and the Truth than the Essayists. The only result of such a wild clamour must be to make people believe that the voice of authority alone, and not of calm reason, can meet the theories of the Essayists, and thus to wholly give up Truth, and the love of it, to the other side. . . . As far as I have seen, those who have written against the Essayists have been profoundly ignorant of the elements of the difficulties out of which the Essays have sprung.[2]

Westcott wished both Hort and Lightfoot to join with him in the projected study, which would be 'a true mean between the inexorable logic of Westminster and the sceptical dogmatism of orthodoxy';[3]

41. *Life of Dean Church*, p. 342.
1. Arthur Westcott, *Life and Letters of B. F. Westcott* (1903), I, 213.
2. *Ibid.*, p. 215.
3. *Ibid.*, p. 214.

but Lightfoot decided that he could not take part in the undertaking and Westcott abandoned his scheme. *Lux Mundi*, when it appeared in 1889, was the kind of volume that Westcott had seen was necessary as early as 1861.

It was necessary because in intellectual circles the Church was being accused of a 'calm and unobtrusive alienation in thought and spirit from the great silent multitude of Englishmen, and again of alienation from fact and love of fact; mutual alienations both'.[4] During the year following the publication of *Lux Mundi*, J. G. Frazer came out with his entertaining folklore treatise, *The Golden Bough*. Although the first edition was noncommittal about religion and its truth, the second edition was openly hostile. Religion 'stands in fundamental antagonism to science, which takes for granted that the course of nature is not determined by the passions or caprice of personal beings, but by the operation of immutable laws acting mechanically.'[5] Like Auguste Comte, Frazer believed that religion was superseded by science, the new faith of humanity: 'the hope of progress—moral and intellectual as well as material—in the future is bound up with the fortunes of science. . . . every obstacle placed in the way of scientific discovery is a wrong to humanity.'[6] Frazer knew that the Victorians were still willing to say 'I believe' rather than 'one does feel', and few said they 'couldn't care less' about religious matters.[7] The creative minority in the Church also knew this, and it had no intention of abandoning 'love of fact', 'Truth', and 'Reason' to the advocates of the old religion of humanity which was evolving into the new religion of sociology.

Lux Mundi: a Series of Studies in the Religion of the Incarnation was a collection of twelve essays written by eleven Anglican teachers and edited by Charles Gore, who was then Principal of Pusey House. Each of the essays, and the work as a whole, represented the new development that theology had taken in England since *Essays and Reviews*. It was a presentation of the Gospel in terms of new movements in secular thought.

> The real development of theology is . . . the process in which the Church, standing firm in her old truths, enters into the apprehension of the new social and intellectual movements of each age: and because 'the truth makes her free' is able to assimilate all new material, to welcome and give its place to all

4. *Life of Hort*, II, 290, Hort to Archbishop Benson.
5. J. G. Frazer, *The Golden Bough* (New York, 1900), I, 63.
6. *Ibid.*, III, 460.
7. David Lack, *Evolutionary Theory and Christian Belief* (1957), p. 110, taken from R. A. Knox, *Absolute and Abitofhell* (1912).

new knowledge, to throw herself into the sanctification of each new social order, bringing forth out of her treasures things new and old, and shewing again and again her power of witnessing under changed conditions to the catholic capacity of her faith and life.[8]

Gore and the other contributors represented a new 'liberal catholic' party in the Church, which had inherited much from Pusey, Liddon, and others who had emerged out of Tractarianism. But it was also indebted to theologians like Maurice and Westcott. The nature of the Church was of great concern to these new 'catholics', but its role in society was of most importance to them. As in the thought of Maurice and Westcott, the Incarnation was the dominant theme in their theology—the Incarnation which they believed influenced every part of God's Creation. 'We deny the verity of the Incarnation in its principle if we deny the Christian spirit the privilege, aye, and the obligation, to concern itself with everything that interests and touches human life'.[9] The Church, they believed, had to be not only 'implicitly' catholic, but also catholic in the sense of world-wide extension. 'The Catholic Church is that which contains within its resources what can supply the needs of all sorts of men, of all sorts of nations, at all sorts of times, and under all circumstances. This universal resourcefulness and applicability of the Gospel is involved and signified in the word Catholic.'[10]

By the 1880's, the evolutionary theory was influencing every field of research and endeavour, including theology and history. The writers of *Lux Mundi* knew this, and knew that if they hoped to present a 'new theology' to a generation which was influenced by evolutionary theory on all sides, the traditional insights of the Gospel had also to be re-interpreted in terms of the popular way of thought.

> The last few years have witnessed the gradual acceptance by Christian thinkers of the great scientific generalization of our age, which is briefly, if somewhat vaguely, described as the Theory of Evolution. . . . Organisms, nations, languages, institutions, customs, creeds, have all come to be regarded in the light of their development, and we feel that to understand what a thing really is, we must examine how it came to be. Evolution is in the air. It is the category of the age; a *partus temporis*; a necessary consequence of our wider field of comparison. We cannot place ourselves outside it, or limit the scope of its operation. And our religious opinions, like all things else that

8. *Lux Mundi: a Series of Studies in the Religion of the Incarnation*, ed. Charles Gore (1895), p. viii. This is the fourteenth edition.
9. *Report of the Church Congress of 1896*, pp. 566–67.
10. Charles Gore, *Two Addresses on Sin Delivered in Exeter Cathedral* (1899), p. 21.

have come down on the current of development, must justify their existence by an appeal to the past.[11]

Gore and his companions knew as well as Beatrice Webb that belief in science and the scientific method was the most important and most original element in the new thought of Victorian England. They also agreed with her that their generation's impulse of self-subordinating service was turning consciously from God to man. To comprehend the new way of thought and the new ethical concerns, they developed in *Lux Mundi* a theology of the Incarnation, which borrowed more from Greek than Latin theology, and was primarily concerned with God's immanence in history rather than man's deliverance from sin.[12] Aubrey Moore in his essay entitled 'Christian Doctrine of God' refused to accept the 'division of territory' between religion and science suggested by Herbert Spencer—where 'religion is allotted to faith, and philosophy and science to reason'.[13] He scorned the devout who accepted this division. 'The present gaps in science are their stronghold, and they naturally resist every forward step in knowledge as long as they can, because each new discovery limits the area in which alone, according to their imperfect view, faith can live'.[14] Christianity has to do with the whole of man's existence.

> Religion . . . claims as its own the new light which metaphysics and science are in our day throwing upon the truth of the immanence of God: it protests only against those imperfect, because premature, syntheses, which in the interests of abstract speculation, would destroy religion. It dares to maintain that 'the Fountain of wisdom and religion alike is God: and if these two streams shall turn aside from Him, both must assuredly run dry![15]

The only essay that referred at length to the Latin theology that was so important to both the Evangelicals and the Tractarians—'the relation between human sin and the Divine righteousness'—was that of Arthur Lyttleton on the Atonement. But it differed widely from either Evangelical or Tractarian doctrinal standards by repudiating the idea that the Atonement consisted chiefly of Christ's vicarious endurance of punishment deserved by man. Such a belief arises only when the Atonement is isolated from other parts of Christian doctrine. Like the rest of the work of Christ, 'the beginning and the end of the

11. J. R. Illingworth, 'Incarnation and Development', *Lux Mundi*, p. 132.
12. For comment on this development *v.* James Carpenter, *Gore, a Study in Liberal Catholic Thought* (1960), p. 53.
13. *Lux Mundi*, p. 43.
14. *Ibid.*, p. 44.
15. *Ibid.*, p. 81.

Atonement is the love of God';[16] but this can only be realized when the doctrine is presented in its proper relationship to the Incarnation. 'Pardon for the past, deliverance from guilt, propitiation of the just wrath of God, are necessary and all-important; but they cannot stand alone. They must, for man is helpless and weak, be succeeded by the gift of life.'[17] The essay is wordy and confused in argument, but enough emerged from it to upset many conservative churchmen.

W. Lock, the Sub-Warden of Keble College, in his essay on the Church, also stressed the need for it to be able to meet the intellectual challenges of the time. He was more interested in the Church being 'catholic' in terms of social and intellectual influence than in its affirming spiritual prerogatives like that of the apostolic succession, which had been so dear to the Tractarians. The Catholic Church, he said, 'contains in its message truths that can win their way to every nation. . . . it has enshrined, protected, witnessed to the truth; both as an "authoritative republication of natural religion", keeping alive the knowledge of God, and of His moral government of the world, and as a revelation of redemption'.[18] This was the great task of the Church in the age of *Lux Mundi*—the proclamation of the truth through reason and revelation.

> Amid the increasing specialization of studies, amid all the new discoveries of science and historical criticism, with all the perplexities that arise as to the interpretation and inspiration of the Bible, now, if ever, there is need of a Church, which conscious of its own spiritual life, knowing that its spiritual truths have stood the test of centuries, has patience and courage to face all these new facts and see their bearing and take their measure; which all the while shall go on teaching to its children with an absolute but rational authority the central facts of the spiritual life, and shall never doubt the ultimate unity of all truth.[19]

The essayist who dealt with the 'perplexities' caused by the application of evolutionary theory to biblical criticism was Gore himself. His contribution, entitled 'The Holy Spirit and Inspiration', excited most public attention because the vast majority of English Christians still believed that the Old Testament account of creation was strictly historical, in spite of the publication of *Essays and Reviews* and Colenso's work on the Pentateuch. Gore argued that the Old

16. *Ibid.*, p. 226.   17. *Ibid.*, p. 220.
18. *Ibid.*, p. 293.   19. *Ibid.*, p. 295.

Testament records the divine action within the arena of history, in a particular national life. The story of this action is given to us by inspired writers who discern the hand of God in history, and interpret his purpose. But they do not give us an infallible record in the sense of exact historical truth. The writers idealize history (as in the book of Chronicles) and they attribute to first founders what really emerges from later, developed, institutions.

Gore also said that the earliest narratives of the Old Testament, before the call of Abraham, pass out of history into myth. These myths, or allegorical pictures were the earliest way in which man's mind apprehended truth. A story like the account of Creation given in Genesis is not to satisfy curiosity, nor to provide the answers demanded by a scientific age, but to reveal certain fundamental religious principles. In giving us these principles the writers were supernaturally inspired.

> The first traditions of the race are all given there from a special point of view. In that point of view lies the inspiration. It is that everything is presented to us as illustrating God's dealings with man. . . . As we go into the history, we find the recorders acting like the recorders of other nations, collecting, sorting, adapting, combining their materials, but in this inspired—that the animating motive of their work is not to bring out the national glory or to flatter the national vanity, nor, like the motive of a modern historian, the mere interest in fact, but to keep before the chosen people the record of how God has dealt with them.[20]

To Gore the Old Testament is above all a book of development, a record of the spiritual evolution of man: 'The essence of the Old Testament is to be imperfect because it represents the gradual process of education by which man was lifted out of the depths of sin and ignorance. . . . in consequence the justification of the Old Testament method lies not in itself at any particular stage, but in its results taken as a whole.'[21] Though it is impossible to maintain the historicity of the Old Testament in all its parts, yet it forms 'an organic whole which postulates a climax not yet reached, a redemption not yet given, a hope not yet satisfied'.[22]

Gore views the New Testament in a different light. In it 'fact is of supreme importance. . . . the evidence has none of the ambiguity or remoteness which belongs to much of the record of the preparation.'[23] Because of this reliable evidence, which reflects the rational attitude of the early Church towards Scripture, the Church should insist upon

20. *Ibid.*, p. 252. 21. *Ibid.*, p. 240.
22. *Ibid.*, p. 254. 23. *Ibid.*, p. 260.

the historical character of the Gospels, including matters like the Virgin Birth, and the 'trustworthiness of the other apostolic documents'. Gore admits that 'at this stage' the evangelical records are 'not historical so as to be absolutely without error, but historical in the general sense so as to be trustworthy'.[24] He never wavered from this approach to New Testament criticism, and many later theologians believed that his failure to advance on this position reflected his desire to force on the Church a new orthodoxy built around *Lux Mundi*.[25] Perhaps he held his ground over the historicity of the New Testament because, like Huxley, he could foresee a time when churchmen might attempt to avoid the problem of the historical Jesus by proclaiming 'a Faith no longer in contact with fact of any kind, standing for ever proudly inaccessible to the attacks of the infidel'.[26]

5. The Church and the Evolutionary Theory

HOW SIGNIFICANT in the development of the mind of the English Church was the contribution made by the Broad-Churchmen of *Essays and Reviews* and the Liberal Catholics of *Lux Mundi*? The only answer that can be given is that both volumes were landmarks; they represented the struggle of the Church to adapt to the changing climate of thought—which was being accepted and in some cases being formed by churchmen. This point cannot be made too strongly. The writers in the popular reviews, and men like Herbert Spencer and Charles Bradlaugh, did much to promote evolutionary thought. But so did the writers in *The Guardian*. And, because of the intense interest in religion at the time, the violent controversy over both volumes contributed much to public interest in the whole question of evolution—and the relationship between religion and science. Not only did the two books succeed in propagating the new evolutionary way of thinking, but to a large extent they succeeded in 'baptizing' the new way of thought.

The biographer of Mandell Creighton has told us that when he

---

24. *Ibid.*, p. 249.
25. Carpenter, *Gore*, p. 100.
26. Benn, *Rationalism in the Nineteenth Century*, II, 485, from Huxley's *Collected Essays*, IV, 238.

went up to Oxford in 1867 the *Essays and Reviews* and Bishop Colenso controversies had both 'left a feeling of uneasiness and suspicion'.

> The prevailing intellectual atmosphere of Oxford was distinctly non-theological rather than anti-theological. Probably one of the chief causes of intellectual agitation was the supposed opposition between science and religion. The old views as to the creation and the position of man in the animal world had been rudely shaken by the revelations of the comparatively new science of geology, and by the publication of Darwin's great work on 'The Origin of Species'.[1]

Creighton was one of those undisturbed by the conflict, because he saw the intellectual difficulties in trying to 'extend principles from the natural world to the spiritual'. This, he said, could only be done by 'appealing to one of the lowest of man's intellectual qualities, viz., his desire for simplicity rather than for truth'. He believed that in 1871 science was 'in exactly the same position as metaphysics was in the Middle Ages'.[2] It still needed much intellectual refinement.

There was much truth in Creighton's insight. Many Darwinists wandered from science into the metaphysics of 'scientism', and the public needed the labours of the essayists of 1860 and 1889 to protect them from the charlatinism of pseudo-scientific and anti-religious writings, like those of Frederick Harrison. The Victorian world needed, and received, through the writings of the creative minority of churchmen who produced *Essays and Reviews* and *Lux Mundi*, a mentality towards science which would 'accept its truths and disregard its hypotheses'.[3]

Churchmen began to see that there could be an approach, other than hysterical denunciation, to the problems raised by evolutionary thought. Reason need not be feared as a threat to what had long been considered to be the truths of Revelation. Frederick Temple revealed this way of thinking about the insights of science when he preached before the University of Oxford, 1 July 1860, at the time of the meetings of the British Association for the Advancement of Science: 'The student of science now feels himself bound by the interests of truth, and can admit no other obligation. And if he be a religious man, he believes that both books, the book of nature and the book of Revelation, alike come from God, and that he has no more right to refuse to accept what he finds in one than what he finds in the others.'[4]

1. Creighton, *Life and Letters of Mandell Creighton*, I, 44–45.
2. *Ibid.*
3. *Ibid.*, p. 46. H. D. McDonald, *Theories of Revelation: An Historical Study* (1963), pp. 33–36, sees the value of *Lux Mundi* in its clarity of presentation.
4. *Christian Remembrancer*, XXXVIII (1860), p. 244.

Essays and Reviews and *Lux Mundi* challenged churchmen to use the new evolutionary manner of thought. The fact that the latter volume was as successful as the former in exciting theological thought, but without anything like the same scandal, reveals the degree to which the issues raised were being solved. Even the disturbing theological ideas which came out of Germany were being assimilated, and used by the Church to strengthen its rational presentation of the Gospel. Perhaps the influence of the essayists of both books is most clearly revealed by the appearance, in 1897, of Samuel Driver's *Introduction to the Literature of the Old Testament*. This work of the Regius Professor of Hebrew at Oxford, who succeeded E. B. Pusey, completed and systematized the higher criticism which had appeared in the earlier works. Driver's volume was so well received that for the next fifty years it remained a standard work on the subject.

One last question remains. Why did so many intelligent churchmen oppose these attempts to find rapprochement with secular learning? Why could they not commend those who were 'trying to capture science, criticism, philosophy and the new social spirit'?[5]

The conservatives fell into three main groups. First of all there were the bishops who, like Tait, feared that 'taken as a whole' the teaching of *Essays and Reviews* was 'not consistent with the true doctrine maintained by our Church as to the office of Holy Scripture'.[6] But most of them, like Tait, listened to responsible individuals like Temple, who argued the liberal case well.

Many years ago you urged us from the University pulpit to undertake the critical study of the Bible. You said that it was a dangerous study, but indispensable. You described its difficulties, and those who listened must have felt a confidence (as I assuredly did, for I was there) that if they took your advice and entered on the task, you at any rate would never join in treating them unjustly if their study had brought with it the difficulties you described. Such a study, so full of difficulties, imperatively demands freedom for its condition. To tell a man to study, and yet bid him, under heavy penalties, come to the same conclusions with those who have not studied, is to mock him. If the conclusions are prescribed, the study is precluded.[7]

Eight years after this letter to Bishop Tait, Temple was consecrated as Bishop of Exeter; by the time that *Lux Mundi* appeared he was Bishop of London, and in 1897 he was translated to Canterbury. As Henry

5. Morley, *Recollections*, I, 262.
6. *Life of A. C. Tait*, I, 288.
7. *Ibid.*, p. 291.

Scott Holland, one of the writers in *Lux Mundi*, said: they 'feared furies'[8] when their work became public, but a new liberalism reigned on the bench of bishops by 1889, and no episcopal censures tried to repress the 'evolution' of theological thought.

Then there were intellectuals like Hort, the critics of *The Guardian*, who condemned *Essays and Reviews* as a whole,[9] and Dean Stanley, who really came to the rescue of only Temple and Jowett in his *Edinburgh Review* article. They were intellectual liberals, who considered the publication of the book premature, and the work of a writer like Baden Powell a contribution to radicalism rather than to reform. They knew the excitable state of public opinion, the spiritual anxieties of their generation, and they considered such a volume a blunder. The defensive alliance of High and Low Church which rose against the essayists was feared by these men because they knew its hysteria would impede the progress of intellectual thought which was called for. They also recognized that the issues being raised were probably more complex than even the essayists realized—particularly the question of the relationship, if any, between biological evolution and moral values. There were many thinkers of this school who saw, as Huxley did, that Gore's position in *Lux Mundi* was an uncomfortable one, when he was willing to 're-mythologize' the Old Testament in evolutionary terms, but insisted upon the historicity of the New Testament. They were not conservatives, but they had some appreciation of what Liddon meant when he said of the *Essays and Reviews* crisis: 'The Girondins of revolution have their day, but they make way for the Jacobins. . . . All might have been saved if Newman had remained with us . . . to recover the hearts of English churchmen to the principle of authority.'[10]

H. P. Liddon and Archdeacon G. A. Denison are representative of the old Tractarian and High-Church party which, like those churchmen of the Newman era, resisted the *Zeitgeist* and the liberalism which supported it. They were the Tertullians of their time, and the ideas of a liberal like J. R. Illingworth, who contributed two essays to *Lux Mundi*, were anathema to them. His description of Christianity, like that found elsewhere in the book, they believed to be 'naturalistic and Pelagianizing'.[11]

8. *Henry Scott Holland, Memoir and Letters*, ed. Stephen Paget (1921), p. 280.
9. Pusey and Keble still considered *The Guardian as a* 'liberalized' journal, in spite of its condemnation of the book. *Life of Pusey*, IV, 49.
10. R. Prothero and G. G. Bradley, *Life and Correspondence of A. P. Stanley* (1893), II, 169.
11. Johnston, *Life and Letters of H. P. Liddon*, p. 372.

Christianity . . . welcomes the discoveries of science as ultimately due to Divine revelation, and part of the providential education of the world. It recalls to art the days when, in catacomb and cloister, she learned her noblest mission to be the service of the Word made flesh. It appeals to democracy as the religion of the fishermen who gathered round the carpenter's Son. It points the social reformer to the pattern of a perfect man, laying down His life alike for enemy and friend. . . . it crowns all earthly aims with a hope full of immortality.[12]

They believed such imprecise natural theology to be typical of the liberals. 'The writers seem to think it a gain when they can prune away, or economize the Supernatural, or the great and awful doctrines of Grace, which are the heart of Christianity.'[13]

During the *Essays and Reviews* crisis, their forces were led by Pusey, who was not upset greatly by the doctrinal content of the essays—as he said they 'contain nothing with which those acquainted with the writings of unbelievers in Germany have not been familiar these thirty years'[14]—but rather by the effect on the Church of the decision of the Judicial Committee of the Privy Council about Williams and Wilson, the essayists who were prosecuted. Like Bishop Wilberforce he was dismayed because the *Times* had said 'the teaching of the Essayists is recognized', and the Church could do nothing to undo this decision of the highest ecclesiastical court in the land. As far as Pusey was concerned, this appeared to make the Church 'the destroyer of souls' in the nation; and he joined with Wilberforce in a scheme to draw up a declaration on the divine authority of Holy Scripture, and a request to the Queen asking her to institute a Commission to inquire into the constitution and practice of the Judicial Committee of the Privy Council.[15] Pusey was above all anxious for souls, and he protested against both the lack of real scholarly research in many things the essayists said, and the folly, as he saw it, of the Privy Council judgment.

Pusey was never an obscurantist. He denied any fear of 'scientific facts' on the part of the Church; but he was a conservative scholar who warned his contemporaries against any over-hasty adoption of scientific theories, which seemed to fit the biblical record.[16] He died in 1882. Liddon and Denison looked upon him as the great champion of orthodoxy, and represented his school of thought in 1889—a

12. *Lux Mundi*, p. 156.
13. Johnston, p. 372. The militant Denison loved litigation, led the opposition to the volume in Convocation, and left the English Church Union because of it.
14. *Life of Pusey*, IV, 42.
15. *Ibid.*, p. 53.
16. *Ibid.*, p. 80.

theological position which was abandoned by Gore and his companions. They said of *Lux Mundi*: 'It is practically a capitulation at the feet of the young Rationalistic Professors, by which the main positions which the old Apologists of Holy Scripture have maintained are conceded to the "literary" judgment of our time. Not only could Dr. Pusey never have written these pages, it would have been difficult to have written anything more opposed to his convictions.'[17]

Less than a year after *Lux Mundi* came out, Liddon died; and Denison followed him six years later. They were intransigents who dreaded compromise with secular thought. They could not understand the Liberal Catholicism of Gore, Scott Holland, or Edward Talbot—men who were not primarily concerned with abstract theological principles like apostolic succession, or the prerogatives of the Church, but rather with a catholicism of mission or extent. The new men represented what the Church had to offer the nation as it entered into its 'golden age of pastoral endeavour'—a generation of churchmen who looked upon themselves as a creative minority, who would interpret the Faith for the men of their generation in the English nation. These Liberal Catholics, like their fellows of *Lux Mundi* fame, regretted 'that theologians were unduly slow to recognize the vast amount of evidence on which reposes the scientific theory of evolution through natural selection'.[18] They were willing to use evolutionary thought—even in their presentation of the Gospel found in Holy Scripture—provided it assisted the mission of the Church to the world.

Unlike the old Evangelicals, they did not expect a mass conversion of the nation, nor were they concerned in nurturing traditional piety. Rather, as a creative minority, they were willing to use the spirit of the age, even the new evolutionary thought and fascination with science, to reveal the power of the Incarnation at work throughout creation. If the *Zeitgeist* was turning from theological speculation about God in the abstract to man and his problems, they were not only willing to go along with this development in thought, but even to lead it.

> We should not look for... change of spirit to arise from any simultaneous conversion of men in masses. If we accept the teaching of past experience, we should expect the general alteration to arise from the influence in our society of groups of men, inspired probably by prophetic leaders, who have attained to a true vision both of the source of our evils and of the nature of the true remedies; and who have the courage of faith to bind them together to act and

17. *Life of Liddon*, p. 368.
18. Charles Gore, *Mission of the Church* (1892), p. 99.

to suffer in the cause of human emancipation until their vision and their faith come to prevail more or less completely in society at large.[19]

19. Charles Gore, *Christ and Society* (1928), p. 156. Liddon was never as separated in thought from Gore as he believed. *V.* H. P. Liddon, *St. Paul's and London* (1871), p. 27, where he says: 'not for one moment would I place the completion of this cathedral in competition with the claims of humanity, or of Christian education, or of Christian missions.'

V. The Church
and
Education

*If the course of politic affairs cannot
in any good sort go forward
without fit instruments, and that
which fitteth them be their
virtues, let Polity acknowledge
itself indebted to Religion.*

RICHARD HOOKER

*1. The Church and the
    Universities*

ONE OF the most remarkable
developments in Victorian
England was the growth in
the size of Oxford and Cambridge. Admissions to both universities
had diminished in the eighteenth century during a period of general
decline, but when reform came after 1800, numbers began to increase.
At mid-century those admitted to each university were between three
and four hundred a year. After 1880 admissions increased more
rapidly and by the end of our period were about doubled.[1]

Most of those who attended the universities belonged to the landowning class, though sons of families engaged in commerce and
industries mingled with them. The ethos of both universities was
decidedly Anglican. Dissenters were excluded from Oxford until
1854, and could not take a degree at Cambridge until 1856, and
fellowships and other distinctions were reserved for churchmen until
1871. Apart from some overly earnest Evangelicals, the clergy were
generally accepted as fellow gentlemen by the young men who
attended the universities.

EPIGRAPH: *The Laws of Ecclesiastical Polity*, V, i, 2
1. Clark, *Making of Victorian England*, p. 256.

Though the Tractarians turned Oxford into an 'ecclesiastical cock-pit', the picture given by many contemporaries seems to reveal that most of the young gentlemen were untouched by theological or any other kind of intellectual stimulation. Thomas Hughes went up to Oriel a year after the condemnation of Tract XC, while Hawkins was still Provost, and Newman was still at Littlemore. Oriel had had its moment of glory, but as Hughes says in his biography of James Fraser, Second Bishop of Manchester, 'with the exception of Christ Church, there was at this juncture probably no college in Oxford less addicted to reading for the schools, or indeed to intellectual work of any kind.'[2] There were only fifty or so undergraduates at Oriel, including half a dozen gentlemen commoners who paid double fees for the privilege of dining at the Fellows' table in silk gowns and velvet caps. They were 'immune' from lectures and, in fact, the real work in the college was carried out by four scholars and one or two other studious men. The remaining undergraduates were strenuous athletes, sport being 'the main object of residence at the university'.[3]

As we have seen in an earlier chapter, the Tractarians did nothing to bring about university reform, and Goldwin Smith, A. J. Froude, and Mark Pattison, among others, have witnessed to the need of academic reform. There were hardly any intercollegiate lectures, as the instruction of the students was in the hands of the College tutors. The system of serious examination for a degree was a recent innovation, the scope of the examination was as narrow as the standard of instruction was low, and the quality of the degree of not much significance. Men went to the universities for the education considered appropriate for a gentleman; and this did not necessarily include knowledge of modern history, natural science, or modern languages.

The twin shadows of an established church and a self-satisfied order of society still lay thickly over the entire University. The undergraduate was governed and taught exclusively by clergymen, and the way that Fellows were appointed 'left no place for any qualification of learning, even if learning had existed at all in the University'.[4] Over this clerical society ruled the oligarchy formed by the Heads of the Colleges—in Oxford these remote individuals became the villains of the Oxford Movement. If any reform was to be brought about, they had to initiate it, for the colleges in the unreformed

2. Hughes, *James Fraser*, p. 26. *V.* V. H. H. Green, *Religion at Oxford and Cambridge* (1964), p. 255, for the easy-going atmosphere of pre-Tractarian Oxford, and D. A. Winstanley, *Unreformed Cambridge* (1935).

3. Hughes, p. 26.

4. Faber, *Oxford Apostles*, p. 53.

universities were everything, and the university itself of little importance.

In his novel *Loss and Gain*, Newman has given us a Tractarian view of the Heads of Houses, whose domestic indulgence was so upsetting to the earnest clergy of the Oxford Movement. Charles Reding sees them as:

> ministers of Christ with large incomes, living in finely furnished houses, with wives and families, and stately butlers and servants in livery, giving dinners all in the best style, condescending and gracious, waving their hands and mincing their words as if they were the cream of the earth, but without anything to make them clergymen but a black coat and a white tie. . . . I don't impute to the dons ambition or avarice; but still what Heads of houses, Fellows, and all of them evidently put before them as an end is, to enjoy the world in the first place, and to serve God in the second. . . . their immediate object is to be comfortable, to marry, to have a fair income, station, and respectability, a convenient house, a pleasant country, a social neighbourhood.[5]

These were not the type of men to reform a university, particularly if reform meant admission of Dissenters and a disturbance of such a comfortable existence. Like the privileged who battled against the temporal reforms sought by bishops like Blomfield and statesmen like Peel, the university lobby sought to keep both Oxford and Cambridge the closed preserves of the Church that they had been since the reign of James I. As late as 1850, when a Royal Commission was appointed to inquire into the state of the universities, this lobby was strong enough to persuade Lord John Russell that religious tests should not be abolished.

What made reform by the legislature inevitable was the failure of the Church to initiate a reform programme within the universities. The Church never had an academic Blomfield who could work with the State to assist the older universities to adjust to the needs of the new society of Victorian England. While the universities tried to keep Dissenters from obtaining degrees at Oxford and Cambridge, a charter was granted to the University of London in 1838 which made it open to all 'without distinction', and free to compete with the older institutions. Statesmen like Peel and Russell hoped that this might satisfy those who criticized the education provided by the old universities. But as long as the Heads of Houses remained in control, criticism could not be avoided.

Their mismanagement of the Tractarians made State intervention inevitable. Just as much as the Tractarians, the Heads were part of the

5. J. H. Newman, *Loss and Gain* (1962), pp. 145–46.

'ecclesiastical cock-pit'; and while they fought with Newman and his followers they had no time for academic reform. In 1841 they condemned Tract XC without giving Newman a chance to defend himself. 'The majority of the Heads were too angry or too panic-stricken to obey that elementary rule of justice which prescribes that the worst criminals shall be heard in self-defence before their condemnation.'[6] It has often been argued that with more understanding on the part of the Heads of Houses, Newman might never have left the Church of England.

Pusey knew that the quarrelling in the university was ultimately going to be harmful to the image of the Church in the nation: 'What we fear is lest a deep despondency about ourselves and our Church come over people's minds, and they abandon her, as thinking her case hopeless or lest individuals who are removed from the sobering influence of this ancient home of the Church should become fretted and impatient at these unsympathetic condemnations, and the continued harassing of the unseemly strife now carried on.'[7] Unfortunately the 'unseemly strife' did carry on, and the person it next influenced was Pusey himself. When, in May 1843, Pusey preached before the University of Oxford a sermon entitled 'The Holy Eucharist a Comfort to the Penitent', the sermon was examined by the Vice-Chancellor and six doctors of divinity. They came to the conclusion that the teaching within it was erroneous and, without giving Pusey opportunity for defence, suspended him from preaching before the university for two years. When the sermon was published the soundness of its doctrine was revealed to all.

Scarcely had the Heads completed this blunder than they continued their wild crusade against Tractarianism by persecuting W. G. Ward, Fellow of Balliol, for his controversial *Ideal of a Christian Church*. As far as the Heads were concerned, the book maligned the English Church and eulogized that of Rome. They said that certain passages in the book were utterly inconsistent with the Thirty-Nine Articles. Because of this, Ward was degraded from his degrees of B.A. and M.A. It was also proposed by the Vice-Chancellor that anyone suspected of unsound doctrine should be made to declare that 'he subscribed to the Articles in the sense in which he believed them to have been originally drawn up, and to be imposed by the university at the present time.'[8] This would have meant that the university

6. *Life of Pusey*, II, 174.
7. *Ibid.*, p. 242.
8. *Ibid.*, p. 416.

was imposing a doctrinal test which the bishops did not impose at ordination.

One of those who saw the danger and folly in this proposal of the 'Hebdomadal movement at Oxford' was Gladstone. In a letter to Samuel Wilberforce he said: 'I do think that the proposition itself is a violent blow to the whole doctrine and practice of subscription; and that, if it be tenaciously adhered to, it will break down subscription altogether'.[9] The Heads also saw this danger and the proposed test was withdrawn. But the Heads had lost much of their prestige. When an attempt was made to condemn Tract XC in Convocation in February 1845, at the same time that Ward was deprived of his degrees, the Proctors, one of whom was R. W. Church, vetoed the censure. An address to the Proctors thanking them for their conduct was signed by men of all parties in the university. Church later said about this unhappy episode: 'If the men who ruled the university had wished to disgust and alienate the Masters of Arts, and especially the younger ones who were coming forward into power and influence, they could not have done better.'[10]

Canon Liddon in his biography of Pusey named the condemnation of Tract XC in 1841, Pusey's suspension in 1843, and the deprivation of Ward in 1845 as the three blunders which took from the Heads of Houses their moral authority and ensured university reform.

> So far as the University is concerned, this act [Pusey's suspension], in connection with the similar acts of 1841 and 1845, may be said to have sealed the doom of the old *régime*—the authority of the Heads and the old ecclesiastical polity of Oxford. Tories must have seen the hopelessness, Liberals the impossibility of things remaining as they were. It was a call for great University Reform. So far as the Church was concerned, it was very disastrous. . . . It made men either despair of Anglicanism, or realize what they had to expect if they remained true to their Church awaiting its deliverance.[11]

After 1850 serious reform began in the universities. Not only were Dissenters allowed to enter them and to take degrees, but the curriculum was liberalized and the university authority built up at the expense of the colleges. The Heads of Houses fought these developments and refused to assist the Royal Commission on the universities; and intransigents like Archdeacon Denison attacked in Convocation proposals that sought to establish a School of Modern History at Oxford. But most of the proposals of Russell's Commision, which reported in 1853, were carried out.[12]

9. *Life of Wilberforce*, I, 253.
10. Church, *Oxford Movement*, p. 290.
11. *Life of Pusey*, II, 363.
12. For details of these proposals *v.* Carpenter, *Church and People*, pp. 183–91.

During the struggle between the Hebdomadal Board and the Tractarians, it had been said 'If you crush Tractarianism . . . you must fight "Germanism".'[13] Some men, like Pusey, Keble, and Liddon could not see how the loss by the Church of influence in the universities could do other than contribute to the increase of heretical thought which was coming in from the continent. They had no appreciation of the theological help that Nonconformity might provide them. They considered its thought to be as intellectually barren as that of popular Evangelicalism within the Church. Only the Catholic Faith as taught by the Church had any chance of resisting Rationalism.

They also believed that the initiation of university reform by the State was another act of aggression designed to weaken Christian influence in the nation: 'we are simply asked to surrender our Endowments and Franchises, and the control of our teaching into the same hands which already hold the appointment of our Bishops and the determination of our doctrines.'[14] It was unlikely that the State, or a secularized university, would be concerned with the threat of German heresy; which would undermine the Christian teaching and moral influences which the Church had traditionally provided.

Pusey, Keble, and Liddon agreed with Newman that the university was the place where the young would receive a 'persevering, gentle, oversight' during their transition from boyhood to manhood: 'a University training is the great ordinary means to a great but ordinary end; it aims at raising the intellectual tone of society, at cultivating the public mind, at purifying the national taste, at supplying true principles to popular enthusiasm and fixed aims to popular aspiration, at giving enlargement and sobriety to the ideas of the age, at facilitating the exercise of political power and refining the intercourse of private life.'[15] Universities controlled by the Church were an essential part of a program of education designed to 'ensoul' the nation. State interference, which encouraged the secularization of the universities, as well as the admission of Dissenters, would do much to weaken the Church's influence upon the young men of the privileged classes—surrender the universities to secular influences which would welcome Rationalism, and the very moral fibre of the nation would be weakened.

The rearguard action against change in university affairs was fought

13. *Life of Liddon*, p. 67.
14. John Keble, *A Few Very Plain Thoughts on the Proposed Admission of Dissenters to the University of Oxford* (1854), p. 12.
15. *Idea of a Liberal Education: Selections from the Works of Newman* (1952), p. 104. Cf. Green, *Religion at Oxford and Cambridge*, 300–301.

in the post-*Essays and Reviews* period by the remnants of the old Tractarian party, led by H. P. Liddon. His continuing resistance to the liberalism of churchmen like Jowett and Stanley,[16] which was assisted by 'his intimacy with Pusey and Bishop Wilberforce, and his social relations with a very large number of the junior and senior graduates of the University',[17] was not without value. Liddon never flagged in presenting his case, and even his opponents respected the role he played in the dialectic. Stanley was impatient when he refused to preach for him because churchmen like Jowett and Maurice had also been asked to preach, but he never completely ignored Liddon's cautions: 'You speak, my dear Mr. Dean, of a period of transition. "Transition" to what! One current of thought flows towards Mr. John Stuart Mill and Positivism beyond; another towards Baur and the school of Tubingen, and the desolate waste beyond that.'[18] Much of Liddon's influence reflected the recognizable charity which he exercised towards those whom he opposed. As the Rt. Hon. George Russell noted: 'He "differed" from Dean Stanley on almost every point in controverted theology, but strained charity even to bursting point in belauding his attractiveness, unselfishness, and sincerity.'[19]

From 1862 until his death in 1890, Liddon had rooms in 'Tom Quad', Christ Church. Here he came increasingly under the influence of Pusey, whose biographer he was to become. In turn he had great influence with the undergraduates. C. Kegan Paul wrote about the impression Liddon made on the university in an article in the *Theological Review* of October 1867, and directly compared him with the great conservative of a preceding generation: 'What Newman was to the men of his time in his University, that is Mr. Liddon to those of the present.'[20] When Liddon protested against this identification, Kegan Paul replied:

> I have been several times in Oxford lately, and from undergraduates and dons I hear the same story. You are looked on as practically the great influence in the reaction against Liberalism which is so marked just now in Oxford. This I hear from Liberals and High Churchmen alike, and leading men on the Liberal side consider you their most dangerous opponent. I only mention this to show that I have not, as I think, exaggerated your influence.[21]

16. Liberalism was also represented in the schools by Mill's 'nominalistic views', and later by the idealism of T. H. Green, the first layman to become a fellow at Balliol.
17. *Life of Liddon*, p. 67.
18. *Ibid.*, p. 74.
19. G. W. E. Russell, *Dr. Liddon* (1905), p. 138.
20. *Theological Review*, XIX (1867), 589.
21. *Life of Liddon*, pp. 80–81.

Kegan Paul at this time had fallen under the influence of Positivism and was on the point of leaving the Church of England in which he had been ordained in 1852. He was well acquainted with the theological liberals at Oxford, and his estimation of Liddon's authority was verified by the reception given to the Bampton Lectures on *The Divinity and our Lord and Saviour Jesus Christ*, which were delivered by Liddon in 1866. The lectures attempted 'in a popular form, to refute the negative criticism of Renan, Baur, and Strauss',[22] and though they lacked originality of content, they reflected considerable theological knowledge, were well argued, and deserved the high repute they were accorded.

A great preacher, whose sermons were often extempore, and of an hour or more in length, Liddon was very widely known. Sermon-tasting, as we have seen, was then a popular pastime; and Liddon records in his diary, apparently as a matter-of-course, that he preached to two thousand people in Newbury parish church during a mission.[23] He also had great influence at the university as a preacher— publishing two series of sermons he delivered at Oxford in 1865 and 1879. Popular notice was also taken of him because he steadfastly refused to be nominated to a bishopric. The only preferment he accepted was the canonry at St. Paul's, which provided him with opportunity for preaching, and the chair of exegesis at Oxford, which enabled him to influence the university.

Like Pusey, Liddon was a great theoretical supporter of the episcopal office. At the consecration of Bishop King to the see of Lincoln, he preached a sermon under the title 'A Father in Christ' which idealized the episcopal office to the great dismay of churchmen of many parties. But when Archbishop Tait openly declared his desire that the use of the Athanasian Creed in public worship should be discontinued, he found himself confronted by a rebellious Liddon who called the proposal by the primate a 'wound and insult to fundamental truth'.[24] For the rest of his life, Tait's opinion of the Athanasian Creed was used against him; and in Convocation he was accused of 'deliberate contempt for the faith of the Church Catholic', and of having 'publicly stepped over to the side of the Socinian and the infidel'.[25] Liddon made it quite clear that he would consider the primate a traitor to the Church if he meddled with the Athanasian

22. *Ibid.*, p. 85.
23. *Ibid.*, p. 68. When he preached at St. Paul's in 1864 he said 'there seemed to be literally no standing room down to the west end of the nave.' *Ibid.*, p. 76.
24. *Life of Tait*, II, 137.
25. *Ibid.*, p. 143.

Creed. 'The destructive energy of the unbelieving school will not stop with the creeds, as your Grace's knowledge of the existing condition of controversy with respect to the books of Holy Scripture would assure you. Would that it might not be reserved for your Grace's Primacy to 'give the tiger'—as far as our poor English Church is concerned—his first taste of blood!'[26] Like Pusey and Keble, Liddon considered that the ultimate authority in ecclesiastical affairs lay with the whole Church, and Tait's 'primacy' was responsible to it. This letter was sent to Tait in 1872. Five years later the *Church Times* noted that: 'the theoretical champion of Apostolical Succession is in practice a rank Presbyterian or Independent.'[27]

The man who could harry Tait, and bring him to heel in doctrinal matters, became between 1870 and 1890 the chief teacher of the English Church. He was free from the duties of executive office; his chair at Oxford gave him a position of great advantage, as did his canonry at St. Paul's; and he used to great effect his notable gifts as a preacher. His year was divided between London and Oxford; and though his Lenten lectures, like those of 1870 at St. James's, Piccadilly, had great influence when they were published as *Some Elements of Religion*, his real importance lay in his work at Oxford. He was singularly free from responsibility; even as a professor he taught only those who freely came to him, and was unfettered even from the necessity of holding examinations. He was free to brood over the fate of the university as secularism grew, and to rally the conservatives who resisted the change and idealized the Oxford of the Newman era.

In the *Church Quarterly Review* of April 1881, he wrote an anonymous article entitled 'The Recent Fortunes of the Church in Oxford' in which he summed up university history from the standpoint of an old Tractarian. He said that, before 1854, 'the Church was still everything and everywhere.' But she failed 'to make due use of the splendid opportunities which her relation to the University placed at her disposal'. Even 'the day of Grace' which was Oxford's during the Newman era was despised—because the Heads of Houses had allowed the Tractarians no time to breathe their new spirit 'into work as well as into prayer, into literature as well as into philanthropy, into art— whether music or architecture or poetry—as well as into scientific theology, a reality and vigour that had long been wanting.'[28]

---

26. *Ibid.*, p. 139.
27. *Cf. supra*, p. 125. Liddon also defied his diocesan after the Purchas Judgment prohibited the Eastward Postion at the altar. *V. Life of Liddon*, p. 151.
28. *Life of Liddon*, p. 253.

Liddon believed that the Universities Test Act of 1871, which 'de-Christianized' the colleges by throwing open all Fellowships, except one or two in each college, to laymen and Nonconformists, was designed to satisfy 'the demands of the anti-Christian Liberals'. Those who implemented this policy were helped by the 'plausible arguments which you get, in a distorted form, in *The Guardian*'. Because of the meddling of the State without, and the subversion of liberals within, the university, Liddon could 'see no future whatever on which a Christian can look with any approach to hope'.[29]

> The question before us is . . . the present and apparently future circumstances of the English Church in Oxford. . . . The prospect is, to a great extent, a dark one. The days are gone when those who knew the real state of the case could talk of Oxford as one of the 'eyes' of the Church, or could do other than smile when they read the conventional, or sometimes the almost mystical utterances of the Episcopal and other authorities on the subject. The plain truth is that henceforth Oxford will belong to the Church of England just as much and just as little as does the House of Commons. It is still a centre of social and intellectual interests; but as a centre of religious force it is no longer what it was, and is unlikely in its future to be what it still is.[30]

Liddon's influence did much to retard the appearance of liberalism in theological studies at Oxford. When it did appear in 1889, it took the form of *Lux Mundi*—a mild explosion after a long period of intellectual repression, but to Liddon a complete tragedy. He confessed that he was never more isolated in Oxford in his whole life than he was in 1890, the last year of his life. He believed that there was an 'absolute contradiction' between the thought of Charles Gore and that of E. B. Pusey. When *Lux Mundi* appeared he asked the former to try to see how his essay looked from Liddon's conservative viewpoint:

> Is there not a temptation in an age like ours to 'purchase the goodwill of the barbarians by repeated subsidies' drawn from those treasuries of Revelation which we have no right to surrender? I have felt keenly the pressure of this motive myself; I wish I could be quite sure that I had always resisted it. For a time, no doubt, a concession may ensure a truce between Revelation and its enemies. But not for always, or probably for long. The *nexus* between Truth and Truth and error and error forbids this.[31]

The Church lost many of its old prerogatives at Cambridge, as it had at Oxford, but Cambridge never produced churchmen as opposed

---

29. *Ibid.*, p. 251.
30. *Ibid.*, p. 254.
31. *Ibid.*, p. 363. For an insight into the theological tensions at Oxford raised by the fear of Liberalism *v.* E. W. Watson, *Life of Bishop John Wordsworth* (1915), p. 69 ff.

as Pusey and Liddon were to the liberalism that was coming out of Germany. Rather there arose a school of theologians, more influenced by Evangelicalism than by Tractarianism, whose theology was 'leavened' by the new spirit of scientific history displayed by men like William Stubbs at Oxford, and Mandell Creighton at Cambridge. Liddon had no high regard for their way of thought. One of their most prominent members, Brooke Foss Westcott, the future Bishop of Durham and Regius Professor of Divinity from 1870 to 1890, he dismissed as 'a thoughtful Latitudinarian, covered all over with a thin pietistic varnish, which has the effect of leading the *Record* and other Low Church persons to suppose that he is a variety of Evangelical'.[32]

Westcott, together with J. B. Lightfoot and A. F. Hort, in spite of the denigrating of people like Liddon, did much to make the foundations of theology secure in their generation—even when the process involved the abandonment of cherished beliefs. They set themselves the task of examining biblical records critically to discover what they actually said, and how they would have been interpreted by the original hearers. In doing this they ushered English theology into a golden age. In the words of Hastings Rashdall, these Cambridge scholars 'raised English theology . . . from a condition of intellectual nullity up to the level of the best German work, while they infused into it a characteristic English spirit of caution and sobriety'.[33]

Lightfoot and Westcott might have been even more influential as scholars if they had not both become Bishop of Durham; Westcott succeeded Lightfoot in 1890. Many people thought the elevation of the two men a tragedy for scholarship at Cambridge. R. W. Dale, the Congregationalist leader, wrote to Westcott in 1883 to say: 'do not let them make you a bishop. I do not know what Dr. Lightfoot may have done for Durham; for those of us who are outside he has done nothing since his elevation.' In a later letter, written in the same year, Dale said: 'If he had not been made a bishop we should have had two or three books from him by this time. His silence gives us Congregationalists another argument against Episcopacy.'[34] By 1890 the threat to Anglican scholarship came from the demands of the Establishment, rather than from any obscurantist ecclesiastical party.

By the time of Hort, Lightfoot, Westcott, Stubbs, and Creighton, churchmen were being recognized as scholars of note by the nation at large. Contemporaries were well aware of the intellectual ascendancy

32. Russell, *Dr. Liddon*, p. 77.
33. Hastings Rashdall, *Principles and Precepts*, ed. Major and Cross (1927), p. 164.
34. A. W. W. Dale, *Life of R. W. Dale of Birmingham* (1902), pp. 524–25.

of churchmen in this generation. Few churchmen disagreed when Hensley Henson said: 'It has ever been the boast of the Church of England, and on the whole justly, that her clergy are the most learned clergy in the world; to accuse her of indifference or hostility to education is to convict the accuser of ignorance alike of the past and of the present.'[35] By 1889 the Church had lost much temporal authority in the universities, but had gained a new intellectual respect.

2. The Church and Public Elementary Education

HENSLEY HENSON could boast of clerical enlightenment by 1894, but earlier in the century many churchmen were uneasy about the use the clergy made of their education—particularly in their instruction of the young in the parishes of the nation. Popular legend, in some parts of the country, spoke of an unholy pact which had existed between squire and parson, from time immemorial, in which the former said to his clerical crony about the education of the villagers: 'You keep 'em ignorant, and I'll keep 'em poor.'[1] To read some clerical comment on the education of the poor in the pre-1833 era is to realize that this class myth probably had some basis in fact. The Archdeacon of Stowe in his visitation of 1826 saw positive danger in any attempt being made to take the minds of the poor from the manual employment and necessary labour which went with their occupation in life.[2] Even the College of St. Mark, Chelsea, which sought to train schoolmasters for the poor, was careful not to train them 'above their station' in life—the studies of the schoolroom were designed 'not to exalt but to humble'.[3]

Most people in the early part of the century considered education in the nation to be a responsibility of the Church, or other religious societies. But there were many weaknesses in a system of education which depended upon voluntary societies, or the goodwill of individuals in a parish, to provide for the enlightenment of the masses.

35. *Church of the People: Sermons Preached at All Saints, Notting Hill, May, June, 1894*, p. 11.
1. Or so said Mr. Richard Harvey, late publican of Black Horse Inn, Appleford, Berkshire, in the autumn of 1958.
2. H. V. Bayley, *A Charge delivered to the Clergy of the Archdeaconry of Stow* (1826), p. 12.
3. F. Warre Cornish, *English Church in the XIX Century* (1910) Part 1, p. 202.

Compared to what was provided for the masses in countries like Prussia, Switzerland, or France, elementary educational facilities in England were not good. Sometimes the only education available in the country would be the poor instruction provided in independent dame schools; at other times that directed by the priest in the parish. In the towns and cities, the schools might be those provided by the Nonconformist British and Foreign School Society after 1814; Lord Brougham's Utilitarian answer to the need for public education—the 'Society for the Diffusion of Useful Knowledge', which was founded in 1827; or the High Church 'National Society for the Education of the Poor in the Principles of the Established Church throughout England and Wales', which was incorporated in 1817. The latter proved to be by far the most popular society. By 1831 it taught almost half a million children, and in 1847 it had almost a million students receiving daily instruction. 'The Commission of 1858 to 1861 found that at the time of their report the Church of England possessed about nine-tenths of the elementary schools in the country with three-quarters of the children, the Roman Catholics about 5½ per cent., the Wesleyans 4 per cent., and the Congregationalists 2 per cent.'[4]

Elementary education was also provided in Sunday schools. The first of these was founded by a Gloucester journalist, Robert Raikes, with the help of an Anglican clergyman. The idea spread to other large towns, and by 1803 a Sunday School Union had come into being, whose activity influenced the whole of England. In 1834 there were a million and a half children in these schools.

There was much wrong with this education. Many schools used a cheap mass-production type of teaching, which suited the age—the 'monitor system'. In it, one master, with the aid of many masters who repeated by slate and voice what he gave to them, could offer instruction in reading and writing to a multitude of children at one time. But even the use of such a mechanical system of mass education failed to solve the nation's needs. By 1838 the *British Critic* reported that less than two and a half million children were being taught in all schools, out of the nearly four million who needed instruction.[5]

The Benthamites could not tolerate this chaotic situation. In 1833, John Roebuck laid before the reformed parliament the educational programme of his group—a plan for the universal education of the whole population. Education was to be made compulsory between the

4. Clark, *Making of Victorian England*, p. 175.
5. *British Critic*, XXIII (1838), 347. A report had been made in 1838 by a Parliamentary Committee on Education of the Poorer Classes in England and Wales.

ages of seven and fourteen; the nation would be divided for educational purposes into districts; local school boards would be democratically elected; and over all would be a minister of education, with a seat in the Cabinet. He would allocate funds granted by the State, authorize the construction of new schools, and supervise the system of education. Both the High-Churchmen and the Evangelicals drew together to defend the practical monopoly of popular education enjoyed by the Church of England; and, because the Dissenters and the Free-Thinkers of the Benthamite school distrusted each other as much as they did the Church, Roebuck abandoned his idea which had been based on American and Prussian examples.[6]

The Benthamites had to backtrack because Church strength was growing. The Reformed Parliament granted assistance for the National Society and the British Society to build new schools; and, at first, each received an equal grant. But soon the schools of the Established Church were granted more; priority was given to 'those applications where, by a small expenditure, they can forward the education of the largest number of scholars'.[7] This rule aided those communities most able to help themselves, and virtually guaranteed more schools for churchmen than for Dissenters. At the end of five years, the National Society had received £70,000, while the British Society had received only £30,000.

Part of the failure of the British Society to thrive may be attributed to the Dissenters' attitude to education. They believed it was one area that should not be controlled by the government. Because of this belief, many of them devoted such money as they gave for education to schools which did not apply for a government grant—although even among those schools which received no grant, the Church of England foundations outnumbered those of Dissent. Many Dissenters were making considerable fortunes, but they apparently chose to give little to their schools—certainly not as much as came from the pockets of the clergy of the Church, often at the cost of severe self-sacrifice. Probably the Dissenters preferred to give their money to Sunday schools, foreign and home missions, and adult education. They could justify their position by pointing out that 'the most effective adult education a young intelligent man of the working or lower class could receive, was to become a member of, and possibly a lay preacher in, a Dissenting congregation.'[8]

6. *Hansard*, XXVI (1835), 495 ff.
7. Raymond G. Cowherd, *Politics of English Dissent* (1956), p. 118.
8. Clark, p. 176.

198

Brougham later tried to resurrect Roebuck's scheme but in a modified form. He disclaimed any desire to introduce into British legislation a Prussian form of compulsory education; but the religious bodies noted that he wanted a board of public education which would, among other duties, control the management of the many religious foundations of ancient origin which were then so poorly administered. Once more reform was put off. Yet something had to be done for the millions of children without elementary education; and in 1839 Lord John Russell proposed the appointment of a committee of the Privy Council, which would be comparable to the education board which Brougham had suggested. The proposed committee would allocate the grants to the societies, and establish a normal school or training college for teachers in the schools.

When the committee was brought into being by an Order in Council, it protested against the foundation of a training college, because it would have been undenominational; and this project was dropped. It also declared its intention of setting up a body of inspectors, who would investigate any school that received a grant from the committee. The Evangelicals and the High-Churchmen once more closed their ranks to resist the government, and the Wesleyans placed their powerful organization at the service of those who opposed the Whig scheme. Lord Ashley denounced the scheme as a threat to the Constitution, to the Church, and to revealed religion in the midst of a long and bitter debate. The Church, he said, could not condone the State's having control of both 'the temporal and eternal destinies of countless millions'.[9] Parliament was deluged by petitions against the scheme. Archbishop Howley led the Lords in a body to request the Queen to halt these developments. She graciously received them, but firmly refused to comply with their requests. The Committee of Council on Education was to remain.

The strength of public opinion was so strong, however, that an agreement with the Church had to be reached. James Kay (later Sir James Kay-Shuttleworth) became secretary of the committee in August 1839, and his appointment did not help matters. The son of a Lancashire cotton manufacturer, he had, at one time, both taught and acted as superintendent in a Dissenting Sunday school. Although he was a deeply pious and able man, who had also acted as an Assistant Poor Law Commissioner, and had studied the Scottish school system in this capacity, Kay was not acceptable to the members of the High-Church party. They tried to have him removed as secretary; and,

9. *Hansard*, XLVIII (1839), 270.

although they did not succeed in this, they did force the Whig government to abandon its plan for state inspection of schools.

Russell was forced into a concordat with the bishops. After a conference with the Archbishop of Canterbury and the Bishop of London, Russell agreed that inspectors of National Society schools should send reports to the bishops as well as to the Committee of Privy Council. By an order in council in 1840, the archbishops were given power to approve the appointment of inspectors, who were to report on religious as well as secular teaching. In effect the state inspectors had become adjuncts to the parochial system.

The Tory victory at the polls in 1841 assured the Church that the concordat would be reinterpreted in terms even more favourable to the Establishment. The Home Secretary was now Sir James Graham, who was resolved to increase the aid to education and to enlarge the powers of school inspectors. In 1843 he introduced his Factories Education Bill. He planned to establish in the urban areas of the nation schools for factory children, who were to be given time off from their labours to attend them. The cost of these schools was to be met from public funds, but they were to be under the control of the Established Church. In the schools, the ministers of the different sects would have the right to give religious instruction to children whose parents requested it. The children of parents belonging to the Church of England would be instructed in the catechism and liturgy of the Church separately from the other children.

The direct management of the schools was to be in the hands of seven trustees; the clergyman of the district, two churchwardens, and four others nominated by the magistrates. Two of these men were, if possible, to be mill-owners. When opposition was raised about this scheme of management, Graham proposed that one of the churchwardens should be elected, and also the other four trustees, under conditions which would allow the minority its just share in representation.

The scheme was well received in the House. Lord John Russell said that it would be not only foolish, but wicked to oppose its passage.[10] But Dissent closed its ranks, and the welfare of the poor was forgotten as ecclesiastical politicians took over. The Dissenting newspaper, *The Patriot*, declared that the education bill combined the evils of a church-extension bill, a test act, and a church-rate; it was designed to drive Dissenters out of national education.[11] In Man-

10. *Hansard*, LXVIII (1843), 95.
11. Cowherd, p. 127.

chester the bill was considered to be Graham's retaliation against manufacturers for having supported repeal of the Corn Laws. The issue became so controversial that even the Wesleyan Methodists, who had supported the formation of the Privy Council committee, joined the campaign against the bill which 'placed the people wholly at the mercy of the Church'.[12] They feared that Church domination of national education would mean the wide dissemination of Tractarianism, which was then at the height of its influence. Graham wrote to Peel in April 1843: 'It is quite clear that the Pusey tendencies of the Established Church have operated powerfully on the Wesleyans, and are converting them rapidly into enemies.'[13]

With the loss of Wesleyan support Peel came to the conclusion that the help of Dissent could not be counted upon, and that the bill should be abandoned: 'It is but a sorry and lamentable triumph that Dissent has achieved.'[14] Ashley agreed with Peel.

> Let this last trial be taken as a sufficient proof that 'United Education' is an impossibility. It ought never again to be attempted. The Dissenters and the Church have each laid down their limits, which they will not pass; and there is no power that can either force, persuade, or delude them. Your government has nothing to regret, except the loss of a healing measure. You would have much to regret had you not propounded it. But you have endeavoured to remove a great evil, and in so doing have thrown the responsibility before God and man on the shoulders and conscience of others.[15]

Religious strife had ensured that a national system of education under Church control could not possibly be introduced. The way had been opened up for the idea of a 'dual system' of education to appear; where the government would finance and inspect the voluntary schools of the nation, but control of them would remain under direction of the national societies.

Bishop Blomfield was a supporter of State intervention in national education. He realized that it was no more possible for voluntary societies to carry on such a programme, than it was for the government to exist by voluntary contributions rather than by taxation. He was largely responsible for churchmen accepting Russell's plan for school inspectors in 1840, and said he would not hesitate to accept State aid: 'If the Government would grant us money, and be content, as they ought to be, with an inspection authorized by the Church, we

---

12. *Hansard*, LXVII (1843), 1417.
13. C. S. Parker, *Sir Robert Peel* (1899), II, 560.
14. *Ibid.*
15. *Ibid.*, p. 562.

should act very preposterously, I think, if we were to refuse their proffered assistance.'[16]

Blomfield, as we have seen, was not popular in many circles and was dismissed as 'an ecclesiastical Peel'[17]—a reproach which he considered to be a compliment. But even more unpopular, because of his liberalism in matters of education, was W. F. Hook, the Vicar of Leeds. Like Blomfield he was directly acquainted with the lives and the needs of the poor. To him their education was not a political but a pastoral concern, as he pointed out in a public letter he wrote to the Bishop of St. David's in 1846. His ideas about national education were those of 'the working clergy of the manufacturing districts'.[18]

Hook was not happy about the work of the voluntary societies: 'when I look upon all that has been done I ask what is the result? I must contend that, compared with the educational wants of the country, we have done next to nothing; we have lighted a lantern which only makes us more sensible of the surrounding darkness.'[19] Neither had he faith in the monitor system then used; it was quite common for a child to spend two years in a school and still not be able to read. What was needed was for Church and State to work together, along with the Dissenters, in a programme of education which would make use of the new concept of 'duty' now exhibited by the upper classes instead of their old 'ungodly selfishness'.[20]

Although Hook suggested that money for education could be raised by sale of some Church property—'it would be better for the Church to have a pauperized hierarchy than an uneducated people'[21]—and he believed that financial aid from the State should go to Dissent as well as to the Church, his plan was not welcomed by the Dissenters. They particularly objected to his suggestion that the teachers in state-supported and state-inspected schools give 'literary or secular instruction', with parish clergy and Dissenting ministers supplementing this education with Christian teaching on Sundays, and Wednesday and Friday afternoons. They wanted no separation of secular and religious education by the State; nor did they want state interference with the voluntary system.

This was the era when Edward Miall's periodical, the *Non-*

---

16. *Memoir of Blomfield* (1863 ed.), I, 271.
17. *Ibid.*, p. 303.
18. W. F. Hook, *On the Means of Rendering More Efficient the Education of the People: Letter to the Lord Bishop of St. David's* (1846), p. 4.
19. *Life of Hook*, II, 205.
20. Hook, *Education of the People*, p. 5.
21. *Ibid.*, p. 39.

conformist, preached the need to reduce to a minimum the activities of the State. Supported by the *Leeds Mercury*, it attacked those wealthy members of the middle class who had lost their anti-clericalism, and were willing to join with the Church in receiving the favours of Establishment. In 1844 an Anti-State-Church Conference, composed of seven hundred Dissenters from all parts of the country, met in London to declare war against every form of alliance between the State and any religious community.[22]

Dissent feared to surrender its voluntary schools to any domination by the Church because, if it did, sooner or later they would be tainted by Ritualism. On the other hand, it also feared a purely secular system of education which would be separated by the State from any religious influence. As far as the Dissenters were concerned, only in their schools, which were free from Church or State control, where secular and religious education were not separated, was true religion able to flourish.

By mid-century, however, the need for a national system of elementary education for the masses, with the State somehow assisting the voluntary societies in ways other than building grants, could no longer be ignored. The question that had to be worked out was how much control the State would have over the public service it supported. Answers to this problem formed the basis for the educational politics of the years between 1850 and 1870—a time when general prosperity produced an environment which was favourable to discussion of national education. Bill after bill came before parliament, some private, some government measures. These bills were valuable because, although none of them became law, they contributed much to the final solution found in Forster's Act of 1870.

In 1861 a Commission of Inquiry which had been set up under the chairmanship of the Duke of Newcastle submitted its report. It had started out to discover the best means of providing 'sound and cheap elementary education to all classes of the People',[23] and it came to the conclusion that the voluntary system as administered by the Education Department of the Committee of Council should be retained. Only through the voluntary system could the religious character of popular education be ensured; and the Newcastle Commission believed, with the ruling classes of the nation, that the moral instruction it provided was preferable to purely secular education.[24] Life in the slums of the

22. Arthur Miall, *Life of Edward Miall* (1884), p. 92 ff.
23. J. W. Adamson, *English Education, 1789–1902* (1930), p. 203.
24. Sometimes even the working class shared this sentiment. When addressing 3,000 workers in Blackburn in 1870, James Fraser, who had acted as an educational commissioner,

great cities was hard; and, as Sir James Kay-Shuttleworth pointed out, the parents of working-class children were often 'dissolute' and 'rude', sometimes 'brutish immigrants'. His faith was that the voluntary schools at least gave them an alternative to 'that bad school, the street, with its republic of vagrant little ruffians'.[25]

The Newcastle Commission was mostly concerned with financial and administrative reforms. One of their recommendations was that 'payments' should be made to schools according to the 'results' obtained at them. This idea of 'free competition' in the schools, which reflected the 'Manchester' point of view, was opposed by many churchmen, who saw in 'payment by results' an attempt to emphasize the 'Three R's', to the neglect of moral training: 'the reclamation of these children from barbarism is a good, greater far than mere technical instruction in the three lowest elements.'[26]

Kay-Shuttleworth knew, from first-hand experience, the need for the working classes in the slums to help themselves out of their lives of brutality and squalor. But he also knew their appreciation of help from both Church and Dissent in their emancipation. The schools of the voluntary societies acted as agencies of civilization, bringing both secular education and moral influences to the immediate neighbourhood in which they were founded. Few people who were directly acquainted with the lives of the working class wished to eliminate the moral education provided by the voluntary societies. It is true that this training was sometimes resented. Clerical inspectors in the schools were often painfully condescending and, as William Lovett pointed out, preferred teachers who were at home with the poor, but cultured enough to converse with a clergyman. At the same time Lovett did not overlook the need for the lower orders to exercise 'self-sacrifices' in trying to help themselves: 'The working classes . . . still, unhappily, undervalue mental and moral effort for raising their class.'[27] There was need for a change in England's social structure; but there was also need for moral improvement among the workers. Many reformers saw 'self-help and socialism not as incompatible but as in some sense complementary'.[28]

The Reform Act of 1867 doubled the number of voters; and, with

---

asked them 'whether they wanted a purely secular education for their children, and not a voice was raised.' Hughes, *James Fraser: a Memoir*, p. 202.

25. James Kay-Shuttleworth, *Four Periods of Public Education as Reviewed in 1832, 1839, 1846 and 1862* (1862), p. 590.

26. *Ibid.*

27. William Lovett, *Life and Struggles* (1920), p. xxxi.

28. Asa Briggs, *Victorian People*, p. 138.

the threat of the assumption of full citizenship by an unknown number of illiterates, the matter of national elementary education became of immediate concern. It was obvious from the findings of the Commissioners, who had reported in 1861 that universal elementary education could not be provided by voluntary effort alone.[29] There was a striking reversal of public opinion, and many Dissenters began to demand a comprehensive system of State education which should be free and compulsory, and even undenominational. Churchmen began to see that to educate the nation there was need for not only the resources of the State, but also its powers of compulsion: 'the work of civilization, which no doubt the activities of the Churches furthered, needed also the assistance of such powerful allies as the school attendance officer, the sanitary inspector, the temperance legislator and above all the police.'[30]

Two rival educational associations were formed during this period; the National Education League, which had Joseph Chamberlain and R. W. Dale, the Congregationalist leader, among its members; and the Tory-dominated National Education Union with its centre in Manchester. The former organization favoured national education, financed and inspected by the State, which would be non-sectarian, free, compulsory, and universal.[31] The Manchester association wished to supplement the existing system with denominational religious instruction modified by a conscience clause.

In the midst of intense lobbying by both movements, the Vice-President of the Committee of Council, W. E. Forster, submitted a government education bill. Assent was finally given to it 9 August 1870, and it became the Education Act of 1870 (33 & 34 Victoria, c. 75).

From the standpoint of the National Education League, the Act still favoured the Church by allowing its voluntary schools to remain, though they were not to receive aid from the rates. New denominational schools could also be built, to remain outside the control of the school boards. These were bodies set up in areas where existing school accommodation was considered to be inadequate. Most of the school boards were established in towns; and they had power to build schools, to ensure attendance, and to supervise the education provided.

29. *Report of the Commissioners Appointed to Inquire into the State of Popular Education in England*, XXI (1861), Pt. 1, II, *Cf.* Kay-Shuttleworth, p. 555 ff. for criticism of the Report.
30. Clark, p. 195.
31. *Life of R. W. Dale*, p. 270 ff.

By the Cowper-Temple amendment to the bill, the religious instruction in board schools was to be free of any catechism or other denominational teaching. Disraeli said this amendment set up a new 'sacerdotal class' in the persons of the masters who taught an 'undenominational religion', and J. W. Adamson has described the new board-school religion as the appearance of a religious sect whose standard was the English Authorized Version, interpreted in any way that did not agree with a creed, catechism, or other institutional formulary.[32]

After 1870 religious instruction, which for so long had been the basis of all teaching in English schools, became a mere adjunct to other subjects; in many schools only a small portion of time was allotted to it, or even none at all. When the Salisbury government of 1885–1886 appointed a royal commission, under the chairmanship of Sir Richard Asheton Cross, the Home Secretary, to inquire into the working of the Elementary Education Act, its report noted the absence of religious teaching in some schools and expressed concern over the decline of moral training.

The voluntary schools which suffered most by the Act of 1870 were those of the Dissenters. The Church schools and those of the Roman Catholics kept struggling to compete with the board schools; but many Wesleyan and other Nonconformist schools lacked financial resources and disappeared. This was a tragedy to Methodist leaders like Hugh Price Hughes. He saw that one of the reasons for the failure of these schools was the alliance of Dissent with secularism for the sake of ecclesiastical politics. He deplored a situation where 'men of our thinking begin to care more for wretched party and sectarian issues than for the whole Church of Christ and the teaching of the Christian religion in our schools'.[33] Distrust of the Church and fear of Ritualism was so great that the Nonconformist policy in education had become thoroughly negative: 'to protest and protest, but never to produce any alternative policy for which any sacrifice was made'.[34] The result was that in the 'dual system' of English elementary education, after 1870, Dissenting schools began to disappear, to be replaced by State-sponsored schools where religious teaching was either non-existent, or considerably weakened.

The negative attitude of the Dissenters towards any settlement of the education issue is understandable, when the intransigence of some

---

32. Adamson, *English Education*, p. 359.
33. Dorothea Hughes, *The Life of Hugh Price Hughes. By his Daughter* (1905), p. 495.
34. W. T. Whitley, *History of British Baptists* (1923), p. 289 ff.

members of the High-Church party is considered. One of these was Joshua Watson, treasurer for many years of the National Society, who was devoted to the Establishment, which he believed could provide ideal direction of society by Church and State. He refused to consider the Church as a voluntary society formed by man; rather it was 'a society of divine institution, assembled under ecclesiastical government and holding communion in Christian fellowship and in the public service of religion after the apostolic pattern'.[35]

Watson wanted the sort of agreement between Church and State which had brought about King's College, London, as an answer to Brougham's foundation of London University on 'godless Gower Street'. In 1828 the Rector of Lambeth, George D'Oyley, a chaplain to Archbishop Manners-Sutton, held a meeting for this purpose which had been attended by three archbishops, seven bishops, Wellington the Prime Minister, and the principal nobility of the nation. This last great alliance of Church and State, just before the repeal of the Test Act and Catholic Emancipation, was the kind of action that Watson wished to have continued.

Watson gloried in the Establishment, and never lost his vision of what might be accomplished by Church and State working together for the moral elevation of society. In this benevolent concordat, the Church was to be responsible for national education, which had to be of a moral nature. He agreed with his fellow High-Churchmen that 'the way to prevent crime, and to diminish pauperism, is by educating the working classes.'[36] But he also agreed with the Duke of Wellington, who had cautioned enthusiasts for national education that without religious content in their teaching they would be 'only making so many clever devils'.[37] This necessary religious education would be provided by the clergy in their parishes, under direction of the bishops, and assisted by devoted laymen, like Watson himself, who would use their privilege for the benefit of all.

Such Tory benevolence has often been dismissed as feudal paternalism, which reflected only the desire of the privileged classes to keep the workers in their place in society. This is unfair to people like Watson, who gave unstintingly of themselves in the cause of education of the poor. Apart from his 'unbounded munificence' in charitable gifts, he was one of the three actual founders of the National Society;

35. The words are those of Archdeacon Daubney another leading member of the High Church Hackney Phalanx or Clapton Sect. *British Critic*, X (1818), 117.
36. Charles Marriott, *Two Sermons on Civil and Social Duties, Especially On the Duty of Educating the Poorer Classes* (1853), p. 1.
37. Arthur Bryant, *Age of Elegance, 1812–1822* (London, 1950), p. 270 n.

was chiefly responsible for the Church Building Society begun in 1817; and devoted to the work of the S.P.G., the S.P.C.K., and the Additional Curates Society. His great failure was his belief that the traditional Church-State relationship was immutable. He resigned as treasurer of the National Society because of a government grant to St. Mark's College, Chelsea, in 1846; and the introduction of State inspectors into church schools. Watson interpreted both State grants and State inspectors as moves by the secular body towards the eventual take-over of national education. He had no faith in the possible philanthropy of the middle class which had come to power in the legislature.[38] Only the spirit of *noblesse oblige* of the High-Church party would bring to the poor the blessings of education. This would in time, if it was of a religious nature, be of benefit to the whole nation.[39]

George Anthony Denison, Archdeacon of Taunton, would have made 'a first class medieval chancellor, Archbishop and Cardinal' according to Thomas Mozley; and it was Denison who, more than any other man, carried on the opposition of men like Watson to State encroachment on the Church's educational prerogatives. Forster's Education Act of 1870 was to Denison a 'huge national sin'. 'Better I say ten times better, have no schools at all into which upon any pretext, the Civil Power, indifferent and irreligious, can set its foot, than a school under provisions of the Act of 1870, or any modification of that Act, save only its unconditional repeal.'[40] He was another old-fashioned High-Churchman who believed that the Church had, as part of 'the trust committed to her of God', the education of the people of the nation.[41] The State was not to meddle in educational matters which for so long had been the concern of the Church alone. Denison was shocked when a churchman like Gladstone could express his 'view of the right of the Civil Power, i.e., of a House of Commons of "all denominations" to judge of what ought, or ought not, to be the constitution and form of management of a Church school'.[42]

This is not to say that Denison played with the idea of a 'purified' Church, led by its ecclesiastical officers, which would be entirely free of the State. Unlike the Tractarians, he had no great faith in bishops;

38. S. E. Maltby, *Manchester and the Movement for National Elementary Education, 1800–1870* (1918), p. 26 reveals the mentality of some manufacturers who argued 'that to make children dead tired was good for the peace and tranquility of the town.'

39. A. B. Webster, *Joshua Watson: Story of a Layman* (1954), pp. 131–33.

40. *Fifty Years at East Brent: The Letters of George Anthony Denison, 1845–1896* (1902), p. 268.

41. *Ibid.*, p. 26, letter to John Ruskin, 21 March 1851.

42. *Ibid.*, p. 39, letter to Gladstone, 26 June 1852.

and he wished to retain the Establishment. In everything ecclesiastical he wanted 'all the lay co-operation which can be had'; he deprecated the idea of the clergy dominating the Church; and he dreamed of 'the Church, Laity and Clergy labouring to make Crown and Parliament more "Church", in the tradition of Hooker.'[43]

He supported the Ritualists against the bishops and said that he appreciated the law of Church and State which protected them during their persecution. In 1881 he revealed to the Lower House of Convocation that he did not hold a Tractarian view of episcopacy.

> It is worth while to remind churchmen that, when, in 1850, Bishop Blomfield introduced into the House of Lords his Bill for amendment of the Court of Final Appeal in matters ecclesiastical, and proposed a Court consisting of Archbishops and Bishops he was met at once by the lay Peers with the objection which defeated the Bill, viz:— that this would enable the Archbishops and Bishops for the time being, to pronounce what is, and what is not the Doctrine and Discipline of the Church of England. I commend the objection to the churchmen of 1881.[44]

Denison believed that the State was trying to alter the terms of the Establishment. Whenever help came from the State in his day, 'conditions' were insisted upon 'as the price of aid'.[45] What the State really wanted was to give the people knowledge in secular schools which would be of a 'speculative character and steeped up to the lips in "the Pride of Life".'[46] He feared that 'the Church corporate of England, with all its revival by mercy of God, is rather being taught by the People, as represented in a Parliament of all faiths and no faith, than is teaching the People.'[47]

He refused to consider disestablishment, which would make 'the State to be of no religion, in place of maintaining, among many forms of faith, the Primitive Catholic Faith as the Truth of God'. The one sure effect of the victory of secularism, which would inevitably accompany disestablishment, would be the loss of the people— 'handing them over either to Roman Catholicism or to Infidelity'.[48] With prophetic insight he saw that the victory of the secular State would draw together all Christian churches to withstand a common

---

43. *Ibid.*, pp. 17 and 41. He also believed the 'secular position of the Bishops was a great evil' in a society 'which is not only not Catholic, but of no particular religion.' G. A. Denison, *Notes of my Life* (1878), p. 178.
44. *Fifty Years at East Brent*, p. 246.
45. *Ibid.*, p. 25.
46. *Ibid.*, p. 294.
47. *Ibid.*, p. 292.
48. *Ibid.*, pp. 101–2.

enemy. 'I entirely believe that the State and its influences are even a worse enemy to the Church of England than Rome is, and I think it not impossible that a day may be not far off when England and Rome will have to fight side by side against infidelity.' [49]

The tragedy of the position taken by Joshua Watson and Archdeacon Denison was that it belonged to an age that was quickly passing away. Their scheme of national education, provided by the Church, was certainly altruistic in intent and national in scope—but, in the pluralistic society that slowly emerged during the century, it could not be implemented. Denison knew the significance of the Act of 1870: from that time schools identified with the Church of the nation would be 'an exception instead of what they ought to be, the rule'.[50] All their sacrifice, for so long cheerfully given in the cause of universal elementary education, seemed to them to have been in vain.

The intransigents played a valuable role in the creation of England's dual system of education. They ensured that Church schools did continue to exist in the pluralistic society which was emerging. But they also contributed much to national education as an end in itself. Even those who brought the new system into being recognized this. Forster paid public tribute to the Church's efforts,[51] and Earl Russell said of churchmen like Denison: 'They have subscribed to the utmost of their means for the promotion of education, solely, as I believe, from a desire to make their parishioners better men and better Christians, and for the general welfare of society.'[52] It was the Church more than any other body in the nation which had fought the common 'prejudice against educating the poor too highly' then held by the privileged classes.[53]

Unfortunately the redoubtable Denison could never really appreciate the pragmatic approach taken by a churchman like Hook to universal education. He was more caught up in the ecclesiastical policies formed in Convocation than he was in the life of the poor in the great cities. To him the appearance of school boards revealed that the State had become demonic. A radical alteration in the historic relationship between Church and State was underway: 'The supremacy of the Crown in all causes, Ecclesiastical and Civil means that the Crown as the fountain, under God, of all justice, is charged with the

---

49. *Ibid.*, p. 21.
50. *Ibid.*, p. 279.
51. C. K. F. Brown, *Church's Part in Education, 1833–1941* (1942), p. 101.
52. *Hansard*, CXCIV (1869), 807.
53. The words of William Thomson in his primary charge at York. Kirk Smith, *William Thomson*, p. 133.

careful keeping of the two jurisdictions, and with the careful guarding against all undue interference of the one with the other.'[54] As far as Denison was concerned, the Act of 1870, and all that it stood for, was an 'undue interference' in Church affairs by the State.

It is not often realized that much of the thought that lay behind the Act of 1870 came directly from Thomas Arnold—but this may help to explain the antipathy of some High-Churchmen to the new legislation. William Forster was a Quaker, although he had married Jane, daughter of Thomas Arnold; and it would seem that his wife had some influence on his thinking about the Church's role in education. Mrs. Humphrey Ward, who was a distant member of the Arnold family, said: 'It has always been clear to me that the scheme of the Bill was largely influenced by William Forster's wife, and through her, by the convictions and beliefs of her father. . . . it would never have taken the shape it did . . . but for the ardent beliefs of the young and remarkable woman . . . a devoted daughter of the Church, as Arnold, Kingsley and Maurice understood it'.[55]

As we shall now see, the High-Churchmen generally had a difficult time to appreciate the role of the Church in education as it was viewed by Arnold, Kingsley, and Maurice—the Broad-Churchmen of their age.

3. The Church and the Public Schools

IN THE same year that the Newcastle Commission gave its report on elementary education, a royal commission was set up, under the chairmanship of the Earl of Clarendon, to enquire into the state of the nine 'public schools' in the nation.[1] The *Cornhill Magazine* in May and December 1860, and again in March 1861, published letters by 'paterfamilias' which criticized the education provided for the 2,800 sons of the landed and propertied classes who attended these schools. The author of the

54. G. A. Denison, *Supplement to Notes of My Life, 1879, and Mr. Gladstone, 1886* (1893), p. 96.
55. Mary Augusta Ward, *Writer's Recollections* (1918), I, 36.
1. The nine schools were Eton, Winchester, Westminster, Charterhouse, St. Paul's, Merchant Taylors', Harrow, Rugby, and Shrewsbury. In 1862, 467 boys left these schools. *V.* I. L. Kandel, *History of Secondary Education* (1930), p. 290 ff.

articles was obviously a well-informed Old Etonian, and his writing influenced the setting up of the new commission.

After three years of inquiry, the commission revealed that the public schools were considered to be Church institutions; the senior members of the staff, at least, were clergymen of the Established Church; and there was no opposition to the strong ecclesiastical atmosphere which prevailed. Regular attendance at chapel was the rule; boys were prepared for confirmation by the school; and most of them received Holy Communion regularly. This produced in public-school pupils what Moberly of Winchester called 'a strong religious feeling of a very moderate, sober and traditional kind'. This 'public-school religion' influenced the character of the boys and gave them 'a stamp, not a very showy kind, but distinguished by a self-reliance, a modesty, a practical goodness'.[2]

Two questions interest us about this 'public-school religion'. Was it deliberately fostered by the Church? What was the effect it had on the social behaviour of the sons of privilege who attended these schools?

It seems clear that there was little real religious influence at work in the public schools early in the century: 'the recognized defect of the Public Schools in the reign of George III was a moral rather than an intellectual one.'[3] John Keate, who was headmaster of Eton from 1809 until 1834 took for granted that every boy would lie to him, and that he respected only the threat 'I'll flog you.'[4] It was also the age of student mutinies—the most famous Eton uprisings being those of 1810 and 1832, similar demonstrations taking place at Harrow and Winchester in 1818, and at Rugby in 1822. The stock question that George III addressed to Old Etonians was: 'Have you had any rebellions lately, eh, eh?'[5]

By the time an Eton boy was ready for the university he had been introduced to gluttony, drunkenness, an aptitude for brutal sports, and, probably, sexual vice. Between 1832 and 1841 it was common for seventy boys to be locked in the old Long Chamber between 8 p.m. and the following morning, without any supervision in this 'great, bare, dirty room'. Order was kept by the sixth-formers—when they were sober.[6] Because of the brutality at the school, particularly the

---

2. F. D. How, *Six Great Schoolmasters* (1904), p. 55: Moberly's evidence to the royal commission in 1864.
3. Adamson, *English Education*, p. 66.
4. Kandel, *History of Secondary Education*, p. 289.
5. J. W. Adamson, 'Education' in *Cambridge History of English Literature* (1934), XIV, 387.
6. G. R. Parkin, *Edward Thring* (1898), I, 22 ff.

system of fagging, those who left the public schools were the product of a very unsavoury system: 'the boy begins as a slave, and ends as a despot.'[7]

On 2 March 1825, the Hon. E. A. Cooper, younger brother of the future Lord Shaftesbury, was beaten to death in a fist-fight at Eton. The whole college turned out to witness the fight; between rounds the contestants were plied with neat brandy. When Cooper dropped dead, a verdict of manslaughter was returned against the other boy and some of the masters. They were later acquitted on the grounds that Cooper had died as the result of the amount of brandy consumed, rather than from the fight itself.[8]

The situation was no better in the other public schools. Samuel Butler, who was headmaster of Shrewsbury from 1798 until 1836, told of a boy drawing a knife to attack him when an attempt was made to chastise the boy for being drunk. Other pupils terrorized local farmers by killing their pigs in a mock boar hunt. Their reputation was such that no farmer would come forward to identify the offenders. Butler allowed his pupils to settle their differences in fist-fights; though he did write to one boy's parents when their son was caught carrying a loaded pistol. His masters also had their moral failings. The man in charge of the Shell was an insomniac who insisted upon teaching his class at 4 a.m. during the winter months.[9]

It was Butler, however, who began the scholastic and moral revolution in the public schools. He slowly introduced habits of hard work at Shrewsbury, which enabled his pupils to excel at the universities; and he also developed the idea that moral excellence was the chief end of education. He argued that if he could train his pupils to be honourable and virtuous he was conferring a much greater benefit upon them, and upon society, than if he simply imparted to them useful knowledge.

Better known in the history of the English public schools is Thomas Arnold. He was educated at Winchester; became a Fellow of Oriel College, Oxford, in 1815, and was elected Headmaster of Rugby at the end of 1827. Only then did he take full priest's orders. Hawkins, the Provost of Oriel, prophesied that if he were elected headmaster of Rugby, he would change the face of education throughout the public schools of England, and Arnold seems to have had the same idea

---

7. *Edinburgh Review*, LI (1830), 76.
8. J. W. Bready, *Lord Shaftesbury and Social-Industrial Progress* (1928), p. 19.
9. Samuel Butler, *Life and Letters of Dr. Samuel Butler, 1798–1836* (1896), I, 49 *passim*. Butler was also Archdeacon of Derby. In 1836 he became Bishop of Lichfield.

himself. He wrote to his friend George Cornish about his candidature: 'If I do get it . . . I should like to try whether my notions of Christian education are really impracticable, whether our system of public schools has not in it some noble elements which, under the blessing of the Spirit of all holiness and wisdom, might produce fruit even to life eternal.'[10]

Arnold's 'notions' were what distinguished him from Butler. Butler was a good churchman, and a great headmaster, whose personality allowed him to achieve a great deal. Arnold possessed not only the virtue and personal capacity of Butler, but also a clear Idea of the part the Church could play in the shaping of society according to Christian principles. His vision was shared by countless public school masters who were influenced by what he accomplished at Rugby.

To the masters of the Arnold tradition, education was primarily the religious and moral training of a boy. 'He is not well educated who does not know the will of God, or knowing it, has received no help in his education towards being inclined and enabled to do it.'[11] Their pupils were educated to be morally superior gentlemen, who would leave school to engage in their duty—the Christianizing of the English nation. This did not mean engaging in activities like the disseminating of Evangelical tracts, or the supporting of purely ecclesiastical concerns. Rather, it was the furthering of Christian principles which formed the common bond of English society. As Basil Willey has written of Thomas Arnold: 'For him the worst apostasy, the source of all woes, was the separation of things secular from things spiritual: this meant, on the one hand, the handing over of all temporal concerns to the devil or to the operation of natural laws, and on the other, the retreat of religion into priestly inutilities.[12] It was no accident that so many of Arnold's own pupils became workers for social, economic, and political reform.

Arnold's moral fervour 'worked an extraordinary change in the life of Rugby, and through Rugby, in public schools and in English education at large. In his view, "the forming of the moral principles and habits" alone constituted education.'[13] Arnold was quite willing to introduce modern studies such as history, geography, and modern languages, or any discipline which he believed would assist his pupils

10. Stanley, *Life of Arnold*, I, 79.
11. J. J. Findlay, *Arnold of Rugby* (1897), p. 133.
12. Basil Willey, *Nineteenth Century Studies* (1949), p. 54.
13. Adamson, 'Education' in *Cambridge History of English Literature*, XIV, 414.

in their future service to the nation. But it never occurred to him, or to his followers, that education need not be connected with Christianity.

It should be noted here that Arnold did not propagate the 'muscular Christianity' which *Tom Brown's Schooldays* did so much to popularize, and was so welcomed by men like Charles Kingsley. He was the prophet of moral idealism who 'imbued his pupils with a zest for righteousness . . . to use the metaphor of "Rugby Chapel" he set them on the road to the City of God.'[14] The 'moral priggishness' of a disciple such as A. P. Stanley, is more characteristic of Thomas Arnold than is the 'muscular Christianity' of Thomas Hughes: 'Arnold's ideals were altogether loftier than this. He pointed to horizons which a Tom Brown could only dimly descry.'[15] As David Newsome points out in his excellent study *Godliness and Good Learning*, the important fact that we need to remember is that Stanley knew Arnold, and Thomas Hughes did not.

It is true that by about 1870 Arnold's teaching had begun to give way to a new way of life among boys which encouraged manliness, showing of spirit, and prowess at sports rather than moral excellence; but the original religious zeal of the great headmaster was never completely lost, and was an integral part of what was inherited by later generations of 'muscular Christians'. We will look at Arnold's ecclesiastical thought in some detail in Chapter VII; here our concern will be to trace its influence on churchmen who were concerned with the education of the young in the public schools.

One of the most prominent of these men was John Percival, who was successively Headmaster of Clifton College, President of Trinity College, Oxford, Headmaster of Rugby, and Bishop of Hereford. Immediately after his ordination to the diaconate in 1860, he went to Rugby as a classics master. At that time, the headmaster was Frederick Temple. When Thomas Arnold died in 1842 he had been succeeded by Archibald Campbell Tait, the future Primate; the next headmaster had been F. M. Goulburn, the future Dean of Norwich, who had as one of his assistants Edward White Benson, who was also to become an Archbishop of Canterbury. Temple had succeeded Goulburn and carried on the Arnold tradition. Soon after taking up his position, Temple had preached a memorable sermon in the College Chapel on 'The Rich Young Man', which caused Benson to say: 'He is the man to improve us all'.[16]

14. F. J. Woodward, *Doctor's Disciples* (1954), p. 32.
15. David Newsome, *Godliness and Good Learning* (1961), p. 37.
16. W. F. Aitken, *Frederick Temple* (1903), p. 4.

Rugby was a breeding ground for future headmasters of public schools. Benson left to launch Wellington and G. G. Bradley had gone to Marlborough just before Percival's arrival. Among his contemporaries was James Robertson, the future Headmaster of Haileybury. Temple was impressed with Percival from the time of his arrival at Rugby, particularly by his strong sense of duty. When Charles Evans, the fifth-form master at Rugby decided to accept the Headmastership of King Edward's School, Birmingham, instead of that of Clifton College, Temple suggested the daring appointment of Percival to the latter post, although he was only twenty-seven years of age.

Like those masters who had left Rugby before him, Percival went to Clifton to carry on the moral revolution that Arnold had begun in the English public schools. The masters that he brought to the school were those that he believed had the 'individuality and character' to promote the moral improvement of the school: 'whose words somehow rang true in the ears of the not naturally religious boy, and enlisted him on the side of right, of public spirit, of purity, of large-heartedness and courage, of virtues which appeal to a boy.'[17] His appeal to this type of young master was such that one of them later said: 'In the early days of teaching I went to Percival rather than to Clifton.'[18] Another, Sir Herbert Warren, who became President of Magdalen, said of Percival: 'his main secret was that he swept us all along, boys and masters together, with a great moral impulse.'[19]

> It was his constant effort to lift up the soul of this School above the heavy mists of indifference, sloth and self-complacency . . . to awaken every one of the young souls before him to their possibilities as children born of God, born with the very life of God in them, born to be God's fellow-workers in the creation of a society of high ideals. . . . his conviction was so strong and so contagious that he attained it to a degree to which in schools I know no parallel.[20]

In 1879 Percival left Clifton to become President of Trinity College, Oxford: to instil a 'greater sense of religious and moral and political leadership of the nation' at Oxford.[21] He was succeeded by J. M. Wilson, whom he had known at Rugby. Wilson continued the Arnold tradition which Percival had brought to Clifton.

While Percival was at Clifton and Oxford, Rugby began to lose

17. William Temple, *Life of Bishop Percival* (1921), p. 20.
18. *Ibid.*, p. 25.
19. *Ibid.*, p. 29.
20. *Ibid.*, pp. 21–22. The eulogy of Canon Wilson in the College Chapel after Percival's death.
21. *Ibid.*, p. 53.

the moral impulse which Arnold had given to it. When Temple left Rugby for the see of Exeter in 1869, he had suggested that Percival might succeed him. But the fact that he was 'one of Temple's men' led to his rejection by the Trustees of the school who wanted an indisputable Conservative as headmaster. Reaction to the 'moral earnestness' of the Arnold tradition had fostered a party among the Trustees who resisted the reform movement. During four short years their candidate, a Dr. Hayman, precipitated a crisis at the school, which went literally to pieces; its 'bright-shining sun setting in clouds of conservative haze and High Church incense'.[22]

The governing body was reformed; bitterly contested law-suits were begun; and Hayman was dismissed, to be appointed by Disraeli to a crown living in the diocese of Carlisle.

Once more Rugby was offered to Percival, much to the dismay of Clifton College, but in 1874 the appointment went to T. W. Jex Blake, another Old Rugbeian, who was the conspicuously successful Principal of Cheltenham. He succeeded in restoring peace and harmony in the school; numbers began to rise again, and a new building programme was begun. When Jex Blake resigned in 1886, his position was offered to Percival.

Jex Blake had restored the prosperity of the school, and his rule had been a necessary period of consolidation. But the moral impulse was gone; bullying and immorality among the pupils had once more begun, and intellectually the school was slack. Percival began a reformation. He expelled five boys on the spot, striking their names publicly off the school list, and sent many others away at the end of the term. Percival fully accepted Arnold's dictum: 'The first, second, and third duty of a Headmaster is to get rid of unpromising material.'[23] A contemporary has described the scene with which Percival lashed the vice of the school 'with white-hot scorn and disgust', and the 'moral cowardice' of those who had for so long tolerated it.

> Nobody who was present at that gathering in New Big School will ever forget it. One could feel the School wincing and writhing—the tall stern figure on the platform (he seemed about forty feet high), the white face lit up with intense but controlled moral indignation—the pause, and then the word or phrase that fell like a lash. And behind it all the feeling of power and righteousness and judgment to come. The School went out smarting, some of them angry, all of them frightened.[24]

22. *Ibid.*, p. 43.
23. *Ibid.*, p. 102.
24. *Ibid.*, p. 101.

Between 1887 and 1895, when he was made Bishop of Hereford, Percival led Rugby back to the way of life it had known between the headmasterships of Arnold and Temple. He freed the school from its over-emphasis on athletic distinction; reminded the sixth form of its moral responsibility for the welfare of the whole school; and combated sloth by treating schoolboy idleness as a grievous moral fault. He added once more to the staff men of brilliant promise—such as George Smith, future Headmaster of Dulwich, and A. A. David, future Headmaster of Clifton and Rugby. When he finally left Rugby, his successor, H. A. James, said of the state of the school:

> I found little or nothing to be attempted beyond the continued maintenance of the high traditions which he had so sedulously developed. He left me a loyal and capable staff of assistant-masters, and an equally loyal and capable Sixth Form, both alike largely imbued with his own sense of responsibility and of the possibilities, as well as the dangers of public school life. The Arnold tradition of governing through the Sixth had, in his eight years of rule, received a new stimulus and a new life.[25]

Perhaps the headmaster who contributed most to the development of 'muscular Christianity' in the public schools was Edward Thring, a product of the infamous Long Chamber of Eton in the days of Dr. Keate. When he came to Uppingham in 1853 he found it a small country grammar school of sixty-one boys; when he left it thirty-four years later it was a great modern public school of the first rank. Thring was an excellent athlete himself, and he tended to play down 'over-intellectualism' in the school.[26] What he wanted from his boys was not merely a good performance in scholarship, but the development of a strong moral sense of service to society. The boys of the school assisted in a mission to North Woolwich in 1870—a practical lesson in giving personal help to the poor: 'England has never before had this fastening of a school on to real life work in the world outside'.[27]

Thring was instrumental in forming a regular conference system among headmasters of public schools, which sought to provide an alternative to state-directed secondary education. By 1875 the schools which regularly sent a contingent of boys up to Oxford and Cambridge were members of this Headmasters' Conference. They were members of a federation of educational societies which served a common cause

25. *Ibid.*, p. 107.
26. Newsome, p. 221.
27. Parkin, I, 314.

—the shaping of national character through lives of 'service' offered to society by those boys who had attended public schools. The spirit in the schools continued to be that of Thomas Arnold—however much 'muscular Christianity' began to displace earlier 'moral fervour'. As new public schools like Cheltenham, Marlborough, and Wellington appeared, 'the ideals of outlook and discipline were those of the Public School, Rugby being the pattern'.[28]

Perhaps the importance which the public schools gave to moral training and character building may be revealed most clearly by the evidence on secondary education in these institutions given by Edward Bowen, a Harrow classics master, who was interviewed by the Royal Commission on Secondary Education, 25 July 1894.

Q. You do not think that there are certain mental laws or processes common to, or applicable to, the teaching of all scholars alike, whether primary, secondary, or University, which it is possible to understand better by having one's attention systematically called to them, and the use that may be made of them?

A. No, I do not think so, although it seems rash to say it, because a bad man teaching history well is a far worse thing than a good man teaching history badly.

Q. But what is suggested is that a good man might teach history better?

A. Still, all the same, I venture to suggest that the man himself is so much more important than the details of school-work, that it is not worth while thinking of the second in comparison with the first.

Q. (A Commissioner.) You said that the teachers of the public boarding schools were chiefly moral and social forces. Does it not occur to you that it is possible that the moral and social force, even in a most admirable person in that capacity, may be largely discounted and counteracted in schools by want of ease and power in the art of teaching?

A. Yes.

Q. And I suppose it often happens that a graduate going from a university to a school of the type we are now considering finds he is inclined to be a failure in the art of teaching and has to give up the work?

A. Very seldom, if he is such a person as we are thinking of.

Q. But there is no guarantee that he is likely to be a suitable person for the work to which he goes?

A. The headmaster would never think of taking him unless he was.

Q. I am thinking of the pedagogic qualification. Neither the assistant master nor the headmaster can know that this particular graduate is likely to be successful as a teacher?

A. I can hardly agree with that, because when you know a man you can pretty well form an estimate beforehand as to whether he will be likely to succeed. One can gauge to a very large extent his qualifications: for instance, say, good humour, good health, the tone and justness of his mind.

Q. Then you take the view that the art of teaching in practice, and discipline in particular, may be considered as very largely the reflex of a man's character upon the children?

28. Adamson, *English Education*, p. 256.

8*

A. Yes.

Q. And therefore nothing but inherent character can go a very long way towards effective teaching?

A. I would go a very long way towards that.[29]

How much the 'inherent character' of the public school masters was the result of direct religious influence is often difficult to estimate. George Moberly of Winchester was influenced by the Oxford Movement and was a personal friend of John Keble. Not surprisingly his rule in school was described as an attempt 'to make the boys religious', and in all he did he was an ecclesiastic before anything else. But the influence of Arnold upon him was great—as he acknowledged in a letter to A. P. Stanley. After describing the 'irreligiousness' of the undergraduates at Oxford, just before the Tractarian movement began, he describes the influence that Arnold's Old Rugbeians had at the university:

> It soon began to be matter of observation to us in the University, that his pupils brought quite a different character with them to Oxford than that which we knew elsewhere. I do not speak of opinions; but his pupils were thoughtful, manly-minded, conscious of duty and obligation, when they first came to college; we regretted indeed, that they were often deeply imbued with principles which we disapproved, but we cordially acknowledged the immense improvement in their characters in respect of morality and personal piety, and looked on Dr. Arnold as exercising an influence for good, which (for how many years I know not) had been absolutely unknown to our public schools.[30]

Just as much as Arnold, Temple, or Percival, George Moberly believed in later years that education was primarily the religious and moral training of human nature.[31]

Few of the other great headmasters were as religious as Moberly. Charles J. Vaughan, who began the regeneration of Harrow, increasing the school's numbers from 69 to 469 during his headmastership, had been a member of Arnold's inner circle of favourite pupils, and his 'intense holiness' of life had its influence on his students and masters. But Vaughan's religion was less ecclesiastical in its outlook, and the men who succeeded him were concerned more with the moral improvement of boys than with churchmanship. Edward Bowen said that 'Vaughan invented discipline', and it was his emphasis on character-building that endured, rather than holiness of life.[32]

29. W. E. Bowen, *Edward Bowen: a Memoir* (1902), 365–66.

30. *Life of Arnold*, I, 183.

31. Charlotte Moberly, *Dulce Domum: George Moberly, his Family and Friends* (1911), p. 31.

32. Bowen, p. 56. *V.* P. Grosskurth, *John Addington Symonds* (1964), p. 35 ff.

This pattern seemed to be followed in most of the great schools during the century. After Marlborough was founded in 1843, it fell into disrepute; and the headmaster, Matthew Wilkinson, resigned in 1852 after a rebellion. The Council sent to Rugby to get a strong man to put the school in order. The man they received in 1852 was G. E. L. Cotton, one of Thomas Arnold's assistant masters. He approached his task as a kind of missionary work in the educational field, and was so successful that by the time of his departure to become Bishop of Calcutta, six years later, 'a self-respecting corporate spirit had been inspired'.[33] His successor, G. G. Bradley, who was also from Rugby, continued Cotton's work, though he put increasing emphasis on games because of the moral discipline they taught. He could hardly have been called a religious headmaster; though he did grimly inspire in his boys a sense of the value of truth, honour, and the meaning of duty and responsibility: 'Do your duty, do it quickly and don't make a fuss about it.'[34] By the time that Bradley left Marlborough in 1870, excessive intellectualism as well as excessive piety was no longer as acceptable as it had been at Arnold's Rugby. Bradley agreed with his contemporary at Rugby, Frederick Temple: 'I do not think the diminution of religious zeal an evil; I think much of it unhealthy. What I want is a quiet sense of duty'.[35]

Thomas Arnold's 'moral fervour' was succeeded by Temple's 'quiet sense of duty' as the religious ethos of the public schools. F. C. Hawtrey, who succeeded the infamous Keate at Eton in 1834 tried to win the loyalty of his pupils by trust, and his life was viewed as that 'of a Christian gentleman living a blameless life among his fellows'.[36] Other headmasters who tried to emulate Arnold, like Benjamin Kennedy of Shrewsbury, never quite succeeded in being religious in the way that the great Rugby headmaster had been. Emboldened by Arnold's example, Kennedy also attempted to use the College Chapel and its pulpit as a means of bringing 'religious influence' to bear upon the boys, but 'the impression he gave to his pupils was that his religious teaching was perfunctory.'[37]

The moral discipline and character-building ethos of the public schools has often been referred to as 'public-school religion'. In one sense it was, and the great schools were part of a sectarian movement within the Establishment, with Thomas Arnold as its prophet. This

33. How, *Six Great Schoolmasters*, p. 235.
34. *Ibid.*, p. 262.
35. *Ibid.*, p. 207.
36. *Ibid.*, p. 27.
37. *Ibid.*, p. 106.

sometimes seems to be implied by the religious programme many of the headmasters initiated. Canon J. M. Wilson, who succeeded Percival at Clifton, said of his predecessor's failure to speak of the great doctrines of Christianity, or of the nature of the Church:

> The School, he felt, is our spiritual community. This is our Church: and through loyalty to the School he illustrated what the Church was in the mind of Christ. He taught how 'Christ's first act was to gather a society round Him in the midst of the common working-day world, and to build up His Kingdom on the foundations of social life'. That building up of the kingdom must be begun in schools. None who knew him could doubt his fervent belief in such a church, loyal to its Head, as the only means for calling out men's highest powers in the great world.[38]

When one considers the flattering, if not adulating, biographies of schoolmasters, and the accounts of public-school life, which appeared in the latter part of the century, it would seem that loyalty to the old school had become almost religious in expression.

What is clear is that the public schools, and their religion, had great appeal to the new wealthy middle class of the nation. They clearly demonstrated 'what could be achieved by an individual headmaster enjoying freedom from interference, whether from a state authority or his own governors'.[39] The appeal of the Arnold tradition to middle-class parents was that it gave an education which 'fits a boy for life, which develops his intelligence, trains his judgment and gives him inward resources which promote his happiness and make him master of himself'.[40]

Churchmen generally were well satisfied with English public-school education, the formal religion of the school chapel, and the religion of 'service' which was brought into society by those who attended the schools. But, as the middle class grew in numbers during the century, satisfaction was marred by the realization that few of the sons of the lower stratum of the middle class found places in these schools of privilege. There was also some lingering suspicion, on the part of churchmen like Archdeacon Denison, over the 'Arnoldian' religion of the public schools. We must now look at the work of Nathaniel Woodward, who decided to provide schools for this neglected class of the community—schools which Denison believed were 'real Church schools'.[41]

38. Temple, *Life of Percival*, p. 22.
39. Kandel, p. 311.
40. *Life of Creighton*, I, 390–91: A letter of 7 Nov., 1899 to the *Worcester Herald* on ideal secondary education.
41. Denison, *Fifty Years at East Brent*, p. 279.

4. The Church and the Education of the Middle Class

THOMAS ARNOLD noted the growing power of the 'middling classes', and believed their education in Christian principles to be 'a question of the greatest national importance'.[1] Another churchman who arrived at this belief was Nathaniel Woodard. He had been appointed, by Blomfield, as curate-in-charge of the new district of St. Bartholomew, Bethnal Green, with the expectation that he would become first vicar when the mission became a parish.[2] He knew the working class of the area intimately, and he came to the conclusion that for the Church to reach the masses it had to have strong support from the laity of the middle class. If the numerous members of the latter class could be filled with a spirit of service, rather than one of selfishness, they would not only assist the Church in its mission, but would help to ease the tension which existed between themselves and the workers. He persuaded many middle-class people to help him during his time in Bethnal Green, and he always acknowledged that without their help he could have done little to influence the working-class population. Many of them later assisted him in his educational efforts.

Unfortunately for Woodard, Bishop Blomfield took exception to a sermon he preached on sacramental confession in 1843. After some months of correspondence, he was told that he would not become Incumbent of St. Bartholomew's because he preached and maintained doctrines 'at variance' with those of the Church of England. Woodard was a friend of Frederick Oakeley, one of the Tractarians who went over to Rome, but Woodard was never tempted to follow him. Rather he accepted from Blomfield a curacy in the parish of St. James', Clapton, although he was never happy there. Apparently, curate and bishop continued to respect each other, and Blomfield later invited Woodard to found schools in London.

In 1846 Woodard accepted the curacy of New Shoreham in Sussex, and it was here that his real work began. It was a place of some importance for coasting vessels, but there were few educational opportunities offered to the sons of the coasting captains. Because of what he had seen in Bethnal Green, Woodard knew the social unrest which followed neglect of education; and a few months after his arrival in the parish he decided to establish a grammar school where the boys could be taught subjects like navigation, and the French language, which would assist them in their future work. He also

1. Findlay, *Arnold of Rugby*, pp. 198–99.
2. John Otter, *Nathaniel Woodard* (1925), p. 9.

hoped that if the sons of prominent citizens of Shoreham were educated in Church principles, they would in turn influence the lower-class people who would work in their ships and shipyards.

From his experience in Bethnal Green, and from what he observed in the school he set up in his rectory at New Shoreham, Woodard evolved his idea of establishing schools for the middle classes of the nation, which would be based on Christian principles. Woodard was a practical man whose genius included a great ability to obtain financial support for his enterprises. One of the ways that he won the attention of the well-to-do who supported his schemes was through his suggestion that the revolutionary violence of 1848 in Europe was due in large part to the increase in irreligion among the masses. With the aid of privileged people in England, the Church had to begin widespread education of the middle class, who would in turn begin to act in Christian charity towards their employees. This plan had to begin immediately: 'It is a matter of life and death, security to the State, peace to society, and the regeneration of the masses of the people.'[3]

Woodard's plan had merit because it was then rare for thousands of workers to be employed in a single business. Employers knew their workers intimately, and they influenced them greatly. If the employers with small businesses could be imbued with Christian principles, a nation-wide moral education of the masses could begin to the benefit of all.

By 1848 Woodard's thought had matured sufficiently for him to present it to the public in a remarkable pamphlet entitled *A Plea for the Middle Classes*. He pointed out the difficulties experienced by 'gentlemen of small incomes, solicitors and surgeons with limited practice, unbeneficed clergymen, naval and military officers etc.' when it came to providing adequate education for their children. The Church might have some influence with these people; but it hardly touched the lives of the 'trades-class', whose members were 'so linked together by common interests that it moves as one body'. The tendency of the clergy was to visit the wealthy, or the very poor, but to neglect these middle-class people, who were of increasing social importance in the nation. This folly had come to an end if the Church was to serve the people: 'till the Church does educate and train up the middle classes, she can never effectually educate the poor'. The support of the middle classes was necessary to break down the 'unpleasant feeling' that existed between the clergy and the mass of the people.[4]

3. *Ibid.*, p. 38.
4. Nathaniel Woodard, *Plea for the Middle Classes* (1848), pp. 1–7.

Woodard's answer to the social unrest in the nation and to the needs of the poor, was the Christian education of the sons of middle-class parents—the employer class of the next generation. 'If we wish to work for the good of souls we cannot do better than work in this way . . . since hereby we shall get hold of the main strength of the nation—the best disposed people in the Kingdom, if fairly dealt with; and if God give His blessing, if we gain them, a way opened for effectually securing the poor.'[5] Woodard was a High-Churchman, but his religion was a practical one: 'he was acutely aware of the danger and even the absurdity of the Christian religion divorced from ordinary life, of sacred truth separated from secular knowledge.'[6] The Church as the educator of the nation had to provide training in Christian morality and useful knowledge immediately, to that class which could be of most benefit to society as a whole.

In spite of the fact that his pamphlet was badly printed, unattractive in appearance, and privately circulated, it gained much attention from High-Churchmen like Gladstone and Pusey, and from Broad-Churchmen like Julius Hare, Archdeacon of Lewes. An immediate result of its appearance was a substantial grant for Woodard's work, which was received from Magdalen College, Oxford, the patron of New Shoreham and some neighbouring parishes. This enabled Woodard to purchase houses in Shoreham for his pupils to live in, and the Society of St. Nicholas College came into being. It was dedicated to 'the education of the sons of the middle classes at such terms as will make education available for most of them'.[7] The education to be provided was both sacred and secular. Woodard intended to 'leaven a considerable number of them with a truly religious spirit; while the main portion will be awakened to religious ideas and to more rational views of the social institutions about them.'[8]

By 1850 the scheme had so developed that Woodard was able to give up his parochial duties to devote himself entirely to building up his school, and to planning others. In 1853 a second school was opened with permanent quarters at Hurstpierpoint. Then in 1857 the Shoreham school was moved to Lancing, to become the headquarters for the Society of SS. Mary and Nicolas, Lancing. Another school was

5. *Ibid.*, p. 12.
6. W. B. D. Heeney, *The Established Church and the Education of the Victorian Middle Classes: a Study of the Woodard Schools, 1847–1891*, unpublished Oxford University D. Phil thesis, p. 358.
7. Otter, p. 49.
8. *St. Nicolas College for the Sons of Small Shopkeepers, Artisans, Clerks and Others of Limited Means*, n.d., p. 9.

opened at Shoreham in the following year, to be known as St. Saviour's College, Shoreham. In 1870 this school moved to its permanent home at Ardingly. It was planned that many of the Lancing graduates would pass on to the universities, and that many of the Hurstpierpoint graduates would be qualified teachers who would provide Ardingly with some of its teaching staff. Lancing, with its great chapel, was to be the central school of the system.

By the time these three schools were operating, Woodard was planning to found schools in the industrial midlands; the home of so many of the new members of the middle classes. With this idea in mind Woodard wrote a public letter to the Marquis of Salisbury outlining his educational ideas.

He said that he believed national education to be the concern of the Church, which had traditionally borne this responsibility. At the moment the Church was not as concerned as it might be about 'the peril to society from leaving the great masses of the people to seek out for themselves, as best they may, an education which may fit them to discharge those responsible duties which the State has of late years cast upon them'. The Church particularly neglected the education of the middle classes, who should be 'the principal people committed to her charge'.[9] 'The population of the country . . . has made its chief extension in the direction of those sections of society called the middle and lower middle classes; and the Church being taken unawares and without any machinery to meet the wants of this new condition of things has suffered greatly in its hold upon the country.'[10] Because of neglect by the Church, 'the leading representatives of this energetic and restless middle class' had fallen under the influence of Dissent.

Woodard, like many High-Churchmen, was still inclined to regard Dissenters as churchmen, regardless of their protestations. He believed that 'a large portion of the Dissent of the country is far from hostile to the national religion', and he expected that his schools, when established in the north, would be used by 'good Dissenters' as well as by churchmen. He was saddened by some Dissenters who used religion to forward interests that were purely secular: 'What we complain of is that under the cover of Dissent, political speculators combine to injure the Church.'[11]

Woodard believed the choice for members of the middle classes was

9. Nathaniel Woodard, *Scheme of Education of St. Nicholas College: Letter to the Marquis of Salisbury* (1883), p. 9.
10. *Ibid.*, p. 3.
11. *Ibid.*, p. 32.

not between the National Church or Dissent, but between the Church and secularism. He challenged churchmen to consider whether they could morally abandon the youth of the nation. Which would they choose for the young: 'to be trained in a hard, commercial, un-sympathetic irreligious, and un-English system . . . or to combine and have a great and united scheme of National and Christian Education, *cost what it may* for *all* classes which shall be held to belong, and which shall belong to the Church as an independent corporation'.[12] Wood-ard thought the Church could act as the social catalyst of the nation, by providing centres of education similar to the public schools, but with 'the additional merit of a union of all classes . . . opening a way to the humblest person to reach the highest position'.[13] Church schools need not be dominated, as they so often were, by the clergy and the local gentry. Woodard wanted his schools to 'belong to the public'.[14]

To make his scheme national in scope, Woodard proposed to divide the nation into five areas, each of which would maintain a boarding school for the sons of the middle classes. By the time of his death, schools had been founded in three of his five divisions. The seven schools he founded himself, and the two others added before the end of the century, together with six girls' schools, were the result of his work to bring education, based on Christian principles, to the middle classes.[15]

The schools had their failings. The prominence given to the role of the chaplain in the schools, and the encouragement of sacramental confession, tended to give them a sectarian character. The cheapest schools, Ardingly, Ellesmere, and Worksop began to become too expensive for the boys for whom they were expressly built. And Woodard's reluctance to accept help from the State may be questioned. Like Archdeacon Denison he believed that the State inspectors' 'object is not to examine but to corrupt; to force you to accept their system, or to use the agency of examination to injure and break up the school'.[16]

Quite apart from what the schools accomplished, or the question of what they might have been able to do with State aid, is the problem of their significance in the history of the Church's relationship with State and society at this time. The Woodard schools are almost symbolic of what the Church hoped to accomplish. Accepting the traditional role of the Church as the educator of the nation, Woodard and his

12. *Ibid.*, p. 15.
13. *Ibid.*, p. 22.
14. *Ibid.*, p. 21.
15. For a summary of his work v. Ollard, *Short History of the Oxford Movement*, p. 168.
16. Otter, p. 224.

supporters deliberately set out to capture the middle classes of the nation—to win them over to support the mission of the Church in society. Their hope was the total enlistment of the sympathies and resources of this increasingly powerful social group in the cause of Christianizing the nation.

5. The Church and the Education of the Working Class

ONE OF the truly creative men in the Church at this time was Frederick Denison Maurice. The son of a Unitarian minister, he became a clergyman in the Church of England because of the comprehensiveness, or catholicity of its faith, contrasted with the narrowness of sectarianism. In 1846 he was appointed Professor of Theology at the newly created theological school of King's College, London; but he was forced to resign from this position because he attacked the popular view of the endlessness of future punishment. His critics accused him of teaching 'that there was no hell', and the Evangelical *Record* was unremitting in its attack.

This victim of ecclesiastical obscurantism was as concerned as Woodard with the problem of national education. Like Woodard he was sure that the Church, in spite of its failings, should be the educator of the English people. The Church was the only corporation in the nation that was catholic enough to supply the educational needs of all the people, and to contribute to the need for unity between the classes: 'the Church is the great schoolmistress of mankind, to educate us into the highest knowledge and happiness of which we are capable.'[1] But sometimes, as Maurice knew, churchmen engaged in education did not seek the truth: 'If Schools and Universities do not by their acts and words testify their faith in the truth, they cheat the country of the chief blessing which they are meant to impart, if they deny it by their words and acts, they and the country suffer together.'[2]

When churchmen did not seek the truth, they were not serving the Church but what he particularly abhorred—a Church party, or sys-

1. F. D. Maurice, *Kingdom of Christ* (1838), II, 68. Maurice in 1866 became Knightsbridge Professor of Moral Philosophy at Cambridge.
2. F. D. Maurice, *The New Statute and Mr. Ward: Letter to a Non-Resident Member of Convocation* (1845), p. 15.

tem. He said of the Evangelicals: 'No people are less in earnest for truth as truth, more reckless of their ways of preaching that which they substitute for it.'[3] He much preferred the humble spirit of inquiry of John Stuart Mill to their narrow ecclesiasticism: 'One of the few writers of this day who has made a deliberate conscientious effort to discover and treat fairly the meaning of those with whom he differs most widely, and whose mental constitution is most unlike his own.'[4]

Maurice also had difficulty in appreciating the Tractarians, for two reasons. First of all he castigated them for not being catholic in their thought; he believed they were concerned only with ecclesiastical affairs, not with the mission of the Church to the world. In his quixotic fashion he was willing to defend W. G. Ward at the time of his degradation in the university, but he said of Ward's work: 'he calls it "The Ideal of a Christian Church"; it is from first to last, "The Ideal of an Ecclesiastical System".'[5] The hierarchical ecclesiastical body concerned with its own spiritual existence, which he believed the Tractarians wanted, was to Maurice a direct contradiction of catholicism: 'an inverted idea of that which is really divine, universal, adapted to all wants—the Catholic Church'.[6]

He believed the Tractarians to be obsessed with a theology based on 'notions' of 'Fathers, Schoolmen, Mystical Writers', and not on the living thought which lay behind such pious expressions. He refused to confine himself to the viewpoint of Latin theology, and returned in his thought to the Christian Platonists of an earlier age, to the essentially Incarnational theology of the Greek Fathers of Alexandria. Like 'Clemens and Origen' the Church should not refuse to believe 'that all goodness of every kind must have Christ as its author'.[7] One of the great blessings in Christian history was the Reformation because it destroyed the medieval system: 'The Reformation was necessary because it connected faith and learning with the ordinary work of man; because it would not allow either to be shut up in monasteries and universities.'[8]

Maurice refused to separate the sacred and the profane in life: 'I hold that all our knowledge may be traced ultimately to Revelation

3. *Life of Maurice*, I, 434.
4. F. D. Maurice, *Thoughts on the Rule of Conscientious Subscription: Second Letter to a Non-Resident Member of Convocation* (1845), p. 50.
5. *Ibid.*, p. 27.
6. *Ibid.*, p. 29.
7. Maurice, *New Statute and Mr. Ward*, p. 23.
8. F. D. Maurice, *Learning and Working: Six Lectures in London* (1855), p. 60.

from God.' The clergyman was denying his vocation if he withdrew in any way from the world.

> He separates himself from the others if he assumes that he is spiritual and that they are secular. Then he will become the most mischievous of all beings, the so-called director of consciences, one who may withdraw either the lady or the working-woman from plain homely duties, from the earnest cultivation of her faculties, and tempt her to seek the good of her soul by going out of the path of God's commandments, by crushing the powers He has given her to use, by becoming a servant of His servants instead of his own freed woman.[9]

Although he was suspicious of the Tractarian form of clericalism, which he believed to be ecclesiastical and world-renouncing, the role of the clergy in society was of great importance to him. The clergy had a peculiar opportunity to know the real life of the masses—'the life of the people in hovels, in workhouses, in hospitals, as well as in reformatories and penitentiaries'.[10] Their pastoral role put them in the position where they could bridge the widening gulf between the social classes of the new industrial culture, particularly in the field of education. The blessings that God had given them were not for their benefit alone: 'Let them understand that God has been educating them to educate their brethren of the working class.'[11]

Because the clergy were prone to listen to the blandishments of both the Evangelicals and the Tractarians, and to withdraw from the world into purely ecclesiastical concerns, Maurice wanted them to engage in national education which would bring them out of their cloistered preserves. He wished to bring them 'to work in some college with those of other callings who will not take his words for law, who will have much knowledge in which he is utterly wanting, who will have a keen eye to see where he is passing himself off for that in which he is not'.[12] This would rid them of the idea that the Church was the fellowship of the spiritually elect, or limited to those who attached themselves to an apostolic succession of bishops. They would begin to know the Catholic Church as 'the life giving energy to every body in the midst of which she dwells.'[13]

Maurice was as pragmatic as Woodard in his educational ideas;

9. F. D. Maurice, *Lectures to Ladies on Practical Subjects* (1855), pp. 45–51, lecture on the College and the Hospital.
10. Maurice, *Learning and Working*, p. xvii.
11. *Ibid.*, p. xx.
12. Maurice, *Lectures to Ladies*, p. 23.
13. Maurice, *Kingdom of Christ* (1958), II, 254.

they were based on what he learned in his experiments, such as the Working Man's College, which opened in Red Lion Square, London, in November 1853. The college was non-sectarian because Maurice believed that 'Christ was the head of every man, not only those who believed in Him.'[14] The staff of the college, or 'the clerisy', were university men, artists, scientists, and others, who were devoted to teaching the large body of workers who formed the nucleus of the student body. Their instruction was an alternative to the 'vulgar, exclusive, caste signification' found in the teaching of the universities.[15]

This college became the prototype for others which were founded in the provinces. It was open to anyone who could read, write, and knew the first four rules of arithmetic. Those who were admitted were not spoonfed, and the curriculum sounds almost incredible to modern ears. To Maurice, every aspect of God's creation was worthy of study. Courses ranged from one in sanitary legislation by Thomas Hughes to one on the law of joint stock companies by J. M. Ludlow. Maurice himself lectured on the reign of Richard III as illustrated by Shakespeare's play. There were also lectures in algebra, arithmetic, English grammar, the Bible, geometry, politics, geography, history, practical jurisprudence, and mechanics. The most famous classes were those in art given by Ruskin, Rossetti, and Lowes Dickinson. Following his lectures on law and public health, Thomas Hughes gave boxing lessons to combat the 'round shoulders, narrow chests and stiff limbs' of the students, because he believed their bodies as well as their minds needed cultivation.[16]

In the Working Man's College, class differences began to break down and disappear, as teacher and student sought together the fullness of life which Maurice was convinced all men could appreciate —when they were aware of the activity of God at work in them, and the world in which they lived. Intellectuals of the privileged classes like Madox Brown and Burne-Jones, who lectured at the College, began to see that there was no qualitative difference between men which came from social class; rather, when given the opportunity, all men 'can learn to appreciate Michelangelo, Phidias, and Beethoven, and to perceive and value the glory and beauty of the world in which they live'.[17] One of these was Dr. F. J. Furnivall, the famous philologist. He said of his experience in the College: 'we

14. *Life of Maurice*, II, 304.
15. Maurice, *Learning and Working*, p. xvii.
16. J. F. C. Harrison, *History of Working Men's Colleges, 1854–1954* (1954), p. 64.
17. *The Working Men's College, 1854–1904*, ed. J. L. Davies (London, 1904), p. 36.

studied and took exercise together, we were comrades and friends and helped one another to live higher, happier and healthier lives, free from all stupid and narrow class humbug.'[18]

Maurice was more radical in his approach to education than Woodard. Both men were devoted to the cause of breaking down class suspicions and antagonisms through education. Both men agreed that the Church was uniquely empowered to do this because of its commission to be 'the healer of all privations and diseases, the bond of all classes, the instrument for reforming abuses, the admonisher of the rich, the friend of the poor, the asserter of the glory of that humanity which Christ bears'.[19] But where Woodard was concerned only to provide traditional education to the middle classes, who might be inspired to share their blessings in turn with the poor, Maurice was eager to have the middle and working classes educate each other by engaging in common endeavour. His ideas developed as he tried them out through 'pilot projects' like the Working Man's College. His desire was that 'all thought shall dwell upon action and express itself in action, that it shall not dwell apart in a region of its own'.[20]

6. *The Church and National Education*

IF AN attempt is made to understand the attitude of the Victorian Church to national education, it becomes clear that the Church never had time, in the midst of the tensions of the age, to produce a full and reasoned argument for retention of its traditional prerogatives in education. It felt itself to be a beleaguered city; the interest taken by the legislature in education being but one part of a steady encroachment by the State upon all the privileges of the Church.

In the universities, the liberal ideas which the Tractarians fought, the demand of Dissent for equal educational privileges, and the legislation proposed to 'de-Christianize' the colleges were all looked upon as part of a concerted and diabolic attack by secularism. The attempt

18. *Ibid.*, p. 60.
19. C. F. G. Masterman, *F. D. Maurice* (1907), p. 234.
20. Maurice, *Lectures to Ladies*, p. 60. Maurice had been one of the founders of Queen's College in 1848. To ensure that workers would not be intellectually separated from their wives, he also planned to provide education for working class wives.

to inquire into the way of life in the public schools by the legislature was also viewed with suspicion. Even the work of Woodard, in founding schools for the middle classes, and that of Maurice, in founding schools for the working classes, were not universally welcomed. Secularism had become a bogey which threatened either to take over Christian educational institutions completely, or to set up alternative instruction for the people which would not be based upon Christian principles. The fear that religion might be divorced entirely from national education was widespread. Frederick Maurice has said of his father's anxiety about education in 1839:

> The thing my father most dreaded was the 'attempt to treat a human being as composed of two entities, one called religious, the other secular'. He therefore at first, disliked the idea of money received from the State lest it should bribe the clergy into accepting terms that he believed would vitiate the very principle upon which they ought to educate—the essential oneness of the whole purpose of education. . . . fierce, indeed, was his opposition to the government, who were, as he thought at the time, striving to carry out the very project which he believed to be most mischievous—the transfer from the Church to the State of the education of the people.[1]

As might be expected, there was within the Church a whole spectrum of opinion about how dangerous the secular education provided by the State might be to religion. The extent of this thought is most clearly revealed in the writings of those who defended Church rights in elementary education—the most vulnerable part of the ecclesiastical system.

First of all there were intransigents like Archdeacon Denison and Joshua Watson, who thought that the State had already altered radically the traditional relationship between the two powers, the Church and the State, which Hooker had believed to exist: 'If the Government of England had been identified with the Church of England, as in other days, there would have been no attempt on the part of the Government to interfere with the duties and responsibilities of the Church.'[2]

Few churchmen would have disagreed with Denison when he wrote an open letter to Gladstone in 1847 on the role of the clergy in national education: 'The clergy are directly and solely responsible for all that is taught in the parish schools, for the matter and the manner of it. For the clergy are in virtue of their office 'the dispensers of the Word of God and of His Holy Sacraments' and it is upon the Word of God and upon His Holy Sacraments that all Christian Education in

1. *Life of Maurice*, p. 277.
2. G. A. Denison, *Position and Prospects of the National Society* (1853), p. 5.

any true sense of the word must be based.'[3] He might also have added that in England education had been the child and creature of the Church throughout the Middle Ages—and the State had approved this exclusive care until the Reformation. In a famous case in 1410, the common-law courts had acknowledged that schools were a spiritual matter and their jurisdiction was a concern for the ecclesiastical courts. Even after the Reformation the clergy dominated the universities; it was almost unknown to find any but men in holy orders masters of grammar schools; and it was only after 1700 that private elementary schools, without clerical supervision, began to appear.

The Dissenters naturally objected to the Church dominating national education, but, throughout most of the century, neither were they happy about the prospect of the State replacing the Church as the schoolmaster of the nation. Matthew Arnold believed he represented prevailing sentiment when he said in 1861: 'I believe, as every Englishman believes, that over-government is pernicious and dangerous; that the State cannot safely be trusted to undertake everything, to superintend everywhere.'[4] When Denison said that the State was 'very desirous to avail itself of the vast machinery ready to hand in the parochial schools, provided it could so influence and ultimately alter the character of these schools as to suit its own views and purposes',[5] he expressed the common contemporary fear of 'State absolutism which would deny the right of any other society, whether family or Church, to intervene in education'.[6]

Tory High-Churchmen like Denison and Watson had deep suspicion of the motives of the mill-owning and manufacturing class which was beginning to dominate in Parliament. They suspected that education might be looked upon as a means of preparing the poor to serve in their 'station in life', rather than the instilling of moral virtue in man for the general good of the nation. Philanthropic motives on the part of the middle class were hardly taken for granted. Most of the Evangelicals shared the general distrust of 'useful knowledge' which, without moral content, would only 'elevate man from the brute to approximate him to the fiend'. Canon Hugh Stowell, Vicar of Christchurch, Salford, who was well-loved by rich and poor alike,

3. G. A. Denison, *Church Schools and State Interference* (1847), p. 29.
4. Parliamentary Papers, *Reports of Assistant Commissioners on State of Popular Education in England* (1861), IV, 19.
5. Denison, *Position and Prospects*, p. 5.
6. J. N. Figgis, *Churches in the Modern State* (London, New York, 1913), p. 47, *Cf.* Webster, *Joshua Watson*, p. 41 for the prevalence of this fear.

said that the duty of churchmen was to 'either Christianize education or crush it'.[7]

Maurice has given us the most sustained and reasoned inquiry by a churchman into the nature of education that should be provided for the nation. He was convinced that the Church should be the educator of the people because it alone recognized the 'very first principle of education'—the presence in the world of the indwelling Spirit of God, which united all studies, and guided men 'into all good'.[8] His son said of his writings on national education:

> In 'Subscription no Bondage' he had maintained that it was essential to education, that there should be a study which bound all other studies together and made them one; and that *theology*, rightly understood as the study of existing facts, was the one fitted for the purpose. In the 'Kingdom of Christ' he maintained the existence of the Church under two aspects—one as a great social organization, the other as a great educational organization. He had summed up 'the duty which the State owes to the Church' in the words, 'It is simply this, to give the Church free scope to educate the people.'[9]

In 1839 he said the State was saying to the Church: 'The English poor are in a state of wretched ignorance, you have not cured it—we must.' But Maurice doubted the State's ability to provide the education which the people needed. Only the Church could indicate to men the existence of the divine among them, reconciling not only studies but classes and men. Without the power of 'reconciliation' which the Church alone possessed, secular educators would 'teach those who are indifferent to be more indifferent . . . more intolerant . . . the nation growing . . . more divided and broken.'[10] Secular education he believed to be 'narrow and exclusive.'[11]

Maurice admired 'Forster's . . . determination to do the very best he can, and by some means to utilise all moral and spiritual forces', but he saw the limitations of the Act of 1870: 'under the name of Progress we seem drifting back into the old Bell and Lancaster notion of cramming a number of children into a schoolroom and cramming them with a number of fragments of information—part labelled religious, part secular—which, if they should be able to digest this hard morsel, was to be their education.'[12] Only the Church could provide Catholic or unsectarian education which influenced the whole

7. Maltby, *Manchester and the Movement for National Elementary Education*, p. 53.
8. *Life of Maurice*, I, 257.
9. *Ibid.*, p. 269.
10. F. D. Maurice, *Has the Church or the State the Power to Educate the Nation* (1839), p. 163.
11. *Life of Maurice*, II, 613.
12. *Ibid.*

of man's existence. Secular education could never do this for it 'lies entirely beyond the limits of its province'.[13] Only the Church could educate all of man, and all the nation.

> However clergymen may express themselves—however clerical school-masters may express themselves—there is latent in them both a conviction that they are maintaining not a 'distinctive' theology, but a common theology; that they are teaching not something which separates one class of the people from another, but something which is wanted to make us a people. . . . to that thought the Secularist can do no justice, the Dissenters scarcely any. Therefore I cannot resist the conclusion that they are really imposing on the land not a positive, but a negative Secularism. . . . I do tremble for the loss to the people.[14]

Fortunately for the nation, the rigorist High-Church politicians like Denison, and the independent thinkers like Maurice, did not represent the whole body of churchmen. The pastors developed a different approach to education from that of the theologians, who tended to deal with the problem in the abstract, while engaged in ecclesiastical controversy. Many clergy and laymen began slowly to change their minds about resisting State assistance in education, because they were directly involved in the lives of the people of their parishes, and knew the desperate need for universal elementary education. Like Dean Hook they knew there would never be a radical redistribution of Church wealth to finance a real system of national Church education. If the only answer was to have religion depart-mentalized as a part of the curriculum, they were willing to accept it: 'to assist the government to empty gaols by building schools'.[15]

The situation was truly desperate in many parts of the nation, as the Commissioners of 1861 discovered. When the Rev. Mr. Rogers became incumbent of the Parish of St. Luke, formerly part of St. Giles, Cripplegate, in 1845, he found himself in a district which teemed with poor who had no educational opportunities whatever. When he devoted himself to remedying this situation, by beginning a school in a blacksmith's empty shed, the governors of Charterhouse, which was located in this ecclesiastical district, reluctantly presented him with a grant of land. By 1859 his schools were receiving a parliamentary grant of £15,511, but the heavily endowed parish was contributing only £50 for his work with the 'deserving poor'.[16]

---

13. Maurice, *Has the Church or the State Power to Educate*, pp. 303–4.
14. *Life of Maurice*, II, 611–12.
15. Stranks, *Dean Hook*, p. 81.
16. *Report of Commissioners on Popular Education*, IV, 315 ff.

In the parish of St. Giles, there were small endowed charity schools, like Trotman's Free School, which had an income of £110 per annum to support a resident master, and to provide free stationery for the six boys who attended the school. These schools were to be found in most of the old cities like Bristol, Coventry, York, or London; but the education they provided left much to be desired— certainly they were inferior to the inspected schools of the voluntary societies. At Reigate the Charity Inspector was elected, and the post was usually held by a 'decayed tradesman' who was in no way fitted for his position. These ancient charities were jealous of their endowments, and seldom assisted the extension of education among the poor. When the High-Church intransigents resisted State inspection of schools, they contributed to the continuance of these small but scandalous institutions. The Rev. J. S. Howson, Principal of the Collegiate Institution in Liverpool, revealed that charity schools generally educated children whose parents had a good income, and ignored large numbers of those living in utmost poverty, who were 'in great danger of falling into criminal habits'.[17]

Principal Howson also revealed that the day schools for the poor received help from the Church of England, the Roman Catholics, and the Unitarians. But no aid was forthcoming from Dissenters in the population—who said they preferred to support their own Sunday schools.[18] The principal of the York Training College said that Dissenting suspicions about religious influences were unfounded, even in church-sponsored schools. Not only was it possible for the vicar to avoid completely the actual task of teaching in his parish, but the teachers employed in church schools were seldom religious. They might have virtues such as 'manliness, integrity and truthfulness' said Hugh Robinson, the Principal, but anyone 'would be grievously disappointed who expected to find in the majority any very settled habits or devotion or any great religious earnestness'. The attribute of 'reverence' was only to be found among the small minority who had fallen under High-church influences.[19]

The best of churchmen engaged in elementary education saw that Church and State had to work together to relieve the poor of their dreadful moral, intellectual, and physical condition. One of these men was Richard Burgess, biblical scholar and Prebendary of St. Paul's, who accepted State initiative in educational reform, asking only that

17. *Ibid.*, p. 375.
18. *Ibid.*
19. *Ibid.*, p. 377.

the proposed educational system be truly Christian in nature: 'no schools founded or maintained by any public grant of money will be tolerated, unless the Scriptures according to the authorized version, *and that alone*, be made a part of the daily instruction.'[20] Another of these enlightened educators was Richard Dawes of King's Somborne, who deplored the attitude of those rural clergy guilty of using their schools to perpetuate the rural *status quo*.[21]

Much of the criticism of the education provided by the voluntary system came from churchmen who admitted the failure of their schools to provide nation-wide elementary education. But these critics were reluctant to have the State dictate the terms on which it would take over the traditional task of the Church. They wanted the Church to sacrifice some of its prejudices for the attainment of great national object—the eradication through education of social decay and immorality in the manufacturing districts.[22] But they also wanted the State to safeguard religious teaching in aided schools; and most of them, though with many misgivings, welcomed the 'dual system' compromise in 1870. They knew what Mr. Cowper-Temple meant when he said in 1857 that to expect the schoolmaster to teach virtue without doctrinal religion, and to inculcate a sense of duty without distinctive Christianity, was 'to impose on him a difficult or hopeless task'.[23] But there seemed no other way forward, and reluctantly, for the sake of the commonwealth, the Church agreed to the compromise.

Those who would have refused any compromise did so largely because they were carried away by ecclesiastical politics. Maurice, who saw the inevitability of Church and State working together to implement national education, had little sympathy with Denison, who would have 'no agreement with the Committee of Council at all'. He believed that Denison would have made 'a very capital Lord George Gordon, if he had lived in that day'. Denison often seemed to love the battles he fought for their own sake; and, after one turbulent meeting on the education question in 1849, the Bishop of St. Asaph said to Maurice: 'If I had told the clergy in that meeting, what I am sure is true, that they had better be teaching children in their schools

20. Richard Burgess, *Letter to W. F. Hook on his Proposed Plan for Education of the People* (London, 1846), p. 18. Burgess was then Rector of Upper Chelsea.
21. Richard Dawes, *Remarks Occasioned by the Present Crusade against the Educational Plans of the Committee of Council on Education* (London, 1850), p. 8.
22. Stranks, p. 80. Hook was one who saw this was inevitable. 'I know I am right, and when it is too late Churchmen will see that I am.'
23. *Hansard*, CXLIV (1857), 786.

than making a riot in London, I believe they would have said, "Turn him out!", and that the three-fourths of them would have wished to toss me in a blanket.'[24] Maurice agreed that the bishop was not far wrong in his opinion and that the end result of the Denison-led hysteria was success in 'completely bewildering the minds of their hearers about the whole matter in dispute'.[25]

It may be argued, of course, that the intransigents were only playing their part in the great debate over the Church's role in national education. And it must not be forgotten that because the Church had always assumed the task of educating the people, these conservatives appealed much more to popular sentiment than the extremists who advocated a completely secular education. Without their long-sustained opposition, the compromise of England's 'dual system' of education might not have come into being. At the same time, the churchman who became an ecclesiastical politician ran the risk of neglecting his task of educating in his parish—as the Bishop of St. Asaph had feared.

Fortunately, there were few clergy who did neglect this primary duty. Victorian England was heavily indebted to the education provided by the Church—as Newman once commented, those who attacked the educational policy of the Church owed to the Church their ability to articulate at all. This debt was widely acknowledged. One of Her Majesty's Inspectors of Schools in the year 1846–1847 said:

> I have looked carefully over my lists, and I can find only nine instances out of nearly 200 where I have not reason to think that the clergyman has a deep interest in his school, not shown only by words, but by watchful care and frequent attendance. I could mention instances where . . . besides labour almost beyond his strength, pecuniary help beyond his means has been cheerfully given, poor children paid for, masters' stipends made up to a certain income, repairs done, as it were, by stealth, debts willingly taken upon himself, and contributions offered, liberal to excess, that others might be moved to contribute liberally. . . . I am convinced that no one could see what I have seen, of the truly charitable work of the clergy for the support and success of these schools, without feeling increased respect for them.[26]

The ecclesiastical intransigents have always been noted by social historians. The fact that a conservative like Liddon was a cleric is almost underlined; Jowett's being in Holy Orders is scarcely recognized, as both men would have wished. But both men represented the

24. *Life of Maurice*, I, 547.
25. *Ibid.*, p. 546.
26. Brown, *Church's Part in Education*, p. 15.

Church in Oxford—and churchmen stood for reform as well as reaction in both universities. The 'creative tension' between such people ensured that the Church of England ethos never completely disappeared from the universities.

The churchmen responsible for education in the public school deliberately evolved, with the help of Thomas Arnold, a moral education which, with its ethic of service, had great appeal to the powerful new middle class of the nation. Woodard, just as deliberately, founded his schools for those members of this class who could not afford the cost of education at the more famous public schools. There was nothing reactionary in this policy of setting out to capture ideologically the youth of the most important class in the nation. Maurice in his educational experiments tried to give the members of this same class some opportunity to exercise this new spirit of service, which could break down the class tension in England.

During the long struggle to retain moral influence in elementary education, the Church found its deepening conviction of divine commission to serve the whole of the nation. It had men like Dean Hook, as well as men like Archdeacon Denison in its ranks. And in the long run the pastoral concern of men like the former prevailed over the well-justified fears of the latter—fears which even Maurice appreciated. The Church chose, for the sake of the nation, to go along with the State in providing universal education for the people—to try to 'baptize' national education, to keep it from becoming completely secular.

In the latter part of the nineteenth century, there was little evidence to support the myth of an unholy pact between parson and squire to keep the people ignorant and poor. Rather, the new spirit of service, cultivated through the educational policies of the Church, seemed to be giving both clergymen and the members of that new class who now shared privilege with the squires a new zeal to rid the nation of both ignorance and poverty.

VI. The Church
and
Social Reform

*The clergy with their usual
acuteness seeing the movement
that is coming, has already in
fact begun, are taking it under
their wing.*

EDWARD AVELING

*1. The Traditional Social
Policy of the Church*

A CONTEMPORARY Australian historian, K. S. Inglis, has recently passed critical comment on some writers of ecclesiastical history: 'Some ecclesiastical historians, believing all too literally that the kingdom of God is not of this world, or that "the history of the Church is neither more nor less than the history of its theology," give little attention to the relationship between the act of worship and its social environment.'[1] Mr. Inglis goes on to imply that not only have ecclesiastical historians neglected the kingdom of this world, but this oversight was also characteristic of Victorian churchmen. They were much more interested in theology, or developing moral character, than they were in installing drainpipes in new urban centres.

If it is poor historical method for ecclesiastical historians to neglect the relationship of the Church with society, it is surely equally reprehensible for social historians to write disparagingly about the Victorian Church, because it failed to exist primarily as an agency

EPIGRAPH: Edward Aveling, *Christianity and Capitalism* (1884) p. 5, Aveling was the son-in-law of Karl Marx and a bitter critic of Christianity.
1. Inglis, *Churches and the Working Class in Victorian England*, p. 324.

241

of political, economic, and social reform. The latter-day Benthamite may choose to scorn the churchman of the nineteenth century for being religious, and for not acting in the fashion of an enlightened, modern, social reformer; but when he makes value-judgments of this nature, he does not write good history. You cannot abstract the Victorian churchman, or any other historical figure, from his age and its beliefs, to demand from him the insights of later generations. Wisdom demands that the historian remember the caution of the Rabbi Hillel: 'Judge not a man until thou standest in his place.'[2] Victorian churchmen, like the Christians of any age, were bidden not to be *of* their world, but they were still very much *in* it. If they are to be criticized for their social attitudes, the criterion by which to judge them is the social outlook of their secular contemporaries—not the viewpoint of the historian of the mid-twentieth century.

As might be expected, the attitude of any Victorian to social reform was conditioned by his environment, as well as by his Christian conscience. Like most of his contemporaries, the churchman either lived in, or had recently come from, a rural environment. He was confused by the complexities of the new urban and industrial world in which he was forced to live, and he quite naturally attempted to use the traditional means of improving society which had worked in other times—until he found they were no longer of use. In matters of social reform the approach of the churchman was as pragmatic as that of any Englishman of the period. His adaptation to the demands of the new urban world was slow; but it must be remembered that by mid-century about half the population still lived in rural areas, and thirty years later about a third of the people were still countrymen.[3]

The role of the Church in rural social reform has seldom been appreciated. Parson and squire have been pictured as working hand-in-glove in a common policy of repression, particularly when the interests of the landowning class were at stake. The Hammonds, for example, have given us a vivid picture of the repression initiated by clerical justices of the peace in the years following the French Revolution.[4] But these men represented a minority of the rural clergy.

It is difficult to assess the extent or the value to rural society of the direct relief work carried on by the clergy of the Church. Some clergy

2. *Talmud*, 'Pirke Avod', Chapter 2, Verse 5.
3. It is often forgotten that, because of endowments, the rural parish is still the norm in the Church of England. In 1958, 65 per cent of its 14,332 parishes were still rural. *V.* F. R. Barry, *Vocation and Ministry* (1958), p. 160.
4. J. L. and Barbara Hammond, *Town Labourer* (1920), p. 269 ff.: also *Age of the Chartists* (1930), p. 217 ff.

resented their rustication, and did little for their people. Dean Church spoke of the difficulty experienced by the intelligent cleric called to spend his life among people 'to whom the heavens mean nothing at all, and the earth only the field where day after day, from sunrise to night, they toil in the frost and in the heat for their coarse meals; who know their work, and measure all other knowledge by it; to whom everything outside them is bounded and hidden by an impenetrable cloud, broken only by the most fantastic delusions; whose meagre list of words hardly reaches beyond the expression of the necessities of life, and the simplest elementary emotions of the soul'.[5] Many of the clergy in these circumstances began themselves to become part of the landscape, like the rector Keble served when he was curate at East-leach: 'a lazy old prater, who cares for nothing but fishing and chattering'.[6]

The age was aristocratic; the clergy with better-endowed rectories and vicarages ranked with the gentry in economic status, and temptations to use their position for social and political reasons were offered to them. In 1811 the future Bishop Blomfield was presented to the Rectory of Dunton, in Buckinghamshire, by Earl Spencer. His parishioners were only seventy-two in number; but within two years he was made a Justice of the Peace, Commissioner of Turnpikes, and Commissioner of Property Tax: 'The farmers of the parish long remembered how his union of magisterial and ministerial authority had kept them in order.'[7] When less conscientious clerics than Blomfield had positions of this nature thrust upon them, it is little wonder that the Hammonds and other writers have had their scandalous tales to tell of reactionary clerical magistrates. Tales of indolent, eccentric and fox-hunting parsons are too well known to be repeated here.[8]

Yet many rural clergy were devoted pastors, as the clerical diaries of the period reveal. The Somerset rector, John Skinner, who literally gave his life in service of a 'brutified, vulgar people', assiduously visited dank and fever-stricken cottages, opposed the squire on behalf of the farmers, equipped his parish with schools, and even gave up part of his tithe. Worn out by his efforts to get his people to get rid of the dung before their cottages, to clear their drains during a cholera epidemic, and to spend money he gave them on their sick children, he

---

5. Smith, *Dean Church*, p. 129.
6. Battiscombe, *John Keble*, p. 42.
7. *Memoir of Blomfield* (1863 ed.), I, 39.
8. C. K. F. Brown, *History of the English Clergy, 1800–1900* (1953), pp. 126–64. *Cf. Memories of Dean Hole* (1892), p. 288 for an answer to the question: 'Should a clergyman hunt?'

committed suicide because of his sense of failure.[9] In thousands of parishes throughout the land, the same sort of work was quietly carried on—especially after the Tractarian revival and the pastoral revolution carried out by Samuel Wilberforce.

By the end of the century, Sidney and Beatrice Webb found the clergy in their parishes devoted to protecting the helpless, raising the standard of life of the people, inspecting houses of correction and county jails, advocating prison reform, and generally investigating the position of the labourer: 'we find them among the foremost to recognize that the magistrate had his duty in protecting the helpless and in raising the standard of life of the people.'[10] The wife of the 'resident gentleman' in the parish took blankets and soup around to the cottages of the poor and used her skill to nurse the sick. His daughters taught in the day and Sunday schools and sat reading to the old people. The vicar ran the clothing club, collected the medical money, and dispensed the charities. In the nineteenth century, in many counties, the hiring fair was a feature of the rural scene. This was a time when the farm labourers stood all day long in the market place, waiting for farmers to hire them for the coming year. According to folk-lore, a farmer who had a 'good vicar' in his parish offered the labourers a shilling less than the usual weekly pay.

Many clergy, however, knew that their relief work was not enough; they loved the poor, but often they could do so little. One of those who thought in this fashion was Charles John Ellicott, Bishop of Gloucester and Bristol, who preached on 'The Church and the Rural Poor' in his visitation to the parish church of Stow-on-the-Wold in 1873.

> We who know the real state of the rural poor; we who enter into their cottages day by day—cottages often a disgrace and a reproach to a Christian land . . . we the clergy, how little can we do. . . . we may use our quiet influence with the landowner or the farmer . . . we may set example, as we often do by the assignment of allotments of land. We may further the establishment of friendly societies and working-men's clubs; but when we have done this—and how systematically it *is* done in many a parish—we must all alike feel that the material solution of the problem is still beyond us.[11]

9. Howard Coombs and A. N. Bax, *Journal of a Somerset Rector: John Skinner, 1772–1839* (1930), p. 301.

10. Sidney and Beatrice Webb, 'Parish and County', *English Local Government* (1906), I, 355. After 1878 the Church experienced its worst financial crisis since the sixteenth century with the beginning of agricultural depression. *V.* Best, *Temporal Pillars*, p. 471, and J. A. Venn, *Foundations of Agricultural Economics* (1933), pp. 173–74.

11. C. J. Ellicott, *Church and the Rural Poor* (1873), p. 14.

The Church's answer to the problem of the agricultural labourer was direct relief organized by the clergymen—and the use of 'quiet influence' on the members of the privileged classes who might help the lot of their workers. Even the Tractarian *British Critic* in its last year of publication tried to remind the gentry of the countryside that the opportunity for good works lay right under their casements.

> There was a time when the negro absorbed the pity of the English public. When he was emancipated the factory child took his place. His tale had scarcely been told when . . . the collier is now dragged forth from his subterranean world, and without the smallest wish on his part, compelled to be the hero of a parliamentary and newspaper tragedy, but . . . will the kind gentlemen and ladies excuse us if we call their attention to an object of compassion for which they need not dive either into the bowels of the earth or the smoke of the manufacturing town. We mean the agricultural labourer and his family.[12]

Charles Kingsley, in his own inimitable fashion also tried to stir the consciences of privileged people, and to remind them of their need to serve the rural poor. In a lecture to ladies entitled 'The Country Parish' Kingsley said: 'A lady can go into a poor cottage, lay down the law to the inhabitants, reprove them for sins to which she has never been tempted . . . give them a tract as she might a pill, and then a shilling as something sweet after medicine, and see no more of them until her benevolent mood returns.' But charity of this order was of little help to the poor: 'If you want Christ's lost lambs really to believe that He died for them, you will do it better by one little act of interest and affection than by making them learn by heart whole commentaries. . . . do not apply remedies which they do not understand to diseases which you do not understand.'

Kingsley challenged his listeners to face up to the fact that many of the ills of the rural poor in their dank dwellings came from economic causes: 'it is a mockery to visit the fever-stricken cottage while your husband leaves it in a state which breeds that fever.' He urged them to rebel against their husbands' indifference, and force them to really help the poor countrywomen whom they knew intimately 'as woman to woman'. They were to say to their husbands: 'If you will not new-roof that cottage, if you will not make that drain, I will. I will not buy a new dress, till it is done; I will sell the

---

12. *British Critic*, XXXIII (1843), 248. W. R. Ward, 'Tithe Question in England in the Early Nineteenth Century', *Journal of Ecclesiastical History*, XVI (1965), 70–73, reveals the identification of interest of parson and gentry in the enclosure movement. Commutation of tithe was often made in the form of a land grant to the parson prior to 1836.

horse you gave me, pawn the bracelet you gave me, but the thing shall be done.'[13]

Many churchmen, however, knew that the traditional 'comforting of the afflicted' in rural parishes, or the parson's attempt to 'afflict the comfortable', by urging the privileged to extend their charity, was not enough. No one doubted the good brought about by encouragement of thrift through promotion of friendly societies; or the benefits that came through the schools which were run at the cost of great clerical sacrifice. But the standard of living of the labourer in his rose-covered cottage was abominably low, and had to be raised. James Fraser was an assistant commissioner on children's employment in 1867 and, after a survey of life in ninety-six parishes said that 'the majority of the cottages . . . are deficient in almost every requisite that should constitute a home for a Christian family in a civilized community. . . . Modesty must be an unknown virtue, decency an unimaginable thing, when in one small chamber . . . two and sometimes three generations are herded promiscuously . . . where the whole atmosphere is sensual, and human nature is degraded into something below the level of swine.'[14]

Agricultural labourers, like all countrymen, were conservative, and did not readily accept change. Even though country wages were low, the drift to the cities was slow; and the agricultural population did not fall to the point where landowners had to compete for labour. The only answer was for the labourers to organize themselves, to demand from their employers greater return for their work.

The pioneer in the agricultural labour movement was a clergyman, E. D. Girdlestone.[15] When he came to Halberton in North Devon in 1866, he was shocked by the social conditions he found among the poor in his parish. After private appeals to the farmers' conscience were ignored, he wrote to the *Times* about the situation. The result was that at his next vestry meeting the respectable members of the parish refused to pay a church rate. Girdlestone's letter to the *Times*, however, brought numerous offers of better conditions for labourers in other parts of England and Ireland, and some financial help from philanthropists. Girdlestone immediately began an extensive and regular system of migration from his parish. In the six years he was at Halberton, he sent between four and five hundred labourers, most

13. Charles Kingsley, 'The Country Parish', *Lectures to Ladies at Working Men's College* (1855), pp. 56–59.
14. D. O. Wagner, *Church of England and Social Reform since 1854* (1930), p. 146.
15. F. G. Heath, *English Peasantry* (1874), p. 138.

of them with families, into other counties where they would be better treated. The movement spread to neighbouring counties, and a tide of emigration began from Devon, Dorset, Wiltshire, and Somerset. The result was that the wage of seven or eight shillings paid for a week's work in 1866 rose to become seventeen shillings by 1872.[16]

Two years after he started his work, he also began to consider agricultural labourers' unions which could guard workmen against intimidation by employers. Such an association did arise in Kent in 1866, to protect labourers against 'the evils of their serfdom'.[17] Then strikes were held by farm labourers in Buckinghamshire and Oxfordshire, who had organized themselves to assist emigration, and to demand better wages for those who remained in their counties. Towards the end of 1870, an extensive association was organized in Herefordshire, with an executive of clergy; the president and twenty vice-presidents were churchmen, and the secretary was a Dissenter. Within a year it had thirty thousand members.

Joseph Arch made his appearance on the trade-union scene in 1872. An itinerant hedger who had travelled about the countryside a great deal, he was also a Primitive Methodist preacher, who had a deep resentment of the Church. He has recorded that his parents in Barford, Warwickshire, had to wait for Holy Communion until after the gentry and tradesmen had received it. The village parson cut the family allowance of soup and coal when Arch's mother was not sufficiently humble. These humiliations were long remembered, and underlay much of his opposition to the Church.[18]

In 1872 the labourers in Warwickshire began to join together in an agricultural labourers' union, and Arch became its chief organizer. Several weeks later a congress was held to form a National Agricultural Labourers' Union. Several clergymen were on the platform at this meeting. After Arch visited Canada to investigate emigration overseas, as an alternative to militant trade unionism, he returned to devote himself to the union; and by 1874 it had a membership of 100,000.

The landowners began to organize in turn, and a lock-out of members of the union threw them back on N.A.L.U. funds. When the actual struggle began, few clergy of the Established Church identified themselves with the strikers; and those who did get caught up in the issue usually came out on the side of reaction.[19] During the lock-out

16. Wagner, p. 151.
17. Ernest Selley, *Village Trade Unions in Two Centuries* (1919), p. 36.
18. Joseph Arch, *Story of His Life* (1898), pp. 20–21, 53–54.
19. Wagner, pp. 162–73, discusses the clergy who supported the strike.

at Ascot in Oxfordshire, strike-breakers were called in from outside. When a group of strikers' wives verbally abused the intruders, the clerical magistrates at Chipping Norton charged them with intimidation. Sixteen of them, some with nursing children, were sentenced to seven or ten days at hard labour.[20]

Bishop Ellicott, whom we have already met, knew the hard lot of the labourers, and urged the granting of allotments to them as the solution to the unrest. He also arranged a meeting of the union leaders with a magistrate and a member of parliament, at which grievances could be heard. But he believed many of the ills experienced by the workers came from their drunkenness and low moral tone, and said about the agitators: 'There is an old saying, "Don't nail their ears to the pump, and don't duck them in the horse pond."' At the same time he seemed to indicate such treatment might be salutary for people like Arch.[21]

The Christian Socialists supported the strike; Girdlestone attacked the lock-out, and James Fraser, who was now Bishop of Manchester, wrote an indignant letter to the *Times* pointing out to the farmers the folly as well as the criminality of their action. At most, he said, they might drive the labourers into workhouses, across the Atlantic, or into new employment: 'But will they have settled the wage question, will they have improved their own condition or prospects?'[22] On the other hand, as Arch did not hesitate to point out, most parsons tried to avoid the issue and 'flew around like weather-cocks as squire or farmer or villager grew strongest at the moment'.[23] The *Guardian* refused to commit itself on the justice meted out by the clerical magistrates at Ascot.[24]

Ecclesiastical politics also played their role in the shaping of clerical reaction to the new union, and to the strike. The Primitive Methodists had a great deal of strength in the country districts; and the Rev. Thorold Rogers, who assisted the N.A.L.U. in its affairs, believed that the peasants could not have been aroused but for itinerant preachers like Joseph Arch. The *Quarterly Review* pointed out that class and religious hatred underlay many of the economic grievances that were discussed: 'After all, Joseph Arch is not a labourer; he is a dissenting minister of a rustic type, influenced by the jealousies and

20. Arthur Clayden, *Revolt of the Field* (1874), pp. 31–44.
21. Arch, p. 121.
22. *Times*, 2 April 1874, p. 7.
23. Arch, p. 102.
24. *Guardian*, 11 June 1873, p. 764.

prejudices of his class.'[25] The striker's journal, the *Labourers' Union Chronicle* demanded on its mast-head 'Freedom from Priestcraft and from the Tyranny of Capital'. Many clergy viewed the union as an organization of Dissenters, whose true purpose was the undermining of the Established Church. Even Girdlestone broke with the union in 1873 because of its leaders' 'meddling with the resources of our clergy and . . . with the connection of Church and State'.[26]

Apart from the Primitive Methodists, the Dissenters remained as indifferent to the strike as did the majority of churchmen. Archbishop Manning appeared on the platform in Exeter Hall when the strike first began; but, apart from individual clerics and the Christian Socialists, the strikers were alone when the N.A.L.U. was forced to admit defeat and turn its attention to emigration as an answer to economic grievances. Joseph Arch later entered parliament as member for Northwest Norfolk in 1892.

The Church's conscience was stirred by the nation's failure to show more sympathy for the labourers as they tried to find an economic solution for their misery. Charles Gore later admitted that many clergy had failed in their pastoral task at this time, and that 'the only time in his life when he was very strongly driven to desert the Church was at the outbreak of the agitation against Joseph Arch. The attitude of the Church towards Joseph Arch's movement was lamentable; the clergy and the well-to-do laity were deaf towards the almost inconceivable record of injustice which that movement voiced.[27] Girdlestone's words troubled many hearts when he said at the Church Congress meeting at Bath in 1873: 'When I think of that last great day, when we must all meet together, rich and poor, learned and unlearned, master and servant, pastor and flock, for my own part I feel, and feel it terribly, that the man whom I shall fear most to meet on that great day is the labourer.'[28]

25. *Quarterly Review*, CXXXVII (1874), 503, 'East Anglia: Its Strikes and Lock-outs'.
26. Selley, p. 88.
27. *Convocation of Canterbury Chronicle* (1918), p. 276.
28. Maurice Reckitt, *Maurice to Temple* (1947), p. 116.

2. *The Urban Challenge and the Fear of Class Warfare*

ONE OF the reasons some churchmen opposed the great agricultural strike was the excessive alarm which came with the rebellion of farm labourers, who had been so docile until this time. The *Guardian* argued that the labourer was already able to improve his condition, as the extension of allotments continued and enlightenment spread among the landlords.[1] There was no need for agitation of this kind, which might convulse England, as it had European countries, in social revolution. This disquiet was shared by most members of the privileged classes, particularly in the great cities, where so many of the impoverished countrymen had flocked to find work in the new factories, and a way of life in the great slums. The new slum dwellers, whether from the English or Irish countryside, were not shocked by the conditions which greeted them—considering what they had left behind them— but as time passed they lost their old humility, and the privileged classes began to fear them.

Writing to the undergraduates of Cambridge in the 1860's, Charles Kingsley said of the unrest of the 1833 period:

> Thirty years ago, and even later, the young men of the labouring classes were the 'cads', 'the snobs', 'the blackguards'; looked on with a dislike, contempt and fear, which they were not backward to return, and which were but too ready to vent themselves on both sides in ugly words and deeds. That hateful severance between the classes was, I believe, an evil of recent growth, unknown to old England. From the middle ages, up to the latter years of the French war, the relation between the English gentry and the labourers seems to have been more cordial and wholesome than in any other country of Europe. But with the French Revolution came a change for the worse. The Revolution terrified too many of the upper, and excited too many of the lower classes . . . the old feudal ties between class and class, employer and employed, had been severed. Large masses of working people had gathered in the manufacturing districts in savage independence. The agricultural labourers had been debased by the abuses of the Poor Law into conditions upon which one looks back now with half-incredulous horror. . . . then arose Luddite mobs, meal mobs, farm riots, riots everywhere; Captain Swing and his rickburners, Peterloo 'massacres', Bristol conflagrations, and all the ugly sights and rumours which made young lads, thirty or forty years ago, believe (and not so wrongly) that 'the masses' were their natural enemies, and that they might have to fight, any year or any day, for the safety of their property and the honour of their sisters. How changed thank God! is all this now.[2]

Most Victorians reckoned with the possibility of overt class warfare. The early part of the century saw the introduction of the man-

1. *Guardian*, 13 November 1872, p. 1427; Address of Lord Nelson to Labourers.
2. Charles Kingsley, *Alton Locke: Tailor and Poet* (1884), p. xci.

trap for poachers, and the woods echoed with the sound not only of the spring-gun, but of outright battles between gentlemen, their servants, and poachers. The enclosure of land was resisted; and Tom Mozley mentions, quite casually, that soldiers dined at Oriel after putting down rioters at Otmoor.[3] Many believed with Macaulay that the Chartists would first use their political power to despoil the rich. The year 1848 saw riots in London, Liverpool, Glasgow, and other large towns. London was filled with troops under the Duke of Wellington, the bridges were barricaded, the Bank garrisoned, and the Houses of Parliament provisioned for a siege. In 1866, Life Guards armed with sabres were used to assist the police to break up a meeting of the Reform League in Hyde Park.[4]

Few churchmen were as sanguine as Kingsley in the 1860's about the class conflict within the nation. As late as 1871 John Henry Newman viewed the numerous lower classes as the 'new Goths and Vandals to destroy civilization'.[5] The parish clergy who actually worked among the poor, such as George Campbell Ommanney of St. Matthew's, Sheffield, knew at first hand the violence, and even murder, that occurred in industrial disputes.[6] Others, like Charles Lowder of St. Peter's, London Docks, actually experienced mob violence after they criticized local 'sweat-shops', as we shall see later. The threat of violence and rioting on the part of the masses had to be seriously reckoned with. The tension between what Disraeli called 'the Two Nations' often seemed to be at the breaking-point.

Visitors to England also noted the social misery created by the new industrial economy, and the class hatred it fostered. One of these was Alexis de Tocqueville, who made his second visit to England in 1835, and visited the cotton textile factories of Manchester during his tour. He wrote of the conditions in them:

> These vast palaces of industry shut out the air and light from the human dwellings they overhang; they envelop them in a perpetual fog; here is the slave, there the master; there the riches of a few, here the misery of the vast number; there the organized strength of a multitude produces for the profit of one man whatever society has not been able to offer; here the weakness of the individual is more extreme and more helpless than in the midst of a desert; here are the effects and there the causes.[7]

3. Mozley, *Reminiscences of Oriel*, II, 60.
4. *Illustrated London News*, 4 August 1866, p. 172, gives a picture of how contemporaries viewed this encounter.
5. Ward, *Life of Newman*, II, 344.
6. F. G. Belton, *Ommanney of Sheffield* (1936), pp. 55–56.
7. Max Beloff, 'Can England Avoid Revolution', *Listener*, 29 May 1958, p. 891.

It was clear to him that the hostility between 'haves' and 'have-nots' in England was great and that it was unlikely a peaceful solution to this social and economic inequality would be found. 'In contemporary England a spirit of discontent with the present and hatred of the past shows itself on every side. The human spirit has fallen into . . . excess. It seeks only for what is wrong around it and is much more concerned to correct what is wrong than to preserve what is good.'[8]

Nine years later Friederich Engels, in his report on *The Condition of the Working-Class in England*, spoke of the 'wild rage of the workers against the higher classes'. They were refusing to be degraded to the level of the brute, and sooner or later they would free themselves through violence from 'servitude to the bourgeoisie'. He completely agreed with Carlyle's opinion about the mind of the working class: 'Revolt, sullen, revengeful humour of revolt against the upper classes, decreasing respect for what their temporal superiors command, decreasing faith for what their spiritual superiors teach, is more and more the universal spirit of the lower classes.'[9]

The workers may have had 'decreasing faith', but both de Tocqueville and Engels noted one curious feature in the life of the English proletariat. There was none of the fierce anti-religious bias which was so often found in continental radicalism. In fact, the leaders of all classes not only appeared to have respect for religion, but some even sought to identify themselves with it. When in 1832 there was a gathering of 12,000 workers in Yorkshire to support Michael Sadler's Ten Hours Bill, the marchers from Bradford on this 'Pilgrimage of Mercy' were led by a cleric, 'Parson Bull'. As the columns converged on Leeds the bells of the parish church greeted them. On their return from York, where they had listened to hours of speech-making by their leaders, Sadler, Richard Oastler, and Bull, they sang 'Praise God from Whom All Blessings Flow' as they marched into Leeds in the pouring rain.[10]

It is little wonder that the continental observers found the attitude of the English working man to religion puzzling. During the Chartist period, some militants actually tried to take over churches in towns like Sheffield and Halifax. On the other hand the workers disliked the clergy generally, because of their 'neglect of duty', and the Establishment they viewed as 'ungodly, plundering, villainous, old mother hypocrisy'. The 'superstitious Old Hog', which was the Church, they

8. *Ibid.*, p. 892.
9. *Karl Marx and Frederick Engels on Britain* (Moscow, 1953), p. 151.
10. Gill, *Ten Hours Parson*, p. 52 ff. George Stringer Bull was curate of Byerley.

rejected as well as Wesleyanism, which had become too respectable. But they did not reject Christianity. Most working-class leaders believed 'the mission of Christianity was to bring them freedom and social justice, the only question remaining to be settled was how this object could be best promoted. The English workingman had decided that the only hope lay in the People's Charter. The natural sequence was that Chartism was therefore divine and ordained of God.'[11] The short-lived Chartist churches reflected working-class Christianity.

By the end of the century, the radicals began to see that within the Church there was a creative spirit which led at least some of the clergy to welcome and 'baptize' rather than reject the new social order. Engels was sneering at the people who 'preached Socialism at the parson's Church Congress',[12] and the English Marxist, H. M. Hyndman, admitted that 'many of the rising young parsons themselves denounce the alliance which the ecclesiastical hierarchy has made with the mammon of unrighteousness and proclaim aloud that whatever modern Christianity may find it convenient to allow, the religion of Christ means more or less complete communism.'[13]

When de Tocqueville revisited England twenty-two years later, in 1857, he described the society he found as much like that of the *ancien régime* in Europe, but 'reformed and perfected'. He attributed the general respect still held for law and property by the workers to religious influence among them, as well as to their general acceptance of social stratification: 'What one does see on all sides is union and agreement among all those who form part of the educated classes from the humblest tradesman to the highest ranks of the aristocracy— agreement to defend society, and to conduct its affairs together and in freedom.'[14] To the chagrin of Marx and Engels the working class did not see this alliance as one that would oppose their interests. Engels wrote to Marx in April, 1863, to say 'the revolutionary energy of the English proletariat has to all intents and purposes completely evaporated, and the English proletarian is in full agreement with the rule of the bourgeoisie.'[15]

What particularly puzzled the continental critics of English society was the lack of clear distinction between classes according to the

---

11. H. U. Faulkner, *Chartism and the Churches* (1916), p. 21 ff. R. F. Wearmouth, *Some Working Class Movements of the Nineteenth Century* (1948), p. 188, discusses Chartist churches.
12. *Marx and Engels on Britain*, p. 523.
13. H. M. Hyndman, *Coming Revolution in England* (1884), p. 29.
14. Beloff, 'Can England Avoid Revolution', p. 892.
15. *Marx and Engels on Britain*, p. 493.

Marxist pattern. On the continent the aristocracy was recognized by its land, mercantile wealth, privileges, titles, and official status, and usually lived in the countryside. The bourgeoisie, on the other hand, remained in the cities to become bureaucratic servants of the State, radically separated from the proletariat. But in England there was always a close connection between the privileged class in the countryside and that in the new cities. Intermarriage between the two groups was one of the ways that distinction was broken down. Another was through the meeting of the two classes in the Church. A rising tradesman could ensure gentleman status for his son in society by purchasing for him the advowson of a suitable parish. This assisted the appearance of the English middle class rather than an urban bourgeoisie, servants of the State, isolated from the gentry of the countryside, and at war with the proletariat.

Not only were the differences between the privileged classes in countryside and city blurred by the emergence of a national middle class, but there was also a lack of clear distinction between the middle class and the workers in the cities. In 1858 Engels wrote in disgust to Marx: 'the English proletariat is actually becoming more and more bourgeois, so that this most bourgeois of all nations is apparently aiming ultimately at the possession of a bourgeois aristocracy and a bourgeois proletariat as well as a bourgeoisie.'[16] Marx admitted five years later that the situation had not improved: 'How soon the English workers will free themselves from their apparent bourgeois infection one must wait and see.'[17]

What was the attitude of the Church during this time when bourgeois ideology was being disseminated by the dominant middle class? To begin with, it must be recognized that the Church knew it had no direct means of influencing most of the working class. In 1801 H. W. Majendie, Bishop of Chester, attributed the social unrest in the great towns of the nation to the 'evil of irreligion' among the working class. He said that in one of his parishes '40,000 pass the Lord's day without attention to public worship under any mode whatever'.[18] In 1840 Thomas Mozley estimated that from three-quarters to nine-tenths of the whole of the urban lower classes were not church-going.[19] In 1851 Henry Mayhew reported a contemporary estimation that not

16. *Ibid.*, pp. 491–92.
17. *Ibid.*, p. 493.
18. H. W. Majendie, 'Charge to the Clergy of the Diocese of Chester' *Gentleman's Magazine*, LXXI (1801), 729.
19. *British Critic*, XXVIII, 346.

three out of one hundred costermongers had ever been in a church or knew anything of Christianity.[20] At the end of the century A. F. Winnington-Ingram, who became Bishop of Stepney and Bishop of London, told of a working man who took a religious census in his factory of 2,000 workers. Only five of these men attended a church— three were Roman Catholics, one was Church of England, and the other was a Dissenter. The bishop accepted the fact that the 'immense majority of working men go neither to church nor chapel', and said of the state of Christianity among the masses: 'It is not that the Church of God has lost the great towns; it has never had them.'[21]

Some historians have acted as though the Church's failure to draw the working classes to worship was something of which churchmen were unaware, and remained unaware. The recent study of the relationship between the churches in England and the working classes, to which we have referred, begins with the statement: 'A listener to sermons, and even a reader of respectable history books, could easily think that during the nineteenth century the habit of attending religious worship was normal among the English working classes.'[22] This is a curious statement, for churchmen knew in the nineteenth century that their churches were ignored, for the most part, by working-class people, and it seems incredible that anyone in our day would believe otherwise, be he parson or scholar. Then, as now, the English working class rejected 'the imaginary, impalpable thing called "the Church".'[23] There were exceptions to this rule, like Joseph Arch's father, who went to the Church through habit,[24] or the attempt to set up Chartist churches; but generally the workers viewed the abstraction they called 'the Church' as the preserve of men of another station in society, and their custom was to keep away from it.

The Church knew that the working class would not choose to be directly involved in Church affairs, and it based its social policies on this fact. When Nonconformist opposition ended the government grants for church building in industrial areas, while the slum areas of the great cities continued to expand, and the Church lacked the central authority to direct its resources to where they were most needed, churchmen were forced to face the sad fact that the Church simply could not find the means to serve the masses directly.

This did not mean, however, that the Church abandoned the masses.

20. Henry Mayhew, *London Labour and London Poor* (1862), I, 21.
21. A. F. Winnington-Ingram, *Work in Great Cities* (1896), p. 22.
22. Inglis, *Churches and the Working Classes*, p. 1.
23. Winnington-Ingram, p. 7.
24. Arch, *Story of His Life*, p. 21.

Rather it deliberately set out to create a Christian social climate which would by 'osmosis' influence the lives of even the workers. It did this by an ideological capturing of the middle class (with the aid of Nonconformity), and by giving the middle class the conviction that it should reconcile the divided classes in England. Both the Church and the middle class dreaded class warfare, and they worked together in a mixed spirit of Christian altruism and enlightened self-interest to prevent it.

It took time for this policy to evolve. The Evangelicals of the Church, and many of the Nonconformists, believed the poor should accept the social order as it was. They told the needy that at least their predicament kept them from sinning grandly, and they had the blessing of freedom from either self-importance or attachment to the things of this world. John Newton said 'if the poor believers consider the snares to which their rich brethren are exposed they will rather pray for and pity than envy them. Their path is slippery . . . they live in the midst of the hurries and vanities of the world, are engaged in a large sphere of action, and are incessantly exposed to interruptions and snares.'[25] Henry Venn agreed in his popular Evangelical moral treatise, the *Complete Duty of Man*, that men of commerce were peculiarly prone to the sin of covetousness.[26] But it is doubtful if the Gospel of 'Christian Contentment opposed to a Spirit of Covetousness' did much to relieve the unrest of the have-nots of the nation. Henry Mayhew's informant said of sermons preached on this theme: 'Our preachers seem to be afraid of ascertaining the sentiments, feelings and habits of the more wretched part of the population; and without this, their words will die away upon the wind, and no practical echo answer their addresses.'[27]

Thomas Arnold was the first real prophet of the Church's social policy in Victorian England. In his *Englishman's Register*, a short-lived publication which came out in the spring and summer of 1831, Arnold said the great need of the age was to open the eyes of the rich to the social misery in the nation, and to get the poor to understand the cause of it. He opposed both 'anti-reformers', who would lull the consciences of the rich, and 'ultra-reformers', who appealed to the passions of the poor and taught the inevitability of class-warfare.[28] He knew the opposition of the secular mind of the age, which believed

25. John Newton, *Twenty-six Letters on Religious Subjects* (1775), p. 242.
26. Henry Venn, *Complete Duty of Man* (1841), p. 264.
27. Mayhew, I, 21.
28. *Englishman's Register*, 4 June 1831, p. 65.

that 'to raise the poor in knowledge and to increase their sense of their own importance, would derange the present order of society.'[29] The poor had to be given more than was offered to them by the new Poor Law of 1834, which viewed them as 'the principal authors of their own poverty'.[30] Those who brought the poor their enlightenment would be the members of the privileged classes, who were to accept such 'service' as their 'duty'.

When the *Englishman's Register* died a natural death in a few weeks, because of Arnold's lack of time and resources to direct such a publication, he wrote a series of thirteen letters to the *Sheffield Courant* where he expressed his social idea: 'the dispersion of a number of well-educated men over the whole Kingdom, whose sole business is to do good of the highest kind'.[31] He was sure that if men of privilege, who possessed social, economic, and political power, could be persuaded to accept such an ethic of 'service', and to help the poor as their 'duty', then the whole nation would be 'Christianized'. 'Our duties to them, if avowed and acted upon by individuals ... get transplanted into other parts of the country, and spread there—they find their way through the press, in the course of time, to public notice;—and at length though much more slowly may find their way into general practice.'[32]

Neither the Evangelicals nor the Tractarians were pleased with Arnold's 'Pelagian' interpretation of Christianity, but his social ethics proved to have great appeal to many parsons and to the middle class. Some rejected this ideal of 'service' as dangerous, a policy which would cause unrest among the masses, but, as the century progressed, more and more churchmen accepted it—to foster the creation of the 'bourgeois proletariat' which had so disgusted Marx and Engels. It was because of this Christian idealism that there did not arise in England the ugly anticlericalism which was so common on the continent. There were enough parsons willing to perform their Christian duty so that the Church would not be wholly identified with social privilege. It was also part of the reason why the workers did not create for themselves a secular religion, or a class religion, as did the American negro.[33]

29. Thomas Arnold, *Sermons* (1878), II, 262.

30. The words of T. R. Malthus, *Essay on Population* (1914), II, 278. In his *Englishman's Register*, 7 May 1831, p. 2, Arnold said the 'anti-reformers' speak 'as if all the suffering of the poor was the result of inevitable necessity.'

31. Thomas Arnold, *Thirteen Letters on Our Social conditions* (1832), p. 33.

32. Arnold, *Sermons*, II, 265.

33. There was never any real class identification of Nonconformity and the working classes. The 'Nonconformist conscience' of later labour leaders reflected the dissemination of Arnold's ethic.

This Christian social ethic was at least more altruistic than that symbolized by the new Poor Law of 1834, which Arnold said 'wears an air of harshness, and will, I fear, embitter the feelings of the poorer classes still more'.[34] It gave England's powerful new shop-keeper class an alternative social policy to that of the secular intellectuals, which was based on the political economists' view of man: 'Political Economy presupposes an arbitrary definition of man, as a being who invariably does that by which he may obtain the greatest amount of necessaries, conveniences and luxuries, with the smallest amount of labour and physical self-denial with which they can be obtained in the existing state of knowledge.'[35] Slowly the English middle classes began to accept the Church's ethic of 'service', and to restrain themselves from acting as selfishly as Marx and Engels had expected they would—in the fashion of the continental bourgeoisie.

This was the great accomplishment of the Church in Victorian England. Through the writing, teaching, and preaching of its creative minority, it gave to the powerful new middle classes an ethic of 'service', based upon Christian principles. This did more to save England from open class warfare, and to end what Arnold called 'the continued crime of society . . . allowing the poor to go on in such a state of ignorance and misery',[36] than any 'Morrison's Pill, Act of Parliament or remedial measure' such as those suggested by secular intellectuals—Emigration, Education, Corn-Law Abrogation, Sanitary Regulation, Land-Property Tax, Reform Bill, Ballot-Box, or Five-Point Charter.[37]

It was a slow process 'Given a world of knaves, to produce honesty from their united action',[38] but the Church spoke directly, or through Nonconformity, to the conscience of the middle classes in the way that Arnold had spoken to his sixth form at Rugby; and the manufacturers and shop-keepers of the nation began to listen. 'I can hardly imagine anything more useful to a young man of active and powerful mind, advancing rapidly in knowledge, and with high distinction . . . than to take him—or much better that he should go himself—to the abodes of poverty, sickness and old age.'[39] The Church not only helped to

34. Stanley, *Life of Arnold*, II, 61.
35. W. Nassau Senior, *Four Introductory Lectures on Political Economy* (1852), p. 60, quoted from John Mill's 'Unsettled Questions of Political Economy'.
36. Arnold, *Sermons*, II, 262.
37. Thomas Carlyle, *Past and Present* (1897), pp. 23–24.
38. *Ibid.*, p. 25.
39. Arnold, *Sermons*, II, 170.

bridge the gap between aristocracy, gentry, and urban bourgeoisie so as to assist the middle class to appear in England; it implanted in the new class the old idea of *noblesse oblige* in the form of 'service' and 'duty'—an ethic which helped to ease social tension, and to bring relative social peace to the nation.

It was not only foreign observers like Marx and Engels who noted the change in English society—which the two communists attributed to the 'Christian slavish nature' of the English workingman. Militant class language began to abate after 1848. In 1850 the Earl of Essex was able to congratulate the nation on the sound good sense of the middle classes, and the forbearance of the artisan and operative classes which gave England its state of peace. He particularly congratulated the privileged orders of society for their wisdom, 'which led them to abandon their long-rooted prejudices and to sacrifice their self-interest whenever they were called upon to do so by the public voice for the public good'.[40]

After 1850 the new spirit is represented in the writings of Samuel Smiles, *Self-Help* (1859), *Character* (1871), *Thrift* (1875), and *Duty* (1887)—the Christian bourgeois answer to the needs of the Victorian workingman. Smiles is a great moralist: 'National progress is the sum of individual industry, energy and uprightness as national decay is of individual idleness, selfishness and vice. What we are accustomed to decry as great social evils will, for the most part, be found to be but the outgrowth of man's own perverted life.'[41] Thomas Arnold is frequently mentioned in Smiles' most famous work, *Self-Help*; and, like Arnold, Smiles was sure that the answer to social strife in the nation was a greater sympathy among the classes: 'Want of sympathy pervades all classes—the poor, the working, the middle and the upper classes. There are many social gaps between them, which cannot yet be crossed.'[42] Smiles first presented his message to about a hundred young workingmen in Leeds who had set up an evening school for 'mutual improvement'. They accepted his concern, and that of other men of privilege who were willing to help them to raise the entire condition of the working class, through the encouragement of Christian virtues.

The influence of this new morality in the nation has been noted by many historians. G. D. H. Cole and Raymond Postgate have said about the Trade Union Movement in Victorian England: 'From

40. Hansard, CVIII (1850), 400.
41. Briggs, *Victorian People*, p. 125.
42. *Ibid.*, p. 133.

1850 to 1875 the Trade Union Movement was wholly remodelled by what to-day would be called a youth movement . . . whose objectives little suggested young and hot blood: it was a revolt in favour of prudence, respectability, financial stability and reasonableness, and against pugnacity, imagination and any personal indulgence.'[43]

Beatrice Webb has also remarked about the prevailing social ethic of the Victorians: 'It was the bounden duty of every citizen to better his social status. . . . by this persistent pursuit by each individual of his own and his family's interest would the highest general level of civilization be attained.'[44] John Stuart Mill in his essay 'Theism', 'the carefully balanced result of the deliberations of a lifetime', and the last considerable work which he completed, also stressed the importance of moral change for the good of all.

> A battle is constantly going on, in which the humblest human creature is not incapable of taking some part, between the powers of good and those of evil, and in which even the smallest help to the right side has its value in promoting the very slow and often almost insensible progress by which good is gradually gaining ground from evil, yet gaining it so visibly at considerable intervals as to promise the very distant but not uncertain final victory of Good.[45]

Malthus had said of the poor, 'if they obey their passions in opposition to their reason, or be not industrious and frugal . . . they must expect to suffer the natural evils which Providence has prepared for those who disobey its repeated admonitions.'[46] At the beginning of the nineteenth century, the privileged classes had believed this—that the masses would persist in living their unvirtuous lives, and that the poor would always be with them. But as the Church stirred out of its lethargy, and began to rediscover its mission to the nation, men like Arnold began to urge the middle class to help the workers to help themselves, by exhortation and by example. The middle class began to listen to the ideology of the Church, as well as to that of the political economists, and to accept a new view of society, as fluid and dynamic, where classes would work together for the common good. As they listened to the ideology which was presented to the nation directly by the Church, or through Nonconformity, they began to say to the workers: 'if you will take a little more pains to ask God to give you Grace to get rid of lust, intemperance, all that keeps you down . . . there is no country in the world . . . in which the honest, sober,

43. G. D. H. Cole and Raymond Postgate, *Common People, 1746–1946* (1956), p. 367.
44. Webb, *My Apprenticeship*, p. 13.
45. J. S. Mill, *Three Essays on Religion* (1874), p. 256 ff.
46. Malthus, *Essay on Population*, II, 175.

industrious, thrifty workman has so good a chance of raising himself to a position of independence as in England'.[47]

Such middle-class counsel was the Church's answer to the needs of the industrial poor, and to the threat of class warfare. The working class of England listened to this gospel. They still kept away from the places of worship, which they considered to be the preserve of the classes above them—but they accepted the moral and ethical values propagated by the people who filled the churches. By a process of 'osmosis' the workers received from Victorian society, which was dominated by the middle class, a diffused version of Christianity, which persuaded them that they should serve the commonwealth rather than any narrow class interest of their own. Through their acceptance of middle-class virtues, which reflected Christian values, the English workers joined with their social superiors in the revival of religion in Victorian England. Kitson Clark has called this revival a power almost as dynamic as that provided by the blind forces of population increase and the Industrial Revolution. It 'pervaded all society, challenged men and women of every level of society or of education and became fused with the objectives of most political parties and the hopes of every class'.[48] In the words of R. C. K. Ensor, it made Victorian England, among civilized nations, 'one of the most religious the world has ever known'.[49]

3. The Bishops and Social Reform

EVERYONE has heard the jibe about the bench of bishops, being the Tory party at prayer and few writers have had words of praise for the episcopate of the Church of England in the Victorian age. Critics have been especially scornful of what they judged to be the bishops' lack of social conscience. This is understandable, for the radical social reformers of the nineteenth century bitterly condemned them, one and all, for their timid policies of social reform. William Lovett, the Chartist leader, considered it worth noting in his autobiography when he read

47. Hughes, *James Fraser*, p. 211. Fraser's address to workingmen in Salford in 1871.
48. Clark, *Making of Victorian England*, p. 148.
49. Ensor, *England 1870–1914*, p. 137. *V. supra*, p. vii.

of 'one honest, outspoken bishop'.[1] The problem we must now examine is the social policy of the Church, which was approved and directed by the episcopate, and the question of how justified are the critics who condemn the Victorian bishops for their reactionary social views and activities.

To begin with, there is no doubt that the bishops were aware of the miserable conditions under which the English working classes lived. Many of them had actually worked as parish priests in slum areas, and those who had not were reminded by their contemporaries of the ugliness of life in the teeming courts and alleys of industrial towns and cities. Sir James Kay-Shuttleworth told of his work as a physician for the Manchester Board of Health in streets that were impassable to a cart because they were foul with 'heaps of refuse, stagnant pools, ordure etc.'[2] The people in these streets had 'semi-barbarous habits'; the mothers often worked alongside their husbands in the factories, and the mortality rate of children under the age of five was 12.9 per cent: 'the price paid for the cheap labour of married women is a high rate of infant mortality and of waste in drink'. Cholera, typhus, and other epidemics, which were a threat to the whole community, raged among the poor 'whose health was depressed by moral and physical evils'.[3]

Kay-Shuttleworth's brother, Joseph Kay, who was also interested in the lot of the manufacturing poor, reported in 1852 that the juvenile crime rate in Newcastle was increasing four times as fast as the growth in population, and attributed this crime wave to 'drunken mothers'. He said of the life of the poor: 'We have amongst us a peculiar race or class of people. They have a code of morals of their own—the very reverse of the code prevalent among Christians. They have their own organization, their own ideas and habits, their own temptations and tribulations . . . they are the scandal of our civilization and the grief and shame of the wise and benevolent'.[4]

Hippolyte Taine, the French philosopher, critic, and historian, described in his *Notes on England* his impression of life in the slums of Wapping as he observed it during the late sixties:

> Poor streets of brick under red-tiled roofs cross each other in every direction, and lead down with a dismal look to the river. Beggars, thieves, harlots, the

1. Lovett, *Life and Struggles*, p. 394.
2. Kay-Shuttleworth, *Four Periods of Public Education*, p. 95. This describes the situation in 1832.
3. *Ibid.*, p. 130.
4. Joseph Kay, *Condition and Education of Poor Children in English and in German Towns* (1853), p. 19.

latter especially, crowd Shadwell Street. One hears a grating music in the spirit cellars . . . through the open windows one perceives unmade beds, women dancing. Thrice in ten minutes I saw crowds collected at the doors; fights were going on, chiefly between women; one of them, her face bleeding, tears in her eyes, drunk, shouted with a sharp and harsh voice, and wished to fling herself upon a man. The bystanders laughed; the noise caused adjacent lanes to be emptied of their occupants; ragged poor children, harlots—it was like a human sewer suddenly discharging its contents. Some of them have a relic of neatness, a new garment, but the greater number are in filthy and unseemly tatters.[5]

By the end of our period, General Booth was telling the privileged classes of life among the 'submerged tenth' of the population who existed in 'Darkest England'.

The overcrowded homes of the poor compel the children to witness everything. Sexual morality often comes to have no meaning to them. Incest is so familiar as hardly to call for remark. The bitter poverty of the poor compels them to leave their children half fed. There are few more grotesque pictures in the history of civilization than that of the compulsory attendance of children at school, faint with hunger because they had no breakfast, and not sure whether they would even secure a dry crust for dinner when their morning's quantum of education had been duly imparted. Children thus hungered, thus housed, and thus left to grow up as best they can without being fathered or mothered, are not, educate them as you will, exactly the most promising material for the making of the future citizens and rulers of the Empire.[6]

The bishops were well aware of the 'Bitter Cry of Outcast London' and the misery to be found in every industrial slum. As the century progressed, few of them remained unconcerned about the cause of social reform. There were always prelates like the Dean parodied by *Punch* in January, 1886, who is pictured telling a beggar who has halted him with outstretched hand:

Ah my poor fellow your case is very sad, no doubt. But remember that the Rich have their troubles too. I dare say now that you scarcely realize what it is not to know where to find an investment which will combine adequate security with a decent interest on one's money.[7]

But in the second half of the century, in particular, this mentality was found less and less on the bench of bishops. Most of them were concerned to improve the social life of the poor—especially their moral behaviour, which they believed to be the specific concern of the Church.

5. H. Taine, *Notes on England* (1872), pp. 33–34.
6. William Booth, *In Darkest England and the Way Out* (1890), pp. 65–66.
7. *Punch*, 23 January 1886, p. 45.

Few contemporaries condemned the bishops, or the Church generally, for being concerned primarily for the moral welfare of the poor—
the social evils of drunkenness, prostitution, and crime were too prevalent and too alarming for them to be dismissed as inconsequential.
The crowded insanitary homes of the poor made the public houses
of the period appear warm, cheerful, and attractive; and whole families crowded into them in the evenings. Meetings of friendly and
benefit societies were often held in them, and even wages were paid
there on Saturday afternoons. Alcohol was the chief medicine of the
poor during illness; a drinking party accompanied any important
social function, such as a wedding or a funeral, and licensing acts did
not begin to appear until the 1870's. Drunkenness was a vice not
only of the father of the family but, only too often, also of the mother
and children. A witness to a select committee of the House of Lords
on Public Houses revealed the state of London drinking places in the
neighbourhood of Blackfriars Road in 1854.

> They are full of people drinking; in one house he counted fifty persons
> drinking; they were serving as fast as they could. Amongst the numbers were
> women with children in their arms; upon one butt there was an infant fast
> asleep, and the father and mother were drunk by one side; against the counter
> was a little child, about four years old, fast asleep. At one house the police
> were obliged to stand with their staves to prevent the people from pushing
> the doors in, as the publican and his servants drove them out to prevent their
> getting more drunk.[8]

The situation was the same in other parts of industrial England, and
drunkenness was a social plague among the poor—their opiate to
escape the misery of their environment. 'Drink', it was said, 'is the
quickest way out of Manchester'.[9]

Some of the poor were as concerned as the Church was about their
moral weaknesses, of which drunkenness was the most prevalent.
Temperance movements began among them; like the 'Temperance
Chartism' which drew many moderate Chartists into moral reform,
and the programmes of social improvement which appeared after mid-
century. John Cassell, who published several phenomenally popular
magazines for workingmen, was a leading temperance reformer among
the poor.[10] Few Victorians disagreed with the thesis that prostitution
and crime would decrease if habits of temperance could be built up
among the working classes.

8. Heasman, *Evangelicals in Action*, p. 126.
9. Bready, *Lord Shaftesbury and Social-Industrial Progress*, p. 366.
10. Cole and Postgate, *Common People*, pp. 368–69.

The bishops believed that their part of the nation's task was to relieve the poor by directing the resources of the Church in a way that would bring Christianity and moral reformation into the slums. This was the primary work of the Church—a mission of such magnitude that little time was left for the Church, as an organization, to agitate for social reform in the national legislature. This was often done by individual bishops, and churchmen like Shaftesbury; but the bench as a whole found direction of the unwieldly organization of the Church in mission concerns a full-time occupation. Just as Parliament found by the end of the century that it had less and less time to devote to ecclesiastical concerns, so the hard-pressed Victorian bishops found that they had little time to devote to the work of the State—the relieving of want through legislative reform. As the working-class population, which was largely pagan, began to increase rapidly, the task facing the bishops was one against time. Frederick Temple in his last charge to the diocese of London noted that 'on the previous Easter Day, out of 3,500,000 in the diocese, only 110,000 had presented themselves for Holy Communion'.[11] Most churchmen agreed that the Church could not then make up for the neglect of the poor for the past hundred years, but they devoted themselves, led by the bishops, to the task of beginning a grass-roots spiritual revival campaign among the poor.

The strategy of the bishops was to use the new spirit of altruism among the commercial classes to bring the Gospel and direct relief to the poor. Some historians have levelled much criticism at the middle-class philanthropy they supported, which is perhaps best exemplified by Octavia Hill. She devoted her life to providing housing for the poor, and to knitting together the upper and lower classes in the nation in mutual sympathy and respect. Because she stood for principles opposed to those of the modern welfare state, her work is seldom now appreciated; but from the eighteen-sixties to the first world war she was a power to be reckoned with, and was generally highly respected. G. F. A. Best in his magnificent study of Queen Anne's Bounty, the Ecclesiastical Commissioners, and the Church of England, entitled *Temporal Pillars*, describes her social reform work as that of one who 'was on one of history's losing sides'. Yet her mentality was shared by most of her contemporaries, and by churchmen like the Ecclesiastical Commissioners and the bishops who encouraged her work:

11. *Report of the Church Congress held at London, October, 1899*, p. 38.

her mind ran along fairly conventional and indeed increasingly old-fashioned lines—individualist, moralist, *laissez-faire* anti-centralization, anti-State almost. She took it for granted that life was meant to be a rigorous business, that the poor would be always with us, that God had not intended the race to be to the slow. She rarely strayed far from the safe position of assuming that if you did not get on in life, there was something wrong with you, physically or morally; if the former, then you must be encouraged and helped to get going at whatever economic level you could independently manage; if the latter, it was necessary you should be told your faults and shown how to be better. Character was far more important than comfort. Charity was the greatest of Christian virtues and the most misunderstood and malpractised. ... Real charity meant personal service, the giving of time, self and sense, not just money and emotion. The poor cried out for charity and it was the duty of the comparatively affluent to give it them.[12]

Because the Church managed to 'ensoul' England's commercial classes, and to give them their ethic of 'service' and 'duty'—no mean accomplishment—the affluent heard the cry of the poor for charity in Victorian England. There was a remarkable increase in voluntary charities between 1850 and 1900. In the decade 1850–1860 the number of such charities in London increased by a quarter, and their income by more than a third. This rate of increase was not maintained through the following decades, but it seldom fell short of it and was still noticeable at the end of the century. By 1909 the Royal Commission on the Poor Laws admitted that voluntary charities supplemented rather than competed with State relief.[13] Charles Booth noted their work in the metropolis: 'In the poorer parts especially, in almost every street, there is a mission; they are more numerous than schools or churches, and only less numerous than the public-houses'.[14] Where the Poor Law failed to treat persons as human beings, and where direct aid to the needy was not to be had, the Christian missions and charities did their work. The poor accepted and often depended upon their existence among them. Because there was so much individualism connected with Victorian charity, there was a certain incompleteness in the aid that was offered to the poor, but in spite of the limitations of these charities, their extent and liberality was such that we should 'be astonished not at what was left undone, but by what was achieved'.[15]

This Church-inspired 'ambulance work' by the middle and upper classes was not, as we now know, able to influence significantly the causes of much of the misery known by the poor. In the 1850's Charles

12. Best, *Temporal Pillars*, p. 489.
13. Heasman, pp. 8–9.
14. Charles Booth, *Life and Labour in London*, 3rd series (1902), VII, 270.
15. Christopher Dawson, 'The Humanitarians', *Ideas and Beliefs of the Victorians* (1949), p. 252.

Kingsley rejoiced at the 'growing moral earnestness' of the privileged orders which he believed was fostered by the Church;[16] by the end of the century intense criticism was being directed at the evangelistic and charitable work of both the Church and Dissent. Within the Church and without, critics were urging Christians to work for political, economic, and social reform which could eradicate poverty in the nation—traditional Christian charity was not enough.

> The strange, dark writing mass of human misery lying crouched and helpless beneath our social system cries out in dull despair, and Christianity answering says, 'My Kingdom is not of this world. I cannot interfere in political matters. I know nothing of right or wrong; of justice or injustice', and goes mumbling and droning its way along toward Heaven, scattering meagre handfuls of charity to them, and with outstretched hands dispenses holy blessings upon the cruel Juggernaut that rolls over them. . . . but if you should . . . cast in your lot with the people making common cause with them for right and justice; teaching and leading them; laying bare to them the sources of the evils under which so many of their number are made to suffer; awakening them to a knowledge of their power and of their rights, and directing them towards the emancipation which is within their reach, you will make for yourself an imperishable name.[17]

The bishops always encouraged the Victorian churchman's concern for charity. And there were many reasons why the bishops chose to help the poor in the way they did—through fostering a spirit of Christian altruism among members of the privileged classes. Many of them, like Newman and other churchmen, never considered social questions except in their relation to faith.[18] The poor were the objects of compassion, benevolence—and conversion; and caring for them in a religious sense left many hard-pressed bishops little time for causes which sought to change the environment of the poor. As we have noted, their efforts to improve the lives of the poor through evangelism, charities, and moral exhortation were generally welcomed by the poor, and approved by the rest of society. No one believed the Poor Law alone would remedy the plight of the poor. The bishops urged the upper and middle classes to give liberally of themselves in charity, that class tensions might be eased in the nation. When the Whigs passed their Poor Law of 1834, based on the thought of Edwin Chadwick and Nassau Senior, the bishops and most churchmen regarded the sudden withdrawal of outdoor relief from the wage-earner with some anxiety: 'The Bill had done its part—we ask

16. Charles Kingsley, *Yeast* (1859 edition), p. ix of Preface.
17. Elihu, *Is General Booth's Darkest England Scheme a Failure* (1895), p. 30.
18. Charles Marson, *God's Co-operative Society* (1914), p. 71.

not whether well or ill; it remains for Christian individuals to do theirs; it remains for the rich individually to show that they have no disposition to be the enemies and oppressors of the poor.'[19]

Another reason why the bishops used the middle class to reach the workers was the absence of any other way of doing so. They had to contend with the reluctance of the underprivileged to identify themselves with either the Church or Nonconformity. There was no 'open hostility to religion' among the workers, but rather 'simple indifference'. Walsham How, suffragan Bishop of Bedford in London's East End, told the Church Congress of 1880 that there was no secularism of an intellectual or religious nature that persuaded the workers to reject the Church's spiritual ministrations. Rather it was their conviction that the Church was for the rich and comfortable, and they rejected Christianity for social reasons: 'Because of class feeling . . . you go your way and we'll go ours is pretty much the spirit in which they regard any who make a profession of religion.'[20] Dean Hook said that in Leeds the poor considered 'a man of the working-classes who is a Churchman to be a traitor to his Party or Order—he is outlawed in the society in which he moves.'[21] In the same meeting the Rector of St. George's-in-the-East argued that though the poor did not exhibit either thrift or sobriety, they did have a morality of their own, which reflected the diffused Christianity which was to be found throughout the nation. 'The bulk of the real aid given to the poor does not come from the rich but from the poor themselves. They share too that deep-rooted regard for truth which penetrates every stratum of society in this nation of ours. And, as a class they are honest . . . they unquestionably exhibit toleration . . . they have a shrewd perception of what is fair.'[22] In fact, the rector believed personally that there was much more dishonesty to be found among 'greedily speculative commercial circles' than there was among the poor. The workingmen of Wolverhampton might crowd a meeting to hear the Bishop of Lichfield assure them that, regardless of class, 'if we are really Christians we are all working people';[23] but they did not take seriously such idealistic proclamations. The English worker accepted the existence of social classes in the nation, and to him the Church was the preserve of privilege.

19. *British Critic*, XVI (1834), 487 ff.
20. *Report of Church Congress held at Leicester, 1880*, p. 95.
21. *Life of Wilberforce*, I, 226.
22. *Church Congress Report* (1880), pp. 101–2. Mr. Jones also disliked calling the poor either 'godless' or 'heathen'.
23. *Report of Church Congress held at Wolverhampton, 1867*, p. 234.

The poor welcomed 'the noble army of men and women who penetrate the vilest haunts, carrying with them the blessings of the Gospel'[24]—and they depended upon the welfare provided by missions and Church-inspired charities. The literate workingmen, who knew of the labours of a bishop like Phillpotts of Exeter on their behalf, were grateful that they had a redoubtable champion who did not allow the government to overlook matters like paupers dying of dysentery and neglect, in poorhouses that were as cold and miserable as the hovels they had left.[25] They wanted the paternalism of the Church because they were almost totally neglected by society without it; but they had no desire to identify themselves with it, or with the middle classes in Dissenting chapels.[26]

The strategy of the bishops was also shaped by the reluctance of the privileged orders to identify themselves too closely with the poor. The Church was not composed of the bishops and clergy alone—as we have seen, the laity have always had a good deal to say about Church policy in England, particularly in social matters; and the laity did little to welcome the poor into the churches. The bishops and prominent churchmen like Shaftesbury might persuade them to give to the poor in charity, or even to help people like Dr. Barnardo or Josephine Butler in their labours; but they preferred—like the Benthamites—to keep the underprivileged at arm's length, and to treat 'the problem' of the slums as an abstraction. Any Victorian, whether he was a churchman, Dissenter, or secularist did not like to 'focus' on personal examples of human wretchedness. When the master-sweep ushered his poor little minions into the Victorian drawing-room he was left alone to do his work. The lady and gentleman of the house left, not only because of the soot, but because of the cancerous sores on the knees of the climbing-boys, and their vermin-infested bodies. For the same reason the poor, when they came to church, were seated in a remote corner. Robbie Burns might be amused by a louse on a lady's clothing in kirk, but the sight of human vermin seldom roused a similar reaction from a person of refinement. The truth was that most members of both the working and middle class in Victorian England accepted, and were grateful for, the social 'apartheid' that was practised. The workers could cheer John Lonsdale, Bishop of Lichfield,

---

24. W. C. Preston, *Bitter Cry of Outcast London* (1883), p. 1.
25. *Hansard*, LX (1842), 978 ff.
26. There were, of course, exceptions to this generalization among some of the Methodists and others. *V.* R. F. Wearmouth, *Methodism and the Working Class Movements of England 1800–1850*, pp. 272–73, and his *Methodism and the Struggle of the Working Classes, 1850–1900* (1954), p. 171 ff.

when he said two weeks before his death: 'There has come a new spirit among us, a desire to spend ourselves for Christ, to labour among you.' They could accept with gratitude Samuel Wilberforce's confession that 'the clergy have been stiff and unsympathetic very often in times past . . . they have fled, to a certain degree, from the conflict Christ ordered for them with . . . the difficulties of men and the sins of men.' But they chose to ignore Lonsdale's announcement, 'we want great churches filled with working men.'[27] They knew the reception they got from the laity when they wandered into most churches or chapels, and they left the churches to the upper and middle classes. Lonsdale's successor, G. A. Selwyn, dreamed of having a parish in an industrial area staffed 'by its own servants, drawn from its own people', but neither the middle-class nor working-class people of his diocese showed much enthusiasm for the idea.[28]

The Church Congress Reports clearly reveal the anxiety of the bishops and other prominent churchmen over the failure of the Church to provide pew accommodation for the poor—for the clergy generally still hoped that the middle and upper classes might be persuaded to welcome the workers into the churches, and that the workers might come. In 1867 Archdeacon Moore reported that between 1831 and 1861 church-building, and the provision of clergy for the people, had roughly kept up with the population increase in rural areas of Staffordshire, but the Church was failing completely to provide for the spiritual needs of the masses in the manufacturing districts. Only 36 per cent of the available clergy laboured among the 70 per cent of the total population of the country who lived in the towns and cities.[29] One of the reasons for this was the lack of endowment of parishes in manufacturing centres. Many critics cynically remarked on the tendency of clergymen to seek better-paid country livings.

How could the bishops deal with this problem? They knew that in the 1860's in Birmingham there were only 36,073 church sittings for a population of 296,306 people. The Rector of St. Thomas' parish had the cure of 30,000 souls; the Rector of St. Luke's was responsible for the spiritual direction of another 20,000.[30] They hesitated to subdivide old parishes because of the tendency of the middle class to drift to suburbia, leaving the workers in the centre of the town. This could produce a situation where, in the words of Winnington-Ingram, 'all

27. *Church Congress Report*, 1867, pp. 234–50.
28. H. W. Tucker, *Memoir of George Augustus Selwyn* (1879), II, 256.
29. *Church Congress Report*, 1867, pp. 20–22.
30. J. C. Miller, *Church of England in Birmingham* (1864), pp. 6–8.

who made jam lived in one place, and all who ate jam lived in another'
—a subdivision of parishes could also give 'jam-makers' and 'jam-
eaters' separate places of worship.[31] The bishops chose to build up
funds to support curates in existing parishes, and to find ancillary help
in the form of mission clergy and lay workers. They even accepted
the Ritualists' suggestion of sisterhoods, once they found they could
be kept under firm diocesan control. But such expediency only added
to another problem of the bishops—the great number of underpaid
curates in the Church, and of irregular workers in the parishes.

When a bishop did appear who was concerned about the 'un-
churched poor' he often found that the wealthy parishioners had no
intention of sharing their accommodation with slum-dwellers. By the
Church Building Act of 1818 (58 Geo. III, c. 45) pew rents had been
set for the new churches, which were built under the Act, to provide
them with income. Other churches in the towns and cities followed
this example, and in most churches pews were allocated according to
the 'different qualities and degrees of people', each according to his
rank.[32] By the Church Building Act of 1851 (14 & 15 Vict., c. 97) the
Church Building Commissioners, because of growing agitation against
such distinctions in the Church, were enabled to extinguish pew rents
where a satisfactory endowment had been found for the new churches,
but by this time the custom of renting pews was widespread. There
were some new churches, like St. Jude, Whitechapel, where all seats
were free; but in others, such as Christ Church, Stepney, more than
half the pews were reserved.[33] For a variety of reasons the pew
holders sometimes chose to oppose the suggestion of either the
clergyman or the bishop that all seats in the churches be made free,
and open to use by the poor.

Any reforming bishop found that he had to wage war against 'the
front pew, that is, against the very Faith in money, which has brought
the Church and its clergy into bondage, the poor into vagabondage'.[34]
It was unlikely that any of them considered the abolition of pew rents
as a 'Morrison's Pill' which would automatically bring the poor
flocking into the churches, but they did know that what anti-clericalism
there was among the English workingmen usually revealed itself in

31. Winnington-Ingram, *Work in Great Cities*, p. 4.
32. C. G. Prideaux, *Practical Guide to the Duties of Churchwardens*, 1841 (1895, 16th
edition), p. 288.
33. Port, *Six Hundred New Churches*, pp. 156–57.
34. Thomas Hancock, *Salvation by Mammon* (1890), p. 20. P. J. Welch, 'Difficulties
of Church Extension in Victorian London', *Church Quarterly Review* (1965), CLXVI, 307,
points out the problem of alienating 'the very people who were helping to build and endow
churches.'

scornful criticism of pew rents. The poor quite naturally did not like to be condescended to by 'the quality'. A female street-seller said to Henry Mayhew 'they have no clothes to go to church in, and ar'nt a-going there just to be looked down upon and put in any queer place as if they had a fever, and for ladies to hold their grand dresses away from us as they walked into their grand pews'.[35] The bishops knew that something had to be done about the situation where most urban churches were 'little more than chapels of the privileged few, in which the people at large have no more concern than they have in the Chapel Royal or any nobleman's private chapel'.[36]

To overcome the resistance of the 'front pew' to reform, the bishops again used the tactic of working with the enlightened churchmen who were willing to use their wealth and position to open up the churches to the workers. Some of them really believed that if pew rents were abolished the poor would come to the churches. After the pew-rent agitation at the Church Congress held at Manchester, the Vicar of Brighton wrote to the *Times* to say that, in spite of appearances to the contrary, 'the labouring classes of this country were at heart deeply religious. . . . let the cry of every churchman be "the National Church for the people" and the counter-cry would assuredly ring out "the people for the National Church".'[37] The Dean of Manchester argued that pew rents were 'in all populous districts the chief hindrance to church attendance'.[38] By the 1860's churchmen who thought in this fashion were banding together in organizations like the Manchester 'National Association for Freedom of Worship', the Chester 'Diocesan Open Church Association' and the London 'Free and Open Church Association'.

The London body became known as the Incorporated Free and Open Church Association, and did much to provide propaganda for its cause. One example is a sermon preached by John Keble at the opening of St. Peter's, Sudbury, a church which had no pew rents.[39] The Ritualists generally supported this movement, as part of their clerical reaction to lay tyranny where 'every pew holder looks upon himself as a sort of patron'.[40] Prominent bishops, such as W. C. Magee of Peterborough, Frederick Temple of London, James Fraser

35. Mayhew, *London Labour and the London Poor*, I, 460.
36. Parliamentary Papers, *Deficiency of the Means of Spiritual Instruction* (1857–1858) IX, Appendix J., 610.
37. *Times*, 5 October 1888, p. 5.
38. Dean of Manchester, *Pew-Rents: Injurious to the Church* (1865), pp. 6–7.
39. Incorporated Free and Open Church Association, *Free and Open Church Chronology: Manual for the Use of Preachers, Speakers and Writers in the Public Press* (1892), p. 31.
40. Dean of Manchester, p. 10.

of Manchester, and William Thomson of York, began to identify themselves with the movement. A private member's bill was also introduced into Parliament, sponsored by the association, which sought to put an end to seat-appropriation and pew rents, except where the church building acts had initiated such practices.

This bill lay before Parliament between 1870 and 1890, but nothing came of it, largely because many churchmen did not want the legislature interfering with authority which was supposed to lie with the bishops and the churchwardens. But the agitation did have great effect. By the end of our period, a steady decline in the number of churches that retained rented pews was being reported, and the activities of the Association began to wane. Many churchmen who had at one time taken the pew system for granted were now beginning to think that 'no man . . . can be a good churchman . . . who sits from Sunday to Sunday in an appropriated sitting.'[41]

The 'pew problem' puts the position of the reforming bishop of Victorian England in proper perspective. As Blomfield found when he attempted to redirect the resources of the Church in London, or as Wilberforce discovered in the diocese of Oxford, the laity had much to say about the disposition and the use made of the temporalities of the Church. They were very reluctant to surrender their power of patronage, even to a well-meaning bishop, and if they chose not to assist him in his reform activities, he had even less influence to use against them than he had with the parson in his freehold. The only hope for the bishop was that he could use his office and personal influence to build up a reform movement, among both clergy and laity, which would assist him in his work—like the Incorporated Free and Open Church Association. Most churchmen believed this patient process was preferable to further interference by the legislature in church affairs.

The bishops could do little about pew rents, but there were ardent social reformers among them. One of these was James Fraser, the second Bishop of Manchester. A strong-minded individual, he drew much public attention when he allowed the Rev. S. F. Green, one of his clergy, to be persecuted under the Public Worship Regulation Act for being a Ritualist. When Green was imprisoned in 1881–1882 for contumacy, Fraser defended his action by saying that the Ritualists had to learn that the 'Church is not the clergy', and he was a vigorous opponent of those who opposed the national mission of the Church

41. "C", *Christian Socialism: Two Papers Contributed to the Weekly Churchman* (1884), p. 21.

for theological reasons. It should be noted that he was just as opposed to the Orangemen who attacked the Ritualists as he was to Green and the other members of his party.[42] He soon became known as the 'layman's bishop' because of his absence of clerical pretension, and his custom of chatting with workingmen in tramcars and walking the streets carrying his own bag. He was convinced that the weakness of the Church in society came from the 'apathy of the laity'. The evils of 'priestcraft, sacerdotalism, clerical assumptions and so forth' were symptomatic of this ecclesiastical malady.[43]

Fraser was intent upon uniting all classes in Manchester in a great mission to improve social conditions for the ultimate benefit of all: 'Our National Church cannot afford to be the church of the privileged classes. It must be by its constitution the Church of the whole people, tolerant, catholic, evangelical, comprehensive, conciliatory.'[44] The Church's immediate task was to use all its resources in a great mission to improve the lot of the poor. These resources were in large measure to be supplied by those pious laymen who had social influence and were dedicated in their service to the nation.

By nature Fraser was a practical man, and he did not confine himself to exhortation. He had acted as an Assistant Commissioner to the Education Commission, and one of the reasons Gladstone offered him Manchester in 1870 was that Fraser's educational views were in accordance with the Act of that year. Manchester was a centre of educational controversy, and Fraser did much to persuade the Tories in the city to accept the dual system of national education, which he believed would benefit all.

Fraser believed that churchmen should carry forward the mission of the Church to the nation by taking part in every act of social amelioration of the day, whether it was directed by ecclesiastical or by secular agencies. He drew attention to the merits of the Co-operative Movement, and was the first bishop to speak before one of its congresses. He also attempted to act as conciliator in trade-union disputes in Manchester and Lancashire. He admitted that he was 'no lover of the principles of Trade-Unionism; but they have been forced upon the working classes by the inequitable use of the power of capital.'[45] The *Times* accused him of meddling with a question on

42. Hughes, *James Fraser*, p. 215.
43. James Fraser, *As Things are How Can We Educate: A Question Attempted to be Answered in a Sermon* (1853), p. 15.
44. Hughes, p. 209.
45. *Times*, 2 April 1874, p. 7.

which he was not sufficiently informed;[46] but this did not deter Fraser, who was dedicated in his opposition to all social injustice. During the lockout of agricultural labourers in 1874, Fraser began his protest in the *Times* by asking 'Are the farmers of England going mad?' and he appealed to their intelligence and self-interest as well as to their sense of justice.[47]

Like most of his contemporaries Fraser also engaged in direct charity. He was one bishop who walked the slum streets of Manchester and Salford, and what he saw there led him to give a total of £31,536 to the poor during his episcopate. On his marriage in 1880, he gave to the poor people of Manchester 500 thick Scottish shawls, 50 boys' suits, and Sunday joints for 32 poor families, as well as arrears of rent for 52 homes—regardless of church membership.[48] The example he set to the commercial classes of Manchester was as much appreciated by the poor as the support he gave to the trade-union movement. Charity which helped their immediate misery was not only willingly received, but taken for granted as a social necessity. When it was encouraged by the Church, through the altruism of men like Fraser, the poor applauded religion for doing what it should be doing—providing them with what the Poor Law failed to give. As Henry Mayhew found out, through talking with London's coster-mongers, the poor reckoned 'that religion's the best that gives the most in charity'.[49]

Bishop Fraser's experience as an Education Commissioner had convinced him that the Church had to supplement the parochial structure in the urban areas with a new and more flexible organization which could direct men to where they were most needed—among the 'semi-heathenized' populations of the slums. He was one of the first to advocate a team ministry, a 'body of mission-clergy' to assist both Church and State in the Christian mission to ameliorate the life of the poor: 'Other agencies are needed, more energetic, more free, more flexible, more ready to adapt themselves to every opportunity that offers.'[50]

Fraser's popularity with the workingmen of Manchester did not make him by any means a national champion of the poor.[51] Rather he was considered to be a welcome exception to the usual Anglican

46. *Ibid.*, 11 April 1874, p. 5.
47. *Ibid.*, 2 April 1874, p. 7. *Cf.*, *supra*, p. 248.
48. Hughes, p. 253.
49. Peter Quennell, *Mayhew's London*, n.d., p. 59.
50. James Fraser, *Charge Delivered at his Primary Visitation* (1872), p. 77.
51. Fraser was never a political bishop and was almost unknown in the House of Lords.

bishop, who was believed to think and act like Charles Ellicott of Gloucester, the prelate who advocated a horse-pond ducking for labour agitators like Joseph Arch. When Ben Tillett looked back on his life as a labour leader, he admitted that the strategy for the London Dock Strike of 1889 had been inspired by lectures given at Oxford House, Bethnal Green, by Cosmo Lang, the future Archbishop of Canterbury—though Lang little realized the use that was to be made of his talks on Napoleon's campaigns. He also admitted that during the great strike he had the staunch support of the Ritualists, Samuel Barnett of Toynbee Hall, James Adderley of Oxford House, and the Guild of St. Matthew. But much more important to Tillett was the rejection he received from the 'square-jawed' and 'hard featured' Frederick Temple, then Bishop of London, who had engaged in 'most violent abuse of the docker' before leaving the city for holiday in Wales—only to hurry back when he discovered that Cardinal Manning was stepping in to dominate negotiations.[52] This kind of episcopal blunder, like the foolish babble of Dr. Ellicott, became part of working-class legend and was not easily forgotten: 'During the strike of 1874, the stupidity of two obscure clerical magistrates and the indiscretion of a bishop had over-shadowed the outspoken sympathy of many churchmen. In 1889 Temple's spectacular retirement outweighed the quiet effort of the Christian Socialists.'[53]

During Fraser's episcopate, however, a great change began to take place on the bench of bishops, although it was largely unrecognized until the end of our period. The Anglican bishops began to display a social conscience which was startling in its manifestation. Fraser's idea of a national Church which was catholic in its mission was 'in the air', and even unreligious people like Beatrice Webb were saying: 'I should desire the Church to become the home of national communal aspirations as well as of the endeavour of the individual towards a better personal life.'[54] Here and there bishops began to show that they shared her wish. Interestingly enough, among them were men who were already well known to the public because of their scholarship.

One of them was J. B. Lightfoot of Durham, a shy scholar, who nevertheless joined Fraser in support of the Co-operative Movement, and urged the Co-operative Congress held at Newcastle in 1880 to encourage brotherhood in the nation among all classes.[55] Another

52. Ben Tillett, *Memories and Reflections* (1931), p. 146 ff.
53. Wagner, *Church of England and Social Reform*, p. 257.
54. Beatrice Webb, *Our Partnership* (1948), p. 207.
55. J. B. Lightfoot, *Inaugural Address at the Co-operative Congress* (1880), p. 3 ff.

such bishop was Mandell Creighton, a close friend of Beatrice and Sidney Webb, who acted as mediator during the 1895 boot-trade lockout in Leicester and Northampton, which threw 120,000 men out of work. As Bishop of Peterborough he approached the masters' federation, the trades council, and the secretary of the Board of Trade to try to find a settlement and to ease the misery brought upon the workingmen and their families. After agreement was reached a contemporary wrote of Creighton's work: 'He helped the leaders on both sides to settle the dispute, not only by being a good listener to the statements of their different points of view and the arguments in support of them, but by suggesting at the right moment the method of intervention and the choice of a reference. But the action taken at the critical moment, with such good results, would have been impossible if he had not previously in many ways won at least a certain amount of confidence in many quarters.'[56]

From the standpoint of the social reformer, however, the ideal Anglican bishop was Brooke Foss Westcott, who succeeded his friend J. B. Lightfoot as Bishop of Durham in 1890. He is still celebrated, with Hort and Lightfoot, as a leader of the revival of Anglican theology in the last quarter of the century; but Westcott's scholarship was never an end in itself. It provided him with the basis for a sound Incarnational theology which stressed the redemptive work of Christ as the most important phenomenon to be reckoned with not only in personal religion, but in social development. He said that when he looked at the social movements of his age, Chartism, Corn Law agitation, Factory Reform, the Young England party, and even the Oxford Movement:

> I saw how movement acted upon movement and how all movements pointed to something deeper than any one showed; so I recognized that I was bound to study the problems of the new age no less than the lessons of the old world if I was to take a just view of the office to which I aspired. I seemed to discern, as I looked on the events which were a large part of my training, that all life was one, that no part lay outside my sphere, that national life, social life, civic life, were all forms of the religious life which was the embodiment of the Gospel.[57]

Westcott believed that the Church was called upon to interpret and to commend to society God's will for each generation: 'It will be the duty of the clergy to keep before their people, without weariness

56. *Life of Creighton*, II, 130.
57. B. F. Westcott, 'Social Service', *Christian Social Union Addresses* (1903), p. 2.

and without impatience, the clear vision of the purpose of God for His creation.'[58] Details of how God's will was to be implemented were to be left to the State and 'to men who have a practical knowledge of affairs' but the Church was to shape public opinion so that it demanded God's ordering of society: 'The Church educates and inspires society, which moulds the State.'[59] 'To Christians, I say, and to the National Church, the capacity and the charge are given to commend to our countrymen an ideal fitted to occupy the energies and meet the needs of our generation.'[60]

The great achievement of the Church in the nation during his life-time was the promotion of social harmony and the easing of class conflict. In 1899 he said that he could look back sixty years to the time 'when everyone was speaking confidently of the coming great revolution which it was expected would be wrought in desolation and blood. . . . the revolution had come but silently and peacefully'.[61] The Church had done much to ease social tension through 'declaring with authority what must and must not be done',[62] and through establishing a much closer union between the clergy and the masses of the people, which had shown to the privileged people of the nation that such social agreement was possible.[63]

Westcott confessed to representatives of the chief industries in Durham that his own first desire in life was to bring about closer intercourse and better understanding among all classes.[64] He devoted himself to this cause, whenever it was possible, from the time he became Bishop of Durham, and soon won the confidence of the working class in the area. The people loved a bishop who had won renown as a scholar, yet could find time to have meetings of miners' lodges at Auckland Castle to discuss the question of homes for aged miners; who would allow miners' brass bands to play in the cathedral at their annual special services; who called for a boycott of goods of employers who did not pay reasonable wages; who opened the deer park of Bishop Auckland to the townspeople of Durham; and had four sons in the mission field. The northern penny weekly called *The News* spoke of Westcott as 'one who holds a foremost position in the Episcopate, is revered throughout Europe as a distinguished

---

58. B. F. Westcott, *The Incarnation and Common Life* (1893), p. 38.
59. *Ibid.*, p. 23.
60. *Ibid.*, p. 27.
61. *North Eastern Daily Gazette*, 25 October 1899; address to the Durham Diocesan Church Conference at Town Hall, West Hartlepool.
62. B. F. Westcott, *The Incarnation—a Revelation of Human Duties: Charge to the Clergy of Durham, 19 November, 1892*, p. 13.
63. *Newcastle Daily Journal*, 22 October 1897.
64. *Durham Chronicle*, 27 July 1898.

scholar and theologian, and still more—is known and loved by "workers everywhere".'[65] The *Donnington Star* said that 'few prelates, not even excepting the late Archbishop Thomson, have obtained so firm a hold upon the working classes.'[66]

Soon after his arrival at Durham there occurred a disastrous strike in the pits, which put some 90,000 men out of work between 9 March and 3 June 1891. The bishop was called upon to act as conciliator in the strike, and met with the colliery owners and the representatives of the men at Auckland Castle for discussion about how the dispute might be solved. His office of mediation was successful. In a dramatic moment, the secretary of the Miners' Union rushed from the council table to a window and held up his hands with ten fingers extended, to be recognized by wives and families waiting below as a sign that the men had obtained a ten per cent increase in wages.[67] Incidents like this became as important a part of working-class tradition in the north as the stories of clerical injustice, such as those told by Arch and Tillett, which were treasured elsewhere. Few of the working class disagreed with the opinion that 'the workmen of Durham had a great friend in the bishop.'[68]

In fact, later Bishops of Durham, like Hensley Henson, found themselves the objects of abuse when they avoided using the 'peacemaking potentiality of episcopal influence' in mining disputes. Henson said of the embarrassment that caused him: 'The tradition of Westcott leads the public to think that much is possible in the way of episcopal mediation, which everybody with any real information on economic subjects to-day knows to be wholly beyond the limits of possibility.'[69] Westcott would not have agreed with Henson that economic matters were outside the Church's sphere of influence. To him 'the corporate life of . . . society is a divine life',[70] and it was the Church's task to ensure that God's purpose, which was at work in economics as well as in the Church, was recognized: 'There is, I will venture to say, no spiritual force outside the Church which it is not able to assimilate and to use effectively.'[71]

65. *The News*, 21 April 1899.
66. *Donnington Star*, 13 September 1897. *The Northern Weekly Leader* of 24 July 1897 spoke of his 'high place in the regard of the Durham pitmen.'
67. Westcott, *Life of B. F. Westcott*, II, 129.
68. *Middlesborough Evening Telegraph*, 21 October 1897.
69. Henson, *Retrospect of an Unimportant Life*, II, 25.
70. B. F. Westcott, *National Church and the Nation* (1893), p. 4; a speech delivered at Westminster Town Hall in May 1891.
71. B. F. Westcott, *The Idea and Work of the Church of England* (1893), p. 8, speech at Darlington, December 1891.

Westcott did much to promote his own tradition of reconciling class tensions among the other members of the bench of bishops after he came to Durham. Henry Scott Holland, Canon of St. Paul's, and one of the contributors to *Lux Mundi*, was the founder of the Christian Social Union, which appeared in London in 1889; and Westcott became its first president. One of the aims of the new organization was 'to study in common how to apply the moral truths and principles of Christianity to the social and economic difficulties of the present time',[72] and Westcott did much to persuade his fellow bishops that they should support this movement. Many actively supported the C.S.U. as it grew into a substantial body of churchmen and women, with a respectable leadership, which was pledged to investigate social problems in the light of Christian morality.

The members of the C.S.U. generally agreed with Westcott's Incarnationalist theology; to 'claim for the Christian law the ultimate authority to rule social practice'.[73] At the same time, they agreed with him that the practical answers to 'how shall we bring our Gospel to bear on the evils of our time'[74] might well be provided by men versed in secular affairs who were not primarily churchmen. They had an abiding suspicion of those who sought to provide ecclesiastical blue-prints of how society should be ordered. When Leo XIII issued his encyclical *Rerum Novarum*, which applied traditional Catholic teaching to the new conditions created by the Industrial Revolution, Scott Holland noted how abstract was its wisdom: 'far aloof . . . from the actual dust and heat of the turmoil in which the social world is engaged'.

> There is a patriarchal simplicity assumed throughout. And this gives a far-away, old-fashioned, dreamy tone to all that is said. It reads like some old tale; we enjoy the quiet continuity with which it moves from point to point; it is so clear, so precise, so dignified . . . but it has all nothing to do with the world in which we live: it is the voice of some old-world life, faint and ghostly, speaking in some antique tongue of things long ago.[75]

The C.S.U. preferred a pragmatic approach to the problems created by industrial society. Its tactic was to stir the social consciences of the privileged of the nation, both clergy and laity, and to beg from every source enlightenment which could help the lot of the poor. Unless men of privilege chose to work for the commonwealth, and to redress

72. Wagner, *Church of England and Social Reform Since 1854*, p. 212.
73. B. F. Westcott, *Christian Social Union* (1895), p. 2.
74. *Ibid.*, p. 6.
75. *Economic Review*, I (1891), 460–61.

social grievances willingly, little would be accomplished. Charles Gore, who had become an active supporter of the C.S.U. said that the 'real obstacle to social advance is selfishness or sin. No external reform will remove this.'[76]

The Union published unofficial periodicals to propagate its ideas, like the *Economic Review* of the Oxford branch, which ran from 1891–1914, and *Commonwealth* which Scott Holland edited from 1895 until 1912.[77] Through these publications, study groups, and public lectures and sermons, the C.S.U. appealed to churchmen, and any others who might support its cause, to give support to the various schemes being advanced to help the working class of the nation. Westcott, Holland, and their followers realized the value of the Church as an agency through which they could challenge the privileged classes. For too long the Church had seen as its task the 'comforting of the afflicted'—now its role was to 'afflict the comfortable'. In the words of H. C. Shuttleworth, 'The first step towards social improvement is to make people discontented with things as they are, so long as things are not what they ought to be.'[78] The parish clergy were to be not only a source of charity, but 'tribunes of the people', protecting the workers from those who would rob and oppress them. Scott Holland announced that 'the Church wants the Workers',[79] and challenged the members of the C.S.U. to consider the real reasons why the working class was estranged from the Church.

> Why is it that this Church of ours . . . so rich in her catholic inheritance, so interwoven into England's story . . . should somehow appear to the masses of English workers in country and in town now at the very crisis of their fate, as if she stood aloof from their very life, and was cold to their aspirations and suspicious of their aims and helpless in their needs; why should she wear the aspect to them of something privileged and propertied, jealous and timid, and carry with her so little of the likeness of Christ?[80]

By 1895 the Union had twenty-seven branches and almost three thousand members, and Scott Holland enthusiastically viewed the acceptance of socialism in the Church as a new kind of Reformation in the Church of England.

---

76. *Ibid.*, p. 152.
77. James Adderley of the London Branch also edited the short-lived *Goodwill*, from 1894–1897, an overly religious publication.
78. *Vox Clamantium*, ed. A. Reid (1894), p. 45.
79. H. S. Holland, 'Labour Movement', *Christian Social Union: Three Addresses* (1896), p. 23.
80. H. S. Holland, 'National Penitence', *Lombard Street in Lent* (1894), p. 9.

From every side windows were flung open, barriers were thrown down. . . . we were ready for a call and it came. From over the sea we began to be aware of a Social Philosophy, which however nationalistic some of its tendencies might have become, had had alliance with the spiritual Hegelianism with which we had been touched. It took its scientific shape in the hands of Karl Marx, but it also floated across to us, in dreams and visions, using our own Christian language, and invoking the unity of the Social Body and the law of love and the solidarity of Humanity. It read out the significance of citizenship in terms that were spiritual and Christian. It challenged us to say why we were not bringing our creed into action as the true secret of all social well-being. . . . we woke up to Maurice. His influence which had lain as it were alongside the Oxford Movement now passed within it. . . . Christian doctrine showed itself as the very heart of a Social Gospel, and it was no longer necessary for an interest in drains to be identified with a desire to 'hang theology'.[81]

It is difficult to estimate how much effect such rhetoric had upon the Church as a whole. It certainly marked the passing of the time when clergymen like the Rev. Thomas MacDonald, Rector of Kersal Moor, Manchester, could argue that the deserving poor should be helped not only through alms-giving, but also through parish teas, with readings on 'The Happy Home', 'The Duties and Joys of Friendship', and 'Counsels to Grumblers', which would not fail to reach the workers and 'mingle profit with delight'.[82] It also marked the waning of suspicion which had been shown for so long by the official leaders of the Church, when they considered the ideas of people like Maurice or the Ritualists. The policies of the C.S.U. were cautious enough to be acceptable to even the bench of bishops, and the general encouragement that the prelates gave to the movement led many of the public to hope that it would accomplish much in changing the image of the Church.

> Because it [the Established Church] has been a favoured and a greatly privi-liged religious community its Bishops and clergy and members have laboured to maintain privilege and to perpetuate injustice. . . . But here is the Christian Social Union professing principles that can only be heartily wel-comed if they are the means of breaking down the resistance of the State Church to certain necessary measures of social reform. . . . If the Church of England with all its resources and agencies could throw its influence into the scale against some of the crying evils of our time, reformers would cease to stand almost in despair before the difficulties that confront them.[83]

Contemporaries made many criticisms of the Union. Stewart Headlam of the Guild of St. Matthew thought it too 'academic' and

81. *Ibid.*, Introduction, p. xii.
82. Thomas MacDonald, *How to Reach Working Men* (1877), p. 23.
83. *Leeds Mercury*, 27 November 1900, report of C.S.U. meeting in Albert Hall, Leeds where Westcott had urged class amity.

dominated by 'dignified gentlemen' to be truly a revolutionary body, and he judged its mildness by the fact that Westcott could act as its president.[84] Others criticized its lack of a practical programme. The Unionists might urge state legislation for the housing of the poor, or the taxation of the unearned increment of landowners, but no real social agitation was initiated, apart from a 'white list' of fair employers which was received from the Oxford Trades Council and read at a meeting of the Oxford C.S.U. Some churchmen, like Hensley Henson, attacked it on theological grounds and tended to view the movement as a secular threat to the Faith. No one really expected it to attract the working class into its membership, though Gore later regretted that trade-unionist churchmen were not raised up by the C.S.U. and encouraged to influence the labour movement.[85]

This failure to attract working-class membership is understandable, for 'the leaders of the C.S.U. were unable to free themselves from the accidents of their education.'[86] Most of them had been dons, most came from families of privilege; and though the working-class leaders might welcome their labours to change the mind of the Church about socialism, they identified the C.S.U. spokesmen, as they did most churchmen, with the upper classes. They wanted the classes to work together for the betterment of society generally, but in this mission 'you go your way, and we'll go ours' was the attitude of most of those in the C.S.U., and most working-class leaders. Both groups were content if the Church's social attitudes could be changed sufficiently that the 'distaste for parsons' held by men like George Lansbury could be modified,[87] and grudging recognition be granted to the new spirit that Westcott, Holland, and Gore represented. The English working man could applaud Westcott when he told the Church Congress of 1890: 'Wage labour, though it appears to be an inevitable step in the evolution of society, is as little fitted to represent finally or adequately the connection of man with man in the production of wealth as in earlier times slavery or serfdom.'[88] But at the same time he had no desire to join a body in which he would feel socially uncomfortable. In turn, C.S.U. leaders, like Scott Holland, 'viewed labour rather from outside than inside'.[89]

84. F. G. Bettany, *Stewart Headlam* (1926), p. 90.
85. C. Gore, 'Holland and the Christian Social Union' in Stephen Paget, ed., *Henry Scott Holland* (1921), p. 250.
86. Reckitt, *Maurice to Temple*, p. 139.
87. Raymond Postgate, *George Lansbury* (1951), p. 293.
88. Reckitt, *Maurice to Temple*, p. 144.
89. *Commonwealth* (1918), p. 304. Cf. *Ibid.* (1910), pp. 185–88 on the C.S.U. policy of avoiding political affiliations.

10*

The real importance of the C.S.U. is to be found in the influence it had on the Church as a whole. In the words of Westcott, it fostered 'quiet study' of social problems, and through teaching, preaching, and writing encouraged this activity throughout the Church—including the bench of bishops. Its spokesmen on the bench brought its philosophy into Parliament, and its lesser figures sought to forward its logic in the Church assemblies. But its greatest influence was among the bishops—who welcomed its mild social doctrines. This was a revolutionary development of the time. It was now expected that bishops display a social conscience. When Westcott's friend, Edward White Benson, who had just been translated from Truro to Canterbury, addressed the Rochester Diocesan Society at Lambeth Palace, he showed that he was intimately acquainted with the plight of people like the local poverty-stricken matchbox and ulster makers.[90] The social encyclical issued by the Lambeth Conference of 1897 'might have passed muster as a pamphlet of the Christian Social Union'.[91]

> The bishops, in fact, had been specially affected by the progress of the Union. From its foundation in 1889 to 1913 fifty-three episcopal appointments were made. Of these, at least fourteen appointments, mostly to urban or industrial sees, went to members of the Union. Other bishops were more or less favourably disposed towards its doctrines. . . . 'Oddly enough', said the Rev. Percy Dearmer in 1907, 'under the last two Conservative Governments it was rare for any one to be made a bishop who was not keen about social reform.'[92]

The C.S.U. had become the conscience of the episcopate. Through the writings of Scott Holland and others, it urged that the bishops should recognize the demand of working men for a wage 'on which it is possible to live and save', as 'human, moral, Christian'; a subject upon which the bishops should speak out.[93] By 1909 Earl Beauchamp, a Liberal leader, was complaining that the proposals made by the bishops, in the debate over the Housing and Town-Planning Bill of that year, 'were so extreme that a moderate Government like the present was unable to follow them'.[94]

The new social outlook of the episcopate encouraged the progressive clergy to express similar ideas in Church Congresses:

> The debates at the Church Congress at Hull, of which we report the second day's proceedings this morning, are assuredly not open to the objection that

90. *Christian Socialist*, I (1883), 45.
91. Wagner, p. 241.
92. *Ibid.*, p. 242. The Dearmer quotation is from *Commonwealth* (1907), pp. 294–95.
93. Paget, *Henry Scott Holland*, p. 202.
94. *Hansard*, III (1909), 210.

the clergy these days hold themselves timidly aloof from the treatment of practical problems. Questions of theology, and even of ecclesiastical organization had only a secondary place assigned to them. The clergy of an earlier generation would have stood aghast at the spectacle of bishops . . . and other high dignitaries entering with intense earnestness on controversies about strikes and sanitation . . . not to speak of a problem going so deeply to the roots of the existing order of society as that which is summed up in the word 'Socialism'. They refuse to see that in spite of any conceivable social reforms, under any and every ideal scheme of human organization, economic laws will continue to operate and will often produce painful results.[95]

4. The Ritualist Slum Priests

LITTLE would have come of the mild agitation of the Christian Social Union if most churchmen had not been made aware of the needs of the poor in urban areas by a grass-roots movement which caught public attention —the activities of the minority of clergy who spent their working lives in slum parishes. It has been said that the bishop's task is to confirm, not to baptize in the Church, and this was certainly true in the case of the social revolution which took place in the Victorian Church. The work of the C.S.U. only comes into perspective when it is viewed against the background of work that was carried out by lesser-known, less officially recognized clergy, who lived and died among the poor.

The best known of these slum priests were the Ritualists, whom we met in Chapter III as dissident clergy who vigorously opposed their bishops and advocated disestablishment of the Church. They were dedicated in their service to 'catholicism', by which they usually meant the bringing of the Gospel of Christ to bear on all parts of society. Just as much as the followers of Wesley in an earlier age, they displayed 'enthusiasm', which manifested itself in extravagant use of ceremonial in liturgical services, and called upon their heads the wrath of their diocesans and the prominent Low-Church party. 'The cold and lifeless services of a past age had a natural tendency to beget a taste for excessive display in a succeeding generation. . . . the black bottle, and dirty wine-stained tablecloth, the hurried administration, and hardly concealed impatience of the

95. *Times*, 2 October 1890, p. 7.

celebrant . . . could not but occasion a contrast of something like superstitious reverence.[1]

Because Pusey acted as their 'father-in-God', and they had a 'high' doctrine of the Church, which they conceived to be the conscience of the nation, they have often been considered as spiritual descendants of the early Tractarians. But, as we have seen, they had little of the Tractarian love of episcopacy, and refused to admit that mitred prelates should be granted unquestioning obedience. Another way in which they differed from the Tractarians was in their concern for society. They refused to confine their interests to purely ecclesiastical affairs, and believed that a Church interested only in abstract theological concerns, like apostolic succession, was hardly 'catholic' in its expression.

Wesley Bready, in his study of *Lord Shaftesbury and Social Industrial Progress*, claimed that a 'disastrous consequence' of the Tractarian movement was the direction in which it led the thinking of churchmen: 'It centred attention on dogmas, sacramental and doctrinal, to at least the partial exclusion of ethical considerations.'[2] Scholars have disagreed over the extent to which the Tractarians were guilty of this,[3] but the evidence seems to indicate that like most of their generation they accepted the immutability of economic laws. The poor were always to be with them, and the most the Church could do was to encourage the practice of charity by the privileged orders: 'God has divided the world into rich and poor, that there might be more exercise of charity and patience.'[4] Station in life was to be accepted, and no encouragement was to be given to class envy or strife.

> Differences of rank, power and riches between man and man is no doubt God's appointment, as much as differences of health and strength. And when we speak or think unkindly of our neighbour, for being nobler or richer or of more consequence than ourselves, we do in fact grumble against our Maker, and set up ourselves as better judges than He of what is really good for us. And if we die in such a temper as that, our end can be no other than everlasting destruction. On the other hand, a cheerful submission to authority, a desire to find one's superiors in the right, and such a respect for them and ourselves . . . are real parts of sound Christian wisdom. [5]

1. *Guardian*, 25 October 1865, p. 1073.
2. Bready, *Lord Shaftesbury*, p. 81.
3. *Cf.* Binyon, *Christian Socialist Movement in England*, p. 58 ff. and Peck, *Social Implications of the Oxford Movement*, p. 48 ff.
4. John Keble, *Sermons: Occasional and Parochial* (1868), p. 174, sermon on the poor in Ireland.
5. *Ibid.*, p. 223, sermon in 1830 when introduction of threshing machines led to serious riots in countryside.

The only place in this life where class differences could be forgotten was in the Church during worship: 'there is no difference among you, but what you make yourselves by the minds and tempers and habits you bring with you into Church.'[6]

There were many critics, of course, ready to comment on the Tractarian failure to provide a social Gospel: 'High assumptions of priestly dogmatism and the affectation of a peculiarly exclusive tone of instruction, are surely not the method by which in the present age, a really salutary impression is to be made on the ignorant and ir-religious masses.'[7] Many of those who remained associated with Pusey, and what was left of the Tractarian party after Newman's departure, began to share these doubts about the social policies that had been followed. Charles Marriott, who had become vicar of the University Church at Oxford, said: 'The truth is, that the system of the Church loses its true living character for anyone as soon as he makes it a substitute for the life of the Church, or his own, as soon as he regards the Church as a machine for manufacturing cut and dried dogmas.'[8]

Pusey, himself, as we have noted, could never allow doctrine so to occupy his mind that 'ethical considerations' were driven from it. In 1855 he confessed that he felt his academic duties in Oxford were almost a bondage which kept him from living and working in the slums of London: 'If I had no duties here . . . I would long ago have asked leave to preach in the alleys of London, where the Gospel is as unknown as in Tibet.'[9] He envied the charitable works that could be performed by his brother Philip, member of Parliament for Berkshire, who devoted himself to serving the poor, travelling even to Scotland to relieve those he had heard to be in dire need.[10] We have noted Pusey's own support of Blomfield's church-building programme in East London, and his endowment of St. Saviour's, Leeds. In much of his preaching, he devoted himself to stirring the social conscience of his peers.

> I did not give to the poor; but I paid what I was compelled to the poor rate, of the height of which I complained. . . . I did not take in little children in Thy Name, but they were provided for; they were sent, severed indeed from father

6. John Keble, *Rich and Poor One in Christ* (1858), p. 18.
7. Baden Powell, *The State-Church: Sermon Before University of Oxford* (1850), p. 36.
8. Charles Marriott, *Five Sermons on the Principles of Faith and Church Authority* (1850), p. xii of Preface. Cf. his *God and Not System the Strength of the Church* (1850).
9. *Life of Pusey*, III, 32.
10. *Pusey House Mss.* Pusey to Philip Pusey, 4 March 1845. Cf. *Life of Pusey*, III, 167 ff. for his attitude to Irish famine.

or mother to the poorhouse, to be taught or not about Thee, as might be; I did not feed Thee when hungry, political economy forbade it, but I increased the labour market with the manufacture of luxuries; I did not visit Thee when sick, but the parish doctor looked in on his ill-paid rounds; I did not clothe Thee when naked, I could not afford it, the rates were so high, but there was a workhouse for Thee to go to: I did not take Thee in as a stranger, but it was provided that Thou mightest go to the casual ward. Had I known . . .[11]

The Ritualists' desire to bring the Gospel to the slums through their evangelical preaching, and their 'enthusiasm', has led several scholars to identify them with the Evangelical movement rather than the Tractarians. Yngve Brilioth has wondered whether Pusey was not, in fact, 'one of the great English Evangelicals',[12] representing the second phase of English Pietism, and Dieter Voll in his *Catholic Evangelicalism* has indicated the fervid evangelicalism at the heart of the mission work of priests like George Wilkinson, who succeeded E. W. Benson as Bishop of Truro, and later became Bishop of St. Andrew's.[13] Particularly during his three years at St. Peter's, Great Windmill Street, Wilkinson made effective use of evangelistic street preaching, as well as Ritualist devices such as the processional cross. He found that both 'enthusiasm' and ritual appealed to the people who lived in the squalid alleys around Piccadilly Circus. His introduction of extempore prayer and vivid sacramentalism did much more to bring common people into his church than the traditional Low-Church Protestantism which had been offered to them for so long. A contemporary has left us with a description of one of his processions in the streets, and sermons addressed to the poor.

Mr. Wilkinson in surplice and hood, supported by his curates and followed by choir and churchwardens, walked in procession from the church singing hymns. Such a spectacle seemed so odd in those squalid London streets. . . . Arrived at the place chosen for the sermon . . . we were glad to see a good many of the class we wanted gathered together, besides some of the better people who attend the church. Mr. W. preached with great power. It was a tremendous exertion but his voice was distinctly heard to the very edge of the crowd. He told them . . . how he longed for their souls, picturing to them the life so many of them had been living, and their sore need of a Saviour. A good many listened most attentively, and accepted his invitation to follow him into church for some prayer. It was indeed a singular scene—the tall houses with hideous-looking women hanging out of every window, dirty men with short pipes in their mouths, the tawdry fine work-girl, the jaunty shop boy, the city arab, the fat, prosperous-looking landlady in silk and velvet, a man selling

11. E. B. Pusey, *Christianity Without the Cross a Corruption of the Gospel of Christ* (1875), pp. 27–28.

12. Y. Brilioth, *Evangelicalism and the Oxford Movement* (1934), p. 36.

13. D. Voll, *Catholic Evangelicalism*, p. 53 ff.

apples and ginger beer, with a soldier or two, and rising up in the midst Mr. Wilkinson's refined, thoughtful face and pure white surplice.[14]

This account of Wilkinson's open-air services comes from the governess of his children, and it may be that the social condescension she displays in her writing may also have been projected by Wilkinson himself. Both Lord Derby and Mr. Gladstone were among those who attended St. Peter's, 'to escape from the more fashionable churches of the West End'; and Wilkinson was the guest of the Gladstones at Hawarden.[15] In 1870 he was offered St. Peter's, Eaton Square, in the fashionable world of the metropolis, which was soon 'well-known for its High Church Methodism'.[16] Wilkinson also caught attention through his work in the London Missions of 1869 and 1874, and the hierarchy looked benevolently on his combination 'of the best elements of Wesleyanism on the one side and High Churchmanship on the other'.[17] He prospered in the Establishment because he was wise enough to avoid excessive ritual which might have caused public distress.

Most of the Ritualists were like Pusey, or Wilkinson, in their evangelical fervour, but unlike the latter they did not prosper in the Establishment. When they were humble men, like George Rundle Prynne, who served in the slums of Plymouth, in the new parish of St. Peter, from 1848 to 1903, they were in a position where no one but their own parishioners really appreciated their labours. Prynne's parish was 'the most poverty-stricken and degraded in Plymouth'.[18] During his fifty-five years of labour, mobs were raised against him because of his use of ritual, and he was handicapped in his work by the bitter antipathy of his fellow clergy. But his heroic labours, together with those of Miss Sellon and the Devonport Sisters of Mercy, during the cholera epidemic of 1849, won him an abiding place of affection in the memory of the poor of Plymouth. As Prynne said: 'From a missionary point of view the cholera visitation was a great help to us. It showed the people that the Church cared for them.'[19] Another of these unrecognized saints was Arthur Douglas Wagner, who also served in the slums of Brighton for some fifty years without much public notice. An ascetic who gave his fortune

14. A. J. Mason, *Memoir of G. H Wilkinson* (1910), p. 102.
15. *Ibid.*, pp. 103–5.
16. Voll, p. 70.
17. *Ibid.* p. 73.
18. A. C. Kelway, *George Rundle Prynne* (1905), p. 28.
19. *Ibid.*, p. 51: *Cf.* G. R. Prynne, *Thirty-Five Years of Mission Work in a Garrison and Seaport Town* (1883).

for the building of three churches and most of a fourth, he was much loved by his people. After he was brutally assaulted by hired toughs, their wives and families were supported by him during the time the men were imprisoned for the attack.[20]

It must not be assumed that only the Ritualists had the spiritual zeal needed to work in the slums. Looking back at the work of the Church in East London, Bishop Winnington-Ingram told the Church Congress of 1899 that in 1831 there were only twenty-three places of worship in the area.[21] Among these parishes, the only sign of vigorous spiritual life was to be found in Whitechapel where W. W. Champneys, an Evangelical, tried to bring the people into his church from 1837 until 1860. When he arrived in Whitechapel to live among the people, a noteworthy action in itself, he found that one church, which could hold 1,500 people, provided for a population of 36,000 souls. Only a handful of people came to Sunday worship; sixteen people attended his first monthly service of Holy Communion. When he walked in his parish he was shocked by the lack of sanitation or drainage, the sight of forty people sleeping in one room, and being called to administer Holy Communion to a dying man in a room where twenty others were sleeping. He found hundreds of 'ragged boys' who slept in sugar hogs-heads, or wandered the streets all night, with no one concerned for their physical welfare, let alone their education.[22] At the end of his twenty-three years of devoted service to the poor, Whitechapel had been subdivided into four parishes with churches, vicarages, and schools for each. Champneys had begun to bring the children of the gentry down to visit his parish, to awaken their social conscience, and had persuaded many of their parents to help him in his work. On 30 March 1851, 1,547 people worshipped in his church in the morning, 827 in the afternoon, and 1,643 in the evening.[23]

Unfortunately Evangelicals like Champneys were rarely found to be actually living among the poor. Their spiritual zeal tended to manifest itself in biblical exposition; and when they showed preaching ability their temptation was to move into larger and better-attended

20. H. H. Maughan, *Wagner of Brighton* (1949).
21. *Church Congress Report* (1899), pp. 40–41.
22. W. W. Champneys, *Spirit in the Word: Facts Gathered from a Thirty Years Ministry* (1862), p. 150 ff.
23. *Church Congress Report* (1899), p. 41. The figures are taken from Parliamentary Papers, *Religious Worship in England and Wales* (1852–1853), LXXXIX. There is an article on Champneys in *Dictionary of National Biography*, X, 36–37, and a report on his work in Parliamentary Papers, *Deficiency of Means of Spiritual Instruction in the Metropolis* (1857–1858), IX, 123–37.

parishes, as George Wilkinson did, and to prosper in the Establish-ment. The 'ambulance work' of the Evangelicals was magnificent, and London's East End would have been much the poorer for the absence of the missions which dotted the area, but the members of this school of churchmanship seldom developed a social conscience which would lead them to 'muck in' with the poor, in the way that the Roman Catholics did with the Irish, or the Ritualists did with the slum-dwellers in their parishes. They seemed to make an unconscious division in their thought between matters of religion and matters of this world, even those of social reform. They had the mentality of Newman, who confessed late in his life that 'he had never considered social questions in their relation to faith, and had always looked upon the poor as objects for compassion and benevolence.'[24] Shaftesbury was aware of this deficiency in his co-religionists and said of their attitude to his campaign to help chimney-sweeps: 'I find that Evangel-ical religionists are not those on whom I can rely. The Factory Question, and every question for what is called "humanity" receive as much support from the "men of the world" as from these men who say they will have nothing to do with it'.[25]

The real significance of the Ritualists is the fact that they identified themselves with the lives of the poor in a way that other groups in the Church failed to do. When they did so, the social problems of the poor became their problems; and they realized that for the Gospel to influence the people in the slums it had to be of effect in their temporal as well as their spiritual lives. If it was not so, it was not catholic. Their use of ceremonial in presenting the Gospel was essentially a means of bringing colour and vividness into the drab courts and alley-ways of the slums—a technique which General Booth was later to use with corresponding success. With all the fervour of the early Wes-leyan movement, they took upon themselves the religious task of bringing the Gospel to the poor, and the social task of showing the poor that the Church was concerned about their welfare.

The latter mission was the more difficult of the two—the Evangel-icals could argue they were already engaged in the former—but no group in the Church really attempted to identify itself with the social life of the poor. The *Guardian* said of the 'Social Position of the Clergy': 'The relation of the Anglican clergy to the different ranks of the nation is too much what we might have expected. With the aristocracy they are very influential, more so probably than the

24. Marson, *God's Co-operative Society*, p. 71. This was in a private letter to Marson.
25. Edwin Hodder, *Life and Work of the Seventh Earl of Shaftesbury* (1886), I, 300.

clergy of any other country. Over country labourers, the natural vassals of the landed gentry they have power but not what they ought to have. . . . that the Church has lost its hold on trade is too generally acknowledged to require illustration.'[26] The estrangement from the poor was so 'generally acknowledged' by the Church that the *Guardian* did not bother to refer to them.

At the time the *Guardian* was making this comment, however, a significantly new experiment in reaching the masses was being initiated, through the work of Charles Fuge Lowder. He had been curate of St. Barnabas, Pimlico, where W. J. E. Bennett had introduced innovations like the eastward position taken by the celebrant in Holy Communion, flowers, altar lights, a surpliced choir, and a sung service. Another innovation was the absence of pew rents in this new church, the opening of the building for prayer and services on week-days, and the welcoming of the poor by the congregation. An open sewer ran through the area on its way to the Thames; and, during the cholera epidemic of 1849, Lowder and the other Ritualist clergy were as unsparing in their pastoral work as Prynne and the Devonport Sisters were in Plymouth. Instead of bringing them praise, their heroism brought complaints that they had used prayers for the souls of the departed. With the other clergy of St. Barnabas, Lowder endured the episcopal censures and intolerable rioting which the new ceremonial brought upon them.

In 1842 the Rev. Bryan King was appointed to the Parish of St. George's-in-the-East in London's dockland area. The parish then contained some 38,000 souls, and King's predecessor had visited it only once in seven years, providing a curate who held four services a week. The absentee rector probably felt justified in not living in such an area, for in the 733 houses which constituted the block in which was the church there were 23 public houses, 13 beershops, and 154 brothels.[27] The parishes of Whitechapel, Mile End, and St. George's-in-the-East then contained most of the Jewish coat-making industry; and in King's parish were many of the infamous 'sweat-shops' of the period. The average wage of a girl who worked for a 'sweater' was a shilling to a shilling and sixpence for twelve hours of labour a day, but labour was not hard to find when in the 1860's about one hundred people a year died of starvation in St. George's-in-the-East parish.[28]

---

26. *Guardian*, 10 December 1856, p. 937.
27. An Englishman, *St. George's Riots: An Appeal to Justice and Common Sense* (1860), p. 4.
28. C. F. Lowder, *Five Years in St. George's Mission* (1861), p. 76.

In the 1880's Beatrice Potter worked in one of these Jewish 'sweat-shops' to experience the life of a working girl in this area, and to reveal this life to the 'well-to-do West-enders, unwilling to dedicate persistent thought and feeling to their fellow-citizens'.[29] She found that of the 908,000 labourers in East London, about 314,000 were dependent on casual work. During the winter of 1886, 29 per cent of the people in the parish of St. George's-in-the-East depended on the Mansion House Relief Fund for subsistence. The moral life of the poor reflected the strain of their marginal existence. 'Weary of work, and sick with the emptiness of stomach and mind, the man or the woman wanders into the street. The sensual laugh, the coarse joke, the brutal fight, or the mean and petty cheating of the street bargain are the outward sights yielded by society to soothe the inward condition of overstrain or hunger.'[30]

Life was not much different in this part of London twenty years earlier when, in 1856, Lowder left St. Barnabas, Pimlico, to become one of Bryan King's five curates working among the Irish labourers and others who thronged the Ratcliff Highway, and other parts of Wapping. He had visited France in 1854, read a book on the life of Vincent de Paul, and been persuaded that the only way for the pagan masses in the slums to be brought the Gospel was for Christians to come among them and share their lot. Then by the preaching of the Gospel, and through spiritual 'osmosis' they might begin to understand what God had done for them in Christ. 'It was simply childish to act as if the Church were recognized as the Mother of the people. She must assume a missionary character, and by religious association and a new adaptation of Catholic practice to the altered circumstances of the nineteenth century, and the peculiar wants of the English character, endeavour with fresh life and energy to stem the prevailing tide of sin and indifference.'[31] In his work Lowder was helped by a society of clergy, the Society of the Holy Cross, which was devoted to mission work among the poor.

As King's curate, Lowder shared the unhappy times which came to St. George's-in-the-East in 1859. In his charge of 1842, Bishop Blomfield had told his clergy they were to use the surplice in the pulpit, and to read the prayer for the Church Militant, two directives

---

29. Beatrice Potter, 'Dock Life of East London', *Nineteenth Century*, XXII (1887), 498.

30. *Ibid.*, p. 494. *Cf.* her other articles, 'East London Labour', *Nineteenth Century*, XXIV (1888), 161–83, and 'Pages from a Working Girl's Diary', pp. 301 and 315.

31. Lowder, *Five Years*, p. 2. *Cf.* Parliamentary Papers, *Deficiency of Means of Spiritual Instruction*, pp. 166–72 for the work done in St. George's-in-the-East parish.

which caused great unease among members of the Evangelical party. King and other Ritualists welcomed this enjoinder, but A. C. Tait, who had succeeded Blomfield as Bishop of London, thought that King, in particular, 'had not the gift, in introducing such changes as he thought necessary, of doing it in a conciliatory manner'.[32] Widespread dissatisfaction arose when King began to use the then almost unheard-of Eucharistic vestments. This led him to lose the support of old-fashioned middle-class parishioners, without his attracting the poor to any extent. The result was that by an old Act the vestry of the parish nominated as 'afternoon lecturer' a rabid 'no-Popery' agitator. Soon rioting began between the morning and afternoon congregations. By September, 1859, the church was practically in the hands of a mob. Dean Stanley intervened the following year and persuaded Mr. King to retire before the rioting got completely out of hand. At one service of Evening Prayer in January 1860, there were 3,000 in the church, including 1,000 boys in the galleries. The mob attempted to smash the altar and the cross on it, shouted down King, Lowder, and twelve white-garbed choristers who were trying to take the service, and pushed and shoved them as they left the service. It took an inspector and a dozen policemen to clear the church, with the help of some sixty to eighty gentlemen who attended the service.[33] After King took a country parish in the diocese of Salisbury, 'and the services were so arranged as to correspond with what was then customary in London churches',[34] the 'anti-Puseyite' rioting ceased.

While this rioting was going on in the mother church, Lowder acted as priest-in-charge of a mission area of the parish in the centre of dockland. A small iron chapel had been built in Calvert Street in 1856, and Bishop Tait gave his blessing to this 'earnest and single-hearted' attempt 'to spread the Gospel . . . through the masses of the metropolis.'[35] Lowder was helped in his work by two other clergy and by Sisters who arrived to assist his rehabilitation of 'fallen girls'. Bishop Tait approved the work of the ladies who formed the Community of the Holy Cross to serve the poor of dockland.[36] Soon after the arrival of the Sisters, Lowder secured an abandoned Scandinavian church in Wellclose Square which he transformed into an Anglican mission.

It took a great deal of courage actually to reside in Wapping as

32. *Life of Tait*, I, 231.
33. *Times*, 30 January 1860, p. 3.
34. *Life of Tait*, I, 247. V. O. Chadwick, *Victorian Church* (1966), pp. 495–561.
35. *Ibid.*, p. 233.
36. P. F. Anson, *Call of the Cloister* (1956), pp. 281 and 356 ff.

it then was. The Ratcliff Highway was crowded with foreign sailors from every nation, and about one-third of the people in the area were poor Irish labouring families. The smell from the Thames was almost unbearable in mid-summer, and the narrow courts and alleys were teeming with people living in wretched poverty. Maria Trench in her biography of Lowder has given us a description of a typical garret which the Sisters would have visited:

> A poor woman lies dying on the floor, huddled into a corner on a bag of straw, covered for the sake of warmth with all the rags which constitute the property of the place. One is half-stifled with the intolerable smell. At a glance we take in the awful poverty, for literally, there is not a stick of furniture, save the crazy-looking table and one broken chair. The children—well I have seen them quite naked like savages. Perhaps even in the depth of winter no fire in the grate. We are told, and we could have guessed it from their faces, that they have not tasted food that day.[37]

The people who lived in such appalling poverty were almost inevitably led into immorality and crime, and what schooling their children received came from the streets, 'abounding in temptation, echoing with profane and disgusting language, and forming a very atmosphere of vice; their examples at home a drunken father and mother, with brothers and sisters already deep in sin; and abroad thieves and prostitutes a little older than themselves'.[38]

Lowder and his two assistants received a total of £250 a year for their work. They arose at 5 a.m., spent two and a half hours daily in worship, and another eight and a half hours among the people. Over a hundred poor were fed daily; within five years six schools were operating with over eight hundred pupils; and a Working Man's Institute was founded in 1861 with four hundred members. Men like F. D. Maurice, J. M. Ludlow, Thomas Hughes, and A. P. Stanley came to lecture in the college, at the request of Lowder. In Lowder's first service he was one of two communicants, but by Easter of 1860 he had 130 attending his church, each of whom risked physical assault to do so. In a period of five years he baptized seven hundred people. Through experience he discovered that the more vivid and ritualistic he made his services, the more the working people appreciated them. When a labourer died in a large sewer in Calvert Street from the foul air within, his funeral service included a procession, the singing of the *Dies Irae* and the Litany, and the preaching of a eulogy in the street. The man's widow walked in the procession.

37. Maria Trench, *Charles Lowder: A Biography* (1883), p. 109.
38. Taine, *Notes on England*, pp. 105–6. A good description of life in Wapping is also provided by Walter Besant, *London in the Eighteenth Century* (1903), pp. 352–53.

The mission in Wellclose Square shared the abuse of the mobs during the riots of 1859 and 1860 in St. George's-in-the-East, and Lowder said that one Sunday there were over a thousand people crowded into the square to intimidate the worshippers.[39] Many of them were there because of Protestant agitation, but others represented the publicans and brothel-keepers whose trade had been damaged by Lowder's mission, or the Jewish 'sweaters' whose practices had been criticized. In spite of this harassment Lowder continued his work, with the help of A. H. Mackonachie after 1858, and began to gain the support of even the Irish, who had long resented his presence among them.[40] Tait had more confidence in Lowder's work than in Bryan King's, because the mission in Wellclose Square did attract the poor. When the storms subsided, the mission district became the parish of St. Peter's, London Docks, and the new church built there was consecrated on 30 June 1866.

The new church was barely in use when the East End was visited by a major epidemic of cholera. The authorities had known it was coming, but showed little interest in trying to improve sanitation in the area. The *Guardian* led in the agitation for sanitation reform, but its warnings fell on deaf ears: 'The probability of a visitation of cholera next year is foretold by no uncertain signs. What is most wanted, perhaps, is an act of self-denial on the part of the upper classes who now commonly stand aloof from the local politics of boroughs or parishes where they reside, as if they were not worth their labour and not consistent with their position.'[41] The first cases appeared in Wapping in July 1866, and for two months raged through the dockland area. As far as the poor could see, the only members of the privileged classes who cared for them in their need were the Ritualist clergy, the Sisters, and the laity who came from other parts of London to work in the cholera wards.

The outbreak was 'confined almost without exception to densely packed and ill-drained neighbourhoods'; and into these areas hurried Devonport sisters and those Sisters who were attached to the Ritualist parishes, All Saints, St. Margaret's, and St. George's. The nurses in the local hospitals were in a state of panic, and without this volunteer work the cholera wards might not have been staffed. The nursing Sisters of St. John the Divine were of particular help because they had

39. C. F. Lowder, *Ten Years in St. George's Mission* (1877), p. 129.
40. The nearest Roman Catholic Church was the newly-opened SS. Mary and Michael, Commercial Road. *V.* Anson, *Call of the Cloister*, p. 359, n. 1.
41. *Guardian*, 8 November 1865, p. 1121.

charge of the men's cholera ward at Westminster Hospital. Their experience was invaluable in the emergency wards that were established throughout the parish.

The heroism of Lowder and the other Ritualist clergy, the devotion of the Sisters in their nursing of the poor, and the sight of men like Pusey and Lord Halifax carrying stricken children into the emergency cholera hospitals won the confidence of East London. When the hospitals in the rest of London were almost empty, yet refused to admit cholera victims from the East End, the poor realized the significance of the devotion shown by the Ritualists, who were willing not only to live, but to die among them. It was during this epidemic that the title 'Father' first began to be applied to Lowder. When Charles Booth investigated the attitude of the poor of Wapping towards religion, later in the century, he noted their toleration of the Ritualists: 'the saintly self-sacrificing life is that which strikes the imagination of the poor as nothing else does.'[42]

Bishop Tait held meetings of the clergy of Bethnal Green, Stepney, and Spitalfields to discuss what might be done to assist the sanitary authorities to clean up the infected river Lea;[43] but the official Church, like the rest of the city, showed comparatively little interest in the epidemic once it was clear it was going to confine itself to the East End. Lowder said: 'It was in the midst of this sad time that the writer received the very kind letter from the Bishop of the Diocese inquiring after his own health and the state of the district, and most considerately adding, "you will not fail to command my services if I can be of any use".'[44] When the emergency workhouse wards were almost empty, Tait came to inspect them, to preach at St. Peter's, and to visit the convent of the Holy Cross Sisters.[45]

Lowder's heroism became an example for most clergy who came in later years to work among the poor in London's slums. In 1872 the assistant curate at St. Peter's, Vauxhall, the Rev. A. B. Goulden, was appointed by Samuel Wilberforce, then Bishop of Winchester, to be priest-in-charge of a mission in the Elephant and Castle area of South London, between the Blackfriars and Southwark bridges. Goulden had been secretary of the Confraternity of the Blessed Sacrament, which sought to promote sacramentalism and ritualism in the Church, and like Lowder he devoted himself to service of the poor in what

42. Booth, *Life and Labour*, VII, 24.
43. *Life of Tait*, I, 470.
44. Lowder, *Ten Years in St. George's Mission*, p. 115.
45. *Illustrated London News*, 15 September 1866, p. 247.

was to become the parish of St. Alphege, Southwark. The area was inhabited by costermongers, stevedores, hospital scrubbers, match-box-makers, and other poor working people, who added to their income by thievery. The first day Goulden came to the mission he was taken for a detective, and for some time was an object of much suspicion.

He began services in an old stable, over a cesspool, and in it he established a Sunday school and began to hold evening services. He was assisted in his mission work by the first members of a new order of Sisters who formed the Community of Reparation to Jesus in the Blessed Sacrament, or the Mission Sisters of St. Alphege as they were more popularly known. The Sisters opened a crèche for the children of working mothers, and completely won the affection of the poor by the saintliness of their devotion. During a smallpox outbreak, the Public Health Officer found one of the nuns, Sister Teresa, trying to comfort a dying child which was in her arms. She sat by the side of a bed where a mother and infant lay ill, with two dead children at the foot. Sister Teresa thought the children were ill because of measles.[46] The nuns did without heat in their convent, which was established just off the Blackfriars Road; and when their pipes burst during one winter they went without water. The local women liked to 'blood each other' in a Sunday morning fight, but no one laid a hand on 'the lambs' as the Sisters were called, although the Mother Superior admitted she had, on different occasions, a stale haddock, a quart of beer, and a bag of flour thrown in her face. Few failed to appreciate the 5,000 free meals of soup given to children during a bad winter like that of 1876, or the more substantial food brought to those who were ill.[47]

Like most Ritualists, Goulden was a sturdy nonconformist who had trouble with his ordinary. Wilberforce was comparatively tolerant of his liturgical aberrations, and appreciated the fact that none of Goulden's costermongers seemed to resent his playing 'at being a Popish priest'. When Wilberforce came to bless the work that was being done in the mission, the costers drove off Protestant agitators who had come to protest, chasing them the full length of Blackfriars Bridge. He also chose not to make an issue of a theological college which Goulden founded in Blackfriars Road, a quasi-brotherhood of

46. Most of the information about the work of Goulden has been gathered from back copies of *The Elephant*, the St. Alphege parish magazine of this period, and from the memoirs of Rev. Mother Catherine, the first Superior of the Order, which are kept in the community house, Rushworth Street.

47. *Church Times*, 6 April 1877, p. 202.

young men, without university degrees, who experienced 'late vocations' to the priesthood. But in 1879 the mission was transferred to the Diocese of Rochester, and Goulden's new ordinary was A. W. Thorold. Thorold showed no sympathy for Goulden's work, particularly for his use of Eucharistic vestments, which the new bishop said should no longer be worn. He also told Goulden that he would refuse to ordain anyone trained by him in his theological college, which had to be abandoned in 1882.

In spite of the refusal of his bishop to encourage his mission work, Goulden persevered with the help of clergy like Pusey (who was his confessor), T. T. Carter, the Rector of Clewer, who had founded the prominent Community of St. John the Baptist, and Canon Robert Gregory of St. Paul's Cathedral, who had served a curacy among the poor of Lambeth. His parish had no endowments, and Goulden himself received only £156 a year; but prominent laymen, among them Sir Henry Graham and Sir Frederick Milner, often came to assist the hard-pressed missioners. By this time the Ritualist movement had become almost a party within the Church, ready to lend its resources to help slum priests who received little encouragement from their ecclesiastical superiors.

By 1876 Goulden had 8,257 working-class communicants attending a chapel which had been built on the site of the Shamrock Public House in Friar Street. Seven Sunday services were held, and three during the week; 800 children attended the schools he established; and clubs were established for working men and working boys. Goulden was now known among the poor as 'the Coster Parson'. When he died in February 1896, vast crowds of working people lined the street to attend the funeral procession.

The Ritualists also laboured in the slums of Holborn, in central London, which was then a veritable 'thieves' kitchen' where 'poverty, sin, disease, crime and misery in a thousand forms surrounded the church'. Lord Leigh granted a freehold site in these slums upon which a pious layman, J. G. Hubbard, later Lord Aldington, built and endowed the church of St. Alban the Martyr. The first vicar of the new parish was A. H. Mackonochie, whose 'burning zeal for souls' had been displayed between 1858 and 1862 when he worked with Lowder in Wellclose Square. Hubbard wanted not only a Ritualist, but also a good pastor to act as vicar of the new church, and Mackonochie proved to be both.

Unfortunately, from 1867 he was the victim of persecution by the Church Association for the Ritualistic practices at St. Alban's—

persecution which forced his resignation in 1882 after a series of law-suits had impoverished him. Few of the public, outside his parish, and none of the bishops appreciated his pastoral zeal. Mackonochie became increasingly intransigent during his persecution and, as we have seen, was one of the Ritualists who longed to see the Church disestablished, so that it could be free to promote its catholic mission to all parts of society, including the neglected poor. In the midst of his tribulations, Mackonochie saw himself, and his companions, as followers of Wesley rather than of Newman.

> Let me ask you Sir: Who drove Wesley from the Church of England? The Bishops and the Upper Middle Classes in Church and State. In fact the 'Chief Priests with the Scribes and Pharisees'. Who are now trying to drive from the Church those who are the fruits of the labour of Wesley and the old Evangelicals? The same 'Chief Priests with the Scribes and Pharisees'. An old and highly respected priest of the Evangelical section of the Church, lately gone happily to his rest, used to say 'If you want to find an old Evangelical, you must look for him in the ranks of the extreme High Churchmen.'[48]

St. Alban's, Holborn, is also remembered as the church of Mac-konochie's remarkable curate, Arthur Henry Stanton, who remained there as an assistant priest for fifty years. Stanton came from a family of means, and while at Oxford he fell under the influence of H. P. Liddon. With other undergraduates he was indignant over the rioting at St. George's-in-the-East, and became a member of the choir of the beleaguered church. He met Mackonochie at this time, and at the suggestion of Liddon decided to go to St. Alban's when he completed his theological training at Cuddesdon. When he told Bishop Tait of his wish, he was bluntly told: 'If you go to Mackonochie of St. Alban's, you must never expect any Church preferment.'[49] Stanton had already refused the advowson of Tetbury, which his father had purchased for him, however; and he had no intention of becoming an ecclesiastical careerist; to the slums of Holborn he went, to work among the poor from 1862 until his death in 1913.

Tait's attitude toward the Ritualists helped to ensure that Stanton would mature into a typical 'poor Puseyite'. He said of his own opinions that he was 'politically socialistic, in faith papistical, in Church policy a thorough-going Nonconformist'.[50] He had none of

48. A. H. Mackonochie, *Letter Addressed to the Record* (1870), p. 13. For a life of Mackonochie v. E. A. Towle, *A. H. Mackonochie* (1890); E. F. Russell, *Alexander Heriot Mackonochie: a Memoir* (1892); and W. A. J. Archbold in *Dictionary of National Biography*, XXXV (1893), 185.
49. G. W. E. Russell, *Arthur Stanton: a Memoir* (1917), p. 34.
50. *Ibid.*, p. 138.

the veneration of episcopacy which had been displayed by the Tractarians. Stanton believed spiritual authority rested in the whole
Church, not in the office of its chief administrative officers. In a letter
he wrote to his mother in 1866, he said: 'You talk of Bishops and
Archbishops as if they were infallible. Of course they act as they do;
they were selected out of the clergy in order that they might, notoriously under political partisanship; but the doctrines of my Bible and
Prayer Book are dearer to me than a whole bench of Political
Pastors.'[51] He agreed with Mackonochie that the Church should be
disestablished now that there had appeared a 'growth of zeal within
the State Church'. He wanted bishops elected by the people of the
Church, not appointed by the State—a system which came 'peril-
ously near blasphemy'.[52]

His tilting with the episcopate ensured that he was inhibited from
preaching anywhere but at St. Alban's. Tait was Archbishop of
Canterbury by 1875, but at that time he told Stanton: 'I should not
be candid with you if I did not say that, were St. Alban's in my
Diocese and were you really to preach the sermons which are attributed to you in the public newspapers, I should very seriously consider whether it was not my duty to withdraw your licence.'[53] It is
interesting to note that Tait, and most bishops, were concerned more
about Stanton's power as a preacher than they were about his use of
ceremonial in the Eucharist. Stanton pointed out that it was the poor
parish of St. Alban's that was persecuted 'while rich parishes, where
the same ritual was used, were left undisturbed'.[54] Samuel Wilberforce was more kindly disposed towards Stanton than most bishops,
and he described his preaching as 'useful, practical . . . thoroughly
evangelical, but rather an imitation of Liddon'.[55] The poor of St.
Alban's appreciated this preaching also, and agreed with the man
who shouted aloud at the end of one sermon: 'Can't he chuck it orf
'is chest!'[56]

Without the episcopal inhibitions, Stanton might have been
tempted to become an itinerant Anglo-Catholic preacher, wandering
from pulpit to pulpit like so many Evangelical clergymen of the day.
But he confined his power of preaching, which was based on sound
biblical exegesis, to the people of his parish, who loved the special

51. *Ibid.*, p. 86.
52. *Ibid.*, p. 108.
53. *Ibid.*, pp. 159–60.
54. *Ibid.*, p. 155.
55. Joseph Clayton, *Father Stanton of St. Alban's, Holborn: A Memoir* (1913), p. 64.
56. *Ibid.*, p. 68.

services he encouraged, like the annual Watch Night vigil on New Year's Eve, or special evangelical services on Monday evenings in Advent, Lent, and August. When he did not base his sermons on the Bible he built them around the lives of people he worked with in his parish. A contemporary said of his preaching: 'he passed from the sublime to the ridiculous, from the grave to the gay, more swiftly than any man I have ever heard: at one moment a lump was in your throat with the amazing pathos of his story, at the next you were laughing at the quip of some street-Arab.'[57]

Stanton's power as a preacher reflected his genius as a pastor. He could give his people answers to the spiritual questions they were asking because he had his ear to the ground—he knew their lives intimately because he lived among them for half a century. They knew he was not one of them, but they also knew that all he had was freely given to them—as well as the wealth of friends like T. M. Talbot, the son of a Welsh M.P., who had inherited a large amount of money. He was converted to Stanton's cause after hearing him preach during the London Mission of 1869, and from then until his death in 1876 he worked alongside Stanton to bring the Gospel to the poor, and to improve their social conditions.

Stanton was devoted to the cause of uniting the social classes in the nation, and of making the Church the spiritual centre of all men, not just those of privilege. He was one of the pioneers in this venture, and was helped not only by his own financial means, but through the contribution made by Talbot. They founded the Brotherhood of Jesus of Nazareth, which had the express purpose of uniting men of different social classes in the work of the Church. They bought the lease of a beer-shop, which became the 'St. Alban's Club'; in it the working man could relax in the manner of his social superiors in their West End Clubs, calling for beer, spirits, cards, dinner, or whatever other amenities were provided. One of the gentlemen who worked with Stanton in the club wrote:

> I first got to know Stanton in 1871. . . . He used very often to come to my rooms at 'Bart's' where he had a flock of admirers. . . . I was a member of the St. Alban's Club. The Club-rooms were half way up Brooke Street, on the left going up. I think my joining that Club did me a lot of good. Stanton asked me what I could do to help the young fellows. I suggested teaching either boxing or swimming, and we decided on the latter. I used to take a party of the very dirtiest you can imagine two or three times a week to the bath. . . . Ever

57. Russell, *Stanton*, p. 254.

since then I've got on exceedingly well with those who are so often erron-
eously called the Lower Orders.[58]

Stanton made sure that the workingmen understood that this was not
a religious trap, a club where they could be 'got at' by the parson. It
was an institution governed by the men themselves, its sole object
being the alternative life it offered to that of the streets. The workingmen appreciated what Stanton and Talbot were about, but many
clergymen were distressed by what they considered an encouragement
of the poor to indulge themselves in drunkenness, gambling, and
other vice. They could not understand a club where no religious
newspaper was allowed, and no provision was made for social improvement classes. By 1871 the club had two hundred working-class
members.

It is easy to dismiss this mission work by the Ritualist clergy and
laity as 'ambulance work', or 'Tory Benevolence', but it took place
even before the settlement-house movement began, and well before
Beatrice Potter began her short-term expeditions into the slums. It
should not be overlooked that both Stanton and Talbot gave the
whole of their working lives to the poor of St. Alban's parish. 'It must
be borne in mind that the mission work in St. Alban's was begun and
carried on for years before the passing of the Education Act, or the
Public Health Act, and before what seems to be a great wave of
reviving spiritual life had begun to be felt in London; before too it
had become the fashion to visit in the slums.'[59]

As Charles Booth discovered from his research later in the century,
the poor understood the meaning of sacrificial love—and men like
Lowder, Goulden, Mackonochie, Stanton, and Talbot lived long enough among them that they could not fail to recognize its presence.[60]
Perhaps it was because of the labour of such men that anti-clericalism
was never a problem in Victorian England. The thousands who lined
the streets between Holborn and Waterloo Station for Stanton's funeral
procession in 1913 were a reverent testimonial to a good pastor.

Another of Stanton's organizations brought into the Ritualist
cause a remarkable Ulsterman, Robert Dolling, who became as well
known as Stanton for his work in the slums. This was the League of
St. Martin, which provided houses where postmen could rest and read

58. *Ibid.*, p. 128.
59. Baldwyn Leighton, *Recollection of Theodore Mansel Talbot* (1889), p. 22.
60. Charles Booth, *Life and Labour*, VII, p. 45, said of the Ritualists that they 'bring to
their work a greater force of religious enthusiasm ... which is also more definitely
professional.'

during their off-hours. It was another attempt by Stanton to throw 'a bridge of friendship across the gaping chasm which separates clergy from the working classes'.[61] Dolling threw himself wholeheartedly into the work of the League, and was affectionately known to the postmen as 'Brother Bob'. His work among the postmen, and talks with Liddon convinced Dolling that he had vocation for the priesthood, and he went to Salisbury Theological College in 1882. While he was there he was greatly inspired by reading the lives of St. Francis of Assisi and John Wesley. After ordination to the diaconate he went to serve in London's East End.

He was appointed as missioner of a district in Holy Trinity parish, Stepney, and there he carried on the type of work begun by the earlier Ritualists. Dolling believed that 'the secular and spiritual elements should interpenetrate in one religious unity of social life',[62] so the chapel and religious services were confined to the top floor of a house, the lower floor being used for meetings and other secular activities. He also believed that the Church should provide a meeting ground for the social classes of the nation, and in 1884 he visited Magdalen College, Oxford, to persuade undergraduates to come and visit the mission in Stepney, and to assist in its work. Dolling had a great deal of personal charm and a wide experience among working-class people, and so the mission flourished.

Dolling's relationship with the hierarchy was not to be any happier than that of the other Ritualists, however; and his first mission venture came to an unhappy end. As a deacon he was under the direction of Walsham How, the Evangelical Suffragan Bishop of Bedford, who recognized and appreciated Dolling's peculiar gifts. How had hoped that when Dolling was ordained priest he would be granted a licence from the Bishop of London, Frederick Temple, which would enable him to carry on his mission work under the Bishop of Bedford. But Temple refused to consider the mission as a special work which Dolling might build up. He insisted that Dolling be licensed only as an ordinary curate to the Vicar of Holy Trinity, to be used in whatever work the Vicar chose to give to him. After ordination to the priesthood, Dolling left the mission, which shortly afterwards disappeared.

In 1886 he was appointed missioner in charge of St. Agatha's Mission, Landport, Portsmouth; and it was here that Dolling performed his most memorable work. The authority in the mission was

61. Russell, *Dolling*, p. 18.
62. C. E. Osborne, *Life of Father Dolling* (1903), p. 48.

divided between the Bishop of Winchester, Dr. Harold Browne; the mother parish of All Saints, which had a population of 23,000 souls; and Winchester College, which provided the temporal wealth needed by the mission. This situation enabled Dolling to play off one authority against the other while he used his exceptional pastoral abilities to work among the poor.

Dolling's task was not an easy one. Landport was a 'huddled mass of miserably small and overcrowded dwellings', filled with slaughter-houses, public houses, and brothels. Because of the local garrison and the men from warships in the harbour, the streets were full of life and laughter, 'horseplay and street-romping'. Saturday night in Landport had a carnival air to it. It was no place for a 'peelywolly' parson, but it was made to order for Dolling to 'muck in' with the lads of the town. A burly, jovial man, filled with exuberant energy, the life of Landport stimulated him to see within it the possibilities of great good rather than evil: 'Amid the streets of Landport Father Dolling was no deplorable misfit. Excitement did not weary him, it stimulated his efforts; and Portsmouth, whatever its faults, is not dull.'[63] It was not as disconcerting to Dolling, as it might have been to another cleric of the age, to have a brothel next door to the mission, and to have its patrons mistakenly waken him up at all hours of the night. Nor was he upset by the petty persecution of its madam, who sought to interrupt Dolling's services, such as the dedication of the newly-built parsonage in 1889.

> A procession of choir, acolytes, and priests was moving from room to room with lighted candles and clouds of incense. At the end came Father Dolling, in a gorgeous cope, saying the office of benediction for each part of the building, the crowded congregation meanwhile filling up all the vacant spaces in the house and the gymnasium. In the intervals of the devotions raucous shrieks were heard proceeding from the harridan who was responsible for the house next door, and who in its back-yard was heard invoking many curses both loud and deep upon the heads of 'old Dolling and his pack of Catholics'. Like the silversmiths of Ephesus, she felt, no doubt, that her gains were likely to be interfered with.[64]

In Landport Dolling once more ensured that what the mission of the Church offered to the people was not purely spiritual. A gymnasium was set up which drew young men (as well as blue-bottle flies) from 'Bloody Row', the neighbouring street of slaughter-houses. Dancing classes were also organized, as were classes in good

63. *Ibid.*, p. 72.
64. *Ibid.*, p. 98. Dolling later succeeded in buying out the brothel.

manners; and card-parties were encouraged. He won the confidence of the Winchester College boys, who were stirred by his preaching in the school to come and work in Landport; 'there can be no doubt that many a Wykehamist has been helped by Dolling's influence and Dolling's example to form a higher resolve for life, to recognize the obligation, in whatever profession he might adopt, to do something for the bettering of his fellow men—to find his ideal in serving rather than in enjoying.'[65]

Dolling kept a 'common table' in his parsonage, which was the real heart of the mission; and here soldiers, sailors, marines, and down-and-outs sat down with benefactors of the privileged classes.[66] Dolling's personality ensured that there was none of the social stiffness which characterized similar efforts attempted by other clergymen —such as Samuel Barnett.

> The atmosphere of the parsonage was surprisingly free from either officialism or pietism, the former the evil genius of Established churches, and the latter of sectarian Christianity. The house did not suggest 'the resident gentleman in every parish', upholding the sober decencies of the National Establishment, but neither did its tone lead one to suspect that its friendliness and humanity were crafty bait, to conceal some soul-hunting design. Yet, broadly human as was the tone of the place, it was also genuinely Christian. Dolling's personality as its presiding influence secured it both from pious sentimentalism—or, in other words, cant—on the one hand, and irreligious rowdiness on the other.[67]

The men of privilege who supported Dolling's mission were usually Ritualist sympathizers from outside the parish, because Dolling's work was not appreciated by many of the good citizens of Plymouth. There was some opposition to his Ritualism, but not as much as might have been expected, considering that St. Agatha's became one of the most advanced centres of Puseyite practice. This was because 'Dolling had a clear sense that ritual was made for man, and not man for ritual'.[68] He boxed the ears of a precious young Ritualist who was distressed by his 'incorrectness' while at the altar. To Dolling, Ritualism was utilitarian—a necessary means in that age to serve the great end of propagating the Gospel of Christ—and it was always balanced by his fervent evangelical preaching. After his death, a Roman Catholic writer in the *Pilot* made a shrewd assessment of Dolling's Ritualism and its significance:

---

65. *Ibid.*, p. 101.
66. *Annual Report of St. Agatha's Mission, Landport* (1894), p. 10.
67. Osborne, p. 96.
68. *Ibid.*, p. 109.

Incredible as it may sound to Protestants who looked upon him as a Roman-
iser of the extremist type, he was, in spite of his easy adoption of nearly the
whole system of Catholic dogma and practice, an Evangelical to the backbone;
that is to say, his whole interest was in the saving of those individual souls—
and they were thousands—with whom he came in contact, and not in any
ecclesiastical system for its own sake. He cared as little for theology and
scholarship as did S. Francis or John Wesley, as it was because he discovered
by intuition and experiment that Catholic beliefs and practices were efficacious
for the sole end he cared about, that he adopted them fearlessly without much
deference to Bishops or Articles. For the same reason he took over boldly, and
to the scandal of ecclesiastical dilettanti, such elements of Methodism as by
their efficacy with the multitude had proved their right to survive. A lawless
mind it might seem to some, but only because it was governed by a somewhat
neglected law which puts the absolutely necessary end before any dispensable
and less necessary means.[69]

Dolling's troubles with the local middle-class people came from his
complete identification of himself with the lives of the poor: 'Every
lad staggering in drink through the Landport slums, every poor girl
flaunting her tawdry finery along the streets by the Hard, was to him
a brother or sister.'[70] When he discovered the owner of a brothel or
low drink-shop, he threatened to expose him in public; and, though
legal proceedings were threatened, Dolling welcomed such proceedings. By exciting public indignation, he managed to close 'at least
fifty houses of shame' in his parish. He gathered facts about the close
connection between public houses and prostitution, and formed a
'Portsmouth Social Purity Organization', which consisted of clergy,
Nonconformist ministers, doctors, working-class labour leaders, and
other prominent citizens. This committee called on the Mayor to
present their facts, in spite of his protest that Portsmouth was 'in
quite an excellent condition as to sobriety and moral temptation'.
When Dolling put pressure on the Mayor and other civic officials to
clean up this situation, he carried his policy of public exposure so far
that he wrote about it, and preached on the subject in London. He did
not hesitate to label Portsmouth a 'sink of iniquity' when preaching
for the Christian Social Union in 1894 at the Church of St. Edmund
the King, Lombard Street.[71] He also publicly exposed the life in the
streets of Landport:

My first Sunday afternoon, as I was walking in Chance Street, I saw for the
first time a Landport dance. Two girls, their only clothing a pair of sailor's
trousers each, and two sailor lads, their only clothing the girls petticoats,

69. *Ibid.*, p. 113.
70. *Ibid.*, p. 133.
71. Robert Dolling, *Ten Years in a Portsmouth Slum* (London, 1896), p. 137.

were dancing a kind of breakdown up and down the street, all the neighbours looking on amused, but unastonished, until one couple, the worse for drink, toppled over. I stepped forward to help them up, but my endeavour was evidently looked at from a hostile point of view, for the parish voice was translated into a shower of stones, until the unfallen sailor cried out, 'Don't touch the Holy Joe; he doesn't look such a bad sort'. I could not stay to cement our friendship, for the bell was ringing for the children's service.[72]

Respectable Portsmouth was furious when Dolling disclosed matters like the poor children of Landport eating raw meat and drinking blood which came from the nineteen slaughter-houses in his parish, but it was his preaching in London against liquor traffic and prostitution that led the Mayor to speak out publicly against Dolling. This attack in no way daunted Dolling, who even had the courage to criticize the Patriotic Fund, which provided for the widows and orphans of soldiers and sailors. He said publicly that the fund was 'mismanaged and kept back with culpable dilatoriness by the authorities',[73] and refused to allow his parish to contribute to the organization.

Dolling's troubles with his diocesan first came to a head because of his political views. Dolling labelled himself a socialist, and invited Stewart Headlam of the Guild of St. Matthew, whose work we will look at in the next section, to speak at the mission in 1890. Headlam advocated Henry George's idea of a 'Single Tax' as a needed social reform, and after his speech the Bishop of Winchester suggested that Dolling should publicly disassociate himself from Headlam's radical group. He said that he now had to 'consider whether the good of your mission is not more than counterbalanced by the evil of those whom you associate with yourself, and whether I can suffer it to go on under my authority'.[74] Dolling offered his resignation at this time, but then withdrew it when there was public protest made on his behalf.

When he finally left St. Agatha's mission six years later, he did so because he was emotionally exhausted by his labours, and because of tension with the bishop over the issue of saying masses for the dead. But he also left because of a sermon he had preached for the Christian Social Union, during Lent, 1895, which had done much to weaken whatever faith his new bishop, Randall Davidson, had in him. He spared no words in pointing out the failure of the Establishment to show any interest in the working class of the great towns. He said

72. Osborne, pp. 135–36.
73. *Ibid.*, p. 156.
74. *Ibid.*, p. 127.

that if the Establishment still continued to impede the mission of the Church it would have to go:

> A free Church can reform herself, a fettered Church never. And if your heart is aflame to defend the Church of England, first, at any rate, see that you cleanse her. And you will never do this until you have the courage, not only to think, but to speak the truth about her; to put away from ourselves all tall talk and in a spirit of true and real humility begin by confessing where we fail. Let those in authority put the question to the test, let them through Convocation propose the needed reforms; and if our Establishment forbids us to reform, let us burst our bonds and set ourselves free.[75]

After this sermon, as Dolling's biographer says, 'No wonder that, apart from "third altars" or "extra services", Dolling's relations with the ecclesiastical authorities were seriously strained when he left St. Agatha's at the beginning of 1896.' To Dolling's dismay, even Bishop Westcott refused to allow him to take a parochial mission in his diocese because 'submission to authority is essential for the corporate life of the Church.'[76]

For a time after leaving Landport, Dolling was out of work. The parish of St. Nicholas, Deptford, in the Diocese of Rochester was vacant, and strong influence was brought upon the patron to offer it to Dolling. It was another slum parish, again inhabited by people engaged in slaughter-house work; and it would have suited Dolling admirably. But the bishops did not want Dolling at Deptford: 'it really seemed as if the rulers of the Church of England, *semper pavidi*, did not want such men as Dolling, and as if the Anglican, self-complacent temper had learnt nothing from the terrible examples of its failure to deal with Wesley.'[77]

Dolling visited America in 1897–1898, and during this tour was offered charge of the Cathedral in Chicago. When he was in America, the Rector of Poplar, who was also patron of the living, offered him the vicarage of St. Saviour's, Poplar. He then returned to England to labour in the slums of the East End until his death in 1902. The Rector of Poplar was the Rev. Arthur Chandler, a thorough-going Sacramentalist, and treasurer of the Poplar Labour League. When Protestant agitators objected to Dolling's appointment, he told them their talk of a 'crisis' in the Church of England over Ritualism was nonsense. Dolling saw clearly that the Church was failing because it was not catholic—it did not have a universal sense of mission to all classes

75. *Ibid.*, p. 213.
76. *Ibid.*, p. 214.
77. *Ibid.*, p. 222.

in the nation. 'As to the present so-called crisis, the *real* crisis, the one that ought to make Churchmen, cleric or laic, on their knees in penitence before God, confess their negligence, is that the vast majority of English people care nothing for the Church, many even nothing for God.'[78]

St. Saviour's, Poplar, was a very depressing slum parish. Even the vice in the area lacked colour, and the people were totally apathetic about religion. But Dolling began, once more, to try to bring the Gospel to the labouring poor whom the Church had so long neglected. In typical fashion, his first task was the altering of the drainage for the schools, vicarage, and mission house. He begged the money from wealthy laymen, to whom he said: 'I speak out and fight about the drains because I believe in the Incarnation.'[79] He also continued to present the Gospel to the poor through the unique use of Ritualism and Evangelicalism which he had developed at Landport—though he had little success in Poplar.

Dolling is often represented as a victim of episcopal persecution— the devoted Ritualist who suffered because of his love of ecclesiastical ceremonial. But Dolling himself knew clearly why he received so little encouragement from the bishops. It was because he had a radically different idea of what was the 'Catholick and Apostolic Church' in England.

He disliked those prelates who venerated their own respectability, and their assurance of authority which came to them through apostolic succession; he also disliked those churchmen who were devoted to maintenance of the Establishment as an end in itself. Dolling believed the 'sober worldliness' of the Church of England to be its greatest evil, for it kept the common people out of the parish churches of England. It was Dolling's hatred of Erastianism and his suspicion of the Establishment as it was, together with his lack of respect for the ecclesiastical authority in the Church, that was 'the underlying root difference between Father Dolling and the Bishops'.[80] He cared little for the ecclesiastical Church; his concern, like Wesley's, was to 'build the City of God'. He was not convinced that the bishops always knew what was best for the Church: 'The mere fact that the Archbishop says a thing does not necessarily make it a spiritual utterance from a spiritual authority.'[81]

78. *Ibid.*, p. 255.
79. *Ibid.*, p. 264.
80. *Ibid.*, p. 299.
81. Robert Dolling, *The Lambeth Opinion: Speech to the English Church Union*, October, 1899, p. 5.

Dolling believed the National Church had to become truly catholic.

> If the Church of England is in any sense to be National . . . she must represent the highest interests of the whole nation; she must not represent one class in the nation; she must not ever represent one body of influence in the nation. If she is to claim her share of the great title of Catholic, which means in one of its senses Universal and touching all true human interests, she must recognize the just political aspirations of the people; she must become the National Church in reality, as well as merely in name . . . by furthering every true measure for the social uplifting of the whole population of the nation which God has elected her to spiritually represent and minister to.[82]

Three months before his death, Dolling contributed to the *Pilot* of 15 February 1902 an article entitled 'The Genius of the Church of England', which summed up his criticisms of the official Church and its mission to the people, particularly the persecution of the Ritualists by the bishops:

> What of the ignorant riots of St. George's-in-the-East; the sending of priests to gaol; the closing of perfectly harmonious centres of work, due always to a vulgar mob, with the Bishop's authority behind it? And though to-day nearly all the things which the Bishops condemned twenty years ago they recognize and approve, still, they have but one opportunist canon of conduct: Be commonplace, be respectable after the sober manner of the ritual of the Church of England. On the day of Pentecost it was said of some that they were drunk with new wine. Would to God we could see our prelates thus inebriated, or, at any rate, permitting some of their followers to be so. . . . I wonder if it is true that there is a bedroom in Lambeth that each prelate sleeps in on his first visit; that in that room there is a bed which has the power of elongating or compressing each occupant to a certain uniform stature. At any rate, we can see the effect of this process. . . . On no question of any importance, religious or social, have the Bishops given any leading to their people unless they have been driven to it by the man in the street, and the advice they invariably give is *festina lente*—very wise, indeed, when you occupy the whole position, but fatal when you are leading a forlorn hope.[83]

5. Maurice and the New Catholicism

PETER ANSON has pointed out in his *Call of the Cloister* that many of the sisterhoods which came into being at this time in the Church of England had their origin in some attempt made by ladies of privilege to overcome a

82. J. Clayton, *Father Dolling: a Memoir* (1902), p. 51.
83. Osborne, pp. 306–7.

specific social evil. The theological rationale for the sisterhood usually followed this social and religious involvement. So it was with the Ritualist movement generally. In many ways it was purely pragmatic; the movement had no real intellectual basis, and few of its priests had either the time or the inclination to develop a theoretical justification for what they were about. When Lowder advocated sacramental confession to the Bishop of London he argued his case from the standpoint of pastoral experience, not from that of sacerdotal authority.[1] Stanton thought little of the ecclesiastical ideas of Newman—'Too subtle, too subtle; he could make everything seem true'[2] —and said he much preferred the thought of the 'more human Manning'. Dolling, as he admitted himself on many occasions, was not a theologian and possessed an essentially 'unspeculative mind'. By trial and error he found a way of bringing the Gospel to the poor, but his churchmanship was never a reflection of systematic, firmly held, theological principles: 'the sympathies of Dolling and of those who worked at S. Agatha's with him were at once Catholic and democratic rather than of the usual Anglican High Church type. They were at once more advanced in one sense and broader in another than the distinctively "Via Media" or "Moderate High" school . . . which still is singularly ill-adapted for kindling and sustaining enthusiasm, especially among the multitude and the ignorant.'[3]

Some ecclesiastical historians have considered that this lack of an ideology, particularly a social philosophy, was the great failing of the whole Church in the new industrial order, and that the Ritualists shared in the Church's general obliviousness to the needs of society: 'the major defect of the nineteenth-century Church . . . was a failure of prophecy, a failure to understand and interpret the phase of history into which the age had come. . . . in an age of revolution it becomes the one thing needful'.[4]

It may be argued, however, that the failure in prophecy was not confined only to the Church—it wasn't encouraged by secular reformers any more than it was by churchmen, for the Victorian Englishman preferred to be pragmatic in his approach to society and its needs. Victorian social reformers showed significantly little enthusiasm for the system of thought which lay behind either the *Communist Manifesto* or *Rerum Novarum*, and the mass of the people

1. C. F. Lowder, *Penitent's Path* (1869), and *Sacramental Confession Examined by Pastoral Experience: a Letter to the Bishop of London* (1874).
2. Clayton, *Father Stanton*, p. 138.
3. Stanton, *op. cit.*, p. 79.
4. E. B. Wickham, *Church and People in an Industrial City* (1960), p. 191.

did not welcome the application of Benthamite ideas in Chadwick's Poor Law. Victorian people were impressed with what worked and arose out of a tradition that was identifiably English. The real influence of the Ritualists came from the fact that they could reach the poor—in the way that other churchmen could not—though it may well be argued that, like the Fabians, they had a good press.

The writings of the Ritualists indicate that the two theologians of the age who influenced them were E. B. Pusey and F. D. Maurice. Pusey and Maurice differed greatly over theological matters, such as the meaning of some of the Thirty-Nine Articles, but Maurice, just as much as Pusey, had a passionate love of the poor. It was his pastoral 'digging' which influenced the later Ritualists and the Settlement House workers who, inspired by events like the rioting in St. George's-in-the-East, began to move into the slums in the 1880's.

Maurice was Professor of Theology at King's College, London, in 1848, when London was gripped by panic because of the revolutions in Europe and the Chartist agitation in England. Heavy gun batteries were brought into the city from Woolwich; volunteers made up an emergency police force of 150,000; Wellington brought regiments of troops into the city; all public conveyances stopped, and the streets were deserted. In the midst of this excitement, Maurice received a letter from John Malcolm Ludlow, a young barrister who had just visited Paris. Ludlow was a student of law, politics, economics, and theology; he was a skilled linguist, and had witnessed the troubles in Paris at first hand. He expressed to Maurice his belief that 'Socialism was a very great power which had acquired an unmistakeable hold, not merely on the fancies but on the consciences of the Parisian workmen, and that it must be Christianized, or it would shake Christianity to its foundation, precisely because it appealed to the higher and not to the lower instincts of the men.'[5]

Maurice interpreted Ludlow's letter as a summons to lead an 'English theological reformation, as the means of averting an English political revolution'; of putting an end to the 'semi-Atheistic' religion in England with its passionate concern for 'theories of sin, of justification, of apostolical succession', and its ignoring of God, 'the root and ground of all things'. Maurice believed himself called upon to prophesy within the Church: 'I see my way but dimly; this, however, I do see, that there is something to be done, that God Himself is speaking to us and that if we ask Him what He would have us to do, we shall be shown.'[6]

5. *Life of Maurice*, I, 458.
6. *Ibid.*, pp. 458–59.

The first thing Maurice did was to introduce Ludlow to Charles Kingsley, who became the great propagandist for Christian Socialism, the movement which the three men began to lead—with Maurice the theologian of the group. Archdeacon Julius Hare of Lewes also lent his support to what was undertaken. The immediate venture decided upon was the publication of placards addressed to the Chartists; and Kingsley's first effort 'delighted' Maurice, who was 'in great excitement'.

WORKMEN OF ENGLAND!

You say you are wronged. Many of you are wronged; and many besides yourselves know it. Almost all men who have heads and hearts know it—above all, the working clergy know it. They go into your houses, they see the shameful filth and darkness in which you are forced to live crowded together; they see your children growing up in ignorance and temptation, for want of fit education; they see intelligent and well-read men among you, shut out from a Freeman's just right of voting; and they see too the noble patience and self-control with which you have as yet borne these evils. They see it, and God sees it . . . you cannot stop their working for you. . . . You think the Charter would make you free—would to God it would! The Charter is not bad; *if the men who use it are not bad*! But will the Charter make you free? Will it free you from slavery to ten-pound bribes? Slavery to beer and gin? Slavery to every spouter who flatters your self-conceit, and stirs up bitterness and headlong rage in you? . . . Will the Charter cure *that*? Friends, you want more than Acts of Parliament can give. . . . A nobler day is dawning for England, a day of freedom, science, industry! But there will be no true freedom without virtue, no true science without religion, no true industry without the fear of God, and love to your fellow-citizens.[7]

Maurice also addressed the Chartists, and held them spell-bound. Kingsley reported: 'Chartists told me this morning that many were affected even to tears. The man was inspired—gigantic. No one commented on what he said. He stunned us.'[8] Kingsley went on in his writing to address himself to the conscience of the clergy, particularly the *working* clergy, who were willing to live among the poor. 'I assert that the business for which God sends a Christian priest in a Christian nation is, to preach freedom, equality, and brotherhood in the fullest, deepest, widest meaning of those three great words; that in as far as he so does, he is a true priest, doing his Lord's work with his Lord's blessing on him; that in so far as he does not he is no priest at all, but a traitor to God and man.'[9] He also addressed himself to the con-

7. *Life of Kingsley*, 1883 edit., pp. 117–18, the 'living in darkness' that Kingsley refers to is physical—the window tax was not then taken off.

8. Thomas Hughes, 'F. D. Maurice as a Christian Socialist', *Economic Review*, I (1891), 209.

9. Charles Kingsley, *Alton Locke* (1881), Eversley Edition, Prefatory Memoir by Thomas Hughes.

science of the manufacturing class under the pseudonym 'Parson Lot' in novels like *Alton Locke*, which came out in 1850, condemning the sweated labour and industrial ethics of the period.

Christian Socialism speedily attracted public attention, and the scorn of the privileged orders of society.

> Incredible as it may appear, there is, it seems, a clique of educated and clever but wayward-minded men—the most prominent of them two clergymen of the Church of England—who from, as it seems, a morbid craving for notoriety or a crazy straining after paradox—have taken up the unnatural and unhallowed task of preaching in the press and from the pulpit not indeed open undisguised Jacobinism and Jacquerie but Christian Socialism—the same doctrines in a form not the less dangerous for being less honest.[10]

The *Edinburgh Review* sneered at Maurice and his followers as 'anti-economic philanthropists', but admitted that when socialism in England was being made respectable by clergymen supporting it, the subject could no longer be ignored, although 'all schemes of social amelioration which violate the principles of economic science must come to nought.'[11]

The Christian Socialists followed up the placard experiment with a series of *Tracts on Christian Socialism*, and then, after 1851, with a penny journal, *The Christian Socialist*, which sought to promote the co-operative movement, and to oppose the political economists who had 'no morality but that of buying cheap and selling dear'.[12] Other supporters appeared: Thomas Hughes and Arthur Stanley of the Thomas Arnold school of churchmanship; Edward Ellison of the Young England camp, Carlyle and Ruskin. After 1850 the group also received much help from E. V. Neale, a barrister of means who, although he was not an orthodox Christian, donated large sums to the cause of Christian Socialism.

Maurice was convinced by his contact with little groups of Chartists throughout 1848 that it would be valuable to attempt pilot projects in co-operative industry, in which men of the working class and others could work together. This led to the founding of the Society for Promoting Working Men's Associations, which had workshops in London and the provinces for producing goods such as boots, printed books, and bread. Neale helped in the founding of other associations for distribution as well as production.

The Society did not prosper because it lacked capital, and it erred

---

10. *Quarterly Review*, LXXXIX (1851), 524.
11. *Edinburgh Review*, XCIII (1851), 11–32.
12. *Christian Socialist*, 5 April 1851, p. 178.

through lack of experience. Maurice had little to do with the later movement, for after 1854 his interest shifted to education of the poor in his Working Men's College, which we looked at in Chapter V. But he was the initiator of the early experiments, and his approach was typically English and pragmatic, as he recognized himself: 'We thought it un-English to begin with a large scheme. We judged it best to make a particular experiment which, with all our different blunders, will be a lesson to us hereafter, and a still more valuable one to our successors.'[13] The great value of these experiments, which began the Co-operative Movement in Great Britain, was their establishment of 'co-operative industry on an ethical basis'.[14] This was what Maurice wanted—the working men of England to see that there was an alternative to the ruthlessness of Victorian economic theories. This alternative was to be based on the Christian Gospel, which they could recognize 'as the law of their public and private life, of their inner selves, of their outward transactions'.[15] Maurice's Society also helped in the passing of the Industrial and Providential Societies Act of 1852, and Neale and Hughes became leaders in the larger Co-operative Movement.

Maurice's experiments in co-operative industry, like his Working Men's College, were important; but in the long-run his greatest influence was through his prophetic writings. More than any of his contemporaries he convinced churchmen that man need not be interpreted as the economic creature of the political economists: 'If divines do not perceive that fact, our Owenites, with a much clearer and juster instinct, do perceive it.'[16] He believed his vocation was to show his contemporaries the divine at work in the secular social movements of the age, and to inspire them with the 'modest ambition of converting a nation of competing shopkeepers into a family of loving Christians'.[17] This was the task accepted by the Ritualists and the Settlement House workers of late Victorian England, who sought to unite the social classes of the nation in a war on moral and social evils, and to make England more Christian.

13. F. D. Maurice, *Reasons for Co-operation: a Lecture, to Which is Added God and Mammon, a Sermon to Young Men* (1851), p. 16.

14. Beatrice Webb, *Co-operative Movement in Great Britain* (1930), p. 154. For detailed studies of Christian Socialism *v.* C. Raven, *Christian Socialism, 1848–1854* (1920), and C. K. Gloyn, *Church in the Social Order*, 1942.

15. Maurice, *Reasons for Co-operation*, p. 48.

16. F. D. Maurice, *Christian Socialism: Dialogue Between Somebody (a Person of Respectability) and Nobody (the Writer)*, n.d., p. 6. This was No. I of Tracts on Christian Socialism.

17. *Ibid.*, p. 16.

Maurice was convinced that only the Church, because of its divine commission, could act as the Universal Society needed in England— the catalyst which could dissolve class tensions and bring in a new era of social harmony and national purpose. When properly interpreted, the Gospel had the answer for the masses and one which secular movements based on the idea of class warfare could never provide: 'the people . . . have become impatient of class divisions, have turned to this language, have recognized in it a message addressed to them.'[18]

Because trade unions were used as class instruments, Maurice was suspicious of what they really sought to achieve: 'every successful strike tends to give the workmen a very undue and dangerous sense of their own power, and a very alarming contempt for their employer, and . . . every unsuccessful strike drives them to desperate and wild courses.'[19] The *Christian Socialist* said of the trade-union movement: 'Notwithstanding their ultimate benefit to all classes trade-societies are always in the first instance the embodiment of class interest and tend to foster class selfishness.'[20] What Maurice wanted in the nation was not a combination of working men who would refuse to work, but a combination of men of all classes for the purpose of work.[21]

Maurice and Ludlow also assailed the Chartist programme because it did not consider the good of the commonwealth first. It claimed to seek the abolition of class government, but the Chartists followed their leaders as blindly as party men in Parliament did, and Ludlow accused them of trying to set up an alternative class government, that of the proletariat—'the very quintessence of competitive selfishness'.[22]

At the same time Maurice did not welcome the ideal systems devised for society by continental theorists such as Fourier and Louis Blanc, nor those of Robert Owen in England. He had no faith in any system devised by man as a solution for England's social misery.

God's order seems to me more than ever the antagonist of man's systems; Christian Socialism is in my mind the assertion of God's order. Every attempt however small and feeble to bring forth God's order, I honour and desire to assert. Every attempt to hide it under a great machinery . . . I must protest against as hindering the gradual development of what I regard as a divine

18. F. D. Maurice, *Social Morality* (1872), p. 381.
19. *Life of Maurice*, II, 48.
20. *Christian Socialist*, 7 December 1850, pp. 43–44.
21. *Ibid.*, 18 January 1851, p. 95.
22. *Ibid.*, 14 June 1851, p. 258, 'The Chartist Programme'.

purpose, as an attempt to create a new constitution of society when what we want is that the old constitution should exhibit its true functions and energies.[23]

His criticisms of the social attitudes of churchmen were as severe as those he levelled at trade unionists, Chartists, and theoretical socialists. Like most Broad-Churchmen, he particularly disliked the condescension with which many Evangelicals attempted to bring the purely spiritual blessings of the Gospel to the poor (in the words of Baden Powell): 'surely not the method by which in the present age a really salutary impression is to be made on the ignorant and irreligious masses'.[24] He would have applauded the press indictment of the activities of churchmen in the Workmen's Hall, Portland Road, Notting Hill, near the Kingston Potteries, which had been opened in March, 1865, to provide a 'good public house' for local indigents. 'It is obvious that as matters now stand the hall is not so much a club as a clubhouse ... not an effort by workingmen themselves to meet a social want of their own in their own way ... but rather a centre of propagandism; a place where the workingman finds himself in a state of tutelage, which of all things he abhors. The Hall in fact is specially devoted to the diffusion of teetotal principles and the dissemination of religious tracts.'[25]

He admitted the great spiritual benefit brought to the Church by the Tractarians, who had reminded many a poor curate that he held a commission from the King of Kings, and was not the creature held in contempt by those of privilege.[26] But he disliked the social attitudes of the Tractarians, particularly the clergy, who were influenced by 'chivalric and feudal feeling'.[27] They were too much identified with the aristocracy and landed gentry in sentiment, and wanted a return to an age when 'the priest, the landlord and the retainer were the only elements of society'. He said of Tractarian teachings:

High-minded young converts like these new notions because they have learnt on the authority of Charles II that Romanism or something approaching it is the only religion for a gentleman; that young ladies find the calling of a nun to be much more graceful and poetical than the calling of a district visitor;

23. J. L. Davies, 'Social Doctrine of F. D. Maurice', *Sermons on Social Subjects: St. Paul's, Covent Garden* (1904), p. 185.

24. Baden Powell, *The State-Church: Sermon Before the University of Oxford* (1850), p. 36.

25. *The Workmen's Hall, Portland Road, Notting Hill: Narrative of Proceedings* (1865), p. 9. The curriculum of the club is on pp. 9–15.

26. Maurice, *On the Right and Wrong Methods of Supporting Protestantism: A Letter to Lord Ashley*, p. 11.

27. *Ibid.*, pp. 8–12.

that men in professions prefer a faith which separates them from tradesmen; that priests admire that which severs them from the laity, that in fact a system has been set up with which the middle class has no fellowship, which insults its habits and feelings.[28]

He did not share the traditional faith that the Catholic Church had always had in the spirit of *noblesse oblige* among the wealthy: 'The rich . . . if left alone, would assist their poor brethren out of their wealth.'[29] Rather, he remarked to Lord Ashley, 'they brought to their religious committees all the shrewd business-like habits which they had acquired in their different avocations.'[30]

Maurice particularly disliked the tendency of both the Evangelicals and the Tractarians, with their distinctly Augustinian theology, to concentrate upon the personal sins of the poor, and to separate religion from the social concerns which were of such immediate consequence to those who actually lived in the slums. 'How would the proclamation to our Chartists and Socialists that they had baptismal purity once and that they have lost it now; that they must recover their ground by repentance, by prayer and fasting; that they must submit to discipline . . . how can such a proclamation as this meet any of the confused, disorderly notions which are stirring in their minds or set them right.'[31]

This did not mean that Maurice despised theology—he always described himself as first and foremost a theologian.[32] But, whereas the Evangelicals and the Tractarians began their consideration of man and his place in society by stressing the original sin which held man in bondage, Maurice began with God, His mercy and goodness, and the freedom which He had given to man. Rather than a sinful creature in need of regeneration, Maurice saw man as an ignorant creature in need of education: 'a spiritual being with an animal nature who, when he has sunk lowest into that nature has still thoughts and recollections of a home to which he belongs, and from which he has wandered'.[33] Repentance, to Maurice, was the turning of man to confess the Presence of Christ which he had always had with him. The great fact of human existence to Maurice was the universal

---

28. *Ibid.*, p. 11.

29. *Why no Good Catholic Can Be a Socialist: Paper Read to the Brothers of the London Oratory* (1890), p. 32.

30. Maurice, *Letter to Ashley*, p. 8.

31. Maurice, *Kingdom of Christ* (1958), II, 336.

32. F. D. Maurice, *Theological Essays* (1853), p. 445 says: 'Any basis of fellowship but a theological one, must be narrow and exclusive.'

33. F. D. Maurice, 'Essay on Archdeacon Hare's Position in the Church, With Reference to the Parties that Divide it' in J. C. Hare, *Victory of Faith* (1874), p. xl.

and never-ceasing activity of the living God, with which man could co-operate.

He believed that the Church's task was to bring the Gospel to the poor, 'that there is a Spirit guiding and educating the thoughts of . . . all men awakening us to activity . . . keeping us at one when we are most inclined to be divided'. This Spirit is 'latent in the most brutal',[34] and even to these 'Christ tells men the good news that they may have a will in accordance with the Law, that they may overcome that in themselves which leads them to violate it.'[35] Maurice wanted the Church to indicate to men everywhere the presence and activity of this Spirit: 'to bring it to light, to act as if it existed'.[36] By educating the poor to the presence of the Spirit, the Church raised the poor into men. This was the mission of the Church, to reveal the Spirit at work in the world by living among those who did not recognize its presence, and by witnessing to it. 'The Church ought to meet men as men, not according to their rank or social privileges, not according to the degree or measure of their faith, but as men of whom Christ is the Lord, whether they acknowledge Him as such or not, for whom Christ died, whether they feed upon His sacrifice or not, for whom He lives to make intercession, whether they draw nigh to the Father of all through Him or not.'[37]

The Church failed in its mission when it became overly concerned with theological abstractions such as those which occupied the ecclesiastical parties of the age—the biblical discourses of the Evangelicals, the Tractarian concern for apostolic succession, or the Broad Church's absorption in liberal theology. It must be primarily concerned with the real world, and the revealing of the Spirit at work in all parts of the redeemed Creation. In 1852 he wrote to Ludlow to try to make himself clearly understood:

Let people call me merely a philosopher, or merely anything else, or what they will, or what they will not; my business because I am a theologian, and have no vocation except for theology, is not to build, but to dig, to show that economy and politics (I leave physics to dear Kingsley . . .) must have a ground beneath themselves, that society is not to be made anew by arrangements of ours, but is to be regenerated by finding the law and ground of its order and harmony, the only secret of its existence, in God. This must seem to you an unpractical and unchristian method; to me it is the only one which makes action possible, and Christianity anything more than an artificial religion for the use of believers. I wish very earnestly to be understood on

34. Maurice, *Social Morality*, p. 385.
35. *Ibid.*, p. 390.
36. Maurice, *Christian Socialism*, p. 8.
37. F. D. Maurice, *Nineteen Sermons Preached at Lincoln's Inn* (1851), p. xxix.

this point, because all my future course must be regulated on this principle, or on no principle at all. The Kingdom of Heaven is to me the great practical existing reality which is to renew the earth and make it a habitation for blessed spirits instead of for demons. To preach the Gospel of that Kingdom, the fact that it is among us, and is not to be set up at all, is my calling and business.[38]

The idea of unity was a passion with him: 'the desire for unity and the search for unity, both in the nation and in the Church, has haunted me all my days.'[39] Within the Church, which he believed to be the great social catalyst in the nation, there had to be a meeting of men of all classes and all vocations, who were to engage in the mission of exposing the Spirit at work in every part of the material and social world: 'God is to be sought and honoured in every pursuit, not merely in something technically called religion.'[40] Maurice was influenced by Coleridge's idea of 'the clerisy', which referred to the body of university men, artists, scientists, tradesmen, and others—like those who taught in the Working Men's College—who sought to reveal to the whole of society the power of the Incarnation at work. Because the divine order they were uncovering by their 'digging' was a moral order, real fellowship was possible among those who served in 'the clerisy'—regardless of their social backgrounds. They in turn could help others to become citizens by first making them into men.

Maurice was a prophet, and he was supported by a creative minority of churchmen. It is difficult to evaluate the influence of a prophet and his followers, but there is little doubt that both Victorian society and the Victorian Church would have been poorer without their existence. To society Maurice gave his Working Men's College, the experiment which showed that the classes could work together for mutual benefit in education. He also gave to society an alternative to political economy, 'benevolence under the guidance of science', which Ludlow dismissed as the 'spirit of economic popery'.[41] His followers ensured that his idea of unity was maintained in the co-operative movement also, and that within it there would be room for every social class. Hughes argued the theory of class conciliation in the House of Commons when he was sent to Parliament as the representative of the radicals of Lambeth—after his election campaign was organized by G. J. Holyoake, a militant secularist. He reminded the

38. *Life of Maurice*, II, 137.
39. A. M. Ramsey, *F. D. Maurice and the Conflicts of Modern Theology* (1951), p. 99.
40. *Life of Maurice*, II, 319.
41. J. M. Ludlow, *Christian Socialism and Its Opponents* (1851), p. 21.

privileged orders that their economic and social policies were estranging the skilled artisans of the nation, driving them into emigration, and that 'Labour is here at the door, asking respectfully that it may be opened.' During his time as M.P. for Lambeth, and later for Frome, Somerset, Hughes appealed to the enlightened self-interest of the middle class, as well as to their sense of duty to the nation: 'The middle class . . . had better not bang the door in labour's face, lest it be kicked down.'[42]

The greatest contribution of Maurice and his followers, however, was made to the Church. They gave to contemporaries, and to succeeding generations, a new concept of what was the Catholic Church. Maurice had looked at the Tractarian form of sectarianism, and wished that they had been truly catholic in their thinking—concerned with all aspects of the faith, especially the mission of the Church to society. In the same way he had questioned the lack of comprehensiveness in the other Church parties—none of whom were catholic in their outlook. To Maurice the Church was only catholic when it was revealing the Divine at work in the created order, through a universality of mission to all parts of the created order, and of society. The Church ceased to be the Catholic Church when it devoted itself to purely ecclesiastical affairs, and refused to recognize that the Spirit was at work in all parts of the created order. Society was never purely secular to Maurice.

> The Catholic Church, I think, has established itself in the East and the West, and is acknowledged by God as His kingdom upon earth. It has been preyed upon by diseases of all kinds in the shape of human systems: by the Romish system, which is the most successful parody and counterfeit of its Catholic character, and practically contradicts and outrages that, as well as its spiritual character; by Protestant systems which parody its distinct and personal character, and really outrage that as well as its principle—universal human fellowship. Yet in spite of these, and other different systems which have attempted to make a middle way between them, and so, I think, to combine the mischiefs of both, the Church, I think, is coming forth, and will manifest itself as something entirely distinct for them all.[43]

Maurice wanted churchmen to join with him in 'digging'—the making 'manifest' the Kingdom to men, so that they could identify themselves with the power at work in the world. This power was at work in all parts of man's social order—even in movements that unenlightened churchmen called secular. By identifying itself with

42. Mack, *Thomas Hughes*, p. 150.
43. *Life of Maurice*, I, 307.

this power, and witnessing to its presence, the Church would become 'the life giving energy to every body in the midst of which she dwells'.[44] To be truly catholic, the Church had to be concerned with every part of society where the Spirit was at work, and in the lives of all men, whatever their circumstances. The Church was not catholic if it established for itself a life divorced from the world which God had created and redeemed. Speaking of the State, Maurice said that if anarchy were to prevail, and two or three citizens proclaimed 'the dignity of Law', then 'those one or two would constitute a State, and till the Majority joined with them, the Majority would be no State at all.'[45] Similarly the Church was represented by those who proclaimed the existence of God's Kingdom as already existing here upon earth, and identified themselves with it. While the Tractarians began their theological life at the altar, and the Evangelicals with the Bible, Maurice chose to begin his in society where the Incarnate Son was already at work.

It is paradoxical that the churchmen who drew most attention to the social implications of Maurice's theology were a group of Ritualists who worked in the slums of London's East End. Maurice had disassociated himself from Pusey when he concluded that the latter's Tract on Baptism denied God in nature, and restricted Him to the supernatural. By 1864 Maurice and Pusey had agreed, through a correspondence in the *Times,* that they did not believe in the same God.[46] But just as the ideas of both Maurice and Pusey were used by the writers of *Lux Mundi,* so they were borrowed to justify the social activity of priests such as Headlam, who taught Maurice's doctrine that the Incarnation unified and sanctified man's physical and social life. Headlam, like most of the Ritualists, argued that this theological truth was revealed through the social implications of the Mass.

Headlam was one of the most colourful and erratic social reformers that the Church of England produced in the nineteenth century. He had sat at the feet of Maurice while studying theology at Cambridge, but he also developed a strong sympathy, with most of his generation, for the persecuted Ritualists in the slums of the City. He was ordained in 1872, but his acceptance of both the ideas of Maurice and those of the Ritualists did little to endear him to episcopal authority. During the next ten years he held four curacies—the most important being at St. Matthew's, Bethnal Green.

---

44. Maurice, *Kingdom of Christ* (1958), II, 254. *Cf.* p. 246, *supra,* p. 230.
45. Maurice, *Social Morality*, p. 123.
46. *Life of Pusey*, IV, 60.

This was one of the old parishes of London; in an area where Blomfield's industry resulted in ten churches being built during the forties.[47] Early in the century, the Rector had been Joshua King (from 1809 until 1861), a typically absentee incumbent who had chosen to live in Cheshire, leaving the work in the parish to his curates. At the time Headlam came to St. Matthew's, the Rector was the redoubtable Septimus Hansard, who also chose to live outside the parish, in Kensington because of his love of 'clean air'. On most days, however, from 1864 until his death in 1895, Hansard drove to work in Bethnal Green for a few hours. When Winnington-Ingram succeeded Hansard, he said that the area had long been served by misguided men who had tried to live and work in urban slums as though they were country squires. Hansard's relationship with his wardens, and his attitude towards the poor, were certainly those of the worst type of country parson of an earlier age.[48] His tendency to leave the real work in the parish to his curates was a blessing to Headlam, however, until Hansard chose to dismiss his troublesome curate because he supported the unpopular cause of the ballet and the music hall.[49]

Headlam's work among the poor convinced him that the Church was in large measure neglecting the great mass of the English people—what Maurice had called 'the stuff of humanity after class distinctions have been removed from it.'[50] In 1876 this led him to express his ideas in his first substantial work, *The Secular Work of Jesus Christ, His Apostles, and the Church of England*, a passionate call for the Church to free itself from its preoccupation with purely religious affairs, and to co-operate with the secular movements of the age that were seeking social reform.[51] Then, in 1877, with the help of Frederick Verinder, Secretary of the English Land Restoration League—for Headlam was converted to Henry George's economic theories—Headlam organized the Guild of St. Matthew, a fellowship of churchmen who sought to reinterpret the traditional doctrines and rites of the Church, to reveal their significance in common life:

47. Port, *Six Hundred New Churches*, p. 110.

48. There is an interesting account of Hansard by Denis Shaw in *Church Times*, 16 August 1963, p. 7. J. J. Woodroffe, who was his curate, kept a parish diary from 1889 to 1895 to inform Hansard of what went on at Bethnal Green during his absence. It is very illuminating.

49. Bettany, *Stewart Headlam*, pp. 41–44, 79–80. When Headlam tried to win the support of Frederick Temple, Bishop of London, for a Church and Stage Guild, the bishop inhibited him from preaching for many years.

50. F. D. Maurice, *Lectures on Learning and Working* (1865), p. xviii.

51. This work, published by the Guild of St. Matthew was originally a lecture delivered to the East London Branch of the National Secular Society.

'to get rid, by every possible means, of the existing prejudices, especially on the part of the Secularists, against the Church, her sacraments and doctrines, and to endeavour "to justify God to the people".'[52]

At first the Guild had only forty members, and was a purely parochial organization. But when Headlam was forced to leave St. Matthew's, Bethnal Green, its leaders determined to extend their 'study of social and political questions in the light of the Incarnation'[53] to the Church as a whole. It became a propagandist organization for Headlam's version of Christian Socialism. Headlam used his personal wealth to purchase *The Church Reformer*, which became the unofficial organ of the Guild, and a means for Headlam to express his ideas about the ballet and the music halls, and other causes he embraced. The Guild members sought to preach or lecture to any group of interested people, and to set up branches in various parts of England. Prominent among its members were H. C. Shuttleworth, Rector of St. Nicholas, Cole Abbey, and his curate, Thomas Hancock. Both of them were friends with trade unionists and social reformers such as Annie Besant, the Rev. W. E. Moll, an executive member of the Independent Labour Party, and the Hon. and Rev. James Adderley, who was for a short time Head of Oxford House.

From the standpoint of numbers, the Guild was almost insignificant; but its noisy followers, who totalled about a hundred in 1884, when Headlam considered it was most successful, did have great effect among churchmen. It also had influence among secular labour leaders such as Tom Mann, Keir Hardie, and George Lansbury,[54] and did much to convince many people, who were unaware of the heroic labours of the Ritualists in the slums, that the Church did not belong to the privileged classes alone.

The years 1886 and 1887 were ones of great distress among the working classes; and during this period Hancock, who had a flair for rhetoric, labelled the *Magnificat*, the Hymn of the Social Revolution, and preached a sermon at St. Paul's entitled 'The Banner of Christ in the Hands of the Socialists'. Headlam rejoiced in the Christian influence which revealed itself among the workers who attended the service. He said about the banners they carried: 'I noted that inscribed on those banners and flags there were words taken not from Karl Marx, or Lasalle, or Mr. Hyndman, or Mr. Morris, or

52. Binyon, *Christian Socialist Movement*, p. 120.
53. *Ibid.*
54. J. G. Adderley, *In Slums and Society* (1916), pp. 210–13, 220.

Mrs. Besant, or Mr. Champion, or any who were supposed to be leaders, but taken in almost every case from the sayings of Jesus Christ or His great apostles.'[55]

Another Christian Socialist, H. H. Champion, who was a little less Christian and a little more Socialist than Headlam, suggested at this time that the poor should stage a 'sit-down' in Trafalgar Square until the authorities did something for their situation. The unemployed were too disorganized for this to be attempted, but during the bad winter of 1887 groups of them began to gather in Trafalgar Square to listen to speeches. When they attempted to hold a mass meeting on Sunday, 13 November, the police, Guards, and Life Guards were all called upon to use force to keep the people out of the square. Both Headlam and Moll were with the demonstrators on this 'Bloody Sunday'. Headlam later preached the funeral eulogy of Alfred Linnell, who was killed during the struggle.

Champion, in an address at the Church Congress of 1877, said that the £17,000 spent in fitting up Westminster Abbey for the Queen's Jubilee might have been better spent helping the unemployed, and this blunt statement was typical of the shock-tactics used by people like Headlam to gain the attention of churchmen. The latter argued that Christ was not the teacher of religion that He was popularly supposed to be, but the 'servant of Humanity'.

> It is not washing the sin-defiled soul but washing the dusty tired feet that our Lord does to-day, and commands us to do also. . . . he meant us to work for health against disease, to fight against the evil circumstances which make the death rate of St. Luke's so much heavier than the death rate of Belgravia. He meant us to be an organized society to work for the physical as well as for the moral and spiritual well-being of the Humanity He lived and died to save. . . . Holy Brethren, as you kneel to-morrow before the Crucified, remember that it is a Socialistic Carpenter whom you are worshipping, remember that He founded a Society in which equality and brotherhood were to be distinguishing features: think, therefore, how grievously you have failed, since last Good Friday to do much to make that equality and brotherhood a reality.[56]

This power of rhetoric made Headlam the chief propagandist for the new idea of catholicism which was being developed by those Ritualists who were influenced by Maurice. They believed that the Church to be catholic has to 'promote great causes', and had to cease worrying about 'minor matters' such as ritual, or even establishment.

55. Stewart Headlam, 'Christian Socialism' in *Socialism and Religion* (1908), p. 11. This was a Fabian tract; a product of Headlam's short impatient association with this group.

56. Headlam, *Service of Humanity and other Sermons*, p. 13 *passim*.

The great causes were the battles against the evils which enslaved the poor: 'the tyranny of liquor sellers, the scandals of commercial fraud, the evils of sweating, the unjust conditions of female labour, the increase of jerry building, and the continuation of slums; hundreds of such like bad things would be dealt with drastically by the State if there were a great united demand pressed forward by the whole body of Christians.'[57] The clergy as God's priests had to be found in other places than at the altar and in the confessional—clericalism had to die within the Church. The revolt of the working class against the Church was justified because the clergy had long neglected the workers. But, guided by Maurice, Headlam and his followers were now going once more to present Christ to the people as the servant of Humanity: 'the prejudices of Atheists and Agnostics and others against the Church are largely due to the fact that the secular and social side of Christian teaching has been too much neglected in the past.'[58]

Maurice had always believed the Church to be the means by which each class in the nation was saved 'from the selfishness which is the destruction of all' because it was 'the great instrument of intellectual and social improvement'.[59] He also believed that the one class which had really been influenced by Christianity was the much maligned trading class.

> The enemies of the Middle Class may say, but too truly that it has defiled the principles which have been entrusted to it, with all its evil tendencies, that trade and religion have become miserably confused through its influence. They may say this, but if they do not acknowledge also, that its faith has alone preserved its evil tendencies from becoming omnipotent over it, over the nation, they exhibit gross ignorance both of history and of passing events. Take away its Protestantism and it becomes a trading class indeed; that and nothing else.[60]

Maurice was sure that this class with its new political power had a social conscience to which the Church could appeal—a conscience which would save it from becoming merely an urban trading class, hated by the poor, as the Marxists expected.

The Ritualists also had this faith, and the great desire of churchmen like Headlam was to stir the social conscience of privilege—to bring its political and economic power to the aid of the masses in the slums.

57. J. G. Adderley, *Catholicism of the Church of England* (1908), p. 88.
58. Stewart Headlam, *An Appeal to Churchmen* (1890), p. 8; *Cf.* also *Priestcraft and Progress* (1876), p. 97 ff.
59. *Life of Maurice*, II, 92.
60. Maurice, *Letter to Ashley*, p. 5.

Tom Mann, the labour leader, who was a great favourite in clerical circles, was one of those who shared the faith of Maurice and the Ritualists that the power of the middle class could be used for the benefit of the whole nation, and the eradication of slums and other social evils. He called upon the leaders of this class 'to use that power to wipe out these stains on our national and Christian character. . . . The work will be done with or without you, but quicker with you than without you.'[61]

Churchmen were generally unaware of the work of men like William Champneys, the Evangelical rector of Whitechapel; but the rioting in St. George's-in-the-East during Lowder's regime, and the long persecution of the clergy of St. Alban's, Holborn, drew the attention of many clergy and laity to the state of the Church in working-class areas. Here and there, men who had been inspired by the teaching of Maurice and the work of the Ritualists began to work in parishes like Limehouse, Whitechapel, and Stepney. One of these was Edward Denison, son of the late Bishop of Salisbury. He was convinced that London's slums needed 'resident gentlemen' as much as any rural village, and went to live for a short period in Stepney, shortly before his death. Already labouring there was J. R. Green, the historian; and another friend, Brooke Lambert, was a vicar in Whitechapel.

The Ritualists had done much, through their battle with the Establishment and through their pastoral zeal, to appeal to the consciences of the privileged orders, and from the 1870's a series of articles and pamphlets were produced by those who worked in the slums. Sometimes they took the form of argument that the clergy should be consulted whenever any social relief project was initiated, because of their experience among the poor.[62] Sometimes they took the form of the famous *Bitter Cry of Outcast London*, produced by Congregationalist clergy, which urged the State to provide for the poor 'the right to live as something better than the uncleanest of brute beasts', because the Church could do little to help the inhabitants of the slums unless the secular authority first provided them with better social conditions.[63] Others, like the articles that Brooke Lambert wrote for the *Contemporary Review* urged that the great need of the poor was the presence of clergy and laity among them, who would act as a leaven of culture and religion.[64] Scott Holland urged

61. Tom Mann, 'Preachers and Churches' in *Vox Clamantium*, p. 314.
62. Henry Whitehead, 'Mendicity from a Clerical Point of View', *Contemporary Review*, XXI (1873), 365.
63. Preston, *Bitter Cry of Outcast London*, p.15.
64. *Contemporary Review*, XLV (1883), 916 ff., and XLVI (1884), 373 ff.

young men to 'come and be the squires of East London',[65] and James Adderley argued that 'personal contact' could do more for the poor than 'cheque charity' could ever accomplish.[66]

Journalists like James Greenwood, who wrote his *Wilds of London* in 1874, and George Sims, who described the East End to the writers of the *Daily News* and the *Pictorial World*,[67] joined the churchmen in calling for men of privilege to do something for the dispossessed, and these appeals reached young men who were willing to follow the Ritualists and other clergy into the slums. Oxford, in particular, was going through a 'non-theological' phase following the uproar over *Essays and Reviews* and the Colenso controversy; and the new call for a social Gospel was welcomed. Undergraduates like Charles Marson, who became a devoted follower of Stewart Headlam,[68] and Arnold Toynbee, began to spend their long vacation working in the slums, as Charity Organization agents and school teachers. Toynbee became convinced that Oxford men should support the work that was going on in London's East End, and on his return to the university he did much to organize meetings to support the missions of clergy like Samuel Barnett, the Vicar of St. Jude's, Whitechapel. He received a great deal of encouragement, for this was a time when even an agitator like Joseph Arch was invited to speak in Oxford's Town Hall in support of the Agricultural Labourers' Union.

Toynbee had given much thought to the role of the Church in society. In the past, he believed, it had fallen into the error of either 'secluding itself from the world', or of attempting to 'spiritualize the world' through a theocratic domination of the State. Both errors had come from the tendency to 'sacerdotalism' within the Church: 'the form of religion which can become fundamentally dangerous to the State'. As Hooker had, he believed the ideal Church in the English nation was a thoroughly Christian State—'a spiritual and secular power'.[69] The nation could make no progress 'until the religious spirit breathes through every act and institution'.[70] His biographer, Alfred Milner, said that Toynbee was always 'intensely conscious of the all-pervading presence of the Divine'[71] which, like Maurice, he

65. Adderley, *Slums and Society*, p. 48.
66. James Adderley, *Looking Upward: Papers on Social Questions* (1891), p. 4.
67. George R. Sims, *How the Poor Live and Horrible London* (1889). General Booth's *In Darkest England and the Way Out* came out in 1890.
68. For the thought of Marson v. *God's Co-operative Society: Suggestions on the Strategy of the Church* (1914).
69. Arnold Toynbee, *The Ideal Relation of Church and State* (1879), an address given at Balliol College in the spring of that year.
70. Arnold Toynbee, *Progress and Poverty* (1883), p. 49.
71. Alfred Milner, *Arnold Toynbee: a Reminiscence* (1895), p. 36.

saw at work redeeming all aspects of society. Like Maurice also, he believed that all classes had to unite together for the moral and physical well-being of the nation: 'The way we have got reforms carried in England is not by, as a rule, class war, but by class alliance.'[72]

He was haunted by the collective sin of the class he represented. In one of his lectures he confessed on behalf of his fellows to the working class, 'we have sinned against you grievously', and he promised 'reparation' for those who had for so long been offered charity instead of social justice.[73] Beatrice Webb attributed the origin of the social ferment of the eighteen-eighties to this 'new consciousness of sin among men of intellect and property'; a new class consciousness of the social evil which had given to the privileged classes rent, interest, and profit on a stupendous scale, but had failed to provide tolerable living conditions for the great majority of the people of England.[74] Young men like Toynbee helped to propagate this conviction of social sin, and the need for a new form of Christianity which would be concerned not only with a purer theology but also with social reform. The result of their preaching was the Settlement House movement. The inspiration for this way of thought came directly from the teachings of Maurice—'a leaven, leavening the whole of English society' at this time.[75]

The person who was directly instrumental in founding the first Settlement House was Samuel Barnett, a quiet, gentle, yet powerful personality who had studied law and modern history at Wadham College, Oxford, before being ordained in 1867. He was one of the founders of the Charity Organization Society, which sought to discourage indiscriminate charity among the poor, and to provide a rational method of distribution, through the society's acting as a central collection agency, and a clearing house for information. In 1873 he was made Vicar of St. Jude's, Whitechapel, where he remained until 1894. His pastoral experience here, and his work in the Charity Organization Society convinced him that the charity given by the West End in time of social panic was not sufficient to relieve the nation of the social evils perpetuated by the slums.[76]

72. Toynbee, *Progress and Poverty*, p. 53.
73. Arnold Toynbee, *Lectures on the Industrial Revolution* (1884), p. 220 ff.
74. Webb, *My Apprenticeship*, p. 179.
75. Binyon, *Christian Socialist Movement*, p. 117.
76. When windows were broken by the unemployed in Pall Mall on 8 February 1886, the Mansion House Fund for relief of the poor stood at £19,000. Two days later it had risen to £72,000. *V.* Binyon, p. 130.

It had become customary for slum priests like Brooke Lambert, or laymen like Theodore Talbot, to return to Oxford colleges to seek help from undergraduates for Whitechapel or Holborn, and on 17 November 1883, in the room of Cosmo Lang at St. John's College, Oxford, Barnett read a paper which suggested that university men should begin communal settlements in slum areas, to assist the poor by providing them with leadership. The response to this paper was so enthusiastic that immediate pledges were taken to support a Settlement House in Barnett's parish, and the new venture was called Toynbee Hall, in memory of Arnold Toynbee, who had died that year.

The house was near St. Jude's Church, a commodious structure which suited the missioners' usual way of living. Barnett did not want affectation, or false asceticism, in the experiment. The 'settlers' were there not as missioners, to build up a parish, but as men who sought to learn as much as to teach. Mrs. Barnett engaged in some traditional 'rescue work' among young girls, but the main work was the formation of clubs and guilds to assist the poor through education. The house had accommodation for twenty-two residents; and in 1888 there were fifteen men living there while they worked in the area as teachers, almoners, Poor Law Guardians, and administrators of organizations like the C.O.S. and the Children's Country Holiday Fund. Between 1884 and 1911, one hundred and eighty-eight residents stayed in Toynbee Hall.[77]

Besides working in the settlement, the residents acted as social agitators in Whitechapel, organizing the people to vote for a public library and to support labour agitation such as the Docker's Strike of 1889. Their lobbying also resulted in the bringing in of fresh water for much of East London.

Like most slum priests, Barnett was not an intellectual. Beatrice Webb was distressed by his 'chaotic thought', which Barnett described as that of an 'empirical socialist'. The one clear influence in it was that of Maurice, particularly his idea of the classes working together for the good of the commonwealth, and the need for the privileged people of the nation to directly involve themselves in the lives of the poor.[78] As time went on, Barnett also insisted that the State had to do more to assist the poor through municipal hospitals and national old-age pensions. His socialist ideas also led him to

77. For the work of Toynbee Hall v. Werner Picht, *Toynbee Hall and the English Settlement House Movement* (1914), p. 31 ff.

78. Henrietta O. Barnett, *Canon Barnett* (1918), I, 156; S. A. Barnett, *Settlements of University Men in Great Towns* (1884), p. 10; S. A. Barnett, *Some Urgent Questions in Christian Lights* (1889), p. 80.

suggest redistribution of property, as a Christian action—a concern of many clergy of the time. 'Interference with property . . . if it is not dictated by the lust of spoliation, but by a desire to do a duty as in the sight of God—can never impugn the sacredness of property or damage its security, since it means when it is thus conducted that there is a public desire to use the material things which God has lent us more worthily—a deliberate desire to carry out His will upon earth.'[79]

Barnett was never a Ritualist, but like most active clergy in the slums he resented the Establishment, which tolerated 'indolent, incapable and unworthy incumbents'. He also disliked the class complexion of the Church, its clericalism, and its inefficient hierarchy whose main concern was to maintain the privileges of Establishment rather than the mission of the Church. As far as he was concerned, the Church existed 'to spiritualize life', and within it the ultimate authority should be 'the people', who should choose not only bishops, but clergy, churchwardens, and other officials. He had little sympathy for episcopal pretension in any form, particularly ideas like apostolic succession.[80]

Inevitably there was an ecclesiastical reaction to Barnett's Broad-Church ideas. Many churchmen believed that a Settlement House to be really Christian had to be more closely identified with the parochial structure of the Church. They were also unhappy about the unobtrusive role that religious practice had in Toynbee Hall. Few attended the optional prayer meetings, and often the Sunday lectures were not Christian. The result of this dissatisfaction with what Barnett was attempting was the appearance of a second Settlement House, Oxford House in Bethnal Green. It imitated the earlier establishment in many ways, but its residents were all professed churchmen, and the Settlement House made a point of co-operating with parish churches in the neighbourhood. Less attention was paid to purely educational activities, such as the university extension lectures attempted at Toynbee Hall. Care was also taken not to involve Oxford House in trade-union disputes.

The criticisms of Toynbee Hall, Oxford House, and the other Settlement Houses which were founded by the Church, the Nonconformists, and the Roman Catholics, were many. The 'squire' mentality of the settlers, and the transplanting of many of the

79. The words are those of W. Cunningham, Vicar of St. Mary's, Cambridge, 'Church's Duty in Relation to the Sacredness of Property', in *Church of the People* (1894), p. 29.

80. For Barnett's ecclesiastical opinions *v. Clergy and the Democratic Movement: Address to the Junior Clergy of London* (1884), p. 4 ff. *Contemporary Review*, XLVI (1884), 674 ff; *Practicable Socialism* (1894), p. 2 ff.

trappings of Oxcam college life to the slums was offensive to some serious social reformers. The settlers had no desire to set up a classless society—but, as we have seen, the poor did not want it either. Their object was to ease class tension, by having the classes work together for the benefit of all who lived in Whitechapel, Bethnal Green, or wherever the settlement was. The object of the movement was limited, and the results were limited; but, as Charles Booth said, London would have been poorer without the Settlement Houses. Many a conscience was stirred, to the ultimate benefit of society, by what H. G. Wells called the 'benevolent picknicking' of the gentlemen who came to live, however briefly, among the poor.[81] Many an agitator, like Ben Tillett, had his inherited prejudice against the Church and parsons somewhat lessened by what was attempted by people like Barnett, James Adderley, and the other settlers. Perhaps an insight into the value of these attempts to have the classes meet and understand each other is contributed by G. D. H. Cole and Raymond Postgate when they admit, in their history of the common people of England, that 'there was . . . always a small percentage of parsons with a genuine sympathy with Socialism and the misery of the working class, whose influence prevented the Church and the Chapels being counted wholly as enemies; similarly a strain of religiosity and pietism ran powerfully in the Labour movement and was later to be an effective obstacle to the spread of Marxian philosophy.'[82]

When Cole and Postgate wrote this, few studies had been made of the influence of the Victorian Church in social movements. It had not been recognized that, however small in number were the clergy and laity directly influenced by Socialism, few churchmen were ignoring social problems by the end of our period. Even the bishops, as we have seen in our study of the Christian Social Union, were displaying a social conscience. From the pulpits of the nation, churchmen were proclaiming that 'the Church is not and cannot be opposed to civil society; it is the very leaven of civil society . . . destined to redeem our social life, and to make the kingdoms of this world the kingdoms of Christ.'[83] Many churchmen admitted that this revolution in ecclesiastical thought could be directly attributed to the teaching and

---

81. Maurice Reckitt, *Faith and Society* (1932), p. 98, from a speech made at St. John's College in 1910.

82. Cole and Postgate, *Common People, 1746–1946*, p. 323. Postgate also says in his *1848, Story of a Year* (1956), p. 131, that it was because of Christian Socialism that there was never in England 'a break between organized labour and organized religion'.

83. T. C. Fry, Headmaster of Berkhamsted School, 'City of God' in *Advent Sermons on Church Reform* (1898).

work of F. D. Maurice. 'We have learnt, or are learning, mainly from the teaching of that true prophet, F. D. Maurice . . . [that] we must not dare to say of a thing so divinely instituted as the life of the nation that it is common or unclean, that we must recognize marks of divinity stamped on every true and necessary form of human existence, and perceive working through the Family and the State, as well as through the Church, the operations of the living God.'[84]

6. The Victorian Church and Social Reform

IN 1849 an anonymous cleric wrote: 'there is no Poor Law when the Church is truly Catholic.'[1] At that time many churchmen looked back to an imaginary yet ideal past when squire and parson had kept the poor in a state of social contentment through the exercise of Christian charity. But the majority realized that the world in which squire and parson had been so secure was passing away. A new social class had come to power in 1832, and 'soulless' Benthamite reform, like the new Poor Law, was now attending to concerns which had traditionally belonged to the Church. The Guardians of some unions even decreed that the church bell should not be tolled at pauper funerals.[2]

During the hungry forties, many churchmen recognized the social cleavage that arose as the Poor Law 'bastilles' were filled, to get the destitute out of sight of gentle eyes. Most parish priests were only too aware of the desperate suffering endured by their flocks. They saw clearly that the political reformers of their age were not enlightened social reformers, and the answer of the 'ruthless logicians' of the Benthamite school for pauperism was slowly but surely building up class hatred, which might explode at any time. They saw the Poor Law for what it was, not only an agency to take away from the parish its traditional responsibility for the poor, but a measure of the 'manufactory' to protect the wealth and privilege of the mill-owning class.[3]

84. C. E. Osborne, Vicar of Seghill, Northumberland, 'Church and Nation', Ibid., p. 46.
1. Parish Priest, Diaconate and the Poor (1849), p. 7.
2. Hammond, J. L. and B., Bleak Age, p. 112.
3. British Critic, XXVIII (1840), p. 335.

Some churchmen sought to relieve the situation by pressing for legislation such as the Ten Hours Bill. Others, like the Christian Socialists, sought to identify themselves with the Chartist movement, and to give the working class an economic and political solution to their misery other than that of overt class warfare. But the general answer to this social crisis put forth by churchmen was the conversion of the mill-owning and shop-keeping class from the ruthlessness of political economy to the charity of Christianity. This was the great need of the age, the awakening of a social conscience within the merchant class which had come to political power. The *British Critic* argued in 1838, in support of the Metropolis Churches Fund, that the merchants of London had to awaken to 'a sense of their duties' in social reform: they 'know not the squalid wretchedness which lurks within a few yards of their own palaces. . . . this must be brought by the clergy in detail before them . . . that . . . the negligence of the State has bestowed a privilege upon them, the high honour of providing for the wants of the poorer members of their Lord'.[4]

It is easy to dismiss this instilling of a spirit of philanthropy within the trading class as the mere giving of 'the best ideals of the pre-industrial era—Christian social principles on a basis of inequality of status acquiesced in as right by all classes'.[5] But it was carried out by the Church, it was desperately needed by the age, and it gave to England what the political economists and their theories would never have given—social harmony between the classes, and the avoidance of the class warfare which the Marxists expected. It was largely because of the social mission of the Church that the English middle class never became an urban bourgeoisie at war with the proletariat. It was also because of this social mission that anti-clericalism has never been characteristic of the English labour movement. As Barnett reported to the clergy of London in 1883, there was no hostility to the clergy as a class in the slums, some were loyally supported as the leaders of an oppressed minority, some were loved, and all were tolerated. Abusing the parson was not done, for 'he is at any rate not as bad as the landlord.'[6]

The bishops of the Christian Social Union, the Ritualists, the workers in the Settlement Houses, even the scornful Fabians, were all products of this bourgeois morality, which Marx and Engels had sadly to admit was appreciated and admired by the workers of England with their 'Christian slavish nature'. However unsystematic,

4. *Ibid.*, XXIII (1838), p. 189.
5. Binyon, *Christian Socialist Movement*, pp. 63–64.
6. Barnett, *Address to the Junior Clergy*, p. 7.

ill-organized, and unscientific was the social 'ambulance work' fostered by the Church, it was necessary in Victorian England. As in the field of education, there was no real alternative offered to what the churches (including Nonconformity) provided for the relief of the poor. As Christopher Dawson has argued, when we look at the social service work of the Victorian Churches, we should be astonished not at what was left undone, but by what was achieved.[7]

Not only did the Church provide an ethic of service for the trading class of England, but through the experiments and thought of Maurice and his followers it gave to late Victorian England a social policy which even dared to question the divine right of property. With most of their contemporaries, Victorian churchmen were suspicious of State-inspired social legislation, but Maurice's theological view of the Spirit working through secular as well as religious agencies did much to lessen their fears. Yet they seldom waited for State initiative. They believed the task of easing class tension in the nation to be peculiarly the vocation of the Church—which had to be the conscience of the nation in social as well as religious matters. The work of the Ritualists drew the attention of 'the quality' to specific social evils like improper drainage in the slums, and secular reform often followed agitation initiated by the Church. Most Victorian churchmen who laboured in the slums, like Barnett, emerged as 'empirical socialists' —churchmen who sought to combat specific social evils, and then found that the ideas of the Christian Socialists provided them with a reasoned apologetic for what they were about.

No institution was of greater interest to Victorian Englishmen than the Church—particularly after the mid-century when the mission of the Church to ensoul the nation, to make England peculiarly Christian was well under way. By the seventies and eighties, few thoughtful people of the privileged classes were unaware of the work of the Ritualist saints in the East End of London, or the noisy propaganda of people like Headlam, or the social concern shown by even the bishops in the Christian Social Union. If one had ideas of social reform to propagate, the best medium through which to express them was the religious press. Beatrice Webb noted in her diary: 'Sidney spending all the morning writing articles for all sorts of papers—especially the religious organs such as *The Guardian, The Church Times* etc.'[8]

Unfortunately the Victorian Church has always had a bad press. Small groups of secular reformers, like the Fabians, who were experts

7. *V. supra*, p. 266.
8. Webb, *Our Partnership*, pp. 69–70.

in advertising, knew how important it was to announce their activities.[9] On principle, the Church could not set out to seek popular approval; and most of those who did the truly heroic work of 'mucking in' with the lives of the poor deliberately shunned publicity. Often their work was an offering of reparation, of atonement, which sought to establish a new social relationship between the upper and lower classes in the nation. Men like Scott Holland, Fr. Stanton, and Theodore Talbot, together with many of the ladies who laboured with Fr. Lowder along the Ratcliff Highway, were people of great wealth. Supporting them was the social conscience of notable families, the Talbots, the Cecils, the Lyttletons, the Palmers, the Pagets, and the Gladstones.[10] As Charles Booth pointed out, their lives of sacrifice touched the poor as nothing else would have, but a life like that of George Rundle Prynne, who spent fifty-five years in the slums of Plymouth, never received the publicity of Beatrice Webb's brief visits to East London sweat-shops.

Victorian churchmen made no pretence of serving any abstract scheme of social amelioration, and perhaps this is what ensured the permanency of what they accomplished. They bridged the chasm between the classes, and helped to save England from overt class warfare and anti-clericalism. Inspired by Maurice, they rejected the theology of the Tractarians to find a peculiarly English form of Catholicism, which reaffirmed Hooker's view of the sanctity of public secular life, and sought to make the Church catholic by bringing the fruits of the Gospel to every class in the nation, and every aspect of society. They also sought to make England a Christian nation, as they jogged the conscience of a mercantile people, and persuaded the middle class to inherit the spirit of *noblesse oblige* of the aristocracy whose political and economic position they had usurped. They even persuaded some of them to act as 'squires' in Whitechapel and in Bethnal Green. This was no mean accomplishment.

The Church failed to provide spiritual resources for the masses in the new towns, in the same way that the State failed to provide sanitation. It may be argued that Convocation did not begin to meet as an operative body until 1854, and that the Church did not have the organization needed to put its house in order. It should also be noted

9. Herman Ausubel, *The Late Victorians: a Short History* (1955), p. 69 says of the Fabians: 'Even modern scholars have taken them at their word and made them appear more influential than they really were among the late Victorians.'

10. *V*. Henson, *Retrospect of an Unimportant Life*, I, pp. 156–57. For the class composition of the early sisterhoods *v*. Maria Trench, 'English Sisterhoods', *Nineteenth Century*, XVI (1884), pp. 339–52.

that every reform initiated by the Church could be resisted by the secular authority—including the summoning of Convocation itself, or the creation of new dioceses in industrial areas. But it must be admitted that, though the Church was generally in advance of the State in advocating social reform, and that it produced a creative minority which acted as the conscience of Victorian society in the way that no secular body did, the Church could have done much more. Far too much of its time and energy was spent battling over the abstract issues raised by the Tractarians, or in tilting with Nonconformity, or in fighting rather than in transcending the restraint of mission imposed by Establishment. The Church failed the masses religiously and socially in the nineteenth century—but then so did the nation, of which the Church was an integral part.

But—and this is the only explanation of the Christian character of late Victorian England, which so many historians have noted, and is the only explanation of the Church's golden age of pastoral work—the Church did capture the middle class ideologically (with the aid of Nonconformity). The significance of this in the development of English social history is hard to overestimate.

> The Christian religion coloured what many Victorians, particularly lower and middle-class Victorians, thought about everything. Mid-nineteenth-century England was very heavily charged with religious feeling, or religiosity. . . . All religious denominations engaged with ever-increasing zeal in the attempt to re-convert England, churches and chapels were built, missions despatched, revivals staged; what was spent on that work in the way of human effort and sacrifice, and for that matter of financial expenditure, is one of the really important facts of English history of the nineteenth century.[11]

11. Clark, *Making of Victorian England*, p. 284.

PART III
CHURCH
AND NATION

VII. The Idea
of the Church
in Victorian England

> *I cannot understand what is the
> good of a national Church if it is
> not to Christianize the nation and
> introduce the principles of
> Christianity into men's social and
> civil relations.*
>
> THOMAS ARNOLD

1. *The Role of the Church in the Nation*

IN ALL that has been said in the preceding chapters, it seems to have been assumed that, in spite of the fierce party strife which characterized the Victorian Church, churchmen were forming a new and conscious policy of social involvement. The question must now be asked—was this really so? Were Victorian churchmen as a whole seeking and finding an idea of the Church's role in the nation which was significantly different from that held by earlier Anglicans?

Another assumption implied, in the last three chapters at least, is that Church policy alone had significant social influence in the nation. But what of Nonconformity? Could it not be argued that, at least until 1880, Dissent and Liberalism were closely identified, that a very large part of the powerful new middle class practised its Christianity in a chapel rather than in a church, and because of traditional prejudice would have refused to accept anything as important as a conscious social policy from the Establishment?

To conclude this study, these two assumptions are considered. It is argued that not only did the Victorian Church develop a significantly new idea of its role in the nation, but that this idea was implemented, often consciously, by many Dissenters.

EPIGRAPH: A. P. Stanley, *Life of Thomas Arnold* (1844), I, 274.

As we have examined the Church's attitude to the State, and its social policies, constant reference has been made to the innumerable pamphlets which came out of sometimes obscure rectories or vicarages. They have given us something of the thought of the ordinary churchmen about the role of the Church in the nation. But these writings did not influence their contemporaries in the way the thought of the intellectual giants of the Church—Newman, Pusey, Gladstone, Arnold, and Maurice—did.

We must now look at the theories of these important men, bearing in mind that they seldom represent systematic thought. Just as much as the pamphlets produced by the parish clergy, their theories arose out of crises, such as the Hampden and Gorham affairs, which forced churchmen to admit there was some need to redefine the relationship of the Church with the State, and its function in society.

When Arnold Toynbee addressed Balliol College in 1879, he chose to discuss what could be the ideal relationship between Church and State—a matter of great importance to someone as concerned as he was about the moral regeneration of industrial England: 'Material prosperity, without faith in God and love to our fellow-men, is as little use to man as earth to the plants without the sun.'[1] He noted that at times in its history the Church had attempted, with the aid of the State, to guide and direct the social order, reshaping it according to ecclesiastical precepts. At other times the spiritual power had been content to view itself as the servant of the State, leaving national concerns completely in secular hands, that the Church might confine its activities to worship and prayer. Toynbee believed that the Church of England had always sought to avoid either extreme—theocracy or Erastianism—and, at the cost of much conflict with the State, and lack of sympathy from extremist churchmen, to maintain the *via media* that Hooker had once defined, and Toynbee then favoured.[2]

At the time Toynbee wrote there were among churchmen many different interpretations of what was the Church of England, and what was its function in the nation. We must now examine the ideas of the chief protagonists of the main schools of thought, beginning with the 'right wing' of theorists; those who favoured if not theocracy at least 'sacerdotalism'. The most extreme exponent of this way of thinking in the Victorian Church was, of course, John Henry Newman. He was a political theorist of note, who gave to his generation what

1. Quoted by Binyon, *Christian Socialist Movement in England*, p. 119.
2. Toynbee, *Ideal Relation of Church and State* (1879).

Harold Laski has called 'perhaps the profoundest discussion of sovereignty in the English language'.[3]

2. The Right Wing of Theorists

NEWMAN was a man of cold intellect, untouched by sentiment, and this influenced his theory of the Church. His brother Francis said of his thought: 'I distinctly felt his arguments were too finely drawn and subtle, often elaborately missing the moral points and the main points, to rest on some ecclesiastical fiction.'[1] He displayed a curious indifference to social problems, and in his work he always remained a theologian rather than a pastor. Thomas Allies ventured the opinion that his first concern was 'the noblest aspect of man, not the social, but the intellectual'.[2] Certainly he did display a curious indifference to social problems, in an age when they were of increasing interest to most churchmen; and this has been noted by many scholars. Georgiana McEntee has contrasted his social conscience with that of Henry Manning, and said:

> Neither inclination nor the exigencies of his position compelled him to take part in the public life of his time though, had he been so inclined, his duties as a parish priest in the great commercial centre where he lived for a time would have drawn him into it. . . . as far as any effect which it might have had on his own life and work was concerned, the Industrial Revolution with the radical changes which it brought about in the external life of man, and indirectly in his intellectual outlook and spiritual condition, need not have taken place.[3]

Newman was never a democrat, and his avoidance of the common people, and the social misery of the age, may have been justified in his mind by the position in which he was placed as an Anglican at Oxford, and as an Oratorian priest in Birmingham. As an Oxford don during the years of Tractarian controversy, he hardly had time

3. Harold Laski, *Studies in the Problem of Sovereignty* (1917), p. 202, referring to Newman's defence of Papal Infallibility in his *Letter to the Duke of Norfolk on Mr. Gladstone's Recent Expostulation* (1874).
1. F. W. Newman, *Phases of Faith* (1860), p. 8.
2. Allies, *T. W. Allies*, p. 113.
3. Georgina McEntee, *Social Catholic Movement in Great Britain* (1927), p. 15.

for social concerns. As an Oratorian, he believed he was directed by the hierarchy to serve the upper classes alone: 'our great benefactor thirty years ago, Pope Pius IX . . . with that insight which a pope has into the future, and of what is necessary for the Church . . . sent the Oratory, and the Fathers of the Oratory especially to the educated classes, and what would be called the class of gentlemen.'[4]

Another reason why he may have shunned social problems was his dualistic theology, which was very Augustinian in its outlook. Newman looked upon this as a fallen world, a vale of tears filled with evil: 'All our daily pursuits and doings need not be proved evil, but are certainly evil without proof unless they can be proved to be good.'[5] History moved in a cycle, as inevitably man's sin brought on the same bad round again. The world was dark, and the State, together with the secular order it governed, was as corrupt as the men within it. Newman once preached a sermon entitled 'The World our Enemy' based on the text 'We know that we are of God, and the whole world lieth in wickedness.'[6] Lord Acton always thought that, because of Newman's awareness of evil in the world, he divorced morality completely from politics.[7] Perhaps he also divorced it from questions of social reform, which could be of little spiritual value to a fallen world.

Newman believed the great enemy to the Christian in his age was liberalism—'the anti-dogmatic principle and its developments'.[8] Newman wished the Church to be authoritative and dogmatic, to reassert its divine commission, to show the secular world where it was in error, and to restore the State to its proper place of limited functions and services. Newman was obsessed with the problem of sovereignty—a man who by nature longed to be led, if he could not lead himself. In him, if in anyone, can be seen *anima naturaliter Romana*.[9] The true Church was the Catholic Church—the source of spiritual authority in a world of darkness: 'The Church is Catholic, that is she is an organized body, expanded over the whole earth, and in active intercommunion part with part, so that no one part acts without acting on and acting with every other.'[10] He wished the State to respect the Church in the nineteenth century in the way that Roman magistrates

4. W. P. Neville, ed. *Addresses to Cardinal Newman with his Replies* (1905), p. 126.
5. Newman, *Sermons on Subjects of the Day*, p. 123.
6. *Ibid.*, pp. 263–64. *V.* also *supra*, p. 58.
7. H. Paul ed., *Letters of Lord Acton to Mary Gladstone* (1913), p. 181.
8. Newman, *Apologia*, p. 132.
9. Derek Stanford, 'Enigma of J. H. Newman', *Church of England Newspaper*, 23 August 1957, p. 7.
10. J. H. Newman, *Difficulties Felt by Anglicans in Catholic Teaching*, n.d. 4th edition, I, 154.

had reckoned with it in another age: 'a dangerous enemy to any power not built upon itself'.[11]

When Newman discovered that it was impossible to view his Anglican bishop as 'my Pope . . . the successor of the Apostles, the Vicar of Christ . . . his disapprobation . . . the one thing I could not bear',[12] he left the Church of England to seek within the Church of Rome the authority he had to find. There and there alone, he was convinced, was to be found the Catholic Church.

> If the Church is to be regal, a witness for Heaven, unchangeable amid secular changes, if in every age she is to hold her own, and proclaim as well as profess the truth, if she is to thrive without or against the civil power, if she is to be resourceful and self-recuperative under all fortunes, she must be more than Holy and Apostolic; she must be Catholic. Hence it is that, first, she has ever from her beginning onwards had a hierarchy, and a head, with a strict unity of polity, the claim of an exclusive divine authority and blessing; the trusteeship of the gospel gifts, and the exercise over her members of an absolute and despotic rule. And next, as to her work, it is her special duty, as a Sovereign State, to consolidate her several portions, to enlarge her territory, to keep up and to increase her various populations in this ever-dying, ever nascent world, in which to be stationary is to lose ground and to repose is to fail.[13]

By 1843 he was convinced there were 'but two alternatives, the way to Rome, and the way to Atheism'.[14]

Newman's passionate concern for ecclesiastical authority brought into being the Tractarian party. It gave a new lease of spiritual life to clergy who were reminded that their commission was divine, regardless of the 'contempt' they might suffer in the secular world. It also presented to the Victorians a new concept of piety. Finally it introduced the intellectual problem which fascinated churchmen throughout much of the century—what was the nature of the Church of England?

After Newman's departure it seemed that the question of authority in the Church, together with the theory of apostolic succession, would no longer be of much interest to churchmen. But this was not to be. The new type of reforming bishop which began to appear, such as Samuel Wilberforce, had no intention of losing the ideological power that had been attributed to the episcopal office. The Tractarian ideas were used to buttress the authority of the episcopate with increasing frequency throughout the nineteenth century, even by the type of

11. J. H. Newman, *Development of Christian Doctrine* (1878), p. 232.
12. *Apologia*, p. 134.
13. J. H. Newman, *Via Media of the Anglican Church* (1877), I, lxxx–lxxxi.
14. *Apologia*, p. 251.

Erastian bishop that Newman lost faith in when he was an Anglican. A bishop like A. C. Tait had no idea of seeking the early Tractarian dream of a theocratic society, but he had no difficulty in accepting the mystical justification for his office which the Tractarians had built up. Tait would never have agreed with Newman that: 'The Church is a sovereign and self-sustaining power in the same sense in which any temporal state is such. She is sufficient for herself; she is absolutely independent in her own sphere.'[15] But, as he showed in his treatment of the Ritualists, he agreed with Newman that the Church, represented by its hierarchy, 'has irresponsible control over her subjects in religious matters; she makes laws for them on her own authority, and enforces obedience on them as the tenure of their membership with her'.[16] When the Public Worship Regulation Act failed to discipline the Ritualists, Tait fell back on the 'apostolic authority' of the diocesan bishop, arguing that this principle of authority was recognized not by the State, but by the whole of the Anglican communion, represented by the bishops at Lambeth: 'the authority of the diocesan bishops in such cases has been affirmed by the assembly of a hundred bishops at Lambeth.'[17]

Charles Blomfield had thought little of the doctrine of apostolic succession, dismissing such ideas as the fancies of the Nonjuring era; but then he worked closely with Peel, and was a man that any political figure had to reckon with. Later generations of bishops had less social influence and, as it passed from them, they compensated for their loss of prestige by welcoming Tractarian ideas of apostolic authority. Hensley Henson was one of the churchmen who noted this compensatory development as it evolved during the last years of the century: 'The decay of the Establishment, the development of Tractarianism, and the rapid expansion of Anglican Christianity had largely altered the character and functions of the English bishop, weakening his local importance, limiting his personal independence, emphasizing mistakenly his extra-national obligations, and facilitating, if not even compelling, his acquiescence in the exorbitant episcopalian theory of his office.'[18]

Newman's ideas were slow in being accepted, however, even by the bishops, for the descendants of the apostles that he appealed to were almost all thoroughly Erastian in their outlook. Nor had his ideas much lasting influence among the clergy, who were generally

15. Newman, *Difficulties Felt by Anglicans*, I, 157.
16. *Ibid.*
17. A. C. Tait, *Church of the Future: Third Quadrennial Visitation* (1880), p. 28.
18. Henson, *Retrospect of an Unimportant Life*, I, 285.

un-theological beings who shared Archdeacon Hare's suspicions about Tractarian speculation. In consideration of Newman's doctrine of development, Hare said:

> Take a sentence or two here and there from this Father, and a couple of expressions from another, add half a canon of this Council, a couple of incidents out of some ecclesiastical historian, and an anecdote from a chronicler, two conjectures of some critic and half a dozen drachms of a schoolman, mix them up in rhetoric . . . and shake them well together—and thus we get at a theological development. But who except the prescriber can tell what the result will be? and may not he produce any result he chooses?[19]

Most of the clergy were so busy with the mission of the Church in their parishes that they showed little interest in supporting either the theocratic ideas of the Tractarians or their extravagant veneration of the episcopal office. Bishops and clergy might close ranks in Roman Catholicism to ensure clerical domination of the Church. But in Anglicanism the pattern of authority that evolved in the nineteenth century was formed by an alliance of the bishops and the laity, who used each other's political and economic power to dominate the lesser clergy. The laity generally humoured the bishops, who gracefully accepted the Tractarian ideas which enhanced their spiritual authority. Experience proved that bishops who seemed to take the theory of apostolic succession seriously seldom protested against the restraints put upon the Church by the Establishment. The new apostolic bishop was but the old Erastian writ large.

Newman later admitted that the Tractarians knew more about the saints of the early Church than they did about the Privy Council or the Court of Arches, and there was some truth in what he said. They did underestimate the degree to which the Established Church was an integral part of the nation, and they overlooked the fact that the mass of the clergy were as zealous to defend their social status as they were to protect the doctrines of their Church. As W. G. Ward said later to Anglican friends: 'your church so desired to be a National Church, that it failed to take any security that it should be an orthodox one.'[20]

Neither Keble nor Pusey was ever so naïve as Newman about the nature of the Church of England. Both had roots deep in the English countryside, and both represented the traditional and sober High-Church party, which Newman found so fascinating when he began to

---

19. J. C. Hare, *Contest with Rome* (1852), p. 96. This was a charge to the clergy of the Lewes archdeaconry.

20. W. G. Ward, *Anglican Establishment Contrasted with the Catholic Church of Every Age: Letter to the Guardian* (1850), p. 35.

abandon his Evangelical upbringing. It has been suggested that Newman's concern for authority reflected anxiety about his personal social background, in the world of the gentry which he so uneasily entered at Oxford.[21] Be that as it may, there is no doubt that both Keble and Pusey were thoroughly at home in the old aristocratic Church of England; and this shaped their attitude to the question of authority in the Church, and their idea of the nature of the Church.

Keble's thought about the Church of England was revealed at the time of the Gorham controversy, in his two important pamphlets, 'Trial of Doctrine' and 'A Call to Speak out' which were published together in 1850. He called for the people of the nation to recognize themselves as the ultimate authority in ecclesiastical affairs, and to reform the Church for the sake of the commonwealth. Then he retired to Hursley to begin the practical work of spiritual reform, with the remark that if the Church of England was to be found nowhere else it would be found in his parish.

In the long run, Pusey's idea of the Church was more important than that of either Newman or Keble, for it slowly evolved during a long lifetime. It encouraged the Ritualist movement, which combined with the inspiration provided by Maurice to give England a new conception of what was the Catholic Church. Some scholars have attributed the genius of this new vision to Newman,[22] but it was the pastorally minded Pusey, rather than the abstract-theologian of Oriel College, who influenced the Church of England most.

Pusey was a member of the landed gentry, a man who could move at ease among the privileged people of his day. He spent his three-month honeymoon visiting the Southeys, the Coleridges, Sir Walter Scott, and the Bishop of Oxford. His means were sufficient for him to give £5,000 to Blomfield's Metropolitan Church's Fund in 1836, and to endow St. Saviour's, Leeds, in 1845. Pusey seemed to prize his social position, and his wealth, chiefly for the opportunity they gave him for mortification.

He was just as Augustinian in his theology as Newman, and the foundation of his religious life was his deep and abiding sense of sin.[23] Goldwin Smith described him as going 'about with a sorrowful visage and downcast eyes and looking like the embodiment of his

21. Sean O'Faolin, *Newman's Way* (1952), p. 94, notes that at Oriel, 'among all his colleagues and associates he alone was not by origin a gentleman.'

22. Carpenter, *Church and People*, p. 536: Reckitt, *Maurice to Temple*, p. 142.

23. *Pusey House Mss.*, 26 Sept., 1844, Pusey to Keble, 'amid special mercies and guardianship of God I am scarred all over and seamed with sin, so that I am a monster to myself. I loathe myself; I can feel myself only like one covered with leprosy from head to foot.'

favourite doctrine the irremissibility of post-baptismal sin'.[24] He wore a hair-shirt, longed to use the discipline, walked with his eyes on the ground, and as a final mortification—which Keble said was more of a trial to those he met than to himself—he sought never to smile.[25] But his asceticism was social as well as personal, and the example he set made a deep impression upon many people.

To make his endowments he deprived himself of both servants and carriage. He castigated the luxury in which the undergraduates and dons of the day lived, and the call for self-abnegation was a continuous theme in his sermons for well-to-do congregations. He regarded with horror worldly preferment in Church or State. In later years he wrote to W. J. Copeland about the advancement of Manning in the Roman Church: 'How strange the contrast between the outward lot of Manning and dear J. H. N., but you, I, and dear J. K. would have no doubt which and where we would rather be. Manning's is an awful gain in this world.'[26]

Pusey's father was an inflexible Tory who had ruled the little hamlet of Pusey, Berkshire, as a benevolent autocrat. Pusey's rebellious nature may have come from his reaction to his father's heavy-handedness—he even arranged the date of Pusey's wedding—but his son remembered him more for his 'pious and bounteous' character. To many in the village he seemed the ideal squire. Each winter £100 was given to the villagers for winter clothing—a gift which for many years was considered to be of legal obligation by the tenants of the cottages in the hamlet. He was renowned for his 'lavish generosity', and the example of unostentatious charity which he set was never forgotten by his son.

The gift of St. Saviour's to the city of Leeds was that of a churchman seeking to make reparation for sin—but it was also the gift of a gentleman seeking to be 'pious and bounteous', the work of an 'ideal squire' in a social situation where charity was desperately needed. It was the same religious and social impulse which led Pusey, together with his son Philip, and the Hon. C. L. Wood (later Lord Halifax), to spend the long vacation of 1866 helping to establish a cholera hospital in the parish of Bethnal Green during the epidemic of that year. The same sentiment led him into such political action as his support of Peel's bill for repeal of the Corn Laws. Most important of all it caused him to support those churchmen whom he believed were trying to act as 'squires' to the East End of London—the Ritualists.

24. Goldwin Smith, *Reminiscences*, p. 62.
25. *Life of Pusey*, III, 99–111.
26. *Pusey House Mss.*, 2 January 1870, Pusey to Copeland.

It was Pusey, not Newman, who inspired the Ritualists, and gave to the Church of England a new vision of what was the Catholic Church,—that body which brought the power of the Gospel to bear upon all aspects of man's life, both personal and social. He believed the Church could not wait for the legislature of the nation to redress social evil; nor could it wait on the bishops of the Church to lead the way in a new mission to industrial England. Parliament was dominated by men of business who seldom thought in terms of self-abnegation; churchmen now 'had the Bishops whom they desired; and when they had them, despised them'.[27] Churchmen had to be led by the Holy Spirit in a new mission to the nation, particularly to the poor who had been so long neglected by the Church. Pusey said of the Church's mission to the poor of the nation:

> She herself ought to debate upon remedies and should not leave to individual effort the work of the whole. We need missions among the poor of our towns; organized bodies of clergy living among them; licenced preachers in the streets and lanes of our cities; brotherhoods, or guilds, which should replace socialism; or sisterhoods of mercy. . . . we need clergy to penetrate our mines, to migrate with our emigrants, to shift with our shifting population, to grapple with our manufacturing system as the Apostles did with the slave system of the ancient world. . . . Beautiful as is the relation of the parish priest to his flock, lovely as are the village homes of our village pastors, and gentle as are the influences radiating from those who 'point to heaven and lead the way', yet is there now an appalling need of further organization, for a harder, more self-denying, self-sacrificing warfare, if, by God's help, we would wrest from the principalities and powers of evil, those portions of His Kingdom, of which, while unregarded by the Church, they have been taking full possession.[28]

Pusey supported the Ritualists because they alone seemed to have the spiritual fervour needed to carry through the catholic mission to the nation, as it tried to wrestle with the social problems which accompanied industrial revolution. His opposition to the jurisdiction of the State or to the policies of the bishops was not based on a theoretical rejection of secular or episcopal authority. Rather it represented Pusey's emotional response to both authorities, as they tried to curb the mission work of the Puseyites. He had come to the conclusion that the nineteenth century was too late to begin to think of giving substance to any abstract or ideal relationship of the Church with the State, or with society. If legislative acts like the Public Worship Regulation Act sought to shackle the Church's catholic mission, then they had to be transcended. When bishops were more

27. E. B. Pusey, *Councils of the Church from the Council of Jerusalem to the Council of Constantinople* (1857), p. 14.
28. *Ibid.*, pp. 4–5.

concerned with maintenance of the temporal blessings brought by establishment than they were with the sacrifices demanded by mission, they had to be passively resisted. The Church was called by Christ 'to remedy the evils which hinder or check the fulfilment of her Divine mission . . . to call forth self-sacrificing efforts, proportionate to the greatness of the needs in the whole length and breadth of the land'.[29]

Pusey never really worked out an ideal theory of the Church, what its relationship with the State should be, or how it might influence society most effectively. While he deliberated what the nature of the Church might be, his unsponsored disciples, the Ritualists, or Puseyites, began their penetration of the slums; and the rebel within Pusey rejoiced over their militancy. At the same time he did not approve their self-righteousness: 'Their line seems to me to be "We are certainly right; we shall obey our own consciences, and what we think to be right, and shall obey no authority, spiritual or temporal, which contravenes this."'[30] Nevertheless, the Tory churchman who had at one time rejoiced over affairs like Greek Independence, and the repeal of the Test and Corporation Acts, increasingly allowed himself to be identified with the Ritualist slum-priest movement. Just as his founding of St. Saviour's, Leeds, marked his transition from Tractarianism to that form of missionary churchmanship which was characteristic of early Anglo-Catholicism, so his identification with the Ritualists represented an abandonment of traditional High-Church ideas for the new nonconformity which the Puseyites represented. When the bishops in the Canterbury Convocation of 1867 passed a resolution on Ritualism, which was written in the vague language of popular denunciation, Pusey agreed with the Ritualists that 'extrajudicial censures, or contradictions, or opinions, if directed against faith or truth, condemn none but their authors'.[31] At the end of his life Pusey was allied with the Ritualists, not because of the doctrines they taught, the ritual they used, or the persecution they had endured, but because of their sense of catholic mission. He recognized that 'the Ritualists and the old Tractarians differ both in principle and in object';[32] and though he could not abide those who laid undue stress on unmeaning points of ritual, thereby irritating congregations to no purpose, by 1881—a year before his death—he was writing to the *Times* in praise of the work of Ritualist priests who then served in

29. *Ibid.*, p. 6.
30. *Pusey House Mss.*, Pusey to Wood, 9 December 1876.
31. *Life of Pusey*, IV, 214.
32. *Ibid.*, IV, 271.

the slums of the city. Whatever their failings in the eyes of authority, they were justified by the fact that they now served 'a religious population' in what had once been 'the worse localities in London'.[33]

Another right-wing theorist was W. E. Gladstone, whom Keble once called 'Pusey in a blue-coat'.[34] He had been a fervent Evangelical until he spent the long vacation of 1830 at Cuddesdon reading Hooker; and from this time he became a High-Churchman, fascinated with the idea of the Church as a visible divine institution: 'an organization Divinely charged with the maintenance of the Faith and moral law, and the administration of the sacraments'.[35] At the same time he never shared the Tractarian love of clericalism. Talk of priestly prerogatives he believed to be spiritually perilous for the clergy because it 'exalts their power at the expense of their influence . . . it increases what they cannot use, and takes from them what they could . . . it is by influence, and influence only that our clergy can be really powerful'.[36] He agreed with Dean Hook who once said about the idea of the Tractarians: 'I am afraid that many in their zeal for the Church forget Christ, and in maintaining the rights of the Clergy forget the rights of the laity: who are, as well as the Clergy, priests unto the Most High God, and who indeed have as large a portion of the Sacrifice of Prayer and Praise assigned to them in the Prayer Book as the Clergy.'[37]

His suspicion of clericalism grew in later years when he was bitterly attacked for abolishing compulsory Church rates, and advocating disestablishment of the Irish Church. In a public letter he wrote to the Bishop of Aberdeen in 1852, he quoted with approval Hooker's opinion of clericalism, and the danger it could be in the nation: 'Were it so that the clergy alone might give laws unto all the rest, forasmuch as every estate doth desire to enlarge the bounds of their own liberties, is it not easy to see how injurious this might prove to men of other conditions.'[38]

In 1833 Gladstone produced his first study of the Church, which was entitled *The State in Its Relations With the Church*. In doing so he

---

33. *Ibid.*, IV, 363.

34. Lord Irwin, *Keble*, p. 229.

35. W. E. Gladstone, *State in Its Relations With the Church* (4th edition, 1841), I, 328.

36. W. E. Gladstone, *A Letter to the Right Rev. William Skinner, D.D., Bishop of Aberdeen and primus, on the Functions of Laymen in the Church* (London, 1852), p. 25.

37. W. E. Gladstone, *Church of England and Ritualism* (1875), p. 4.

38. Gladstone, Letter to Bishop of Aberdeen, pp. 18–19. For his view of the Roman clergy *v.* W. E. Gladstone, *Rome and the Newest Fashions in Religion. Three Tracts.* (Leipzig 1875), p. 190.

was influenced by Burke, Coleridge, and Thomas Chalmers,[39] all of whom were in favour of the ecclesiastical establishment in England. But Hooker remained the main source of inspiration for his ecclesiastical thought throughout his life. From Hooker he acquired his basic idea, the 'great doctrine that the state is a person, having a conscience, cognisant of matter of religion, and bound by all constitutional and natural means to advance it'.[40] He rejected Warburton's conception of an alliance between Church and State, because in it the State was restricted 'absolutely to temporal, nay to material ends; and is consequently stripped of all its nobler attributes'.[41] Paley's idea of the Church was also rejected because it avoided recognition of the Church as a visible corporate body, and because it was utilitarian.

In his study, Gladstone decided that it was the duty of the State, because it had a conscience and was capable of deciding between truth and error, to support the true religion of the Established Church, and none other. Gladstone knew that in the nineteenth century the Church was no longer, as in Hooker's day, virtually coextensive with the commonwealth. Yet he argued that the English people were still mainly members of the Church, and that the conscience of the nation, 'the result of the general belief of the people', was still formed by the Church and its teaching. Because of this close identification of Church and State in England, the nation was unequivocally Christian. Gladstone had a 'high doctrine' of both Church and State in England.

> The State and the Church have both of them moral agencies. But the State aims at character through conduct: the Church at conduct through character; in harmony with which, the State forbids more than enjoins, the Church enjoins more than forbids. The Church brings down from heaven a divine principle of life and plants it in the centre of the human heart to work outwards and to leaven the whole mass: the State out of the fragments of primeval virtue, and the powers of the external world, constructs a partial and elementary system, corrective from without, and subsidiary to the great process of redemption and spiritual recovery which advances towards it from within.[42]

Gladstone's first study was primarily concerned with the nature of the State; but in 1840 he produced a more theological work entitled *Church Principles Considered in their Results*, which examined the

39. Chalmers was a champion of Establishment at the time of his lectures in London, 1828. *V. D.N.B.*, III, 1361.
40. Gladstone, *State in its Relations with the Church*, I, 14.
41. *Ibid.*, I, 18.
42. *Ibid.*, I, 115, as quoted in A. R. Vidler's study of Gladstone's writings on Church and State, *Orb and the Cross* (1945), p. 45.

doctrines, claims, and circumstances of the Church of England. In it he stressed the divine foundation of the visible Church, which was quite different from any sort of man-created religious association. It is the body of Christ, the organ of His redeeming action in the world, called by God for 'designed and deliberate co-operation in the government and extension of the Kingdom of Christ and the maintenance of His truth'.[43] The Church of England, 'having had the general concurrence of the temporal power, without which it could not be termed national . . . is responsible . . . as an institution . . . for the social condition at large, as being the first and paramount cause which determines it effectually towards well-being or towards the reverse'.[44] The Church ensured the Christian nature of the State. It taught reverence for the State as well as for the Church and bore 'a constant witness to the tasks assigned by God to Church and State respectively'.[45]

Gladstone's ideas were received with mixed feelings by the Tractarians. His writings came out at the time when they considered, with many other churchmen, that 'Church and State are rather at the fag end of an old alliance than identifiable terms.'[46] In the idiom of the age, this was a time for bold action, for nailing colours to the mast, for withstanding a demonic legislature in the fashion of the saints of earlier ages who had withstood the secular power and prevailed. The question that confronted the Tractarians was how the Church could be set free from the state of Erastian bondage it found itself in, so that it could act in its 'free spiritual capacity'.

Keble reviewed Gladstone's first book in the October, 1839 issue of the *British Critic*, and acknowledged his pleasure that such a champion had arisen to further the cause of the Church. 'Here we have no village theorizer, no cloistered alarmist, but a public man and a man of the world, a statesman of the highest talent for business, an orator who commands the ear of the House of Commons; so deeply impressed with the perils of our Church's position at the moment that he makes time to develop and express his views . . . of her connection with the State.'[47] But he also said that he did not think that this was the time for churchmen to be thinking in terms of the 'utility' of the Church in the nation. His fellow Tractarians also had their misgivings over Gladstone's lack of appreciation of priesthood, his men-

43. W. E. Gladstone, *Church Principles Considered in Their Results* (1840), p. 90.
44. *Ibid.*, p. 373 ff.
45. Vidler, *op. cit.*, p. 80.
46. *Life of Wilberforce*, I, 265.
47. *British Critic*, XXVI (1839), 356 ff.

tion of the natural entry of Grace into the soul of man, the self-respect of the masses, and the redemptive work of individuals. Above all they did not appreciate the idea of the State's having a personality, living and active, which 'owns no human superior'.[48]

Gladstone's theory of Church and State as it was revealed in his first book, was also critically reviewed by Macaulay in the *Edinburgh Review* of April 1839. Macaulay believed the Church of England to have been founded at the time of the Reformation, and he believed its genius was to be as latitudinarian as possible. He argued that the work of civil government should be confined to temporal matters—religion was not its business. The State was merely a collection of individuals who combined to seek some temporal end. It was certainly not, as Gladstone thought, 'a person': an organization which was 'as deliberative as an individual: at least as capable, by its nature, of discerning right and wrong'.[49] The State, to Macaulay and the Whigs whom he represented, was not directly concerned with either moral or theological doctrines. Citizens should believe what they liked without guidance or direction. They should also be allowed to do what they liked—provided they did not endanger the existence, or coherence, of the State. The State should accommodate all doctrines, and need not itself make a profession of any. Macaulay attacked Gladstone's idea by seizing on his failure to distinguish between primary and secondary human associations. His argument implied that the burden to seek religious truth rested upon any human association, not only the State: 'requiring all directors and clerks of joint stock banks, and all the members of clubs to qualify by taking the sacrament'. Macaulay also had something to say about Gladstone's embarrassing endorsement of the Church of Ireland as the established Church for that country. The Whigs had little sympathy for the proposition that 'the propagation of religious truth is one of the principal ends of government, as government'.[50]

Gladstone's *Church Principles* came out in the middle of the Tractarian controversy, but little attention was paid to it by any of the warring factions. Newman recognized that it was not a party piece, and merely said: 'Gladstone's book is not open to the objections I feared: it is doctrinaire, and (I think) somewhat self-confident; but it will do good.'[51] Macaulay thought it so theological that it was not worthy of a review.

48. Gladstone, *State in its Relationship with the Church*, I, 69.
49. *Ibid.*
50. D. C. Lathbury, *Correspondence on Church and Religion of W. E. Gladstone* (1910), I, 15.
51. Mozley, *Letters and Correspondence of J. H. Newman*, II, 321.

It may be argued that because of his great respect for the State—which may have represented an unconscious apology for his having entered politics instead of taking Holy Orders—Gladstone does not really belong in the 'right wing' of political theorists. But Keble was right in identifying him with Pusey—for he certainly had a 'high doctrine' of the Church. The rigorist High-Churchmen, such as Denison and Liddon, never trusted him because he supported Kingsley, and defended Maurice at King's College. Pusey refused to have any association with him for over two years because of his 'yielding to the inevitable' in promoting Frederick Temple of *Essays and Reviews* ill-fame. Yet they had to recognize his love for the Church, and support of the position of temporal privilege which had been granted to it by the Elizabethan settlement. He worked for the freedom of the Church in Convocation, protected the existing marriage laws against radical reform, and resisted extension of the influence of the Judicial Committee of the Privy Council in ecclesiastical affairs. He also shared the High-Church dislike of the Erastian episcopate which did so little to promote reform within the Church. During the Gorham crisis he wrote to Wilberforce to say:

> It is high time that there should be a careful argument upon the justice and morality of late ecclesiastical proceedings; that the Archbishop should be awakened of his fool's paradise and made to understand that, though reverence for his office has up to this time, in a wonderful manner, kept people silent about his proceedings, yet the time has come when a beginning must be made towards describing them without circumlocution in their true colours, and it must likewise be shown how judicial proceedings are governed by extra-judicial considerations, and a system is growing up under which ecclesiastical judges are becoming the virtual legislators of the Church while its legislature is silent.[52]

D. C. Lathbury has said of Gladstone's *State in its Relations with the Church* that it 'expresses a theory of the subject which Mr. Gladstone was outgrowing even while he was constructing it. He began the book as an Evangelical; he finished it as, in a great measure, a High Churchman.'[53] But three years after the appearance of his book, in spite of the criticism it received, he presented it in the expanded form of the fourth edition, as representative of protracted and mature thought. It is true, however, that he ceased trying to advocate his idealization of the State, or to think in terms of reviving the traditional alliance of Church and State represented by the Establish-

---

52. Russell, *Mr. Gladstone's Religious Development*, p. 31.
53. Lathbury, I, 18.

ment. But he never ceased to speak as a High-Churchman. He always believed that politics, for all its failings, was a sphere in which man could exercise his spiritual nature. At the same time he 'set to work upon the holy task of clearing, opening and establishing positive truth in the Church of England . . . and the laying of firm foundations for future union in Christendom'.[54] Gladstone had a 'high doctrine' of Church and State throughout his life, and believed his service in both was guided by God. But he could never find an ideal solution to the relationship between Church and State in the nation. Nor could he always reconcile his service to the two powers in his personal life. As Alec Vidler has so aptly remarked: 'He is a symbol of the fact that no satisfactory doctrine of the relations of the State with the Church or of a Christian politics was found in the Victorian era to take the place of the older doctrines.'[55]

Like most Victorian churchmen, Gladstone discovered that it was too late in history for the Church of England to consider a radical change in its relationship with the State, or in its place in society. He was a politician, as well as a churchman, and like Blomfield, Wilberforce, and the other realists of the age he fell back on Hooker's doctrine of Church and State. Then he devoted himself, not to abstract speculation about the ideal Church-State nexus, but to the Church's mission to make England a Christian nation.

3. The Left Wing of Theorists

IF NEWMAN, Pusey, Keble, and Gladstone provided the right wing of intellectuals who helped to form the idea of the Church in Victorian England, Thomas Arnold represented the radical thought of the ecclesiastical left wing —at least in the eyes of the Tractarians.

> I look to the full development of the Christian Church in its perfect form as the Kingdom of God, for the most effective removal of all evil, and the promotion of all good; and I can understand no perfect Church, or perfect State, without their blending into one in this ultimate form. I believe, farther, that our Fathers at the Reformation, stumbled accidentally, or rather were unconsciously led by God's Providence, to . . . the doctrine of the King's Supremacy;

54. John Morley, *Life of W. E. Gladstone* (1903), I, 382.
55. Vidler, *Orb and the Cross*, p. 155.

which is, in fact, no other than an assertion of the supremacy of the Church or Christian society over the clergy, and a denial of that which I hold to be one of the most mischievous falsehoods ever broached—that the government of the Christian Church is vested by divine right in the clergy. . . . Holding this doctrine as the very corner-stone of my political belief, I am equally opposed to Popery, High Churchism, and the claims of the Scottish Presbyterians, on the one hand; and to all the Independents and advocates of the separation, as they call it, of Church and State, on the other; the first setting up a Priesthood in the place of the Church, and the other lowering . . . Law and Government, and reducing them to a mere system of police, while they profess to wish to make the Church purer.[1]

Arnold revered the Reformation settlement of the Church of England; and, as Hooker had, he refused to separate the concept of the Church from that of the State. The State was in need of the Church for inspiration and moral guidance as it sought the highest human welfare for its citizens; and the Church was in need of the State as it attempted to subjugate evil and vindicate good. He refused to accept Warburton's view that the task of the State is only 'the conversation of body and goods'.[2] He also disliked the Evangelicals who through 'ignorance and narrow-mindedness' sought 'to keep the world and the Church ever distinct'.[3] And he was distressed by plans, like those of Lord Henley, which would have removed bishops from Parliament, and kept laymen from 'meddling' with Church doctrine: 'a compound of the worst errors of Popery and Evangelicalism combined'.[4]

Ideally he believed that a Christianized State should be a Church with its executive power responsible to a Christian legislature, which would be the supreme authority for the Church in fact and theory. Such an establishment would be possible as long as men remembered that 'the pretended distinction between spiritual things and secular is a distinction utterly without foundation.' There was no dualism in the thought of Arnold and, like his disciple, A. P. Stanley, he believed that 'the affairs of the nation, both civil and ecclesiastical were the affairs of the Church.'[5]

Arnold was troubled by the existence of Dissent, which weakened the idea of an Established Church serving all the nation. His answer to this problem was comprehension. It would be wicked to persecute Dissenters, to force them into the Established Church. But he believed

1. Stanley, *Life of Arnold*, II, 187.
2. *Ibid.*, I, 376.
3. *Ibid.*, p. 83.
4. *Ibid.*, p. 339.
5. Prothero and Bradley, *Life of A. P. Stanley*, I, 384. Stanley viewed ordination as 'the solemn appointment of important public officers'.

that within the Establishment there could be room for men to retain differing opinions and ceremonies, without their being forced to agree with doctrinal statements or practices that would exclude them.[6] He also championed the cause of the Roman Catholics,[7] but he would have denied the Jews parliamentary rights, and would have provided them with a Liberia to emigrate to—thereby keeping the State Christian. This idea of comprehension did little to endear him to the Nonconformists, who were annoyed by his scorn of their narrowness and sectarian temper. They were also suspicious of his 'liberalism', and they regretted his 'imperfect sense of the deep inherent corruption of human nature'.[8] It also upset the Tractarians, who viewed his religious ideas as 'pure Deism'—'that regenerating spirit of latitudinarianism which Dr. Arnold would invoke'.[9]

Arnold's opinion of 'priestcraft' was even more upsetting to the Tractarians. The only distinction he would have allowed between clergy and laity was that demanded by order in the Church, and he would in no way have allowed the clergy to lay claim to quasi-supernatural powers. Priesthood, he was convinced, had been completely foreign to the mind of Christ, and it was the greatest evil which had ever appeared in the history of the Church. The Tractarian idea of apostolic succession he labelled the 'heraldic view' of salvation, which guaranteed man a heavenly inheritance, like an earthly estate, through a pedigree title. He believed episcopal ordination was a legal qualification for the ministry, but hardly a spiritual one. The idea of a morally necessary priest as the mediator between God and man was 'priestcraft' or the 'essence of popery'. The 'pestilent distinction' between clergy and laity which the Tractarians promoted was anathema to him.

> The Popish and Oxford view of Christianity is, that the Church is the mediator between God and the individual: that the Church (i.e. in their sense, the Clergy) is a sort of chartered corporation, and that . . . by being attached to it, any given individual acquires such and such privileges. This is a priestcraft because it lays the stress, not on the relations of a man's heart towards God and Christ, as the Gospel does, but on something wholly artificial and formal —his belonging to a certain so-called society. . . . it claims to step in and interpose itself, as the channel of Grace and Salvation, when it certainly is not

6. Thomas Arnold, *Principles of Church Reform* (1833), p. 84.

7. Thomas Arnold, *The Christian Duty of Granting the Claims of the Roman Catholics* (1829).

8. Anonymous, *Brief Observations on the Political and Religious Sentiments of the Late Rev. Dr. Arnold* (1845), p. 6. gives the Evangelical *Record* outlook.

9. William Palmer, *Remarks on Arnold's Principles of Church Reform* (1833), p. 35.

the channel of salvation, because it is visibly and notoriously no sure channel of Grace.[10]

Arnold believed that the great threat to the Church in his day came from the Tractarians, not from the attention paid to the Church by the legislature of the nation. 'I will not say that Mr. Newman's favourite doctrines were the very Anti-Christ which corrupted Christianity; I will only say that they did not prevent its corruption—that when they were most exalted, Christian truth and Christian goodness were most depressed.'[11]

Coleridge was a formative influence in Arnold's intellectual development, and Arnold said that he longed to have the poet's mind and Cobbett's language. Certainly he received from Coleridge the vision of what could be accomplished by the clergy—who formed part of 'the clerisy', the learned of the nation—when they worked in their parishes as 'resident gentlemen'. 'To every parish throughout the kingdom there is transplanted a germ of civilization; that is in the remotest village there is a nucleus round which the capabilities of the place may crystalize and brighten. . . . the clergyman is with his parishioners and among them; he is neither in the cloistered cell nor in the wilderness; but a neighbour and a family man, whose education and rank admit him to the mansion of the rich landholder while his duties make him the frequent visitor of the farmhouse and the cottage.'[12] Arnold saw the parsonage acting as a centre of civilization, as well as a meeting place for religious people. It was to provide for the parish not only spirituality but also an example of refinement of manners, for the parson was to give his people knowledge of science and general literature.

Arnold wanted the clergy to be the educators of the nation, and the reconcilers of the social classes which had drifted far apart. He wanted them to use their connection with the privileged classes for the benefit of the oppressed in society, the lower classes which needed to be helped. Much of their work must be secular in its nature, but if the Church was to be truly concerned for the whole of man's existence, then the clergy could not confine their activities to narrowly spiritual work: 'Every outward thing having a tendency to affect man's moral character, either for the better or for the worse, and this especially holding good with respect to riches or poverty, economical questions

10. *Life of Arnold*, II, 66.
11. Thomas Arnold, *Sermons* (1878), p. xxvi.
12. S. T. Coleridge, *Constitution of Church and State According to the Idea of Each* (1830). p. 11.

in all their wide extent, fall directly under the cognizance of those whose object is to promote man's moral welfare.'[13]

He never believed that only the clergy of the Church were responsible for the moral well-being of the nation. The clergy might take the lead in enlightening the rich about the need to educate the poor, for the good of the commonwealth, but the laity had to carry out much of this programme. The Church had to rid itself of the idea of priesthood, 'and to restore its disfranchised members—the laity—to the discharge of their proper duties'. The Church would become a reality, and the nation become Christian, only when the laity awoke 'to their true position and duties'.[14]

As we have seen in Chapter VI, Thomas Arnold was the first real prophet of social reform in the Victorian Church; and the mission, rather than the form of the Church, was always of great importance to him. With social revolution threatening the nation, the Church had no time to prate about apostolic succession, or the glories of the English constitution. It was time that the Church ceased to content itself with lecturing the poor. The time had now come for it to speak boldly to the rich—to challenge them to serve Christ and the nation, through education. He wanted both clergy and laity to turn from purely ecclesiastical concerns—whether they were the scholastic activities of the Tractarians, or the anti-slavery and missionary-society work of the Evangelicals. They had to realize that all the worst evils of slavery and heathenism were to be found in England—and that the Christian Gospel provided the great remedy for these evils, when Christians were willing to bring it to those who were in need.

Arnold's idea of the Church was important, for it was easily understood by the untheological young Englishman, like the young men of Rugby's sixth form who did so much to promote Arnold's religion of 'service'. But it was never appreciated by Newman and the Tractarians, who could not identify themselves with Arnold's passionate love of humanity and his equally passionate distrust of ecclesiastical systems. Newman, and most of the Tractarian leaders, openly feared Arnold, especially after he wrote his famous article entitled 'The Oxford Malignants and Dr. Hampden' for the *Edinburgh Review*, and chose to view their persecution of Hampden as 'moral wickedness' rather than intellectual error. As far as Arnold was concerned, their

13. Thomas Arnold, *Miscellaneous Works* (1845), p. 125.
14. Arnold, *Sermons*, I, xliv, 'Christian Life, Its Course, Its Hindrances and Its Helps'.

idealism could be dismissed as 'busy, turbulent and narrow-minded', where it was not clearly uncharitable.

When the Tractarian leaders and Arnold openly broke with one another, the latter was greatly hurt by Keble's refusal to correspond with him, although he was the godfather of the young Matthew Arnold. Shortly before his death he wrote to Keble to say:

> I am sure that you are not right in breaking off all intercourse with an old friend; in separating yourself from a member of your Church on your own individual authority . . . thus to claim as it were the Church's power of Ex- communication, and pronounced for yourself what opinions ought not to be tolerated as if you were set to judge and to govern. . . . you and your friends constantly assume that you are the only persons who love Christ, and that those who differ from you are merely following their own devices,. . . this I will say confidently, that my opinions have been formed from the Scriptures on no light or careless study of them, and that I sincerely believe not that Christ tolerates, but that He commands me to think of His Church and Ministers as I do, and to protest earnestly against these views which I believe you are advocating. But I am sure also that He commands me to love all that love Him, let the errors of opinion be what they may.[15]

The main source of conflict between Arnold and the Tractarians was their differing view of priesthood. Arnold's inability to compre- hend what the Tractarians were seeking helps to explain the attitude of most members of the educated classes towards them, and towards the Puseyites when they appeared—for most churchmen understood Arnold and appreciated what he was about. It was not that Arnold was simply an Erastian—he had, for example, definite reservations about Gladstone's idea of the State being a divinely appointed govern- ment with a conscience of its own. Nor was he simply an ecclesiastical utilitarian, although he believed the end of an ideal Church-State relationship 'to be the promoting and securing a nation's highest happiness'.[16] He opposed the political economy of his day 'which maintains the game laws, and in agriculture and trade seems to think that there is no such sin as covetousness, and that if a man is not dis- honest, he has nothing to do but to make all the profit of his capital that he can'.[17] He also distrusted the new ethos of secularism which was appearing in the University of London, because he believed it was lacking in morality.

Arnold's real importance for his generation was that he opposed

15. R. J. Campbell, *Thomas Arnold* (1927), p. 15, undated letter to Keble.
16. Thomas Arnold, *An Inaugural Lecture on the Study of Modern History* (1841), p.19.
17. *Life of Arnold*, I, 274.

the Tractarians in the way that Marsiglio of Padua had once opposed the medieval papacy. He castigated Newman for discrediting scripture in order to exalt the Church, for hating the nineteenth century, for dwelling on the virtues of the Middle Ages, and for elevating the office of the clergy. He objected to the narrow intolerance of the Tractarians, which seemed to him to 'put Christ's Church and Christ's Sacraments and Christ's ministers in the place of Christ himself'.[18] Arnold advanced his ideas in his *Principles of Church Reform*, which came out about the same time that Keble preached his Assize Sermon on National Apostasy. Later in the same year he brought out his *Postscript to Principles of Church Reform*. His ideas created more of a stir in the general public than those of the Tractarians, largely because he took for granted the connection of Church and State which history had bequeathed to England—and sought to make the Established Church of utilitarian moral value in the nation. Arnold could not understand how a Church could justify its existence, let alone claim the title catholic, unless it influenced all parts of society in both a spiritual and a temporal sense. As Bishop Sandford of Gibraltar, one of his disciples, put it later in the century, for the clergy to be catholic they 'had to justify their titles and positions as ministers of the National Church'.[19]

4. The Middle Way

ARNOLD always admitted his indebtedness to Coleridge, and praised highly works such as his *Aids to Reflection* of 1825, and his study of Church and State. But Arnold was not the only churchman who was greatly indebted to Coleridge for his idea of 'the clerisy' and his insight into the social evils which were accompanying the industrial revolution. Coleridge was a churchman who said he thought 'the fate of the Reform Bill in itself of comparatively minor importance; the fate of the National Church occupies my mind with greater intensity'.[1] But he was also aware of the threat of class warfare in the nation: 'The

18. *Ibid.*, II, 42.
19. C. W. Sandford, *Duties of Clergy as Ministers of the National Church* (1875), p. 3.
1. S. T. Coleridge, *Table Talk and Omniana* (1917), p. 167.

hollow murmur of the earthquake within the bowels of our own commonwealth may strike direr terror than ever did the tempest of foreign warfare.'[2]

It was the Broad-Churchmen who thought of the Church chiefly in terms of its ethical importance, rather than as the guardian of metaphysical doctrines, and were concerned with its civilizing mission—particularly its value as an agency of social reform and class conciliation. Their chief representative was F. D. Maurice, who also admitted his indebtedness to Coleridge. The Broad-Churchmen sought to provide a *via media* between the extreme interpretations of the role of the Church in the nation provided by Newman and Arnold. They were really closer to Arnold than to Newman, because of their dislike of ecclesiastical systems of thought; but like Coleridge they had a 'high doctrine' of the Church: 'the sustaining, correcting, befriending opposite of the world'.[3] Coleridge recognized that 'Christianity without a Church exercising spiritual authority is vanity and delusion.'[4]

At the time that Coleridge showed interest in the Church of England, it seemed to many people that it was spiritually at its nadir. The *Westminster Review* which preached pure Benthamism dismissed the ideas of Coleridge as amiable Tory fantasy. 'It is easy for a writer of imagination to frame (like Mr. Coleridge) a theory of Toryism, finding a good use for everything that the Tories put to a bad one, and to dream pleasantly enough of a Church and an aristocracy such as might be had in Utopia, but which the partisans of the Church and the aristocracy as they are now would be the last to stir a finger for.'[5]

Many churchmen paid attention to Coleridge's ideas, however; though at times they were difficult to understand. One of those who were directly influenced by them was Julius Charles Hare, the liberal historian and translator (with Connop Thirlwall) of Niebuhr's *History of Rome*, and one of the few English intellectuals acquainted with the new climate of scientific thought in Germany. He was a personal friend of both Coleridge and Thomas Arnold, and the young Maurice came under his influence when he was still an undergraduate at Cambridge. He later married Maurice's sister, and in 1840 was appointed Archdeacon of Lewes.

2. S. T. Coleridge, *The Friend: a Series of Essays* (1818), I, 212, his warning of the year 1810.

3. Coleridge, *Constitution of Church and State* (1820), p. 133.

4. S. T. Coleridge, *Aids to Reflection* (1825), p. 293. Coleridge was very vague on the difference between the Christian and the National Church which he believed coincided as a 'blessed accident' in England.

5. *Westminster Review*, XXVIII (October, 1837), 23.

Hare's idea of the Church was like that of Coleridge and Arnold, a reflection of the traditional view which came from Hooker. Coleridge had always viewed actual institutions as temporary and imperfect embodiments of an 'idea' that was slowly revealing itself on earth—the city of God. Hare also looked upon the institutions of his age in this way, and did not become excited, as did the Tractarians, over the secular power's exercising undue authority in spiritual matters. He believed this was inevitable as the Spirit at work in both State and Church modified the nature of both of them—the secular power gradually becoming more and more spiritualized while the spiritual power grew more secular. Hare refused to regard the cloister as something set up in opposition to the crowd, and argued that one of the blessings of the Reformation was the breaking down of the artificial difference established between what was considered to be secular and what was spiritual in the world.[6]

Because of this principle of unity, Hare showed little appreciation of the Tractarian concern for purely ecclesiastical affairs. He believed that as long as churchmen were passionately concerned about authority and infallibility in the Church, and similar abstract problems, they would have little time to spend on what was desperately needed—a mission to civilize the nation, and to ease the evils brought to society by industrialism. He longed 'to change the uneasy consciousness of certain undefined rights which exist in churchmen into a conscience which shall be alive to their obligations, social as well as individual'.[7]

Hare argued that churchmen had to find a right boundary between the undue appreciation and the inordinate exaggeration of the authority of the Church.[8] As long as the Tractarians were absorbed in their 'system-making' theology, they would add to the party strife that had appeared in the Church, by seeking to impose their ecclesiastical views on churchmen. What they had to realize was the need for the Church to civilize as well as spiritualize the nation; that the 'citizen of heavenly kingdom must be the best citizen of the earthly.'[9] What the Church should immediately concern itself with was the bringing of its spiritual and temporal blessings to the lower classes of the nation. Hare agreed with Coleridge, who had said:

6. Hare, *Victory of Faith*, has an introduction entitled 'Hare's Position in the Church' by Maurice, pp. xvii–cxxxii.
   7. *Ibid.*, p. lxxv.
   8. Hare, *Contest with Rome*, pp. 151–52; this was a charge to the clergy of the Lewes archdeaconry made in the visitation of 1851.
   9. Hare, *Victory of Faith*, p. lxxiii.

'The Church ought to be a mediator between the people and the government, between the poor and the rich. As it is, I fear the Church has let the hearts of the common people be stolen from it.'[10] But the Church could only do this if it opposed the commercial spirit of the age, which created class division—an approach to the problem which was also derived directly from Coleridge.[11] Somehow the Church had to implant in the trading class of the nation, which was now so politically, economically, and socially powerful, the Christian virtue which would overcome the selfishness of the commercial spirit of the age. Then the privileged in society would use their temporal advantages to help the poor of the nation, for the ultimate benefit of all. 'In the middle classes this is especially needful in these times, because the thirst after gain, and the spirit of competition, which have lately been corrupting the trade of England, have beguiled so many of our tradesmen, whose character for honourable dealing formerly stood so high, into all manner of fraudulent tricks. Unless this spirit be checkt, unless these frauds be represt, the glory of England will wane and pass away.'[12]

Maurice carried on the thought of Coleridge and Hare, to become the most significant Anglican theologian of his generation. He failed to impress some of his contemporaries—John Stuart Mill, for example, thought he wasted his time and talents as a theologian: 'There was more intellectual power wasted in Maurice than in any other of my contemporaries. Few of them certainly have had so much to waste.'[13] Leslie Stephen found his mind tortuous, and chose to reject traditional Christianity rather than try to understand the interpretation of the faith provided by Maurice for the Victorians: 'Of all the muddle-headed, intricate, futile persons I have ever studied, he was about the most utterly bewildering.'[14] One has sympathy for both of these critics, for Maurice is often difficult to follow in his writings. His work was largely dictated, and consists of lectures or sermons to be heard, not read. Many of the ideas in these addresses have now become commonplace in the Church, and he seems at times to be labouring what to our generation is obvious. Another obvious criticism of his work is its lack of form. Maurice disliked 'systematic' thought on principle: 'When once a man begins to build a system,

10. Coleridge, *Table Talk*, p. 125, his view of 8 Sept. 1830.
11. S. T. Coleridge, *Lay Sermon to Higher and Middle Classes on the Existing Distresses and Discontents* (1817), pp. 97–100.
12. J. C. Hare, *Education the Necessity of Mankind* (1851), p. 26.
13. John Stuart Mill, *Autobiography* (1873), pp. 153–54.
14. Maitland, *Life and Letters of Leslie Stephen*, p. 240.

the very gifts and qualities which might serve in the investigation of truth, become the greatest hindrances to it. He must make the different parts of the scheme fit into each other; his dexterity is shown not in detecting facts, but in cutting them square.'[15]

Maurice's theology was marked by some characteristics which could not be ignored. Certainly his contemporaries did not overlook them. First of all, there was no dualism in his theology—and this distressed both the Evangelicals and the Tractarians, as they were influenced greatly by St. Augustine. In the Evangelical school, William Wilberforce in 1797 had given his co-religionist what was almost a hand-book of popular theology, and there is no denying the dualistic outlook in it: 'We should not go too far if we were to assert that it [the corruption of human nature] lies at the very root of all true Religion, and still more that it is eminently the basis and ground-work of Christianity'.[16] The world and the flesh were of the devil, and were to be denied, that man's spirit might be free to worship in spirit and in truth. Newman, Keble, and Pusey, and most of the Tractarians shared this outlook. Newman's view of the natural order we have noted, as well as Pusey's obsession with sin. Keble spoke of 'self-abhorrence as a duty, a necessity, a joy'.[17] Maurice, however, viewed this over-emphasis on rejection of the world and human sin as a perversion of the Christian Faith.

He said that both the Evangelicals and the Tractarians made the mistake of making the existence of evil, particularly of human sin, the very ground of their creed. The Fall of Adam seemed more important to them than the regeneration of the world by Christ. Maurice recognized the Fall as a fact which could not be denied, but Christ, not Adam was the root of humanity. The union of God with His Creation, in Christ, was the central mystery of the universe, and nothing was more important than this divine activity. Because of the Incarnation, sin—the condition of separation from, and rebellion against, God—was not man's true state. The Christ who had come to the world in the Incarnation was the head of every man, not only of those who believed in Him, and His activity was universal: 'Mankind stands not in Adam but in Christ . . . the inspirer of all right thoughts, the guide into all truth by His Spirit.'[18] Christ was recognized only in the Church, but he was still the sovereign of every social order.

15. F. D. Maurice, *Lectures on the Ecclesiastical History of the First and Second Centuries* (1854), p. 222.

16. William Wilberforce, *Practical View of Christianity* (1797), p. 24.

17. W. Lock, *John Keble* (1893), p. 233.

18. *Life of Maurice*, pp. 358–59.

Maurice condemned as Manichaeism the idea that the world was an alien society from which the Church of religious people was radically separated. He was convinced that there could be no real separation between nature and grace, the natural and the supernatural, humanity and redeemed humanity, because Christ Incarnate was the Redeemer of all life.

> There are many Christians who would persuade us that the life of a Nation is what they call a secular thing; that it may be very well on mere earthly ground to care for the land in which we have been born and nurtured . . . but that if we would turn our minds to heavenly contemplations and be in the true sense servants of God, we must be looking to a time when all that belongs to us as citizens shall have passed away. . . . I solemnly deny that a Nation is a secular thing . . . if by 'secular' is meant that which belongs to the fashion of a particular age—that which shuts out the acknowledgment of the per-manent and the eternal—that I grant is hostile to Christian Faith, that is the 'evil world' against which we are to fight. But one of the greatest weapons which God has given us . . . is the assurance that the Nation has lived, lives now, and will live in Him, who was, and is, and is to come.[19]

Because he believed the State to be as much God's creation as the Church, Maurice was not upset by matters like the State's insisting at ordination that the clergy should subscribe to the Thirty-nine Articles. He noted that most members of the Church, the laity, did not have to subscribe to them. They were not 'terms of Communion', but a right which the State had to protect the clergy of the Church from a growth of superstition among them. The Gospel protected man from selfish principles of heart and mind, but the Law of the State was there to protect man from the selfish lives of his neighbours. Because the Church and the State worked together to protect citizens from evil within and without, and the people welcomed the Christian faith in England, he was convinced that men had as much right to call England a holy nation as the prophets who once called Judaea holy.[20]

The Church was the body of men who comprehended what God had done for them in the Incarnation. Anyone whose eyes were opened and who understood that he was redeemed was a member of it. But the Church was in no way separated from the rest of society; it was an integral part of it. He could not understand the idea of the Church, established by Christ, which was 'not to love the world, not to save the world, not to convince the world, but to set itself up as a rival competitor to the world, to plot against the world, to undermine

19. F. D. Maurice, *Ground and Object of Hope for Mankind* (1868), p. 45 ff.
20. F. D. Maurice, *Sermons on the Sabbath Day* (1853), p. 71.

the world'.[21] He opposed the system of ecclesiastical thought which the Tractarians developed in Oxford, not only because it separated the Church from the rest of the nation, but because it was so abstract, 'demanding little of its votaries that is positive except an unbounded sympathy with Laud and Charles I'.[22]

> He [Newman] appears to have felt strongly twelve years ago, that he was sent into the world to resist the progress of Rationalism; that the prevalent English system afforded no barrier against it; that we did however possess an adequate barrier in the Apostolic constitution, which we had forgotten or made light of; in the books of the Fathers which our old divines had held sacred; in the reverence for sacraments. . . . He finds the barriers he thought would preserve us from Rationalism insufficient. Is he not right? Are they not insufficient? Will a mere belief in the Fathers or in Succession avail us to answer the question, 'Is GOD really among us or no'? Will Sacraments avail, if we look at them apart from Him, if they do not testify of His presence. The Rationalist has gone beneath all visible things, and has asked what is at the ground of them. If we can, in deepest awe, but also with calmness and certainty give the answer, all forms and orders and visible things will repeat it.[23]

Maurice said that the answer to be given by the Church to the question—what is the ground of all being?—was Christ.

He believed that Newman and all those who promoted religion instead of showing God to the world were guilty of heresy: 'We have been dosing our people with religion when what they want is not this but the living God.'[24] The theologians of the Church were to seek for the evidence of the compassion of God at work in the world in the ordinary life of man, not in the abstract speculations of academic churchmen. 'I am convinced that theology will be a mere *hortus siccus* for schoolmen to entertain themselves with, till it becomes associated once more with the Life of nations and humanity; that politics will be a mere ground on which despots and democrats, and the tools of both, play with the morality and happiness of their fellow-beings, till we seek again for the ground of them in the nature and purposes of the eternal God.'[25] The Tractarians might view the Establishment as bondage, and feel that it forced the Church into 'adaptation to the maxims of our own time', but Maurice believed the secular involvement forced upon the Church by the Establishment

21. F. D. Maurice, *Sermons Preached in Lincoln's Inn Chapel* (1891), I, 249.
22. Maurice, *Thoughts on Conscientious Subscription* . . . (1845), p. 29.
23. F. D. Maurice, *Epistle to the Hebrews* (1846), p. cxxvii–cxxviii of his Introduction, 'Review of Mr. Newman's Theory of Development'.
24. *Life of Maurice*, I, 369.
25. F. D. Maurice, *Gospel of St. John* (1857), p. 475. Cf. *Kingdom of Christ* (1838), III, 319.

to be a blessing. Theology had no meaning unless it referred to the life man lived here upon earth: 'The test of all principles affecting to be moral and human must be their application to the circumstances in which we are placed.'[26]

Maurice argued that the task of the theologian was 'to dig'—to expose the power of the Incarnate Christ at work in God's creation: 'to show that economy and politics . . . must have a ground beneath themselves, that society is not to be made anew by arrangements of ours, but is to be regenerated by finding the law and ground of its order and harmony. . . . the Kingdom of Heaven is to men the great practical existing reality which is to renew the earth. . . . to preach the Gospel of that Kingdom, the fact that is among us, and is not to be set up at all, is my calling and business.'[27] All that Maurice did, in his theological writing, his educational experiments, and in ventures like his co-operatives, was an attempt to expose the Divine compassion at work. The evidence he exposed through his 'digging' he believed to be of more use to the Church, and to society, than the speculations of the Tractarian schoolmen who sought to change State and society by re-establishing the authority of a clerical hierarchy.

Both the Church and the State suffered when they tried to live separate lives. They had to unite in the common task of 'raising the people of England out of their brutality and idolatry . . . to a new and higher life . . . a Kingdom of Heaven, of which God claimed them all as subjects in this present state'.[28] This Kingdom was already in existence in the National Church, which had all the signs of a spiritual and universal Kingdom, but it was also potentially present in the lives of those who did not recognize what God had done for man in Christ.

> He viewed the Church not only as the home of the redeemed, but as the sign that God had redeemed the whole human race and that the whole human race was potentially in Christ. This led them to combine an insistence upon the definite character of the signs of the Church's constitution with an unwillingness to define the Church's present boundaries. Asked about the limits of the Church he answers, 'I cannot answer the question; I believe only One can answer it; I am content to leave it with Him.'[29]

Men would identify themselves with his Kingdom, and raise themselves into their full manhood when the 'digging' of churchmen

26. Maurice, *Social Morality*, p. 371.
27. *Life of Maurice*, II, 137–38.
28. F. D. Maurice, 'On Newman's Grammar of Assent', *Contemporary Review*, May 1870, XIV, 171.
29. Ramsey, *F. D. Maurice and the Conflicts of Modern Theology*, p. 34. The quotation is from Maurice's *Epistle to the Hebrews*, p. cxxiv.

uncovered the Divine compassion at work in the circumstances of their ordinary lives. Many intellectual movements of the age contributed to this exposure of the Divine at work; they were 'half-lights to be cleansed and fulfilled'.[30] The one exception was provided by the Tractarians. They opposed 'the spirit of voluntary association' —which was the spirit of the age—by 'the spirit of submission to Church authority', which was the 'childlike spirit of the fathers'. As long as churchmen were diverted from their task of witnessing to the Kingdom as it was revealed in their generation, as 'the ever-living and acting Spirit of God', they were in error. When they spoke of opposition between the mission of Church and that of State, they reflected the spirit of a former age—and those who were obsessed by it were kept from serving the mission of the Church in their time.[31]

Within society Maurice believed the middle class had the greatest opportunity to serve because of its wealth and political power. It had to be converted for England to become a truly religious nation. When he wrote to Derwent Coleridge, the Principal of St. Mark's College, Chelsea, to acknowledge his indebtedness to S. T. Coleridge, he said: 'If you are permitted to raise up a body of wise and thoughtful teachers out of our trading classes, you will do more for the Church than all the persons together who are writing treatises about it'.[32]

By the time of *Lux Mundi*, the Christian Social Union, and the Guild of St. Matthew, churchmen had begun to 'wake-up to' Maurice, and to possess a permanently troubled social conscience. This new awareness is revealed in the exhortations given by the much-maligned Archbishop Tait to the clergy and churchwardens during his visitations of his diocese. In his first charge he urged them to forsake party differences, to press on with the mission of the Church to the nation. The Church was 'an endowment for the teaching of the Christian religion to the nation', and the questions for churchmen to ask themselves were not the abstract theological truths which were of such concern to many, but rather the soul-searching required of every Christian missioner: 'Am I, in the sphere in which God has placed me, discharging my duty and *responsibility* to the flock of Christ? Am I attending to the poor? . . . am I determined, God helping me, that the Church of England shall at all events have this strength—that it has in my person a godly, self-denying and persevering minister? If so, if this spirit spreads among us, our Zion is secure.'[33]

30. *Ibid.*
31. *Life of Maurice*, I, 226.
32. *Kingdom of Christ* (1958), II, 364. This is taken from Maurice's dedication to the second edition (1842) of the *Kingdom of Christ*.
33. A. C. Tait, *Present Position of the Church of England* (1873), p. 41.

Tait had often listened to Maurice preach at Lincoln's Inn, and he had been influenced as much by him as he had by Thomas Arnold.[34] Like both of them he refused to consider 'a counter system of religious or intellectual thought'[35] to that produced by the Tractarians. As he said in his second visitation in 1876, 'this is not an age in which Christians can afford to quarrel.'[36] The clergy and laity of the Church were to be 'learned, able, religious and zealous', dedicated in their opposition to 'materialistic atheism' as they struggled against vice, and the ignorance of the multitude. But above all, the clergy and laity were to represent the Church—the great social catalyst of the nation—where the social classes could meet and the tension between them be eased, as Christian morality was accepted by all. The Church of England was not to be a class Church, but the Church of the nation, where social grievances as well as personal failings could be overcome: 'The whole of society in this country is charged with dangerous elements from disputes between employer and employed. . . . Our clergy and laity ought to act together to appease strife.'[37]

When Tait heard of the death of Maurice, his thoughts were shared by most churchmen. He wondered who would fill his place, to give to the Church, not only his piety, but the 'remarkable breadth and depth' of his insight into what was Christianity.[38]

5. *The Victorian View of the Church*

WHEN THE ideological conflict within the Church began to ease in the 1880's—because of the demand of society that the Church 'get on with' its service to the nation—the 'operative' idea of the Church which emerged, and upon which the mission of the Church was founded, was still essentially that of Hooker. It is difficult to escape this conclusion. The nation as a whole was weary of ecclesiastical wrangling, and both the State and the parties within the Church were

34. *Life of Tait*, I, 164.
35. *Ibid.*, p. 106.
36. A. C. Tait, *Some Thoughts on the Duties of the Established Church of England as a National Church* (1876), p. 21.
37. *Ibid.*, p. 96.
38. *Life of Tait*, II, 581.

willing to put aside any attempt to alter radically the traditional Church-State relationship. Sober consideration of the alternatives to the *via media* led most churchmen to the conclusion that the Establishment could assist as well as inhibit the new sense of mission which they felt. They agreed with the Cambridge liberals of 1885, Mandell Creighton, Henry Bradshaw, A. T. Lyttleton, and A. J. Hort, that, for all its failings, the Establishment was still a blessing. 'The influence which connection with the State exercises on the religion taught and practised by the Church . . . is a powerful antidote to the inclination to confine religion within the limits of individual emotion or belief, and keeps us a sense of the intimate relations between the Christian faith and character on the one hand and all human interests and social duties on the other.'[1]

There was much to be said for the Church when it was viewed as a 'great national society for the promotion of goodness'[2]—certainly this idea was preferable to the alternatives suggested by 'fierce Protestantism, fierce Rationalism and fierce Catholicism'.[3] The Victorian churchman thought little of those who would turn the Church into a fellowship of the saints to please the Evangelicals, or into a giant mechanics' institute to satisfy the Benthamite mentality, or into a private preserve of the clergy to suit the Tractarians. The parson's freehold, or the control of ecclesiastical affairs exercised by common-law courts might be irksome—but they did protect both the individual and minority parties from any fanatical 'cleansing of the Temple'. No *Syllabus of Errors* came out of the Church of England in the nineteenth century, but rather *The Guardian, Essays and Reviews,* and *Lux Mundi*. There were also the prophetic voices of men like Arnold, Maurice, Pusey, and the Ritualists. Above all, the restrictions of the Establishment, the fact that History could not be undone without a constitutional revolution, forced churchmen to accept the yoking of Church and State, and to get on with their task of being 'the clerisy' in the nation. Those who actively promoted this mission, like the early Christian Socialists, the Ritualists, or the Settlement House churchmen, were at least protected by the Establishment from those who would have opposed what they were about. It may even be argued that when the idea of the Catholic Church as that body which was concerned with universality of mission, not authority, began to be widely accepted, the Establishment encouraged this mission. After

1. L. Creighton, *Life of Mandell Creighton*, I, 349.
2. William Robbins, *Ethical Idealism of Matthew Arnold* (1959), p. 51.
3. *Ibid.*, p. 220.

all, as most thoughtful churchmen recognized, the Church was Established for just this purpose—to serve all classes, through religion and education, to provide them with the moral answer to all their spiritual and temporal needs.

When an attempt is made to assess the contribution made by the representatives of the various church parties to the operative idea of the Church, which gave England its golden age of pastoral work, it becomes clear that Newman's views were least welcomed. The Victorian churchman did not want any radical separation of the spiritual or the secular elements of society, nor did he welcome clericalism in any form. As Bishop Wand has said of popular religion in England: 'The typical Englishman regards religion as something intensely practical. It is a life to be lived in the world. It is identical with his duties as husband, father, citizen. Consequently he is suspicious of any teaching that seems to make of religion a thing apart, that sets a wide gulf between the Church and the world.'[4] In fact, as nineteenth-century experience showed, the English churchman was not really interested in working out in the abstract what the nature of the Church is, its relationship with the State, or its function in society. He had inherited a Church as he had a State, and his concern was to have each of them perform its function to the betterment of society. When a crisis came, like that of the 1830's, he was more impressed by the counsel of Thomas Arnold, or the 'muddling through' churchmanship of Bishop Blomfield, than he was by the theories coming out of Oxford.

The one exception to the almost complete rejection of Tractarian ideology was the English churchman's reluctant toleration of the new justification found for episcopacy—the resurrected doctrine of apostolic succession. The acceptance of this grew as the social influence of the bishops waned. 'The bishops who succeed to the Apostles by an ordination which makes them their representatives are the possessors of that sacerdotal authority and grace with which Christ endowed His Church and which is necessary for her existence. The plentitude of the priesthood is in every bishop.'[5] As we have seen the Anglican episcopate gradually accepted the idea that apostolic succession resided in the bishop's office not only because of ideological conviction, but also because it realized how useful the theory could be. Ideas of the plentitude of ministerial authority being in the bishop, and the clergy receiving a diminished commission, were

4. J. W. C. Wand, *Second Reform* (1953), p. 57.
5. Charles Gore, *The Church and the Ministry* (1882), p. 51.

of benefit in a generation which rejected the authority of the State in spiritual affairs.

Perhaps the higher doctrine of the Church held by most Victorian churchmen could also be attributed, indirectly, to the appearance of Tractarianism. Newman, Pusey, Keble, and their generation of High-Churchmen challenged every party to consider the nature of the Church and its role in the nation. Out of this examination came a general rejection of the Latitudinarianism of the previous century. Even Thomas Arnold, who was so anxious for the Church to be of service to society, could hardly be dismissed as merely an Erastian apologist for the Establishment. 'I would unite one half of the Archbishop of Dublin's theory with one half of Mr. Gladstone's; agreeing cordially with Mr. Gladstone in the moral theory of the State, and agreeing as cordially with the Archbishop with what I will venture to call the Christian theory of the Church, and deducing from the two the conclusion that the perfect State and the perfect Church are identical.'[6]

During the century more and more churchmen realized that the Church was not an appanage of the State, a branch of the Home Civil Service, but a society with a spiritual authority of its own. It could no longer be considered the utilitarian body that Paley had reckoned it to be. There were churchmen who argued that Hooker's identification of Church and State could still be maintained, and that there was no need to talk of the corporate identity, authority, or mission of the spiritual body. Parliament might have taken over the prerogative in ecclesiastical affairs once held by the godly prince, and that same Parliament might now have among its members many opposed to all that the Established Church stood for, but the nature and function of the Church in the nation remained substantially the same. As Canon Shirley has said: 'The mere fact that the process of history has transferred to the Cabinet what was once the ecclesiastical prerogative of Elizabeth, no more destroys the nature of the Church of England than the transfer of the prerogatives of mercy to the Home Secretary jeopardizes the life of any individual.'[7] But the fact of the matter was that Parliament in industrial England had less and less time to devote to ecclesiastical affairs. Like Lord Grey in 1832, it wanted the bishops to put their house in order, not to do it for them. The embarrassment caused by the Public Worship Regulation Act revealed

6. Thomas Arnold, *Introductory Lectures on Modern History* (1842), p. 66. The 'Archbishop of Dublin's theory' referred to is Richard Whately's *Letters on the Church by an Episcopalian* (1826), a high doctrine of the Church.
7. Shirley, *Richard Hooker and Contemporary Political Ideas*, p. 242.

the general desire for churchmen to look after their own affairs. The State welcomed the co-operation of the Church, as churchmen sought to save the nation from class warfare, and to bring some level of civilization to the masses through education and moral exhortation; but it increasingly chose to leave to churchmen the internal affairs of the Church.

The truth of the situation was that Victorian churchmen found themselves living in a pluralistic society. The Church was still the most important corporation in the nation, but only one of many. Its mission was still largely identified with that of the State, and it sought to serve all of society, even when it was rejected. But it was impossible to try to identify it completely with the State as Hooker had once done, and Arnold would still have liked to do.

Experience showed churchmen that any attempt to delineate the boundaries of the Church was fruitless. It only succeeded in fostering party warfare which held up the mission of the Church. When the Church became introverted, and engrossed in abstract theological speculation about its nature and function, it ceased to be catholic. It failed to carry out its mission to 'baptize' each secular movement in society, and to give it a spiritual direction. Though as a body the Church was no longer co-extensive with the State, its mission was to all people of England, and to all parts of society. To try to reconcile the contradictions in this situation through some ideal scheme, or through disestablishment, would have the immediate effect of altering the mission of the Church and its nature. Party warfare in the Victorian Church revealed clearly that when churchmen became obsessed with ecclesiastical problems such as the source of authority in the Church, the mission of the Church faltered, and it lost its catholicity.

6. Nonconformity and the Church   THE EXISTENCE of Nonconformity in England forced churchmen to recognize that they were living in a new pluralistic society, where the Church was the most important corporation, but one whose services were not welcomed by a large part of the population. It was all very well for ecclesiastical theorists to try to maintain some form of

Hooker's vision, at least in terms of the mission of the Church, but the presence of Dissenters and their chapels could hardly be ignored. The Victorian parson took for granted that he was responsible for the spiritual welfare of every baptized soul in his parish, but many of his 'parishioners' had little use either for him or his ministrations.

When Dissenters were so numerous, could it not be argued that if Victorian England was peculiarly a Christian nation, its faith reflected a widespread 'Nonconformist conscience', rather than the ideology of 'service' which was propagated by the Church? Many of the middle class who were 'ensouled' during the century were Nonconformist, and it would seem reasonable to assume that the social policy of Dissent came from the thought of its leaders, not from the Church.

It could never be denied that Nonconformity carried out a great deal of the 'Christianizing' of Victorian England,[1] but for various reasons, which we will now examine, the evidence seems to indicate that much of its ideology of national mission was inspired by the Church. Although the strife between Churchmen and Dissenters only began to flag late in the century, there was a great deal of co-operation between the Church and the various Nonconformist bodies in both evangelizing and social reform. In fact, most Dissenters accepted the necessary existence of the Church. They might choose to ignore, or modify its theological teachings, or its social policies, or even the meddling in their affairs attempted by the village parson—but no Dissenting body tried to establish itself as a national substitute for the Church. In practice, most Nonconformists were not much farther removed from the Establishment than were some parties in the Church—such as the Ritualists.

The religious census which was undertaken by Horace Mann in 1851 indicated that the greatest concentration of Nonconformists was to be found in the cities—in rural areas the Church provided 66.5 per cent of all pew-sittings for worship, but only 46 per cent in urban centres.[2] At first they tended to draw their numbers from the lower middle class of the population, small shopkeepers, artisans, and small farmers.[3] This pattern continued throughout the century, and English Dissent became almost a class religion. As Elie Halévy

1. Rupert E. Davies, *Methodism* (1963), 121 says Nonconformity's emphasis was on individual salvation. This 'atomistic' doctrine of salvation gave people like the Methodists 'an undue preoccupation with the future of their own souls'.
2. Parliamentary Papers, *Religious Worship England and Wales*, 1852–1853, LXXXIX, cxxxvii, table 10.
3. Halévy, *England in 1815*, p. 419 ff.

noted: 'The Nonconformist sects were not churches of the proletariat.'[4] Only the Methodists sought to evangelize the working class, and the members of this class who became Methodists usually also joined the middle class—or if they did not their children did.[5]

The ratio of churchmen to Dissenters in the 1830's was about 120 to 80, but the ratio changed slowly in favour of Dissent until the mid-century mark—particularly in the cities. The religious census of 1851 revealed that the Established Church drew only about 52 per cent of the worshippers in the nation. Then Dissent entered into a period of decline, though Kitson Clark argues that it was 'limited in time and probably in extent'.[6] Lord Robert Montague estimated that in 1860 about 16.5 per cent of the population was Nonconformist, another 16.5 per cent was either Wesleyan or Roman Catholic, about 25 per cent were irreligious poor, and the remaining 42 per cent of the population was Church of England.[7] Until the end of the century, Nonconformists continued to protest that they had more actual worshippers in their chapels and Sunday schools than the Established Church had, but there was a general 'failing vitality' among the sects, and the prevailing belief was that Dissent was in decline: the age was 'on the whole more favourable to the Anglicans than to the Nonconformists'.[8]

The great weakness of Dissent lay in its divisions. It was never a clearly defined social group. Lord Robert Montague noted that the Wesleyan Methodists refused to regard themselves as Dissenters, but rather as a supplementary body of the Established Church. In effect they formed the 'High Church' of Nonconformity, with a hierarchic constitution, and a political and social policy that was frankly conservative. As the century progressed, there was a tendency for Dissent to give birth to a 'swarm of new sects',[9] and in 1851 Horace Mann noted that there were ten major divisions among the Methodists alone.[10] This fragmentation was characterized by great suspicion between the sects, and much changing of allegiance among the Protestants who were Dissenters. It was very difficult for Dissent to speak with a united voice on any issue.

4. Halévy, *Victorian Years*, p. 394.
5. Halévy, *England in 1815*, p. 424.
6. Clark, *Making of Victorian England*, p. 188.
7. Young, *Early Victorian England*, II, 468. For the strength of Nonconformity in the countryside *v.* W. R. Ward, 'Tithe Question in England', *Journal of Ecclesiastical History* (1965), XVI, 67.
8. Elie Halévy, *Imperialism and the Rise of Labour* (1961), p. 176.
9. *Ibid.*, p. 177.
10. For the divisions between Methodists *cf.* Maldwyn Edwards, *Methodism and England, 1850–1932* (1943), p. 219 ff.

One of the chief reasons why Dissent did not increase after mid-century was the rate of defection among its most prominent members. There is much evidence to suggest that Nonconformity provided a transitional creed for those who were rising in the social scale. 'In the normal course the more wealthy Dissenters went over to the Church of England. . . . The unskilled labourer becomes in turn a skilled workman, an artisan, the head of a small business, a business man possessed of a modest capital, and as he rises out of the barbarism in which the working class was plunged, he becomes a Nonconformist. If he himself rises still higher on the social ladder, or if his children rise after his death, he or they go over to the Church of England.'[11]

When Halévy pointed out the turn-over among Dissenters, he was commenting on a continuing phenomenon. In later years there was even a steady drain of Nonconformist pastors to the Established Church.[12] There was a wide gulf separating the respective social positions of the parson and the Dissenting minister; and, when the opportunity presented itself, many of the latter could not resist the temptation to join the Establishment.

Theological justification could usually be found for such a move. If the Church was to influence society, then the Christian clergyman had to be a person who was readily acceptable to the local gentry. The Dissenting minister very rarely received anything more than tolerance from the local squire in the country: in the cities the upper middle class, with its great political and economic power, was usually Anglican. Halévy said of the work of the Nonconformist pastor: 'He was confined to the narrow circle of small farmers and small shopkeepers, who were members of his sect. Everyone else despised or disliked him, or at best regarded him with complete indifference'.[13] The clergy of the Established Church on the other hand were accepted as gentlemen by the upper classes. Many of them were graduates of the public schools, and the two older universities. Some were related to the gentry, and most could move to some degree in circles where social policy was developed. The Nonconformist minister could always argue that if his mission was to society as a whole, and not to the members of his little sect, then he was justified in becoming part of the Established Church. He could even persuade himself that such a change of allegiance would enable him to minister to the poor—for the parson was the accredited mediator

11. Halévy, *England in 1815*, p. 424.
12. Halévy, *Victorian Years*, p. 387.
13. *Ibid.*

between rich and poor in a way that the Nonconformist pastor never was.

Kitson Clark considers this acknowledgment that Established Church clergy were accepted as gentlemen to be the 'consolidation of a caste'. It was without doubt a social movement of this nature, but the clergymen who identified themselves with the ruling classes did not do so only for the social benefits that came with their new status. They brought as much into the class system they became identified with as they received from it. 'In the forties we are aware of a new type emerging from the universities and the public schools, somewhat arrogant and somewhat shy, very conscious of their standing as gentlemen, but very conscious of their duties too, men in tweeds, who smoke in the streets, disciples of Maurice, hearers of Carlyle, passionate for drains and co-operative societies.'[14]

Many of the clergy of the Established Church were part of this new generation; and they encouraged a new middle-class altruism which was to bear fruit, not in traditional philanthropy, but in the mission work of the Ritualists and of the university men in the Settlement Houses. Dissenting ministers were usually not identified with this movement to 'ensoul' the middle class—to give it a spirit of *noblesse oblige*, of duty to the nation, which was based on Christian principle. Until the last decades of the century the gospel of the Nonconformist was usually narrowly religious, and his concept of social reform was that of traditional philanthropy.[15]

The gulf between the Dissenters and the Church was never so great as much of the polemical writing of the time seems to indicate; it was bridged by the Evangelical party. There was growing friction between the sects and the Evangelicals as the power of both began to wane—Mark Pattison said in 1863 that the Evangelical party 'merely covers the grounds with its ruins'[16]—but a giant like Shaftesbury had nearly as much influence in Nonconformity as he had in the Church. He was considered to be almost an embodiment of what was referred to as 'the Nonconformist conscience', and the sects as well as Evangelical churchmen were influenced by his teaching that men's souls were saved, 'that they might, under God, save

14. Young, *Early Victorian England*, II, 474.
15. As Young points out, *ibid.*, II, 346, this philanthropy was also part of the Victorians' 'steadfast determination to perform what they believed to be their duty'. The later Nonconformist leaders such as R. W. Dale, Hugh Price Hughes, Baldwin Brown, Alexander Mackennal, Alex Hannay, Ian MacLaren and others were more conscious of the need for a 'social Gospel'.
16. Mark Pattison, *Essays* (1889), II, 195.

society'. In philanthropic endeavours Evangelicals and Dissenters often worked side by side. The latter might totally reject the 'Catholicity of Institution through sacerdotalism', which characterized the Tractarians; but, at the same time, they accepted Shaftesbury's 'Catholicity of Spirit, through righteous endeavour'.[17]

Halévy had seen the early Methodists as essentially allies of churchmen, and their ministry 'not the enemy but the assistant or *locum tenens* of a clergy which neglected its duties'.[18] A similar conception began to reappear after the mid-century mark, when theological polemics cooled and the idea of the social mission of the Church to the nation matured. The Nonconformists as well as churchmen began to reckon seriously with secularism as a new and militant power, which was willing to engage in battle with them for the souls of the middle class. This confrontation began to convince many Nonconformist leaders that division among Christians assisted the growth of secularism, much more than it withstood the influence of the Established Church: 'for all their freedom of theological difference the sects agreed among themselves and with the national authorities to impose a rigorous ethical conformity on the nation and at least an outward respect for the Christian social order'.[19] The chief 'national authority' the sects agreed with, in this missionary concordat, was the Established Church.

This alliance to make England a Christian nation was continued throughout the century; the spirit behind it was the new catholicism of mission which developed in the Church, and this was welcomed by the sects. It was not always an easy task to persuade the man of business that he should serve the nation in a spirit of Christian altruism, rather than for the commercial goals sought by his class. But churchmen like Matthew Arnold never flagged in their belief that 'the great thing is to drag the dissenting middle class into the great public arena of life and discussion, and not let it remain in its isolation, from which all its faults come.'[20] Slowly the Protestant emphasis on independence and individuality, which prevailed among many Dissenting sects, began to be replaced by a new catholic concern for unity and organization—a movement which reflected a change in theological emphasis from personal salvation to corporate witness in society.

17. Bready, *Lord Shaftesbury*, p. 49.
18. Halévy, *England in 1815*, p. 423.
19. *Ibid.*, p. 425.
20. H. McLachlan, *Records of a Family, 1800–1933* (1935), p. 23.

The younger members of the Nonconformist sects, who had inherited the social privileges acquired by their aggressive fathers,
showed more interest in the Church's attempt 'to capture science,
criticism, philosophy and the new social spirit',[21] than they did in the
old 'dissidence' of Dissent and the 'protestantism' of Nonconformity.
They recognized that a new ideology of mission was appearing within
the Church and that it promised to give to the nation a way of life
which would be infinitely preferable to that offered by the secular
humanists of the day. The new catholicism of the Church challenged
Dissent as much as it did the Church—particularly in the form it
was presented by middle-of-the-road churchmen such as Mandell
Creighton.

> He took his stand for God, and made his great decision at the extreme hour of
> intellectual tension, when the panic roused by the new criticism was at its
> height, and when the victorious efficacy of the scientific and critical methods
> appeared to have swept the field. It is difficult for us now to gauge the dismay
> of that bad hour. At the close of the sixties it seemed to us at Oxford almost
> incredible that a young don of any intellectual reputation for modernity
> should be on the Christian side.[22]

At the time that Creighton was making his decision, Shaftesbury
admitted that he himself had lost faith in the old Evangelical party.
It was 'utterly intolerant', characterized by 'coldness and insincerity', devoted to 'much political, and personal, and very little
spiritual Protestantism'. He said that he received much more ill-
usage from them than he ever did from the Roman Catholics, or the
High-Church party. The Evangelical party had degenerated into a
mere 'theological expression', and many of its members were no
longer concerned for charity and justice. The Ritualists seemed to have
more zeal for Christ than the body of churchmen with whom he had
been for so long identified.[23] Like most of his contemporaries he
recognized the truth of Mark Pattison's comment on the idealism of
the age—that the honey from the T. H. Green school of philosophy
was flowing into the Ritualist hive.[24]

Shaftesbury's disillusionment with Protestantism within the Establishment was shared by many Dissenting leaders when they
looked at the sects, and their lack of corporate social conscience.
Some of the early Dissenters, such as Thomas Binney, the chairman

21. John Morley, *Recollections* (1917), I, 289. *Cf.* p. 142 on Cobden's attempt to 'give
soul' to the manufacturers of Manchester.
22. Creighton, *Life and Letters*, I, 75.
23. Hodder, *Life of Shaftesbury*, III, 254–55.
24. Pattison, *Memoirs*, p. 167.

of the Congregational Union, had agreed with the Wesleyans that their role was essentially auxiliary to that of the Church. Their existence as a separate body was justified because it enabled them to act as the conscience of the nation, in the way that Hooker had believed the Church should do; and this they could not do within the Establishment as it then was. In a famous sermon of 1834, entitled 'Dissent not Schism', Binney said that he was a Dissenter 'because I am a Catholic'. He opposed the political and hierarchical Establishment because it was not performing the mission for which it had been brought into being. Binney's hope was that through the ministry of Dissenters, and those churchmen who might yet find their sense of mission, the day would come in England when 'the world itself shall become the Church'.[25]

Throughout his life, Binney, like most Dissenters, tended to dwell on the inadequacies of the Church, that 'great national evil' whose disappearance was to be encouraged by every lover of God and his fellow man.[26] In pursuit of this goal, the positive mission of Dissent was apt to be forgotten. There were Nonconformist intellectuals such as Edward Baines in the House of Commons, or Robert Vaughan in his *Eclectic Review*, who tried to play down the anti-Church propaganda of the sectarian fanatics, but by 1841 Edward Miall had founded his famous weekly, *The Nonconformist*, which bitterly attacked clericalism in the Church and the excesses of the Tractarians. The only positive note in his paper was its frank endorsement of free trade, the franchise reform wanted by the middle class, and the political rights of the individual. At the mid-century mark it looked as if Binney's dream was reversed—instead of Nonconformity ensouling the middle class, in many sects the opposite had happened, and bourgeois Radicalism dominated Christian social teaching. Nonconformity threatened to become a class religion, concerned with overthrowing the ecclesiastical and political establishment of the age, rather than serving the needs of the nation.

With the religious revival meetings of the 1860's, some of the anti-Church feeling began to wane, as churchmen and Dissenters worked together for the religious conversion of England. Bishop Tait preached out of doors to emigrants, costermongers, railway porters, and gypsies. Lord Shaftesbury and his followers began to hold services in Exeter Hall. A new threat to Evangelicalism was provided by the

25. E. Paxton Hood, *Thomas Binney, His Mind, Life and Opinions* (1874), pp. 26–31.
26. Thomas Binney, *Address Delivered on Laying the First Stone of the New King's Weigh House* (1833), quoted by Halévy, *Triumph of Reform* (1961), p. 150.

revival of the Roman hierarchy, as seen in Cardinal Manning's pastoral aggressiveness. At the same time the appearance of the Salvation Army helped to divert the attention of Dissenters from the failings of the Church. Together with the slow growth of secularism, these developments persuaded Nonconformist leaders that a new corporate approach had to be made by all Christian bodies to the problem of moral and social evil in the nation. The time had come for the Church and the sects to work together.

Even the Congregationalist leader, R. W. Dale, who had no love for the Establishment, realized that as the old vision of what was Christianity began to fade, and the younger generation of Christians showed they were impatient with its traditional presentation, new forms of ecclesiastical life had to appear. Instinctively he rejected the churchmanship of the Ritualists, as he had the theological principles and ecclesiastical claims of the Tractarians, but he admitted that something of the spirit was at work in the life of Pusey and those who were influenced by him—'in the lives and devotion of these men a new endowment of the Holy Spirit came into the life of England.'[27] He knew that if Nonconformity was to survive a decline in contemporary popularity it had to build up a corporate existence similar to the historic organization which gave the Church the means to adapt itself to the changing demands of society. By the 1880's he was writing to B. F. Westcott about the problem of why 'the blood of Christ' which 'avails objectively for the remission of sins, is to be found in that mystical relation between Christ and Humanity which is realized in the Church'.[28] He believed that Congregationalism had drifted into excessive individualism, and that its idea of the Church had degenerated into 'an organization for keeping improper persons from the Lord's Supper, and for securing the election of well-qualified ministers and deacons'.[29] He came under criticism for admiring the attempt of the Ecumenical Council of the Roman Catholic Church 'to reassert the supremacy of the Church throughout the entire domain of thought and knowledge'.[30] He never lost his loyalty to Congregationalism, but his enthusiasm for the Liberation Society which sought disestablishment of the Church was ambivalent,[31] and there is little doubt that he saw the value in the 'public character' of the Church of England which was something the Nonconformist sects had never

27. Dale, *Life of R. W. Dale of Birmingham*, p. 699.
28. *Ibid.*, p. 524.
29. *Ibid.*, p. 243.
30. *Ibid.*, p. 237.
31. *Ibid.*, p. 378.

grasped. As a Congregationalist divine, Dale might choose to ignore the Doctrine of the Church,[32] but as a pastor his concern for matters like the education of the working class convinced him that Christians needed corporate identity if they were to influence the State as they should: 'the religious realm was conceived as that which ought to penetrate and organize the State.'[33]

As might be expected, the Methodists were more appreciative of the Church as the Catholic body of social mission in the nation. Hugh Price Hughes, the well-known Wesleyan divine, who edited the *Methodist Times* from 1885, and became the first president of the National Council of the Evangelical Free Churches, was much influenced by Maurice and Westcott. His daughter commented on this influence by saying: 'Great ideals are never given to one communion, but for all, for they cannot be contained by one.'[34] Her father agreed with this, and never failed to acknowledge his indebtedness to the new ideology of Catholicism which was appearing in the Church. He disagreed widely with Newman, at the same time he admired his saintliness of life, and said he could never take seriously the view that God 'has tied up His grace with the bishops, and is altogether helpless without them'.[35] But the Catholicism of mission which he found among members of the High-Church party, and which he first met in Oxford, moved him greatly: 'If Oxford taught him anything, it was the need of catholic ideas, of wide organization, in Church and State'.[36]

Hughes claimed that certain Nonconformist bodies were just as much an accredited portion of the visible Catholic Church as was the Anglican Church.[37] But the catholicism he referred to was not the abstract justification for an ecclesiastical body, such as that sought by the Tractarians. Rather it was the sense of belonging to a visible body which sought to perform a mission given to it by the Christ who lived within it. His articles in the *Methodist Times* asked his contemporaries 'Is Methodism to be a Dying Sect or a Living Church?' When the celebrated pamphlet entitled the *Bitter Cry of Outcast London* appeared in 1885, and a great meeting was held at Exeter Hall with Lord Shaftesbury in the chair, Hughes represented the Methodists

32. In his *Christian Doctrine*, which first came out in 1894, Dale devotes three whole chapters to the Atonement, and a short note of four pages to the Church, pp. 305–9.
33. *Life of Dale*, p. 719.
34. Hughes, *Life of Hugh Price Hughes*, p. 477.
35. *Ibid.*, p. 390.
36. *Ibid.*, p. 161.
37. *Ibid.*, p. 443.

who wished to join with the Church in a mission to meet the needs of the poor. But he knew, as he once said, that 'Protestantism is a mob'[38]—and this conviction led him to become one of the organizers of the Federation of Free Churches.

Hughes' daughter said that what he sought in the Free Church Federation was an organization that would give to the 'national life . . . such a religious and social environment as shall permit wider ideals and a wider usefulness than has hitherto been possible to many men and women'.[39] His vision of a great Free Church organization was expressed in terms of 'effectiveness'—he wanted Nonconformity to join with the Church in its Catholic mission to Christianize the nation. The Congregationalist divine Alexander Mackennal agreed with Hughes that during the Federation talks of 1888–1894: 'out of the re-awakened perception of the Church as a divine society, came a quickened sense of the unity and catholicity of the Church.' Mackennal also argued that because of the 'comprehensiveness' of the Federation, it actually gave to the nation 'a grander catholicity than was asserted by the Anglicans'.[40]

No one would seek to deny the importance of the 'Nonconformist conscience' in Victorian society: but it is seldom recognized that this social viewpoint was a reflection of the Catholic ideology which matured in the Church, and then by 'osmosis' influenced the major Dissenting sects who joined in the mission to Christianize the nation. Dorothea Hughes claimed that the phrase 'Nonconformist conscience' was first applied to her father by those who opposed his use of the columns of *The Times* to express a Christian viewpoint in political matters.[41] Hughes welcomed the expression, and urged his fellow Dissenters to be worthy of the title which had been bestowed upon them. His ready acceptance of it reflected his satisfaction that Nonconformity was shedding its 'dissidence' and 'individualism' in favour of positive social mission, and corporate identity as part of the Catholic Church of Christ. 'From 1895 onwards he was increasingly constrained to devote his mind and his energies in a strenuous effort to adjust Methodism to the new era, by humanising and spiritualising it, and to achieve what he regarded as even more important and far-reaching, a federation of the various evangelical denominations, on a

38. *Ibid.*, p. 442.
39. *Ibid.*, p. 475.
40. Dugald MacFadyen, *Alexander Mackennal: Life and Letters* (1905), p. 231.
41. *Life of Hughes*, p. 357. A. R. Vidler, *Church in an Age of Revolution, 1789 to the Present Day* (1961), p. 143 refers to Hughes' famous statement about Lord Rosebery—that the Nonconformist conscience would not tolerate a racing premier.

practicable basis, alive at every point to the needs of democracy, yet a conscious portion of the Catholic Church of Christ.'[42]

7. *The Church and Its Press*

IT MAY be argued that the generalizations made in this chapter are not based on statistical evidence, or on specialized studies of issues such as the ideological relationship between the Church and Nonconformity. The truth of such criticism must be acknowledged, for comparatively little research has been done by ecclesiastical historians on the churches of Victorian England. But most of the generalizations are substantiated if an examination is made of the writings of contemporary critics who attempted to assess the influence of religion in the nation. Almost all of them recognized that a new spirit was at work in the Church, and that the result of this development was a new sense of Catholic mission to the nation—a mission which was to be carried out directly by middle-class churchmen, and indirectly through the agencies of Dissent.

Edward Miall, the militant editor of the *Nonconformist*, and vigorous opponent of the Establishment, made one of the first significant studies of the influence of the Church and Nonconformity in society when he published his *British Churches in Relation to the British People* in 1849.

Like Coleridge, Miall recognized the evil which accompanied the 'trade spirit' of the age, and stated his belief that religion could modify it: 'Christianity in one form or another, is fairly grappling with the trade spirit of the age, and gives assurance that when thoroughly aroused, she will be competent to put it down.'[1] He could see no inherent antagonism between what was sought by the trading class, and the goal of Christianity. 'Trade . . . employing the term in the broadest sense of which it is susceptible—is not only not antagonistic in its own nature to the main object of Christianity, but is eminently auxiliary to it. It constitutes one of the principal schools, ordained by the wisdom of Providence, for eliciting, training,

42. *Ibid.*, p. 437.
1. Edward Miall, *British Churches in Relation to the British People* (1849), p. 331.

exercising, and maturing, the spiritual principle implanted in the heart of man by the gospel.'[2] When the truths of the Gospel made 'their civilizing and modifying influence felt' even within 'the ungenial precincts of trade', then middle-class Englishmen would be 'ensouled' to give to the world 'in their own history, a correct picture of a Christian tradesman'.[3] Once the trade spirit was completely overcome, Christian masters would appear who would cease 'looking at work-people through a medium simply of economic laws, and with a reference to commercial profit and loss, to the entire exclusion of Christian impulses'.[4]

Miall admitted that the Church had to promote the mission of overcoming the trade spirit in the nation, because Nonconformity had failed to make a universal appeal. At the time he wrote, he recognized that the aristocracy, 'almost to a man', were members of the National Church, and ranged beneath them in rank were other churchmen who were 'bankers, merchants, members of the liberal professions, manufacturers, farmers and tradesmen'.[5] Although most of the working class lived in a spiritual darkness that was 'truly pagan', when they were influenced by religion at all it was usually by the Ritualists. 'Ritualism is very generally the last resource even of this most hapless class. For if, perchance, such light as is refracted by neighbouring piety disturb their slumbers at the close of life, the visit of a clergyman, and the reception of the sacrament, soothe them to a rest which nothing but the realities of eternity can break.'[6]

The strength of Nonconformity was in those members of the lower ranks of the middle class who wished to find 'religiousness' without 'magisterial authority'. But their loyalty to their chapel often wavered. Miall noted among many of this class 'some latent sense of misgiving' when they became Dissenters, and continuing respect for the religious pronouncements of the legalized system of worship in the nation. 'They are still so far under the spell of authorized priestism, that they hesitate to leave all the approaches to their hearts open to the entrance of divine truth.'[7] The continuing ideological influence of the Church among Nonconformists was a phenomenon Miall much regretted. 'Here in England, and in Ireland too, a considerable proportion of our middle-class are deterred, not merely by fashion, but also by conscience, from seeking any religious guidance or stimulus

2. *Ibid.*, p. 295.   3. *Ibid.*, p. 341.
4. *Ibid.*, p. 329.   5. *Ibid.*, p. 379.
6. *Ibid.*, p. 381.   7. *Ibid.*, p. 375.

from the labours of men not regularly authorized 'by the powers that be'. . . . Nearly one-half of the middle-class, and that half exerting by far the wisest social influence, are prevented by political religion-ism . . . from gaining . . . the . . . spiritual advantage . . . worked outside of the Establishment.'[8] Miall conceded that if anyone sought social status in Victorian England, it was not worth his while to be a Nonconformist: 'To belong to the Church is to side with respecta-bility; to dissent from it is to cast in your lot with the vulgar.'[9]

Miall was dedicated to the cause of emancipating Christianity from its dishonourable domination by the State in England, and he loathed the Establishment. At the same time he had a strong social conscience; and, though he never wearied in his insistence that national regenera-tion would come only through the regeneration of individuals, he did notice that many ostensibly converted Dissenters lacked sympathy for the welfare of the working class, and showed little interest in ideas of social reform. They were men 'who take the lead in our religious institutions, who give princely sums to evangelical societies, and whose names are identified in their several localities with this or that denomination of Christians'. Yet these same men 'are observed to be as ready as others to act almost exclusively upon the hard, inflexible, inexorable maxims of commercial economy'.[10] When he opened the correspondence columns of the *Nonconformist* to letters from working-men who would explain why Dissent had so little appeal to the masses, and suggested that places of Nonconformist worship should also be used for non-religious charitable purposes, he was accused by more orthodox Evangelicals with using his publication and the Anti-State-Church Association for political purposes.

Almost against his will, Miall had to admit that, to influence the nation as a whole, individual piety had to be assisted by the corporate mission of both Church and State. They had to unite to relieve the social misery of the age. He greatly admired Lord Ashley,[11] who showed more concern for the immediate needs of the proletariat than did most dissenting Evangelicals—and was more realistic in the programme he suggested. He would have had Church, State, Dis-senters, and individuals all work together for the Christianizing of England. 'Let your laws, we say to the Parliament, assume the proper functions of law, protect those for whom neither wealth, nor station,

8. *Ibid.*, p. 374.
9. Edward Miall, *Social Influences of the State-Church* (1867), p. 12.
10. Miall, *British Churches*, pp. 229–30. *Cf.* Miall, *Life of Edward Miall*, p. 155 ff.
11. Miall, *British Churches*, p. 351.

nor age have raised a bulwark against tyranny; but above all, open your treasury, erect churches, send for the ministers of religion, reverse the conduct of the enemy of mankind, and sow wheat among the tares.'[12]

Horace Mann was another social commentator who doubted whether the Evangelicals in the Dissenting fellowships would attempt to evolve a national strategy to help the dispossessed of the nation. He published the findings of the religious census of 1851, and it was his belief that such a mission had to be initiated because the census showed clearly that neither the Church nor Nonconformity had much influence among the workers. In the conclusion of his report, which he submitted to Sir George Graham, the Registrar-General, Mann said, 'The middle classes have augmented rather than diminished their devotional sentiment and strictness of attention to religious services. . . . with the upper classes too the subject of religion has obtained of late a marked degree of notice, and a regular Church attendance is now ranked among the recognized properties of life. It is to satisfy the wants of the two classes that the number of religious structures has of late years so increased.'[13]

In the large towns 'an absolutely insignificant portion of the congregations is composed of artizans', and social barriers were such that 'religion has thus come to be regarded merely as a purely middle class propriety or luxury'.[14] The masses had their own faith of 'secularism'—'the creed . . . which virtually though not professedly is entertained by the masses of our working population; by the skilled and unskilled labourer alike—hosts of minor shopkeepers and sundry traders—and by miserable denizens of courts and crowded alleys. . . . these are never or but seldom seen in our religious congregations'.[15]

Mann believed the masses could be deprived of spiritual ministration only at the nation's peril. He took for granted that those who read his report would understand 'to what a great extent the liberty or bondage, industry or indolence, prosperity or poverty, of any people, are the fruits of its religious creed'. 'The religion of a nation must be of extreme solicitude to many minds. Whether we regard a people merely in their secular capacity as parties in a great association for promoting the stability, the opulence, the peaceful glory of a state; or view them in their loftier character, as subjects of a higher kingdom—

12. Hodder, *Life of Shaftesbury*, I, pp. 323–24.
13. Parliamentary Papers, *Religious Worship England and Wales*, 1852–1853, LXXXIX, clviii.
14. *Ibid.*, p. clix.
15. *Ibid.*, p. clviii.

swift and momentary travellers towards a never-ending destiny; in either aspect the degree and the direction of religious sentiment in a community are subjects of the greatest import.'[16] For England to be great she had to be a Christian nation—and all classes in society had to share her common faith.

Because of the individualism of Evangelical piety, and Nonconformity's lack of organization, Mann believed that only the Church could create and sustain a national mission to the spiritually dispossessed. The need for such help from the Church was urgent: 'Doubtless the ill-taught and the wrongly-taught demand her aid as well as the un-taught, but the utterly neglected evidently claim her first exertions.' The Church still held the allegiance of most men of privilege, and it was her task to persuade the wealthy and influential members of the new urban middle class that they should serve the poor in the same spirit of *noblesse oblige* which had long been attributed to the rural gentry. Mann was sure this could be done. If the Church was concerned, as it should be, for the whole of the nation, then the 'heads of great industrial establishments, the growth of recent generations, may perform towards the myriads connected with them by community of occupation those religious charities or duties which the principal proprietors in rural parishes perform towards those connected with them by vicinity of residence.'[17]

An insight into the Evangelical approach to the problem of the poor is provided by Henry Mayhew's monumental study of *London Labour and the London Poor*, which was completed ten years after Mann attempted his investigation of the place religion held in the life of the nation. Mayhew himself recognized the corruptive influence of an environment filled with 'bad amusements and bad institutions', and blamed the existence of much vagabondism on the 'non-inculcation of a habit of industry'. But the Rev. William Tuckniss, who contributed to Mayhew's work an essay on 'Agencies at Present in Operation Within the Metropolis for the Suppression of Vice and Crime', believed the poor brought about their own downfall through the poverty of their spiritual life. His concern was limited to the religious state of the masses who had rejected Christianity. 'Who are those whose souls in countless numbers are now glutting the chambers of hell? Not swarthy Indians nor sable Africans . . . but delicately nurtured Saxon women, who in infancy were lovingly fondled in the arms of Christian mothers and received into the ark of Christ's church

16. *Ibid.*, p. viii.
17. *Ibid.*, p. cxxviii.

in baptism, before a praying congregation. . . . But where are they now? What are their hopes and expectations, and what the probable end of their existence?'[18]

Tuckniss scorned any technique used to help the poor, except traditional Evangelical charity. His call was for pious individuals to give their time and talents to the work of missions such as the Society for the Suppression of Mendicity, the Reformatory and Refuge Union, the Shoe-Black Brigade, and the London Moonlight Mission. No environmental influence would be of any avail—the poor had to be regenerated, to help themselves: 'We have flattered ourselves that education and civilization with all their humanizing and elevating influences would gradually permeate all ranks of society; and that the leaven of Christianity would ultimately subdue the power of evil, and convert our outer world into an Elysium of purity and unselfishness.'[19] Mr. Tuckniss's pessimism about what could be achieved through social reform or education was shared by many Victorians. Mayhew himself gave figures to indicate that juvenile delinquency increased as the Evangelicals provided more and more 'ragged schools'. The reason for this was that these schools quickened the intelligence and increased the power of mischief of pauper children.

When Charles Booth made his analysis of the religious influences in the life of the people of London, he discovered that the idea of 'service' was greatest among members of the upper middle class, 'the great bulk of those of rank and station', who were members of the Church of England. They were steady supporters of the Church, and the part played by religion in their lives was constant: 'with no class is religion more completely identified with duty.'[20] The Catholic party, whose religious expression was far from calm, had its greatest support among members of that class of people 'who fill the principal places in the Civil Service, officer the Army and Navy, and plead in our courts of law'. This class was continually expanding as men rose into it from the class below—the legal and professional men, civil servants, men of business, wholesale traders, and large retailers who were apt to be Presbyterians, Congregationalists, Wesleyans, Unitarians, Quakers, or Baptists. As they rose in the social scale, these men tended to become churchmen, and to share in the ideology

18. Mayhew, *London Labour and the London Poor*, IV, xxxviii.
19. *Ibid.*, p. xii.
20. Booth, *Life and Labour of the People in London*, VII, 395.

of service, based on Christian principle, which was characteristic of the middle class.[21]

Booth had a difficult time in assessing the religious habits of what he called the 'new middle class'—the men of inferior rank in the professions, wholesale and retail trades, and civil service. At one time this class had been strongly Nonconformist, but now it was very fluid in composition, and it was very difficult to be sure what proportion of this large and complex section of people was religious. Apparently many of their number attended either church or chapel, but their loyalties were not strong—they formed the bulk of 'most large religious assemblies'.[22]

There was no difficulty in describing the religious life of the working class. 'The great section of the population which passes by the name of the working classes, lying socially between the lower middle class and the "poor", remains, as a whole, outside of all the religious bodies, whether organized as churches or missions.'[23] Yet the working class were not uninfluenced by religion, however much they kept away from the churches inhabited by the middle class. By a kind of social 'osmosis', which reflected the idea of catholic mission, duty or service, carried out by middle-class churchmen or Dissenters, almost all members of this class were touched by 'practical Christianity' at one time or another in their lives. Their children attended Sunday school, and when times were bad the workers were led 'to open the door to attempts which lie in the middle ground between religious and charitable care'.[24]

Most Victorian writers who were interested in the religious influences in the lives of their contemporaries remarked on the idea which was in the air—that the Church was in some sense a 'moral engine to elevate society'.[25] The Nonconformists were also swept along by this spiritual mission to make England a Christian nation, though they continued to place more emphasis on individual regeneration, and on traditional charity than churchmen did. The work and the writings of Pusey, Gladstone, Arnold, Maurice, Westcott, and so many others convinced the Victorians that in some sense Hooker's view of Church and State in England was still of value from the standpoint of religious practice. This was an age when the Church, with the auxiliary aid provided by Nonconformist sects, sought, and to a large degree, succeeded, in making England a religious nation.

21. *Ibid.*, p. 396.   22. *Ibid.*, p. 397.
23. *Ibid.*, p. 399.   24. *Ibid.*, p. 400.
25. *Life of Mandell Creighton*, I, 121.

Epilogue 1967

The Englishman finds that he was born a Christian, and therefore wishes to remain a Christian; but his Christianity must be his own, no less plastic and adaptable than his inner man; and it is an axiom with him that nothing can be obligatory for a Christian which is unpalatable to an Englishman.

GEORGE SANTAYANA

LOOKING back at the England of Queen Victoria, Basil Willey has said: 'If, after the first World War, we were all debunking the nineteenth century, after the second we are deferring to it, and even yearning nostalgically after it. . . . In that distant mountain country, all that we now lack seems present in abundance: not only peace, prosperity, plenty and freedom, but faith, purpose and buoyancy.'[1]

It has been the thesis of this study that at least a good deal of Victorian 'faith, purpose and buoyancy' reflects the presence and work of the Church of England in the nation: an ecclesiastical body which had entered a Golden Age of pastoral work by the end of the century, as it promoted its catholic mission to bring the light of the Gospel to bear on all aspects of society, and into the lives of the members of all social classes. The Victorian churchman, as well as his Nonconformist brother, accepted that it was his Christian duty to support this catholic mission of the Church. The Victorian citizen

EPIGRAPH: George Santayana, *Soliloquies in England* (1922), pp. 83–84.
1. Willey, *Nineteenth Century Studies*, p. 52.

generally welcomed this form of catholicism because, like Horace Mann in 1851, he believed that the well-being of England depended in large measure upon the faith and virtue of its people.

Churchmen of the late twentieth century are certainly apt to look back nostalgically at the Church of Victorian England when, as Asa Briggs has said, 'the religious climate was more exciting and important than anything else'.[2] This is hardly the case in our own day when the most attention that is paid to anything done by the Church of England is apt to be a polite, though embarrassed, recognition that here and there it still shows signs of life. The embarrassment comes from the fact that most signs of life take the form of a critical exposure of the theological, administrative, and physical weaknesses of the Church. In many ways, in this time of introversion, the Church seems to have returned to the ethos of the Tractarian era. Often its solemn assemblies resemble once more 'ecclesiastical cock-pits' where aging theologians fight the battles of a past age, as they strive to regulate canon law and the wearing of vestments, and to deal with the clerical sloth tolerated by the parson's freehold. Recognition that the Church exists to serve the nation, to act as its conscience and the source of its spiritual strength, seems to have been lost. The clergy, whom the laity expect to lead the patiently waited-for revival of catholic mission, tend to lapse into silence when they are not discussing abstract theological questions. When the Church does discuss its role in society, its primary concern seems to be the physical well-being of the Establishment. Debate is dominated by those bishops, theologians, and administrators who are most devoted in their efforts to maintain the traditional temporal machinery of the Church. The pastors of the Church are apparently either non-existent from the standpoint of the general public, or else they keep away from the Church's assemblies. The only 'working clergy' who seem to be taken notice of by the press are those individuals who in quiet desperation have abandoned the usual clergyman's parish-priest role to labour as 'worker-priests' in secular society.

As many critics have pointed out, this is an age of clerical despondency. Many bishops have compensated for their loss of national influence by gladly accepting the old Tractarian religious view of their office. The laity, on the whole, have been quite content to allow the growth of such affectation. Some secular political figures may even have rejoiced over it. They know from experience that a bishop

2. Briggs, *Victorian People*, p. 27.

who is primarily concerned with a 'high' ecclesiastical or religious interpretation of his office is not apt to be a critic of secular social reform policies. The main concern of many modern bishops seems to be ecclesiastical administrative reform, and some even speak of the need for disestablishment—as once did the Tractarians. The parish clergy who continue to serve dutifully in a traditional way quietly worry over talk of such administrative change. They know that without the Establishment they will be totally dependent on the good-will of ecclesiastically minded bishops, and the largesse of socially conservative laity. At the same time they wonder what their role in society now is, and what is the real function of the Church in the secular world.

What has happened to the Church of England since Cosmo Lang spoke of its having a Golden Age of pastoral endeavour? It is not the purpose of this study to answer the question, but recognition of the obvious disparity in spiritual and physical health between the Victorian Church and the Church of the present day can help us to appreciate the former, and, perhaps, to recognize something of the cause of malaise in the latter.

The Victorian Church had its Golden Age of pastoral work because, after the Tractarian era, it began to abandon its concern to find a theological definition of what was the Church, in terms of dualistic thought which separated the spiritual from the secular in life. It knew that Hooker's view of the *via media* needed to be modified, because the Church was no longer co-extensive with society (if it had ever been). But the essence of Hooker's idea was still of value—the Church was potentially the most influential corporation in the new pluralistic society of industrial England, and its mission was still to all people in the new nation. The Church knew it could and should serve the society in which it existed.

After 1845 churchmen began to think once more in terms of mission. Slowly their attention was drawn from the clerical in-fighting of Oxford to what was represented by the work of churchmen in the slums. The clergy became aware, as they had not been for many generations, that they held a working commission from the King of Kings. They began their catholic mission to serve in the new industrial society. They did not wait for marching orders from the bishops, or from the laity, but pragmatically set out to 'Christianize' England. They began to leave to the bishops questions about ultimate authority in the Church, and to the laymen problems raised by the Public Worship Regulation Act.

The 'working clergy' of the last half of the century paid more attention to Maurice's idea of 'digging', to exposing the divine at work in secular society, than they did to delineation of the areas of prerogative of Church and State. From Maurice, who recognized Chartism as in some way a working-class representation of Christianity, to Stewart Headlam, who sought to 'baptize' secular socialism, the clergy pursued their catholic mission to make all England Christian. They were not surprised, when they did this, to find that the power of the Incarnation was already at work in the world.

Those who carried on this catholic mission were able to accomplish what they did because they won the allegiance of the powerful middle class, and persuaded its members to support their cause—the Christianizing of the English nation. It was largely because the middle class accepted the Christian virtue of self-abnegation, and the ideal of service to the nation which underlay the catholic mission of the Church, that England was spared the class warfare which became so common elsewhere in Europe. The Church of England in turn was spared the ugliness of anti-clericalism, which also became common on the continent. Henry Mayhew found that although the parson and the landlord were often lumped together in tales of oppression told in the casual wards of the workhouses, these yarns of exploitation seldom expressed real anti-clericalism.[3] This was because there was usually a group of clergymen to be found associated with the social movements of the age.[4] For every 'bloody parson' in working-class mythology, there were compensating memories of priests like Lowder of Wapping, Goulden of the Elephant and Castle, and Ommanney of Sheffield. Because of this, the Church was appreciated by both the middle and the working class as the social catalyst of the nation.

In defence of the Church of England, Gladstone read to the House of Commons, on 16 May 1873, an extract from the writings of his friend Dollinger, who had said about it:

It may be said with truth that no Church is so national, so deeply rooted in public affection, so bound up with the institutions and manners of the country, or so powerful in its influence on national character. . . . the cold, dull, indifferentism, which on the continent has spread like a deadly mildew over all degrees of society, has no place in the British Isles. . . . on the whole the Englishman takes an active part in Church interests and questions, and that unnatural hostility and division provided by Ultramontanism in Catholic

3. Mayhew, *London Labour and the London Poor*, III, 390.
4. C. R. Fay, *Life and Labour of the Nineteenth Century* (1920), p. 169.

countries is quite unknown there. . . . what has been accomplished during the last thirty years by the energy and generosity of religious Englishmen, set in motion and guided by the Church in the way of popular education and Church building, far exceeds what has been done in any other country. Attendance at religious worship on Sundays is not, as in France, the exception but the rule, with the higher and middle classes.[5]

The great accomplishment of the Church of Victorian England was its ideological capture of the upper classes of the nation—particularly the powerful middle class, which was encouraged not to develop into a kind of continental bourgeoisie. It was this achievement which allowed the Church to promote its catholic mission to the nation as successfully as it did—with the help of Nonconformity.

This Victorian accomplishment also provided the Church with its later tragedy. By the time of World War I, it was identified almost completely with the middle class in the public mind. When this class slowly lost its influence after the war, the working class, which began to assume political power, was never directly identified with the Church or its mission to society. It is true that many Labour leaders were inspired by Christian ideals or by some form of Christian education, and the whole movement of Labour was steeped in idealism absorbed from the Church through social 'osmosis'. But the Church could never identify itself with the labouring class, as it once had with the middle class of Victorian times. It was still recognized as the largest, and potentially one of the most influential corporations in the pluralistic society of twentieth-century England. But in physical presence it was less and less co-extensive with the nation as the power of the working class grew. In terms of mission, the Church began to lose its genius for providing leadership in every movement of the Spirit in the secular world.

Assuring itself that its retreat was the only tactical—*reculer pour mieux sauter*—the Church began its withdrawal from society. More and more its concerns became those that had once occupied the academic theorists of the Tractarian era, a hundred years before. Its sense of catholicity in terms of mission was lost, and in compensation its adherents protested catholicity in terms of spiritual authority to a society which was less and less interested in what it had to say. If Maurice could have returned to listen to the debates of the Neo-Tractarians of the twentieth century as they looked back on their theological inheritance, he would once more have cried out: 'O that they would be Catholics'.

5. *Speech of Rt. Hon. W. E. Gladstone in House of Commons, 16 May 1873, on Mr. Miall's Motion for the Disestablishment and Disendowment of the Church* (1885), p. 10.

The Victorian clergyman seldom shared the confusion of his twentieth-century counterpart about what his role in society was to be. His task was to 'ensoul' those people who could serve secular society by promoting reform in the nation. He never had to face the problems created by the appearance of the welfare state, the affluent society of the twentieth century, the new technological revolution, the population explosion, or the victory of democracy. But he faced equally complex problems in his age. As he faced them, he knew that his mission was to attempt to 'baptize' each new social movement, and to 'ensoul' each creative individual who could influence the well-being of the nation. Society might be pluralistic, and the resources of the Church so thin that it could not directly enlighten the nation—with which it was no longer co-extensive—but the mission of the Church was still the same. To be catholic, the Church was to expose the presence of the divine at work in all parts of the social order. 'Christians are responsible . . . for what goes on in every area of this world as well as for the inner life of the Church and the salvation of souls. . . . God is interested in the welfare of nations and states as well as of the Church; he is interested in legislation as well as in love, in hygiene as well as in holiness, in work as well as in worship . . . and it is to be presumed that where God is interested Christians should be so too.'[6]

After the Tractarian era the Victorian Church showed a decreasing interest in abstract theological theories which could justify its existence. It believed it was a Catholic Church because its mission was universal—to all parts of secular society. Whatever the intellectual or social movements of the age, the task of the Church was to provide a creative minority to influence them. The glory of the Victorian Church was that it was able to perform this duty. The spiritual power of the Church became concentrated in the clergy as a whole, rather than in the episcopate; and among the clergy appeared the needed creative minority. The Victorian bishop found that his real task was to 'confirm' what was accomplished by his wayward clergy and their lay supporters, rather than to 'baptize' new social movements approved by the Establishment. Because the new spiritual impulse of the Church was 'pastoral' rather than 'theological', it won the allegiance of the responsible orders in society; and England became, as so many historians have recognized, a peculiarly religious nation. There is little doubt that much of the 'faith, purpose and buoyancy'

6. A. R. Vidler, *Christian Belief and This World* (1956), p. 45.

of Victorian England was the direct result of the Church's catholic mission to the nation, and its people. The Church of England had discovered that it was part of the Catholic Church 'which contains within its resources what can supply the needs of all sorts of men, of all sorts of nations, at all sorts of times, and under all circumstances. This universal resourcefulness and applicability of the Gospel is involved and signified in the word Catholic.'[7]

7. Gore, *Two Addresses*, p. 2. As H. R. McAdoo, the Bishop of Ossory, has pointed out in his *Spirit of Anglicanism* (1965), the 'liberal Catholicism' of Charles Gore was simply the perennial expression of Anglicanism which is based not on a theology, but a 'theological method'.

Bibliography

This is offered as an aid to anyone who wishes to identify the most important of the printed works upon which the text is based. It is not an exhaustive list of relevant books, nor a guide to the vast amount of literature concerning the Victorian Church, nor a record of the most recent studies of the era. It does not include newspapers, novels, Parliamentary Papers and Debates, periodicals, or unpublished papers which can be recognized and located through the footnote references.

ABBOTT, EVELYN AND CAMPBELL, L. Life and Letters of Benjamin Jowett. 2 vols. (London, 1897)

ADAMSON, J. W. English Education 1789–1902 (Cambridge, 1930)

AITKEN, W. F. Frederick Temple, Archbishop of Canterbury (London, 1901)

ALLIES, M. H. Thomas William Allies (London, 1907)

ANNAN, N. G. Leslie Stephen (London, 1951)

ANSON, P. F. The Call of the Cloister (London, 1956)

ARCH, JOSEPH. Joseph Arch: the Story of his Life, told by himself (London, 1898)

ARNOLD, THOMAS. The Miscellaneous Works of Thomas Arnold. Ed. by Arthur P. Stanley (London, 1845)

ASHWELL, A. R. and WILBERFORCE, R. G. Life of the Right Reverend Samuel Wilberforce. 3 vols. (London, 1880–82)

BAMFORD, T. W. Thomas Arnold (London, 1960)

BARNETT, HENRIETTA O. Canon Barnett, His Life, Work, and Friends. 2 vols. (London, 1918)

BARNETT, S. A. and BARNETT, MRS. A. Practicable Socialism. New Series (London, 1915)

————. Settlements of University Men in Great Towns (Oxford, 1884)

BATTISCOMBE, GEORGINA. John Keble (London, 1963)

BELTON, F. G., ed. Ommanney of Sheffield, Memoirs (London, 1936)

BENBOW, WILLIAM. The Crimes of the Clergy, or the Pillars of priest-craft shaken (London, 1823)

BENN, A. W. History of English Rationalism in the Nineteenth Century. 2 vols. (London, 1906)

BEST, G. F. A. Temporal Pillars (Cambridge, 1964)

BETTANY, F. G. Stewart Headlam (London, 1926)

BINYON, G. C. Christian Socialist Movement in England (London, 1931)

BLOMFIELD, ALFRED. A Memoir of C. J. Blomfield. 2 vols. (London, 1863) 2nd. edition, 1 vol. (London, 1864)

BOOTH, CHARLES. Life and Labour of the People in London. Religious Influences. 3rd series. 7 vols. (London, 1902–3)

BOOTH, GEN. WILLIAM. In Darkest England and the Way Out (London, 1890)

BOWEN, W. E. Edward Bowen. A Memoir (London, 1902)

BOWLES, JOHN. A Dispassionate Inquiry into the Best Means of National Safety (London, 1806)

BREADY, J. W. Lord Shaftesbury and Social-Industrial Progress (London, 1926)

BRIGGS, ASA. Victorian People. 1851–1867 (London, 1954)

————. Victorian Cities (London, 1963)

BRILIOTH, YNGVE. The Anglican Revival (London, 1925)

————. Three Lectures on Evangelicalism and the Oxford Movement (London, 1934)

BRODRICK, G. C. and FREMANTLE, W. H. A Collection of the Judgments of the Judicial Committee of the Privy Council in ecclesiastical cases relating to doctrine and discipline (London, 1865)

BROSE, OLIVE J. Church and Parliaments: the reshaping of the Church of England, 1828–1860 (Stanford, 1959)

BROWN, C. F. K. Church's Part in Education, 1833–1841 (London, 1942)

————. A History of the English Clergy, 1800–1900 (London, 1953)

BURGON, J. W. Lives of Twelve Good Men (London, 1891)

BUTLER, SAMUEL. The Life and Letters of Dr. Samuel Butler, 1798–1836. 2 vols. (London, 1896)

CAMPBELL, R. J. Thomas Arnold (London, 1927)

CARNARVON, EARL OF. The Advantages of an Established Church (London, 1885)

CARPENTER, JAMES. Gore; a study in liberal Catholic thought (London, 1960)

CARPENTER, S. C. Church and People, 1789–1889 (London 1933)

CARTER, T. T. Parish Sermons on Church Questions (London, 1887)

CHADWICK, OWEN. The Victorian Church (London, 1966)

CHAMPNEYS, W. W. The Spirit in the Word. Facts gathered from a thirty years' ministry (London, 1862)

CHAPMAN, RONALD. Father Faber (London, 1961)

Christian Social Union: Three Addresses delivered at . . . Bristol. December 1st, 1896 (Bristol, 1897)

CHURCH, MARY. Life and Letters of Dean Church (London, 1894)

CHURCH, R. W. Essays and Reviews (London, 1854)

————. Human Life and Its Conditions (London, 1878)

————. The Oxford Movement. Twelve years, 1833–1845 (London, 1891)

————. Occasional Papers, 1846–1890. 2 vols. (London, 1897)

CHURCHMAN OF THE DIOCESE OF CANTERBURY. Laud and Tait: an ecclesiastical study and review (London, 1883)

CLARK, KITSON G. Making of Victorian England (London, 1962)

CLARKE, BASIL. Church Builders of the Nineteenth Century (London, 1938)

CLAYDEN, ARTHUR. The Revolt of the Field (London, 1874)

CLAYTON, JOSEPH. Father Dolling. A memoir (London, 1902)

————. The Bishops as Legislators (London, 1906)

————. Father Stanton of St. Alban's, Holborn: A memoir (London, 1913)

COBBETT, WILLIAM. Cobbett's Legacy to Parsons (London, 1835)

COCKSHUT, A. O. J. Anglican Attitudes (London, 1959)

COLE, G. D. H. and POSTGATE, RAYMOND. The Common People, 1746–1946 (London, 1946)

COLERIDGE, J. T. A Memoir of the Rev. John Keble (Oxford and London, 1869)

COLERIDGE, S. T. Lay Sermon to Higher and Middle Classes on the Existing Distresses and Discontents (London, 1817)

COLERIDGE, S. T. The Friend; a series of Essays. 3 vols. (London, 1818)
———. Aids to Reflection (London, 1825)
———. Constitution of Church and State, according to the idea of each (London, 1830)
———. Table Talk and Omniana. O.U.P. edition (Oxford, 1917)
COOMBS, HOWARD AND BAX, A. N., eds. Journal of a Somerset Rector: John Skinner, 1772–1839 (London, 1930)
CORNISH, F. WARRE. The English Church in the Nineteenth Century. 2 parts (London, 1910)
COWHERD, RAYMOND G. The Politics of English Dissent . . . from 1815–1848 (New York, 1956)
CREIGHTON, LOUISE. Life and Letters of Mandell Creighton. 2 vols. (London, 1904)
CULLER, A. D. The Imperial Intellect: a Study of Newman's Educational Ideal (New Haven, 1955)
DALE, A. W. W. Life of R. W. Dale of Birmingham (London, 1898)
DARWIN, FRANCIS. The Life and Letters of Charles Darwin. 2 vols. (London, 1921)
DAVIDSON, R. T. and BENHAM, W. Life of Archibald Campbell Tait, Archbishop of Canterbury. 2 vols. (London, 1891)
DAVIES, G. C. B. Henry Phillpotts, Bishop of Exeter, 1778–1869 (London, 1954)
DAVIES, HORTON. Worship and Theology in England from Watts and Wesley to Maurice 1690–1850 (Princeton, 1961)
———. Worship and Theology in England from Newman to Martineau 1850–1900 (Princeton, 1962)
DAVIES, RUPERT E. Methodism (Baltimore, 1963)
DENISON, G. A. Church Schools and State Interference (London, 1847)
———, Position and Prospects of the National Society for the Education of the Poor (London, 1853)
———. Notes of my Life (London, 1878)
———. Fifty Years at East Brent: The Letters of George Anthony Denison 1845–1896 (London, 1902)
———. Supplement to 'Notes of my Life', 1879, and 'Mr. Gladstone', 1886 (Oxford, 1893)
DOLLING, ROBERT. Ten Years in a Portsmouth Slum (1896)
DUNN, W. H. James Anthony Froude. 2 vols. (1961–1963)
EDWARDS, MALDWYN. Methodism and England, 1850–1932 (London, 1943)
ELIHU. Is General Booth's Darkest England Scheme a Failure? (Manchester, 1895)
ELLEGARD, ALVAR. Darwin and the General Reader (London, 1958)
ELLICOTT, C. J. The Church and the Rural Poor. . . Visitation to the Parish Church, Stow-on-the-Wold (London, 1873)
ELLIOTT-BINNS, L. E. Religion in the Victorian Era (Greenwich, Conn., 1936)
———. English Thought 1860–1900: the Theological Aspect (Greenwich, Conn., 1956)
ELLMAN, E. B. Recollections of a Sussex Parson (London, 1912)
ENSOR, R. C. K. England, 1870–1914 (Oxford, 1960)
FABER, GEOFFREY. Jowett (1957)
———. Oxford Apostles (London, 1953)
FAIRWEATHER, E. R., ed. Oxford Movement (New York, 1964)
FAULKNER, H. U. Chartism and the Churches (New York, 1916)
FAY, C. R. Life and Labour in the Nineteenth Century (Cambridge, 1920)

FINDLAY, J. J. Arnold of Rugby (Cambridge, 1897)

FRASER, JAMES. As things are, how can we educate? A question attempted to be answered in a sermon (London, 1853)

——. Charge delivered at his primary visitation at the Cathedral, Manchester (Manchester, 1872)

FROUDE, JAMES ANTHONY. Short Studies on Great Subjects. 4 vols. (London, 1901)

FROUDE, RICHARD HURRELL. Remains. 4 vols. (London, 1838–39)

GEE, RICHARD. 'Sixty Years Since' In the Church of England, 1838–1898 (Eton, 1898)

GILL, J. C. The Ten Hours Parson; Christian Social Action in the Eighteen-Thirties (London, 1959)

GIRDLESTONE, CHARLES. A letter on Church Reform . . . with one remark on the plan of Lord Henley (London, 1832)

——. A second letter on Church Reform (London, 1833)

GLADSTONE, W. E. Church Principles considered in their results (London, 1840)

——. The State in its relations with the Church. 2 vols. (London, 1841)

——. Gleanings of Past Years. 1843–78. 7 vols. (London, 1879)

GLOYN, C. K. The Church in the Social Order (Forest Grove, Oregon, 1942)

GOODE, WILLIAM. Some difficulties in the late charge of the . . . Bishop of Oxford (London, 1842)

——. The Case as it is: or, a reply to the letter of Dr. Pusey to His Grace the Archbishop of Canterbury (London, 1842)

——. Address [to] the Inhabitants of All hallows the Great and Less . . . on the recent Act of Papal Aggression (London, 1850)

——. Reply to the letter and declaration respecting the royal supremacy, Received from Archdeacons Manning and Wilberforce and Professor Mill (London, 1850)

——. The doctrine of the Church of England on the two sacraments of Baptism and the Lord's Supper (London, 1864)

——. Remarks on the Episcopal Resolution passed in the Upper House of the Southern Convocation, on the subject of Ritualism (London, 1867)

GORE, CHARLES. The Church and the Ministry (London, 1882)

——. The Mission of the Church (London, 1892)

——. Two Addresses on Sin Delivered in Exeter Cathedral (Plymouth, 1899)

——. Christ and Society (London, 1928)

GRAY, JANE LORING. Letters of Asa Gray. 2 vols. (London, 1893)

GREEN, V. H. H. Oxford Common Room; a Study of Lincoln College and Mark Pattison (London, 1957)

——. Religion at Oxford and Cambridge (London, 1964)

GRUEBER, C. S. Decisions on Ritual. An appeal to the people of the Church of England (London, 1874)

HALÉVY, ELIE. A History of the English People in the Nineteenth Century (New York, 1961)

——. vol. 1 England in 1815

——. vol.2 The Liberal Awakening, 1815–1830

——. vol.3 The Triumph of Reform, 1830–1841

——. vol.4 Victorian Years, 1841–1895

——. vol.5 Imperialism and the Rise of Labour, 1895–1905

HAMMOND, J. L. and HAMMOND, LUCY BARBARA. The Town Labourer, 1760–1832 (London, 1917)

——. The Village Labourer, 1760–1832 (London, 1927)

——. The Age of the Chartists, 1832–1854 (London, 1930)

HAMMOND. The Bleak Age (New York, 1947)

HAMPDEN, R. D. The Scholastic Philosophy considered in its relation to Christian Theology (Oxford, 1833)

———. Observations on Religious Dissent (Oxford, 1834)

HANCOCK, THOMAS. Salvation by Mammon (London, 1891)

HARE, AUGUSTUS. Memorials of a Quiet Life. 2 vols. (London, 1884)

———. The Story of my Life. 6 vols. (London, 1896–1900)

HARE, J. C. Education the Necessity of Mankind (London, 1851)

———. Contest with Rome (London, 1852)

———. The Victory of Faith (London, 1874)

HARRISON, J. F. C. A History of Working Men's Colleges, 1854–1954 (London, 1954)

HEADLAM, STEWART D. The Service of Humanity (London, 1882)

———. The Sure Foundation. An address given before the Guild of S. Matthew (London, 1883)

———. The Guild of St. Matthew, an appeal to Churchmen (London, 1890)

HEASMAN, KATHLEEN. Evangelicals in Action (London, 1962)

HENLEY, 1ST LORD. Plan of Church Reform (London, 1832)

HENSON, H. H. Retrospect of an Unimportant Life. 2 vols. (London, 1942)

HINCHCLIFF, PETER. John William Colenso (London, 1964)

HODDER, EDWIN. Life and Work of the seventh Earl of Shaftesbury. 3 vols. (London, 1886)

HOLLAND, H. S. A Bundle of Memories (London, 1915)

HOOD, E. PAXTON. Thomas Binney: his mind, life and opinions (London, 1874)

HOOK, W. F. A call to union on the principles of the English Reformation (London, 1838)

———. Reason for contributing towards the support of our English Bishop at Jerusalem (London, 1842)

HORNIBROOK, S. Sale of Livings (London, 1873)

HORT, A. F. Life and Letters of Fenton John Anthony Hort. 2 vols. (London, 1896)

HOUGHTON, W. E. Victorian Frame of Mind (New Haven, 1959)

HOW, F. D. Six Great Schoolmasters (London, 1904)

HOWARD, GEORGE B. The future supply of Clergy for the service of the Church of England . . . letter to the Right Hon. W. E. Gladstone (1875)

HUGHES, DOROTHEA. The Life of Hugh Price Hughes (London, 1905)

HUGHES, THOMAS. James Fraser, second Bishop of Manchester. A memoir 1818–1885 (London, 1888)

HUTTON, W. H. Robert Gregory, 1819–1911 (London, 1912)

HUXLEY, T. H. Evolution and Ethics (London, 1893)

INGLIS, K. S. The Churches and the Working Classes in Victorian England (London, 1963)

IRWIN, LORD (Halifax, Lord Edward Frederick Lindley Wood, 3rd Viscount). John Keble (London, 1932)

JOHNSTON, J. O. Life and Letters of Henry Parry Liddon (London, 1904)

KANDEL, I. L. History of Secondary Education (Boston, 1930)

KAY, JOSEPH. The Condition and Education of poor children in English and in German towns (London, 1853)

KAY-SHUTTLEWORTH, JAMES. Four Periods of Public Education as reviewed in 1832–1839–1846–1862 (London, 1862)

KEBLE, JOHN. Assize Sermon on National Apostasy (Oxford, 1833); reprinted 1931

KEBLE, JOHN. A very few Plain Thoughts on the proposed addition of Dissenters the University of Oxford (Oxford, 1854)
———. The Rich and the Poor one in Christ (London, 1858)
KELWAY, A. C. George Rundle Prynne (London, 1905)
KENNY, TERENCE. The Political Thought of John Henry Newman (London, 1957)
KINGSLEY, CHARLES. Charles Kingsley: his letters and memories of his life. Ed. by his wife. 2 vols. (London, 1877)
KIRK-SMITH, H. William Thompson (London, 1958)
LAKE, KATHARINE. Memorials of William Charles Lake, Dean of Durham (London, 1901)
LASKI, HAROLD J. Studies in the Problem of Sovereignty (London, 1917)
LATHBURY, D. C. Correspondence on Church and Religion of William Ewart Gladstone. 2 vols. (London, 1910)
LEATHERBARROW, J. S. Victorian Period Piece (London, 1954)
LEIGHTON, BALDWYN. Recollection of Theodore Mansel Talbot (London, 1889)
LIDDON, H. P. Bishop Wilberforce (London, 1875)
———. Some Elements of Religion (1881)
———. Life of Edward Bouverie Pusey. 4 vols. (London, 1893–97)
LIGHTFOOT, J. B. Inaugural address delivered at the Co-operative Congress (Manchester, 1880)
LITTON, E. A. The Church of Christ in its idea, attributes and ministry (London, 1851)
———. Intellectual Religionism Pourtrayed (Oxford, 1853)
———. Introduction to Dogmatic Theology (London, 1882–92)
———. The Connection of the Church and the State, with particular reference to the Irish Church (London, 1868)
LOCK, WALTER. John Keble (London, 1893)
LOCKHART, J. G. Cosmo Gordon Lang (London, 1949)
Lombard Street in Lent (London, 1894)
LOVETT, WILLIAM. Life & Struggles (London, 1920)
LOWDER, C. F. Five Years in St. George's Mission (London, 1861)
———. Penitent's Path (London, 1869)
———. Ten Years in St. George's Mission (London, 1867)
———. Twenty-one Years in St. George's Mission (London, 1877)
LUDLOW, J. M. Christian Socialism and Its Opponents (London, 1851)
MCCLATCHEY, DIANA. Oxfordshire Clergy 1777–1869 (Oxford, 1960)
MCDONALD, H. D. Ideas of Revelation, 1700–1860 (London, 1959)
———. Theories of Revelation; an Historical Study, 1860–1890 (London, 1963)
MACDONALD, THOMAS. How to reach Working Men (London, 1877)
MCENTEE, GEORGINA. The Social Catholic Movement in Great Britain (New York, 1927)
MACFADYEN, DUGALD. Alexander Mackennal: life and letters (London, 1905)
MAITLAND, F. W. The Life of Leslie Stephen (London, 1906)
MALTBY, S. E. Manchester and the Movement for National Elementary Education, 1800–1870 (Manchester, 1918)
MARRIOTT, CHARLES. Five Sermons on the Principles of Faith and Church Authority (Littlemore, 1850)
———. God and not System, the strength of the Church (London, 1850)
MARSON, CHARLES. God's Co-operative Society (London, 1914)
MARTINEAU, HARRIETT. Autobiography. 3 vols. (London, 1877)
MASON, A. J. Memoir of George Howard Wilkinson (London, 1910)
MASTERMAN, G. F. G. Frederick Denison Maurice (London, 1905)

MATHIESON, W. L. English Church Reform, 1815–1840 (London, 1923)

MAUGHAN, H. H. Wagner of Brighton (Loughlinstown, 1949)

MAURICE, F. C. Subscription No Bondage, By Rusticus (Oxford, 1835)

————. The Kingdom of Christ 3 vols. (London, 1837) new edition, 2 vols. (London, 1958)

————. Has the Church, or the State, the power to educate the Nation (London, 1839)

————. On the Right and Wrong Methods of supporting Protestantism. A letter to Lord Ashley (London, 1843)

————. The New Statute and Mr. Ward. A letter to a non-Resident Member of Convocation (Oxford, 1845)

————. Thoughts on the rule of Conscientious Subscription . . . and on our present perils from the Romish System; in a second letter to a non-resident Member of Convocation (Oxford, 1845)

————. The Epistle to the Hebrews (London, 1846)

————. Sermons on the Sabbath-day (London, 1853)

————. Theological Essays (London, 1853)

————. Lectures on the Ecclesiastical History of the first and second centuries (Cambridge, 1854)

————. Learning and Working: Six Lectures delivered in . . . London (London, 1855)

————. Lectures to Ladies on Practical Subjects (1855)

————. The Gospel of St. John (London, 1894)

————. Ground and Object of Hope for Mankind . . . Four sermons (London, Cambridge, 1868)

————. Social Morality (Cambridge, 1869)

————. Sermons Preached in Lincolns Inn Chapel. 6 vols. (1891)

MAURICE, SIR JOHN FREDERICK. The Life of Frederick Denison Maurice. 2 vols. (London, 1885)

MAYHEW, HENRY. London Labour and London Poor. 4 vols. (London, 1861–62)

MIALL, ARTHUR. Life of Edward Miall (London, 1884)

MIALL, EDWARD. The British Churches in relation to the British People (London, 1849)

————. The Social Influences of the State-Church (London, 1867)

MILL, J. S. Autobiography (London, 1873)

————. Nature, the Utility of Religion and Theism [Three Essays on Religion]. (London, 1874)

————. The Letters of John Stuart Mill. Ed. by Hugh S. R. Elliot. 2 vols. (London, 1910)

MILLER, JOHN CALE. The Church of England in Birmingham (Birmingham, 1864)

MILNER, ALFRED. Arnold Toynbee. A reminiscence (London, 1895)

MOBERLY, CHARLOTTE A. E. Dulce Domum. George Moberly . . . His family and friends (London, 1911)

MOZLEY, THOMAS. Reminiscences, Chiefly of Oriel College and the Oxford Movement. 2 vols. (London, 1882)

NEWMAN, JOHN HENRY. The Arians of the Fourth Century (London, 1833)

————. Parochial and Plain Sermons. 8 vols. (London, 1868)

————. Lectures on the Prophetical Office of the Church (London, 1837)

————. The Idea of a University (London, 1852)

————. Difficulties felt by Anglicans in Catholic teaching. 2 vols. (London, 1858)

————. Sermons on subjects of the day (London, 1843)

————. Apologia Pro Vita Sua (London, 1864)

NEWMAN, JOHN HENRY. Grammar of Assent (London, 1870)
————. Via Media of the Anglican Church (London, 1877)
————. Development of Christian Doctrine (London, 1878)
————. Letters and Correspondence of J. H. Newman during his life in the English Church. Ed. by Anne Mozley. 2 vols. (London, 1891)
————. Correspondence of John Henry Newman with John Keble and Others 1845 (London, 1917)
————. Autobiographical Writings. Ed. by H. Tristram (London, 1956)
NEWSOME, DAVID. Godliness & Good Learning (London, 1961)
OAKELEY, FREDERICK. The Dignity and Claims of the Christian Poor: two Sermons (London, 1840)
O'FAOLIN, SEAN. Newman's Way (London, 1952)
OLLARD, S. L. A Short History of the Oxford Movement (London, 1915)
ORNSBY, ROBERT. Memoirs of J. R. Hope-Scott. 2 vols. (London, 1884)
ORR, JAMES EDWIN. The Second Evangelical Awakening (London, 1955)
OSBORNE, CHARLES EDWARD. The Life of Father Dolling (London, 1903)
OTTER, JOHN. Nathaniel Woodward (London, 1925)
PAGET, STEPHEN. Henry Scott Holland . . . Memoir and letters (London, 1921)
PALMER, WILLIAM (WORCESTER COLLEGE). Remarks on the Rev. Dr. Arnold's Principles of Church Reform (London, 1833)
————. A Treatise on the Church of Christ. 2 vols. (London, 1838)
————. An Inquiry into the possibility of Church Extension (London, 1841)
————. A Narrative of events connected with the publication of the Tracts for the Times (Oxford, 1843)
————. A Narrative of events . . . with . . . supplement extending to the present time (London, 1883)
PALMER, WILLIAM (Fellow of Magdalen College, Oxford). Aids to Reflection on . . . the foundation of a "Protestant Bishopric" at Jerusalem (London, 1841)
PARKIN, G. R. Edward Thring . . . Life, diary, and letters. 2 vols. (London, 1898)
PATTISON, MARK. Memoirs (London, 1885)
PAUL, C. KEGAN. Confessio Viatoris (London, 1891)
PECK, W. G. The Social Implications of the Oxford Movement (London, 1933)
PERCEVAL, A. P. High Christian Principles . . . and the Church of Christ invulnerable (London, 1833)
PHILLIMORE, ROBERT JOSEPH. Study of the Civil and Canon Law in its Relation to the State, the Church and the Universities (London, 1843)
————. The Principal Ecclesiastical Judgements delivered in the Courts of Arches, 1867 to 1875 (London, 1876)
————. The Ecclesiastical Law of the Church of England. 2 vols. (London, 1873–76)
PHILLPOTTS, HENRY. Reply to Lord John Russell's Letter on the Remonstrance of the Bishops against the appointment of Dr. Hampden to the See of Hereford (London, 1847)
————. Letter to the Archbishop of Canterbury (London, 1850)
PICHT, WERNER. Toynbee Hall and the English Settlement House Movement (London, 1914)
PIGOU, FRANCIS. Phases of my Life (London, 1898)
PORT, M. H. Six Hundred New Churches (London, 1961)
POWELL, BADEN. Revelation and Science (Oxford, 1833)
————. The State-Church. A sermon before the University of Oxford (Oxford, 1850)
————. The Order of Nature (London, 1859)

[PRESTON, W. C.]. The Bitter Cry of Outcast London (London, 1883) (also attributed to ANDREW MEARNS)

PRIDEAUX, C. G. A practical Guide to the duties of Churchwardens (London, 1841)

PROTHERO, ROWLAND and BRADLEY, G. G. The Life and Correspondence of Arthur Penrhyn Stanley. 2 vols. (London, 1893)

PRYNNE, G. R. Thirty-five Years of Mission Work in a Garrison and Seaport Town (Plymouth, 1883)

PUSEY, E. B. Patience and Confidence the Strength of the Church (Oxford, 1837)

———. The Holy Eucharist, a comfort to the Penitent (Oxford, 1843)

———. The Royal Supremacy not an arbitrary authority (Oxford, 1850)

———. Renewed Explanation in consequence of Rev. W. Dodsworth's Comments (Oxford, 1851)

———. The Councils of the Church from the Council of Jerusalem to the Council of Constantinople (Oxford, 1857)

———. Christianity Without the Cross a corruption of the Gospel of Christ (Oxford, 1875)

RAMSEY, A. M. F. D. Maurice and the Conflicts of Modern Theology (Cambridge, 1951)

RAVEN, CHARLES EARLE. Christian Socialism, 1848–1854 (London, 1920)

RECKITT, MAURICE. Faith and Society (London, 1932) Maurice to Temple (London, 1946)

REID, ANDREW, ed. Vox Clamantium (London, 1894)

REYNOLDS, JOHN STEWART. The Evangelicals at Oxford, 1735–1871. (Oxford, 1953)

REYNOLDS, M. Martyr to Ritualism: Father Mackonochie of St. Alban's, Holborn (London, 1965)

ROBBINS, WILLIAM. The Ethical Idealism of Matthew Arnold. (London, 1959)

ROBINSON, HASTINGS. Church Reform on Christian Principles (London, 1833)

ROSE, H. J. Internal Union the best safeguard against the dangers of the Church (London, 1822)

———. The Churchman's Duty and Comfort in the present times. (Ipswich, 1833)

RUSSELL, GEORGE WILLIAM ERSKINE. Mr. Gladstone's Religious Development (London, 1899)

———. Dr. Liddon (London, 1905)

———. A Short History of the Evangelical Movement (London, 1915)

———. Arthur Stanton: a memoir (London, 1917)

RYLE, J. C. Our Position and Our Dangers (London, 1885)

———. Disestablishment Papers (London, 1885)

SANDFORD, C. W. The Duties of Clergy as ministers of the National Church (London, 1875)

SANDFORD, E. G., ed. Memoirs of Archbishop Temple 2 vols. (London, 1906)

SELLEY, ERNEST. Village Trade Unions in two centuries (London, 1919)

SIMS, GEORGE R. How the Poor Live, and Horrible London (London, 1889)

SMITH, B. A. Dean Church; the Anglican Response to Newman (London, 1958)

SMITH, FRANK. The Life and Work of Sir James Kay-Shuttleworth (London, 1923)

SMITH, GOLDWIN. Reminiscences. Ed. by Arnold Haultain (New York, 1910)

SMITH, SYDNEY. The Works of the Rev. Sydney Smith, 4 vols. (London, 1839)

STANLEY, A. P. The Life and Correspondence of Thomas Arnold, D.D. 2 vols. (London, 1844)

STEPHENS, W. R. The Life and Letters of W. F. Hook. 2 vols. (London, 1878)

STORR, V. F. The Development of English Theology in the Nineteenth Century, 1800–1860 (London, 1913)

STRANKS, C. J. Dean Hook (London, 1954)

SUMNER, J. B. A Charge to the diocese of Chester (London, 1838)

TAINE, H. A. Notes on England (London, 1872)

TAIT, A. C. The Present Position of the Church of England (London, 1873)

———. Some Thoughts on the Duties of the Established Church of England as a National Church (London, 1876)

TEMPLE, WILLIAM. Bishop Percival (London, 1921)

TILLETT, BENJAMIN. Memories and Reflections (London, 1931)

TOWLE, E. A. A. H. Mackonochie (London, 1890)

TOYNBEE, ARNOLD. The Ideal Relation of Church and State . . . Address at Balliol College, Oxford (Oxford, 1879)

Tracts for the Times. 6 vols. (Oxford, 1833–41)

TRENCH, MARIA. Charles Lowder, a biography (London, 1881)

TROLLOPE, ANTHONY. Clergymen of the Church of England (London, 1866)

TUCKWELL, W. Pre-Tractarian Oxford: a reminiscence of the Oriel 'Noetics' (London, 1909)

VIDLER, A. R. The Orb and the Cross (London, 1945)

———. Christian Belief and this World (Greenwich, Conn, 1956)

VOLL, DIETER. Catholic Evangelicalism. Tr. by Veronica Ruffer (London, 1963)

[WADE, JOHN]. The Black Book; or, Corruption unmasked! 2 vols. (London, 1820, 1823)

[———.] The Extraordinary Black Book . . . an Exposition of the United Church of England and Ireland, Civil List and Crown Revenues (London, 1831)

WAGNER, D. O. The Church of England and Social Reform since 1854 (New York, 1930)

WARD, WILFRID P. The Life of John Henry Cardinal Newman. 2 vols. (London, 1912)

WEARMOUTH, R. F. Methodism and the Working-Class Movements of England, 1800–1850 (London, 1937)

———. Some Working-Class Movements of the Nineteenth Century (London, 1948)

WEBB, BEATRICE. English Local Government: Parish and County (London, 1906)

———. The Co-operative Movement in Great Britain (London, 1930)

———. My Apprenticeship (London, 1950)

WEBSTER, ALAN B. Joshua Watson. The story of a layman (London, 1954)

WESTCOTT, ARTHUR. Life and Letters of B. F. Westcott. 2 vols. (London, 1903)

WESTCOTT, B. F. Social aspects of Christianity (London, 1887)

———. The National Church and the Nation (London, 1892)

———. The Incarnation; a revelation of human duties. A charge to the Clergy of Durham, 19 November, 1892 (London, 1892)

———. The Idea and Work of the Church of England (London, 1892)

———. The Incarnation and Common Life (London, 1893)

———. The Christian Social Union (London, 1895)

WHITE, J. F. Cambridge Movement: the Ecclesiologists and the Gothic Revival (Cambridge, 1962)

WHITLEY, W. T. A History of British Baptists (London, 1923)

WICKHAM, E. R. Church and People in an Industrial City (London, 1952)

WINNINGTON-INGRAM, A. F. Work in Great Cities (London, 1896)

WINSTANLEY, D. A. Unreformed Cambridge (1935)

WILLIAMS, CHARLES. Considerations on the Present State of the Church (Nottingham, 1833)

WOODARD, NATHANIEL. Pleas for the Middle Classes (London, 1848)

————. Scheme of Education of St. Nicolas College in a Letter to the . . . Marquis of Salisbury (London, 1869)

WOODWARD, F. J. The Doctor's Disciples (London, 1954)

WOODWORTH, A. V. Christian Socialism in England (London, 1903)

WORDSWORTH, CHRISTOPHER. Christian Institutes: a series of discourses and tracts. 4 vols. (London, 1837)

YOUNG, G. M. Early Victorian England, 1830–1865 (London, 1934)

Index